TRAVELING
JEWISH
IN AMERICA

The Complete Guide
For Business & Pleasure

TRAVELING JEWISH IN AMERICA

FIRST COMPILED BY
Brynna C. Bloomfield
AND
Jane M. Moskowitz

THIRD EDITION
Revised, Enlarged and Edited By
Ellen Chernofsky

WANDERING YOU PRESS
LODI, NEW JERSEY

TRAVELING JEWISH IN AMERICA
Copyright © 1991
by Creative Resources, Inc., Lodi, New Jersey

Wandering You Press, P.O. Box 20, Lodi, NJ 07644-0020

Library of Congress Catalogue Card Number: 91-065733
ISBN 0-9617104-2-X

Cover & book design by Linda A. Bachert

Population figures throughout this
directory have been excerpted from the 1990 edition
of the American Jewish Yearbook (copyright 1990),
published by the American Jewish Committee and the
Jewish Publication Society, and appear here with the
permission of the American Jewish Committee.

First edition: 1986, Second edition: 1987
Supplement to second edition: 1989

Printed in the United States of America

ACKNOWLEDGMENTS

This book would not have been possible without the gracious assistance of hundreds of individuals throughout the United States and Canada who took the time from their busy schedules to share with us information about their communities. We owe a debt of gratitude to everyone who participated.

Special thanks are due to Tammy Boyd, project assistant, for her patient, cheerful and careful attention to the myriad tasks associated with this project; Colette Kelly and John Treglia for easing our induction into the mysteries of computer typesetting and Deborah Weightman for producing the final galleys.

PREFACE

TRAVELING JEWISH IN AMERICA was originally conceived to serve the needs of the Jewish tourist or business traveler in the United States. With that goal in mind, we have enhanced this third edition to include more information of the kind that we hope will help take the edge off the feelings of strangeness that often beset visitors in unfamiliar territory. New listings include Jewish bookstores, Jewish day schools, more synagogues and more places to stay.

In response to many requests, this edition has been enlarged to include the Canadian Jewish communities; both the larger cities and the smaller towns. We had a good time researching Canada and found that the people we spoke with were delighted to be included, which attitude should presage a warm reception to the traveler.

We trust that the new TRAVELING JEWISH IN AMERICA will continue to make your travel more convenient, enjoyable and productive and that you will take advantage of any opportunities to become acquainted with members of the Jewish communities you visit. We have found that even those staunch remnants of some of the dwindling communities which are scattered throughout the continent often have fascinating histories to share. Personally and by telephone, I have met many wonderful people, and I know that they are out there, waiting to welcome you.

Ellen Chernofsky
Editor

CONTENTS

HOW TO USE THIS GUIDE

Synagogues: The denomination and affiliation appear in parentheses directly after the name of each synagogue, followed by the address, telephone number, name of the rabbi and days on which services are held. The designation "Shabbat" means Friday evening and Saturday. If you are interested in attending services, it is always best to call in advance for exact times.

Eating Out: The establishments listed in this section generally claim some kind of kosher supervision. The address, telephone number, meals served, type of menu and the name of the supervising rabbi or agency are included. We also indicate if the place is closed on Shabbat. In addition to restaurants, delicatessens and pizza shops, we have tried to include any kosher store that has at least a few tables and chairs. You will also find some college campus kosher dining halls and Jewish community center snack bars.

Food: This section provides detailed information on where to buy kosher food. This category becomes particularly important in places where there are no kosher eating out facilities. Listed are kosher grocery stores, bakeries, butcher shops, take-out places and food co-ops (facilities organized by community members in the absence of commercial establishments). As most supermarkets carry some kosher items, we have included only those which feature an unusually wide variety of kosher products or which may be the only source of any kosher food in outlying areas.

Kosher supervision: There are many different kinds of kosher supervision, both public and private, ranging from an individual rabbi to large citywide or national agencies. Where possible, we have included special telephone numbers for kosher information in specific cities. The owner or manager of a particular establishment can give you the name and telephone number of the agency and/or individual responsible for that store's kosher supervision. Some American cities, such as Chicago, Cincinnati, Baltimore and St. Louis, to name a few, have central supervising agencies which support uniform standards in their areas. You will find this to be true throughout Canada.

Only those kosher stores or restaurants which list an "RS:" (Rabbinical Supervision) claim supervision of food preparation. The supervision of kosher butchers' associations is usually limited to checking the meat, to make sure that it is kosher in origin.

We have done our best to list all kosher information accurately. However, since ownership and rabbinical supervision are subject to change, as well as to variation in standards, we cannot take responsibility for the reliability of any kosher supervision information listed in this guide. To resolve any questions in this regard, we suggest that you check with the local rabbinical authority of your choice.

Accommodations: Included in this section are kosher resort hotels and hotels or motels within walking distance of synagogues, with an indication of how long (or short) a trek you can anticipate. Where possible, we have also listed places which offer suites with kitchen facilities. This latter type of accommodation is growing in availability and is becoming increasingly popular with travelers. Also listed in this section are the names and telephone numbers of synagogues or private individuals who are ready to extend hospitality to Jewish visitors.

Mikvah: Address, telephone number and contact information are included.

Day Schools: Except for the five boroughs of New York City (where they proliferate), day schools are listed for the entire United States and Canada. The Conservative, Reform and unaffiliated schools are so indicated.* Most of the others are listed in the Directory of Day Schools in the United States and Canada, which is published by the National Society for Hebrew Day Schools.**

Bookstores: Listed are retail Jewish bookstores, their addresses and telephone numbers. In these establishments, you can shop for a book or gift or possibly have a friendly chat with the owner, who, if not too busy, is usually a fund of information about the community.

---

* Names, addresses and telephone numbers of the national day school organizations are listed on page 304.
** See Sources, p. 490

Population figures: All population figures are approximate, and some may be more current than others. Many include the county or counties surrounding a given town or city. We have put them in to give you a rough idea of what the Jewish population may be in a particular geographical area.

We have made every effort to insure the accuracy of the information in TRAVELING JEWISH IN AMERICA. However, circumstances can change very quickly. If something in the book is incorrect, or if you have information to add, please let us know. You will find a convenient form in the back of this book on page 493.

KEY

J-pop. — Approximate Jewish population figure for the area

Synagogues*

O	— Orthodox	C	— Conservative
Lubav	— Lubavitch	R	— Reform
Trad	— Traditional	Recon	— Reconstructionist

Affiliations

FRCH — Federation of Reconstructionist Congregations and Havurot

NCYI — National Council of Young Israel

UAHC — Union of American Hebrew Congregations

UOJC — Union of Orthodox Jewish Congregations

US — United Synagogue of America

Shabbat — Friday evening and Saturday

Eating Out/Food

b	—Breakfast	d	— Dinner
l	—Lunch	RS:	— Rabbinical Supervision

Vaad or Va'ad — Committee of individuals responsible for kosher supervision

Mikvah — Ritual bath

---

* Names, addresses and telephone numbers of the national synagogue organizations are listed on page 303.

Alabama

BIRMINGHAM Area Code (205) J-pop. 5,100

Synagogues

Temple Beth-El (C-US), 2179 Highland Ave, Ph: 933-2740.
Rabbi S. Glazer. Services: Daily

Temple Emanu-El (R-UAHC), 2100 Highland Ave, Ph: 933-8037.
Rabbi J. Miller. Services: Shabbat

Knesseth Israel Congregation (O-UOJC), 3225 Montevallo Rd,
Ph: 879-1664. Rabbi R. Tradburks. Services: Daily

Eating Out

Jewish Community Center, 3960 Montclair Rd, Ph: 879-0411.
Kosher restaurant and take-out. RS: Rabbi R. Tradburks. Closed
Shabbat.

Food

Browdy's, 2807 Cahaba Rd, Ph: 879-8585. RS: Rabbi R. Tradburks
(bakery only). Some kosher packaged products.

Bruno's, 33 Montclair Rd, Ph: 951-3122. Some kosher groceries,
deli products and frozen Empire poultry.

Accommodations

Private hospitality - call Knesseth Israel, Ph: 879-1664; or Rabbi Y.
Posner, Friends of Chabad, Ph: 871-2406.

Mikvah

Knesseth Israel, 3225 Montevallo Rd. Call Synagogue office
between 9 a.m. and 3 p.m., Ph: 879-1664; 871-3141.

Day School

Birmingham Jewish Day School, 3960-A Montclair Rd,
Ph: 879-1068.

DOTHAN Area Code (205) J-pop. 150

Synagogues

Temple Emanu-el (R-UAHC), 110 N Park Ave, Ph: 792-5001,
Rabbi S. Funston. Services: Friday

FLORENCE   Area Code (205)   J-pop. 150

Synagogues

Temple B'nai Israel (R-UAHC), 210 Hawthorne St, Ph: 764-9242.
  Services: Friday

GADSDEN   Area Code (205)

Synagogues

Congregation Beth Israel (R-UAHC), 761 Chestnut St,
  Ph: 546-3223, Rabbi F. Raskind. Services: Friday

HUNTSVILLE   Area Code (205)   J-pop. 750

For Jewish community information, call William Goldberg,
  Ph: 882-2918.

Synagogues

Temple B'nai Sholom (R-UAHC), 103 Lincoln St SE,
  Ph: 536-4771, Rabbi S. Jacobs. Services: Friday
Congregation Etz Chaim (C-US), 7705 Bailey Cove Rd SE,
  Ph: 881-6260; 882-2918. Services: Shabbat

Food

Bruno's, 1918 Memorial Pkwy, Ph: 880-0693; 9020 Bailey Cove
  Rd, Ph: 882-9200. Some kosher groceries, deli products and
  Empire poultry.

JASPER   Area Code (205)

Synagogues

Temple Emanuel (R-UAHC), 1501 5th Ave, Ph: 221-4000. Services:
  Friday

MOBILE   Area Code (205)   J-pop. 1,100

Synagogues

Congregation Ahavas Chesed - Dauphin Street Synagogue (C-US),
  705 Regents Way, Ph: 343-6010. Rabbi S. Silberman.
  Services: Shabbat

Spring Hill Avenue Temple (R-UAHC), 1769 Spring Hill Ave,
  Ph: 478-0415. Rabbi D. M. Kunstadt. Services: Friday

Food

Call Congregation Ahavas Chesed, Ph: 343-6010 for details
  regarding kosher bakery items under the supervision of Rabbi S.
  Silberman at Bruno's and Welcome supermarkets.
Bruno's, 258 Azalia Rd, Ph: 343-4444. Empire frozen poultry,
  Best frozen hamburgers.
Welcome, Airport and Downtowner, Ph: 341-0710. Some kosher
  products.

MONTGOMERY   Area Code (205)   J-pop. 1,300

Synagogues

Congregation Agudath Israel (C-US), 3525 Cloverdale Rd,
  Ph: 281-7394. Rabbi A. Krupnick. Services: Shabbat; Monday
  and Thursday mornings
Temple Beth Or (R-UAHC), 2246 Narrow Lane Rd, Ph: 262-3314.
  Rabbi D. Baylinson. Services: Shabbat; Monday and Thursday
  mornings
Etz Ahayem (C-Seph), 725 Augusta St, Ph: 281-9819. Services:
  Friday

Food

Gregg's, 2924 Carter Hill Rd, Ph: 834-3354. Some kosher baked
  goods. RS: Rabbi A. Krupnick (kosher baked goods only).
Bruno's, 3433 McGehee Rd, Ph: 284-8110. Challahs and some
  breads. RS: Rabbi A. Krupnick (kosher baked goods only). Also
  Empire frozen poultry.

TUSCALOOSA   Area Code (205)   J-pop. 300

Synagogues

Temple Emanuel (R), 2412 Skyland Blvd E, Ph: 553-3286. Services:
  Friday

Alaska

ANCHORAGE   Area Code (907)   J-pop. 2,000

Synagogues

Congregation Beth Sholom (R-UAHC), 7525 E Northern Lights
  Blvd, Ph: 383-1836. Rabbi H. Rosenfeld. Services: Shabbat
Congregation Shomrei Ohr - Lubavitch Jewish Center (O-Lubav),
  1210 E 26th Ave, Ph: 278-6314. Rabbi Y. Greenberg. Services:
  Saturday mornings and Holidays

Food

Kosher products such as bread, wines, and packaged foods (except
  meat and cheese) are available at the supermarkets.

Accommodations

Golden Lion Hotel, 1000 E 36th Ave, Ph: 561-1522. About seven
  blocks to Congregation Shomrei Ohr.
Shabbat hospitality - call Rabbi Y. Greenberg at Lubavitch Jewish
  Center, Ph: 278-6314.

Mikvah

The mikvah is located on Elmendorf Air Force Base. Call Mrs.
  Esther Greenberg for information/assistance, Ph: 278-6314.
  (Remember the "midnight sun" when summer use is required.)

Arizona

FLAGSTAFF   Area Code (602)   J-pop. 250

Synagogues

Heichal Baoranim (R), 2609 N Patterson Blvd, Ph: 527-8747.
  Services: Call for information.

MESA (See PHOENIX)

PHOENIX   Area Code (602)   J-pop. 50,000

Synagogues

Ahavat Torah Congregation (C-US), 6816 E Cactus Rd, **Scottsdale**. Ph: 991-5645. Services: Shabbat

Beth Ami Temple (R), 4545 N 36th St, (office), Ph: 956-0805. Rabbi F. Grosse. Services: Call for information.

Beth El Congregation (C-US), 1118 W Glendale Ave, Ph: 944-3359. Rabbi H. Silberman. Services: Daily

Beth Emeth Congregation of the Sun Cities (C), 13702 W Meeker Blvd, **Sun City West**. Ph: 584-7210. Rabbi Dr. S. Shoop. Services: Shabbat.

Temple Beth Emeth of Scottsdale (C), 6107 N Invergordon Rd, **Scottsdale**, Ph: 941-4112. Services: Call for information.

Temple Beth Israel (R-UAHC), 3310 N 10th Ave, Ph: 264-4428. Rabbi A. Plotkin. Services: Shabbat

Beth Joseph Congregation (O-UOJC), 515 E Bethany Home Rd, Ph: 277-8858. Rabbi D. Rebibo. Services: Daily

Beth Joshua Congregation (Trad), 10802 N 71st Place, **Scottsdale**, Ph: 998-1565. Rabbi E. Kahn. Services: Shabbat

Temple Beth Sholom (C-US), 316 S LeSueur St, **Mesa**, Ph: 964-1981. Rabbi B. Koppell. Services: Shabbat.

Temple Beth Shalom of Sun City (R), 12202 101st Ave, **Sun City**, Ph: 977-3240. Rabbi B. Kligfeld. Services: Shabbat.

Temple Chai (R), 4645 E Marilyn, Ph: 971-1234. Rabbi W. Berk. Services: Friday.

Temple Emanuel (R), 5801 S Rural Rd, **Tempe**, Ph: 838-1414. Rabbi D. Pinkwasser. Services: Call for information.

Har Zion Congregation (C-US), 5929 E Lincoln Dr, **Paradise Valley**, Ph: 991-0720. Rabbi M. Bisman. Services: Daily

Temple Kol Ami (R), 10210 N 32nd St #213, Ph: 788-0939. Rabbi B.C. Herring. Services: Friday

Temple Solel (R-UAHC), 6805 E MacDonald Dr, **Paradise Valley**, Ph: 991-7414. Rabbi M. Bell. Services: Friday

Tiphereth Israel (O-Lubav), 2110 E Lincoln Dr, Ph: 944-2753. Rabbi Z. Levertov. Services: Daily

Eating Out

Jewish Community Center Lunch for Seniors Program (age 60 and over), 1718 W Marilyn, Ph: 249-1832 ext. 235. RS: Rabbi D. Rebibo. Monday-Friday 12 noon. Call for reservations.

Segal's New Place, 4818 N 7th St, Ph: 285-1515. Meals: b,l, daily; d Thursday. Menu: Continental cuisine, fast food and take out. RS: Rabbi D. Rebibo. Closed Shabbat. All major cards.

Taster's, 3407 N 7th Ave, Ph: 230-2466. Meals: b,l,d. Menu: Vegetarian dishes, frozen yogurt. RS: Rabbi D. Rebibo.

Tiphereth Israel - Chabad Center, 2110 E Lincoln Dr, Ph: 994-2753. RS: Rabbi Z. Levertov. Kosher meals are served regularly. Call for reservations and schedule.

Food

Karsh's Bakery, Cinema Park Shopping Center, 7th St & Missouri, Ph: 264-4874; Shea-Scottsdale Center, Ph: 951-0202. Closed Sunday; 35th Ave & Thunderbird, Ph: 938-5780. Closed Sunday and Monday. RS: Rabbi D. Rebibo.

Midwest Bakery (at Segal's) RS: Rabbi D. Rebibo. Closed Shabbat.

Segal's Kosher Market, 4818 N 7th St, Ph: 285-1515. Meat, kosher groceries and take-out. RS: Rabbi D. Rebibo. Closed Shabbat.

Valley Kosher Meats & Deli, 1331 E Northern Ave, Ph: 371-0999. Prepared meat dishes to go, packaged deli and kosher foods. RS: Rabbi D. Rebibo. Closed Shabbat.

Accommodations

Bridlewood Suites, 5145 N 7th St, Ph: 277-5847. Furnished studios and one-bedroom apartments. Daily, weekly or monthly. Twenty-minute walk to Beth Joseph Congregation.

Manzanitta Apartments, 6110 N 7th St, Ph: 266-6230. Furnished studios with kitchens. Daily and weekly. Five-minute walk to Beth Joseph Congregation.

Private accommodations - contact Rabbi Z. Levertov at Tiphereth Israel - Chabad Center, Ph: 944-2753.

Mikvah

Congregation Beth Joseph, 515 E Bethany Home Rd. Contact Synagogue office, Ph: 277-8858 or 266-3140.

Day Schools

Phoenix Hebrew Academy, 515 E Bethany Home Rd, Ph: 277-7479; 316 S LeSueur, **Mesa**, Ph: 277-7479.

Solomon Schechter Day School of Greater Phoenix (C), 1118 W Glendale Ave, Ph: 944-2464.

Bookstore

Israel Connection, 5539 N 7th St, Ph: 265-6606.

SCOTTSDALE (See PHOENIX)

TUCSON   Area Code (602)

Synagogues

Congregation Anshei Israel (C-US), 5550 E 5th St, Ph: 745-5550. Rabbi A. Oleisky. Services: Daily

Beth Shalom (C-US), 3881 E River Rd, Ph: 577-1171. Services: Shabbat

Chabad-Lubavitch (O-Lubav), 1315 N Mountain, Ph: 881-7956. Rabbi Y. Shemtov. Services: Call for information.

Chofetz Chaim (O), 5150 E 5th St, Ph: 747-7780. Rabbi I. Becker. Services: Daily

Temple Emanuel (R-UAHC), 225 N Country Club, Ph: 327-4501. Rabbi J. Weizenbaum. Services: Shabbat

Young Israel of Tucson (O), 2443 E 4th St, Ph: 326-8362 or 881-7956. Rabbi Y. Shemtov. Services: Daily

Eating Out

B'nai B'rith Hillel at the University of Arizona, 1245 E 2nd St, Ph: 624-6561. Kosher lunches on weekdays and Shabbat dinner. For further information, call Rabbi M. Smith.

Feig's Kosher Market, 5071 E 5th St, Ph: 325-2255. Meals: b,l,d. Menu: Deli-style food. RS: Rabbi A. Oleisky. Closed Shabbat.

Eating Out cont.

The Kosher Deli, Jewish Community Center, 3800 E River Rd,
Ph: 299-3000. Meals: b,l. Menu: (Meat) Deli sandwiches,
snacks. RS: Rabbi L. Barr. Closed Shabbat.

Food

Feig's Kosher Market, 5071 E 5th St, Ph: 325-2255. Fresh meats,
poultry and kosher groceries. RS: Rabbi A. Oleisky. Closed
Shabbat.

Nadine Pastry Shop, 4300 E Pima St, Ph: 326-0735. Breads and
pastries. RS: Rabbi I. Becker.

Accommodations

Private accommodations; contact Rabbi I. Becker at Chofetz
Chaim, Ph: 747-7780 or Rabbi Y. Shemtov at Young Israel of
Tucson, Ph: 326-8362 or 881-7956.

Brauner Apartments, 3537 E 4th St, Ph: 881-7070. Apartments
with kitchens are available for short-term rental.

Catalina Village Apartments, 5324 E First St, Ph: 323-7111.
Apartments with kitchens and single rooms with hot plates.

Mikvah

Mikveh of Tucson (Young Israel), 2443 E 4th St. Call Mrs. E.
Becker, Ph: 745-0958 or Mrs. C. Shemtov, Ph: 326-7739.

Brauner Apartments, 3537 E 4th St. Call Mrs. G. Kraus,
Ph: 881-7070. Winter only.

Day School

Tucson Hebrew Academy, 5550 E 5th St, Ph: 745-5592.

Arkansas

FAYETTEVILLE   Area Code (501)   J-pop. 120

Synagogues

Temple Shalom (R), 607 Storer St, Ph: 521-7357. Rabbi W.
Hamburger. Services: Friday

FORT SMITH   Area Code (501)   J-pop. 160

Synagogues

United Hebrew Congregation (R-UAHC), 126 N 47th St,
  Ph: 452-1468. Services: Friday

HELENA   Area Code (501)

Synagogues

Temple Beth El (R-UAHC), 406 Perry St, Ph: 338-6654. Services:
  Friday

HOT SPRINGS   Area Code (501)   J-pop. 200

Synagogues

Congregation House of Israel (R-UAHC), 300 Quapaw Ave,
  Ph: 623-5821. Rabbi A. Graboys. Services: Friday

LITTLE ROCK   Area Code (501)   J-pop. 1,300

Synagogues

Congregation Agudath Achim (O-UOJC), 7901 W 5th St,
  Ph: 225-1683 or 225-1667. Rabbi S. Weller. Services: Saturday
Congregation B'nai Israel (R-UAHC), 3700 N Rodney Parham Rd,
  Ph: 225-9700. Rabbi E. Levy. Services: Shabbat

Food

Andre's Bakery, 11121 Rodney Parham Rd, Ph: 224-7880. Breads
  and challahs (pareve) and pastries (dairy). RS: Rabbi S. Weller
  (bakery goods only).

Mikvah

Congregation Agudath Achim, 7901 W 5th St. Contact Rabbi S.
  Weller, Ph: 225-1683 or 225-1667.

McGEHEE   Area Code (501)

Synagogues

Meir Chayim Temple (C), 210 N 4th St, Ph: 222-4399. Services:
  Call for schedule.

PINE BLUFF   Area Code (501)   J-pop. 100

Synagogues

Temple Anshe Emeth (R-UAHC), 40th & Hickory, Ph: 534-3853.
  Services: Friday

California

AGOURA HILLS (See GREATER LOS ANGELES)

ALAMEDA (See OAKLAND)

ALHAMBRA (See GREATER LOS ANGELES)

ANAHEIM (See also LONG BEACH)   Area Code (714)

Synagogues

Adat Ari North of Orange County (C), 1250 Lakeview Ave,
  Anaheim Hills, Ph: 970-9304. Rabbi S. Schatz. Services: Fridays
  and last Saturday of the month
Temple Beth Emet of Orange County (C-US), 1770 W Cerritos Ave,
  Ph: 772-4720. Rabbi I. Brandwein. Services: Daily

Food (See **Los Alamitos**)

Accommodations

Temple Beth Emet is near Disneyland and a 15-minute walk from
  many hotels and motels.

Day School

Jewish Studies Institute Day School (C), 1770 W Cerritos Ave,
  Ph: 535-3665.

ARCADIA (See GREATER LOS ANGELES)

BAKERSFIELD   Area Code (805)

Synagogues

Temple Beth El (R-UAHC), 2906 Loma Linda Dr, Ph: 322-7607.
   Rabbi S. Peskind. Services: Friday
B'nai Jacob (C-US,), 600 17th St, Ph: 325-8017. Rabbi M. Samuels.
   Services: Shabbat

BERKELEY (See also OAKLAND)   Area Code (415)

Synagogues

Berkeley Conservative Congregation (C), 1414 Walnut St,
   Ph: 527-9730. Services: Second and fourth Shabbat
Berkeley Hillel Foundation (Independent), 2736 Bancroft Way,
   Ph: 845-7793. Rabbi E. Rammon. Services: Friday
Congregation Beth El (R-UAHC), 2301 Vine St, Ph: 848-3988.
   Rabbi A. Levine. Services: Shabbat
Chabad House of the East Bay (O-Lubav), 2643 College (near
   U.C. Berkeley campus), Ph: 540-5824. Rabbi Y. Ferris.
   Services: Daily
Congregation Beth Israel (O), 1630 Bancroft Way, Ph: 843-5246.
   Rabbi E. Forman. Services: Daily
Kehilla Congregation (Independent), P.O. Box 3063, 94703,
   Ph: 654-5452. Rabbi B. Jacobson. Services: Call for information.

Eating Out

Chabad House, 2643 College, Ph: 540-5824. Kosher meals
   Shabbat: b,d. Call for reservations.

Accommodations

Chabad of the East Bay; Shabbat hospitality and students' residence program for men. Call Rabbi Y. Ferris, Ph: 540-5824.

Mikvah

Mikvah Taharas Israel, 2520 Warring St, Ph: 848-7221.

Bookstore

Afikomen, 3042 Claremont Ave, Ph: 655-1977.

BEVERLY HILLS (See GREATER LOS ANGELES)

BURBANK (See GREATER LOS ANGELES)

BURLINGAME (See also SAN FRANCISCO)   Area Code (415)

Synagogues

Peninsula Temple Sholom (R-UAHC), 1655 Sebastian Dr, Ph: 697-2266. Rabbi G. Raiskin. Services: Friday

CANOGA PARK (See GREATER LOS ANGELES)

CARLSBAD   Area Code (619)

Synagogues

Chabad of La Costa, 9663 Galleon Way, Ph: 943-9985. Rabbi Y. Eilfort. Services: Shabbat and Holidays. (Call for Shabbat hospitality.)

CARMEL   Area Code (408)

Synagogues

Congregation Beth Israel (R-UAHC), 5716 Carmel Valley Rd, Ph: 624-2015. Rabbi N. T. Mendel. Services: Shabbat

CASTRO VALLEY (See also OAKLAND)   Area Code (415)

Synagogues

Congregation Shir Ami (R-UAHC), 4529 Malabar Ave, Ph: 537-1787. Services: Call for schedule.

CHULA VISTA (See also SAN DIEGO)   Area Code (619)

Synagogues

Temple Beth Sholom (C-US), 208 Madrona St, Ph: 420-6040. Rabbi E. Weiss. Services: Shabbat

Beth Torah Congregation (O-UOJC), 4360 Old Valley Rd #211,
  Ph: 267-6049. Rabbi C. Harar. Services: Shabbat

CONCORD (See WALNUT CREEK)

CORONA   Area Code (714)

Synagogues

Temple Beth Sholom (C), 821 S Sheridan St, Ph: 371-9322;
  737-5029. Services: Fridays, first Saturday of the month

CULVER CITY (See GREATER LOS ANGELES)

DALY CITY (See also SAN FRANCISCO)   Area Code (415)

Synagogues

Congregation B'nai Israel (C-US, R-UAHC), 1575 Annie St,
  Ph: 756-5430. Rabbi M. Cohen. Services: Friday

DESERT HOT SPRINGS (See PALM SPRINGS)

DOWNEY (See GREATER LOS ANGELES)

ENCINITAS   Area Code (619)

Synagogues

Temple Solel (R-UAHC), 552 S El Camino Real, Ph: 436-0654.
  Rabbi L. Bohm. Services: Friday

ENCINO (See GREATER LOS ANGELES)

EUREKA   Area Code (707)   J-pop. 500

Synagogues

Temple Beth El (R-UAHC), T & Hodgson Sts, Ph: 444-2846.
  Rabbi L. Trepp. Services: Friday

13

FOSTER CITY   Area Code (415)

Synagogues

Peninsula Sinai Congregation (C), 499 Boothbay Ave, Ph: 349-2816. Rabbi M. Goodman. Services: Shabbat

FOUNTAIN VALLEY   Area Code (714)

Synagogues

Congregation B'nai Tzedek (R), 9669 Talbert Ave, Ph: 963-4611. Rabbi S. Einstein. Services: Friday

FREMONT (See OAKLAND)

FRESNO   Area Code (209)   J-pop. 2,000

Synagogues

Temple Adat Shalom, Jewish Community Center, 5094 N West Ave, Ph: 431-1375. President Fran Ziegler. Services: Friday

Temple Beth Israel (R-UAHC), 2336 Calaveras St, Ph: 264-2929. Rabbi K. Segel. Services: Friday

Congregation Beth Jacob (C-US), 406 W Shields Ave, Ph: 222-0664. Rabbi B. Mazor. Services: Shabbat

Chabad of Fresno (O-Lubav), 6735 N Ila Ave, Ph: 432-2770. Rabbi L. Zirkind. Services: Shabbat and Holidays

Food

Von's, 3043 W Shaw Ave, Ph: 225-8018. Frozen kosher poultry.

Accommodations

Private accommodations for Shabbat; call Chabad of Fresno, Ph: 432-2770.

FULLERTON (See also LONG BEACH)   Area Code (714)

Synagogues

Temple Beth Tikvah (R-UAHC), 1600 N Acacia Ave, Ph: 871-3535. Rabbi H. Asa. Services: Friday

Food (See **Los Alamitos**)

14

GARDEN GROVE (See also LONG BEACH)   Area Code (714)

Food

Sam's Kosher Meat Market, 12432 Lampson, Ph: 534-5621. Fresh meat, poultry, some kosher groceries. RS: Kosher Overseers Assn. of America. Closed Shabbat.

GARDENA (See GREATER LOS ANGELES)

GLENDALE (See GREATER LOS ANGELES)

HOLLYWOOD (See GREATER LOS ANGELES)

HUNTINGTON BEACH (See also LONG BEACH)
Area Code (714)

Synagogues

Chabad of West Orange County (O-Lubav), 5702 Clark Dr #18, Ph: 846-2285. Rabbi A. Berkowitz. Services: Daily

HUNTINGTON PARK (See GREATER LOS ANGELES)

IRVINE   Area Code (714)

Synagogues

Beth Jacob Congregation of Irvine (O), 3415 Michelson Drive, Ph: 786-5230. Rabbi D. Epstein. Services: Shabbat and Sunday

Chabad of Irvine Jewish Center (O-Lubav), 4872 Royce Rd, Ph: 786-5000. Rabbi M. Duchman. Services: Daily

Irvine Jewish Community (R), P.O. Box 19608-638, 92713, Ph: 786-0823. Rabbi S. Elwell. Services: Third Friday of month

University Synagogue (Recon), Office: 4521 Campus Drive #234; Services at U.C.I. Campus Interfaith Center, Ph: 725-9559. Call for information.

Food

Alpha Beta, 18040 Culver Dr, Ph: 262-0407. Kosher meat, frozen dinners and cheeses.

Hughes Market, 5331 University Dr, Ph: 786-0770. Kosher meat and cheeses.

Mikvah (See **Long Beach**)

Day School

Hebrew Academy of Irvine, 4872 Royce Rd, Ph: 786-5000.

LAFAYETTE (See also BERKELEY)   Area Code (415)

Synagogues

Temple Isaiah (R-UAHC), 3800 Mt Diablo Blvd, Ph: 283-8575.
   Rabbi S. Waldenberg. Services: Shabbat

LAGUNA (See also IRVINE)   Area Code (714)

Synagogues

Temple Beth El (R), 30121 Niguel Rd, Ph: 364-2332; Office:
   28892 Marguerite Parkway #210, **Mission Viejo**. Rabbi A.
   Krause. Services: Friday
Chabad of Laguna (O-Lubav), 21462 Ocean Vista, **Laguna Beach**,
   Ph: 499-1432, 786-5000. Rabbi A. Tennenbaum. Services:
   Shabbat

LAGUNA HILLS   Area Code (714)

Synagogues

Beth Torah of Laguna Hills (O), Club House One, Leisure World.
   Rabbi J. Manosevitz, Ph: 458-0170. Services: Shabbat, Monday,
   Thursday and Holidays
Temple Judea of Leisure World of Laguna Hills (C), 24512
   Moulton Pkwy, Ph: 830-0470. Services: Shabbat, Monday and
   Thursday

LA JOLLA (See also SAN DIEGO)   Area Code (619)

Synagogues

Congregation Adat Yeshurun (O), 8950 Villa La Jolla Dr #1224, Ph:
   535-1196. Rabbi J. Wohlgelernter. Services: Daily
Congregation Beth El (C-US), 8660 Gilman Dr, Ph: 452-1734.
   Rabbi M. Levin. Services: Daily

16

Chabad of La Jolla (O-Lubav), 3232 Governor Dr #B, R & N, **San Diego**, Ph: 455-1670. Rabbi M. Leider. Services: Daily

Eating Out

Western Kosher, 7739 Fay Ave, Ph: 454-MEAT. Meals: l,d. Menu: Deli and pareve sandwiches, soups, salads, side dishes. Also take-out. RS: Vaad Harabonim of San Diego. Closed Shabbat.

Food

Western Kosher, 7739 Fay Ave, Ph: 454-MEAT. Butcher, grocery, take-out. RS: Vaad Harabonim of San Diego. Closed Shabbat.

Accommodations

The following motels are a few minutes' walk from Congregation Adat Yeshurun. Both have real keys.
La Jolla Village Inn, 3299 Holiday Ct, Ph: 453-5500.
Residence Inn, 8901 Gilman Dr, Ph: 587-1770.

LAKEWOOD (See also LONG BEACH)   Area Code (213)

Synagogues

Temple Beth Zion-Sinai (C-US), 66440 Del Amo Blvd, Ph: 429-0715. Rabbi C. K. Blueth. Services: Daily

Food (See **Los Alamitos**)

LA MIRADA (See GREATER LOS ANGELES)

Food (See **Los Alamitos**)

LANCASTER   Area Code (805)

Synagogues

Beth Knesset Bamidbar (R-UAHC), 1611 E Avenue J, Ph: 942-4415. Rabbi A. Henkin. Services: Shabbat
Congregation B'nai Israel (C), 43652 Higbee Ave, Ph: 266-9398. Services: Call for information.

17

LOMITA (See also **GREATER LOS ANGELES**)   Area Code (213)

Synagogues

Chabad of South Bay (O-Lubav), 24412 Narbonne Ave,
   Ph: 326-8234. Rabbi E. Hecht. Services: Daily

Food

Food Co. Market, Pacific Coast Hwy & Crenshaw Blvd,
   Ph: 325-0711. Large selection of kosher products.

Mikvah

Mikvas Chana, 24412 Narbonne Ave, Ph: 326-3886

LONG BEACH (See also **GREATER LOS ANGELES**)
   Area Code (213)   J-pop. 13,500

Synagogues

Temple Beth Shalom (C-US), 3635 Elm Ave, Ph: 426-6413. Rabbi
   D. Epstein. Services: Shabbat, Sunday through Thursday
Temple Israel (R-UAHC), 3538 E 3rd St, Ph: 434-0996.
   Rabbi H. Laibson. Services: Shabbat
Congregation Lubavitch (O-Lubav), 3981 Atlantic Ave,
   Ph: 426-5480. Rabbi Y. Newman. Services: Daily
Young Israel of Long Beach, 4134 Atlantic Ave, Ph: 426-9690.
   Rabbi M. Pheterson. Services: Shabbat

Food (See **Los Alamitos**)

Mikvah

Mikvah Yisroel, 3847 Atlantic Ave. Call Mikvah message service,
   Ph: 427-1360.

LOS ALAMITOS (See also **LONG BEACH**)   Area Code (213)

Synagogues

Chabad of Los Alamitos (O-Lubav), 10412 El Dorado,
   Ph: 594-6408. Rabbi Y. Marcus. Services: Shabbat and
   Holidays

Food

Fairfax Kosher Market, 11196 Los Alamitos Blvd, Ph: 594-4600.
Butcher, grocer, deli. RS: Rabbinical Council of CA. Closed
Shabbat.

Bookstore

Ben Yehuda Street, 4382 Katella Ave, Ph: 821-5471.

LOS ALTOS HILLS (See also SAN FRANCISCO)
Area Code (415)

Synagogues

Congregation Beth Am (R-UAHC), 26790 Arastradero Rd,
Ph: 493-4661. Rabbi R. Block. Services: Friday

GREATER LOS ANGELES   J-pop. 501,000

Los Angeles and West Los Angeles Area—Area Code (213)

Synagogues

Congregation Adas Chasam Sofer (O), 8013 Melrose Ave,
Ph: 852-9463. Rabbi H. Schuck. Services: Daily
Ahavas Yisroel (O), 729 La Brea Ave, Ph: 857-1607. Rabbi C.
Citron. Services: Shabbat
Adat Shalom (C-US), 3030 Westwood Blvd, Ph: 475-4985. Rabbi
M. Wallack. Services: Daily
Agudath Israel of California (O), 7114 Rosewood Ave,
Ph: 937-1675. Rabbi A. Teichman. Services: Daily
Temple Akiba (R-UAHC), 5249 S Sepulveda Blvd, **Culver City**,
Ph: 398-5783. Rabbi A. Maller. Services: Shabbat
Anshe Emes Synagogue (O), 1490 S Robertson, Ph: 275-5640.
Rabbi Y. Summers. Services: Daily
Congregation Atzei L'Chaim (O), 8018 W 3rd St, Ph: 852-9104.
Rabbi H. Halbershtam. Men's mikvah. Services: Daily
Temple Beth Am (C-US), 1039 S La Cienega Blvd, Ph: 652-7353.
Rabbi J. Rembaum and Rabbi H. Silverstein. Services: Shabbat
Congregation Beth Chayim Chadashim (R-UAHC), 6000 W Pico
Blvd, Ph: 931-7023. Rabbi D. Eger. Services: Friday

Synagogues cont.

Temple Beth El (R-UAHC), 1435 W 7th St, **San Pedro**, Ph: 833-2467. Rabbi D. Lieb. Services: Friday

Congregation Beth Israel (O-UOJC), 8056 Beverly Blvd, Ph: 651-4022. Rabbi S. Lieberman. Services: Daily

Congregation Beth Jacob (O-UOJC), 9030 Olympic Blvd, **Beverly Hills**, Ph: 278-1911. Rabbi A. Weiss. Services: Daily

Temple Beth Zion (C-US), 5555 W Olympic Blvd, Ph: 933-9136. Rabbi E. Tenenbaum. Services: Shabbat

B'nai David—Judea Congregation (O), 8906 W Pico Blvd, Ph: 272-7223. Rabbi P. Schroit. Services: Daily

B'nai Tikvah Congregation (C-US), 5820 Manchester Ave, Ph: 645-6262. Rabbi D. Zucker. Services: Shabbat

Breed Street Shule/Congregation Talmud Torah (O), 247 N Breed St, Ph: 262-3922. Rabbi M. Ganzweig. Services: Shabbat, Sunday and Monday

Chabad of Bel Air (O-Lubav), 10421 Summer Holly Circle, **Bel Air**, Ph: 208-7511. Rabbi C. Mentz. Services: Shabbat

Chabad of Brentwood (O-Lubav), 11920 San Vincente Blvd, **Brentwood**, Ph: 826-4453. Rabbi B. Hecht. Services: Daily

Chabad of Cheviot Hills (O-Lubav), 32682 Motor Ave, Ph: 474-6685. Rabbi A. Begun. Services: Shabbat

Chabad Israeli Center (O-Lubav), 1520 S Robertson, Ph: 271-6193. Rabbi A. Yemini. Services: Shabbat

Chabad of the Marina (O-Lubav), 714 Washington St, **Marina del Rey**, Ph: 306-4649. Rabbi S. Naparstek. Services: Saturday, Sunday

Chabad of North Beverly Hills (O-Lubav), 409 N Foothill Rd, **Beverly Hills**, Ph: 271-9063. Rabbi Y. Shusterman. Services: Daily

Chabad of Pacific Palisades (O-Lubav), 732 Hartzel Ave, **Pacific Palisades**, Ph: 454-9770. Rabbi M. Shur. Services: Shabbat

Chabad Russian Outreach Center (O-Lubav), 7414 Santa Monica Blvd, **West Hollywood**, Ph: 874-7583. Rabbi B. Zaltzman. Services: Daily

Chabad West Coast Headquarters (O-Lubav), 741 Gayley Ave, **Westwood**, Ph: 208-7511. Rabbi Y. Stillman. Services: Daily

Temple Emanuel (R-UAHC), 8844 Burton Way, **Beverly Hills,**
 Ph: 274-6388. Rabbi M. Heller. Services: Shabbat
Etz Jacob Congregation (O-UOJC), 7659 Beverly Blvd,
 Ph: 938-2619. Rabbi R. Huttler. Services: Daily
Hollywood Temple Beth El (C-US), 1317 N Crescent Heights Blvd,
 Ph: 656-3150. Rabbi N. Weinberg. Services: Daily
Temple Isaiah (R-UAHC), 10345 W Pico Blvd, Ph: 277-2772.
 Rabbi R. Gan. Services: Shabbat
Temple Israel of Hollywood (R-UAHC), 7300 Hollywood Blvd, Ph:
 876-8330. Rabbi J. Rosove. Services: Shabbat
Kehillath Israel (Recon-FRCH), 16019 Sunset Blvd, **Pacific**
 Palisades, Ph: 459-2328. Rabbi S. Reuben. Services: Shabbat
Knesseth Israel Congregation of Beverlywood (O), 2364 S
 Robertson, Ph: 839-4962. Services: Daily
Temple Knesseth Israel of Hollywood—Los Feliz (C), 1260 N
 Vermont Ave, Ph: 665-5171. Rabbi R. Elias. Services: Saturday
Leo Baeck Temple (R-UAHC), 1300 N Sepulveda, **Bel Air,**
 Ph: 476-2861. Rabbi S. Ragins. Services: Friday
Congregation Levi Yitzchok (O-Lubav), 221 S La Brea Ave,
 Ph: 938-1837. Rabbi S. Raichik. Services: Daily
Congregation Lubavitch of S Beverly Hills (O-Lubav), 9017 W Pico
 Blvd, Ph: 657-4363. Rabbi B. Lisbon. Services: Daily
Malibu Jewish Center (Recon-FRCH), 3504 Winter Canyon Rd,
 Malibu, Ph: 456-2178. Rabbi B. Herson. Services: Friday, first
 Saturday
Midrash Od Yoseph Hai (Sephardic), 420 N Fairfax, Ph: 653-5163.
 Rabbi H. Hayward. Services: Daily
Congregation Mogen Abraham (O), 356 N La Brea, Ph: 932-9690.
 Rabbi A. Lowe. Men's mikvah. Services: Daily
Congregation Mogen David (Trad), 9717 W Pico Blvd,
 Ph: 556-5609. Rabbi Y. Kelemer. Services: Daily
Congregation Ohel David (O), 7967 Beverly Blvd, Ph: 651-3594.
 Rabbi E. Adler. Services: Daily
Ohev Sholom Congregation (O), 525 S Fairfax Ave, Ph: 653-7190.
 Services: Daily
Sephardic Congregation Kahal Yoseph (O), 10505 Santa Monica
 Blvd, **Westwood,** Ph: 474-0559. Rabbi M. Benzaquen. Services:
 Shabbat

Synagogues cont.

Sephardic Hebrew Center (C), 4911 W 59th, Ph: 295-5541. Rabbi R. J. Rome. Services: Shabbat

Sephardic Magen David Congregation (O-UOJC), 7454 Melrose Ave, Ph: 655-3441. Rabbi G. Cohen. Services: Daily

Sephardic Temple Tifereth Israel (O), 10500 Wilshire Blvd, Ph: 475-7311. Rabbi J. Ott. Services: Shabbat

Congregation Shaarei Tefila (O-UOJC), 7269 Beverly Blvd, Ph: 938-7147. Rabbi J. Cohen. Services: Daily

Sinai Temple (C-US), 10400 Wilshire Blvd, Ph: 474-1518. Rabbi A. Schranz. Services: Daily

Stephen S. Wise Temple (R-UAHC, Recon-FRCH), 15500 Stephen S. Wise Dr, Ph: 476-8561. Rabbi I. Zeldin. Services: Friday

Synagogue for the Performing Arts (C, R), 1727 Barrington Ct #205, Ph: 472-3500. Rabbi D. Baron. Services: First Friday

Congregation Tifereth Zvi (O), 7561 Beverly Blvd, Ph: 931-3252. Rabbi Y. Ganzweig. Services: Daily

University Synagogue (R-UAHC), 11960 Sunset Blvd, Ph: 472-1255. Rabbi Dr. A. Freehling. Services: Shabbat

Westwood Kehilla (O), 900 Hilgard Ave, (University Religious Conference), **Westwood**, Ph: 475-3686 or 470-1527. Rabbi J. Zeff. Services: Daily

Wilshire Boulevard Temple (R-UAHC), 3663 Wilshire Blvd, Ph: 388-2401. Rabbi S. Donnell. Services: Shabbat

Yeshiva Ohr Elchonon Chabad (O-Lubav), 7215 Waring Ave, Ph: 937-3763. Rabbi E. Shochet. Services: Daily

Yeshiva University (O), 9760 W Pico Blvd, Ph: 553-4478. Rabbi S. Tendler. Services: Daily

Young Israel of Beverly Hills (O-NCYI), 8701 W Pico Blvd, **Beverly Hills**, Ph: 275-3020. Rabbi A. Union. Services: Daily

Young Israel of Century City (O-NCYI), 9315 W Pico Blvd, Ph: 273-6954. Rabbi E. Muskin. Services: Daily

Young Israel of Hancock Park (O-NCYI), 225 S La Brea Ave, Ph: 932-9213. Rabbi Y. Krause. Services: Daily

Young Israel of Los Angeles (O-NCYI), 660 N Spaulding, Ph: 655-0300. Rabbi Z. Teichman. Services: Daily

Eating Out

For kosher information, call:
Rabbinical Council of California, Rabbi B. Lisbon, Ph: 271-4160;
Kehilla, Rabbi A. Teichman, Ph: 935-8383.

Beverly Grand Hotel, 7359 Beverly Blvd, Ph: 939-1653. Meals: d
   Menu: Continental and Mexican. RS: Kehilla. Credit cards. Pay
   in advance for Shabbat meals.
Cellar Cafe, 6505 Wilshire Blvd, Ph: 852-1234. Meals: b,l.
   Menu: (Dairy, meat) Salads, sandwiches, hot dishes. RS:
   Rabbinical Council of CA. Closed Shabbat.
Dan Michaels, 7777 Sunset Blvd, Ph: 851-7557. Meals: l,d.
   Menu: (Glatt meat) Israeli. RS: Rabbinical Council of CA.
   Credit cards. Closed Shabbat.
David's, 9303 Pico Blvd, Ph: 859-7633. Meals: b,l,d. Menu: (Glatt
   meat) Mideastern and European. RS: Rabbinical Council of CA
   and Vaad Ha-ir. Closed Shabbat.
Dizengoff Restaurant, 8107 Beverly Blvd, Ph: 651-4465. Meals: l,d.
   Menu: (Meat) Israeli & European. RS: Rabbinical Council of CA.
   Credit cards. Closed Shabbat.
Elite Cuisine, 7119 Beverly Blvd, Ph: 930-1303. Meals: l,d. Menu:
   (Glatt meat) fish, European style. Also take-out. RS: Kehilla,
   Rabbinical Council of CA and Vaad Ha-ir. Credit cards. Closed
   Shabbat.
Fairfax Kosher Pizza, 453 N Fairfax Ave, Ph: 653-7200. Meals:
   b,l,d. Menu: (Dairy: cholov Yisroel) Pizza and other dairy

Eating Out cont.

dishes. Also take-out. RS: Kehilla and Vaad Ha-ir. Closed Shabbat.

Fish Grill, 7226 Beverly Blvd, Ph: 937-7162. Meals: l,d. Menu: (Dairy: cholov Yisroel) Fish. Also take-out. RS: Kehilla and Vaad Ha-ir. Closed Shabbat.

The Fishing Well, 8975 W Pico Blvd, Ph: 859-9429. Meals: l,d. Menu: (Pareve) Fish. RS: Rabbinical Council of CA. Closed Shabbat.

Grill Express, 501 N Fairfax, Ph: 655-0649. Meals: l,d. Menu: (Meat) Israeli. Also take-out. RS: Rabbinical Council of CA. Closed Shabbat.

I'm a Deli Restaurant, 8930 W Pico Blvd, Ph: 274-2452. Meals: l,d. Menu: (Glatt meat) Deli. RS: Rabbi Y. Bukspan. Closed Shabbat.

Judy's, 129 N La Brea Ave, Ph: 934-7667. Meals: l,d. Menu: (Glatt meat) Lunch: salads, sandwiches, hamburgers; Dinner: International cuisine. RS: Rabbinical Council of CA and Vaad Ha-ir. Closed Shabbat.

Kosher Kolonel, 9301 W Pico Blvd, Ph: 858-0111. Meals: l,d. Menu: Chicken, turkey, burgers, salads. RS: Kehilla. Closed Shabbat.

Kosher Pizza Nosh, 8844 W Pico Blvd, Ph: 276-8708. Meals: l,d. Menu: (Dairy: cholov Yisroel) Pizza, Italian. RS: Rabbi Y. Bukspan. Closed Shabbat.

La Mamounia, 370 N Fairfax Ave, Ph: 930-1891. Meals: l,d. Menu: (Glatt meat) Morroccan cuisine. Lamb, chicken, veal, vegetables, appetizers. RS: Kehilla. Closed Shabbat.

Micheline's, 8965 W Pico Blvd, Ph: 274-6534. Meals: l,d. Menu: (Glatt meat) Fast-food deli, Mexican, American, Chinese. RS: Rabbinical Council of CA and Vaad Ha-ir. Closed Shabbat.

The Milky Way, 9108 W Pico Blvd, Ph: 859-0004. Meals: l,d. Menu: (Dairy: cholov Yisroel) Italian cuisine. RS: Rabbi Y. Bukspan. Closed Shabbat. Call for reservations.

Nagilla Pizza, 9216 W Pico Blvd, Ph: 550-7735. Meals: l,d. Menu: (Dairy: cholov Yisroel) Pizza, Italian, Israeli salads. Also take-out. RS: Kehilla and Vaad Ha-ir. Closed Shabbat.

Olé, 7912 Beverly Blvd, Ph: 933-7254. Meals: l,d. Menu: (Glatt meat) Mexican. Also take-out. RS: Kehilla. Closed Shabbat.

Pat's, 9233 W Pico Blvd, Ph: 205-8705. Meals: l,d. Menu: (Dairy: cholov Yisroel) Italian. RS: Kehilla. Credit cards. Closed Shabbat.

Pico Kosher Deli, 8826 W Pico Blvd, Ph: 273-9381. Meals: l,d. Menu: (Meat) Deli, fish. RS: Rabbinical Council of CA. Closed Shabbat.

Pizza Mayven, 140 N La Brea Blvd, Ph: 857-0353. Meals: l,d. Menu: (Dairy: cholov Yisroel) Pizza. RS: Rabbi Y. Bukspan. Closed Shabbat.

Serravalle Inn, 8837 W Pico Blvd, Ph: 550-8372. Meals: l,d. Menu: (Glatt meat) European cuisine. RS: Kehilla and Vaad Ha-ir. All credit cards. Call for reservations. Closed Shabbat.

Simon's, 8706 W Pico Blvd, Ph: 657-5552. Meals: l,d. Menu: (Glatt meat) Persian. RS: Rabbinical Council of CA and Vaad Ha-ir. Closed Shabbat.

Simon's Downtown, 914 S Hill, Ph: 627-6535. Meals: l. Menu: (Glatt meat) Persian. RS: Rabbinical Council of CA and Vaad Ha-ir. Closed Shabbat.

Simon's L.A. Glatt, 446 N Fairfax Ave, Ph: 658-7730. Meals: l,d. Menu: (Glatt meat) Deli, Chinese and Mexican. RS: Rabbinical Council of CA and Vaad Ha-ir. Closed Shabbat.

Tami's Fish House, 533 N Fairfax Ave, Ph: 655-7953. Meals: l,d. Menu: (Dairy: cholov Yisroel) Fish, dairy dishes. Also take-out. RS: Kehilla and Vaad Ha-ir. Closed Shabbat.

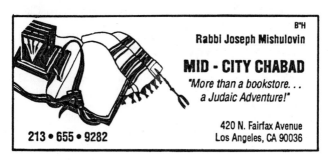

Food

Bastomski's Meats, 7667 Beverly Blvd, Ph: 933-4040. Fresh meat, poultry, deli. RS: Kehilla. Closed Shabbat.

Bazar Market, 451 N Fairfax Ave, Ph: 852-1981. Butcher and kosher grocery. RS: Rabbinical Council of CA. Closed Shabbat.

Beverly Hills Patisserie, 9100 W Pico Blvd, Ph: 275-6873. Breads and pastries (pareve). RS: Rabbinical Council of CA and Vaad Ha-ir. Closed Shabbat.

Bob's Fish Store, 415 N Fairfax Ave, Ph: 655-1126. RS: Rabbinical Council of CA. Closed Shabbat.

Carmel Kosher Meat Market, 8914 W Pico Blvd, Ph: 278-6347. Fresh meat, groceries, frozen foods. RS: Rabbinical Council of CA. Closed Shabbat.

Century City Meats, 8973 W Pico Blvd, Ph: 278-1754. Meat & grocery items. RS: Rabbinical Council of CA. Closed Shabbat.

Doheny Kosher Meats & Poultry, 9213 W Pico Blvd, Ph: 276-7232. RS: Rabbinical Council of CA. Closed Shabbat.

Dove's Famous Bakery, 8924 W Pico Blvd, Ph: 276-6150, Ph: 276-6150. Breads and pastries (Pareve and Dairy: cholov Yisroel). RS: Kehilla. Closed Shabbat.

Eilat Bakery, 513 N Fairfax Ave, Ph: 939-8367; 9233 W Pico Blvd, Ph: 205-8700. Pareve and Dairy: cholov Yisroel. RS: Kehilla. Closed Shabbat.

Elat Market, 8730 W Pico Blvd, Ph: 659-0576. Mideastern kosher products. Closed Shabbat. Closed for repairs.

European Glatt Kosher Market, 360 N Fairfax Ave, Ph: 930-1674. Meat, poultry, fish, fruit, kosher groceries. RS: Kehilla. Closed Shabbat.

Fairfax Family Market, 451 N Fairfax Ave, Ph: 852-1981. Complete kosher grocery. RS: Rabbinical Council of CA. Closed Shabbat.

Fairfax Kosher Market, 439 N Fairfax Ave, Ph: 653-2530. Complete kosher grocery, including cheese and wines. RS: Rabbinical Council of CA. Closed Shabbat.

Hadar Kosher Meats, 440 N Fairfax Ave, Ph: 655-0250. RS: Rabbinical Council of CA. Closed Shabbat.

Kosher Club, 4817 W Pico Blvd, Ph: 933-8283. Kosher groceries. RS: Rabbinical Council of CA. Closed Shabbat.

Kosher Kolonel, 9301 W Pico Blvd, Ph: 858-0111. Prepared meat, chicken and side dishes to go. RS: Kehilla. Closed Shabbat.

Kotlar's Market, 8622 W Pico Blvd, Ph: 652-5355. Complete kosher grocery. RS: Rabbinical Council of CA. Closed Shabbat.

La Brea Market, 345 N La Brea Ave, Ph: 931-1221. RS: Kehilla. Closed Shabbat.

La Mamounia, 370 N Fairfax Ave, Ph: 930-1891. Kosher market, bakery and take-out (Glatt meat). RS: Kehilla. Closed Shabbat.

Little Jerusalem, 8971 W Pico Blvd, Ph: 858-8361. Complete kosher grocery including fresh breads and pastries. RS: Rabbinical Council of CA. Closed Shabbat.

Manes Kosher Meats (in Beverly Square Market), 9238 W Pico Blvd, Ph: 278-6329. RS: Rabbinical Council of CA. Closed Shabbat.

Mehadrin Meats, 7613 Beverly Blvd, Ph: 934-2196 RS: Kehilla. Closed Shabbat.

Menorah Market, 8664 W Pico Blvd, Ph: 854-0447. Deli, full line of kosher groceries and frozen foods. Also take-out. RS: Rabbinical Council of CA (meat and chicken only). Closed Shabbat.

My Kosher Butcher, 415 N Fairfax Ave, Ph: 655-5554. RS: Rabbinical Council of CA. Closed Shabbat.

Rahamim's Kosher Meats, 8730 W Pico Blvd (in Elat Market), Ph: 273-0682. Rabbinical Council of CA. Closed Shabbat. Closed for repairs.

Rami's Market, 505 N Fairfax Ave, Ph: 651-4293. RS: Rabbinical Council of CA. Closed Shabbat.

Real Kosher Meat, 7965 Beverly Blvd, Ph: 653-8355. RS: Rabbinical Council of CA. Closed Shabbat.

Schwartz Bakery, 441 N Fairfax Ave, Ph: 653-1683; 8616 W Pico Blvd, Ph: 854-0592. Pas Yisroel, cholov Yisroel, breads and pastries (pareve and dairy). RS: Orthodox Union and Vaad Ha-ir. Closed Shabbat.

Food cont.

Star Kosher Meat Market, 12136 Santa Monica Blvd, Ph: 447-1612.
Meat, poultry, fish. RS: Rabbinical Council of CA.

Susan's Kosher Market, 656 N Fairfax, Ph: 655-2073. Complete
kosher grocery. RS: Rabbinical Council of CA. Closed Shabbat.

Accommodations

Private accommodations for Shabbat; contact Rabbi Cunin at
Chabad House, Ph: 208-7511.

Beverly Grand Hotel, 7257 Beverly Blvd, Ph: 939-1653. Shomer
Shabbat. Located next to Congregation Shaarei Tefila.

Beverly Laurel Motor Hotel, 8018 Beverly Blvd, Ph: 651-2441.
Some kitchenettes. Walk to Fairfax area synagogues.

Mikvah

L. A. Mikvah, 9548 W Pico Blvd, Ph: 550-4511.

Mogen Abraham Synagogue, 356 N La Brea Ave. Contact
Rebbetzin Lowe, Ph: 935-5415; 930-2690.

Day Schools

Bais Chaya Mushka, 9017 W Pico Blvd, Ph: 859-8840.

Hillel Hebrew Academy, 9120 W Olympic Blvd, **Beverly Hills**,
Ph: 276-6135.

Rabbi Jacob Pressman Academy of Temple Beth Am (C), 1027 S
La Cienega Blvd, Ph: 652-7353.

Samuel A. Fryer Yavneh Academy, 7353 Beverly Blvd,
Ph: 938-2636.

Sephardic Hebrew Academy, 310 N Huntley Dr, Ph: 659-2456.

Sinai Akiba Academy (C), 10400 Wilshire Blvd, Ph: 475-6401.

Stephen S. Wise Temple Day School (R), 15500 Stephen S. Wise
Dr, Ph: 472-7683 or 476-8561.

Temple Emanuel Community Day School (R), 8844 Burton Way,
Beverly Hills, Ph: 275-0209 or 274-6388.

Temple Isaiah Day School (R), 10345 W Pico Blvd, Ph: 277-2772.

Temple Israel Community Day School (R), 7300 Hollywood Blvd,
Ph: 876-8330.

Torat Hayim Hebrew Academy, 1210 S La Cienega Blvd,
Ph: 652-8349 or 652-1533.

Torath Emeth Academy, 540 N La Brea Ave, Ph: 939-1148.
West Coast Talmudical Seminary, Yeshiva Ohr Elchonon Chabad, 7215 Waring Ave, Ph: 937-3763.

Bookstores

Atara's, 450 N Fairfax, Ph: 655-3050.
Chabad Mid-City Center, 420 N Fairfax, Ph: 655-9282.
Herskovitz Hebrew Bookstore, 4421/2 N Fairfax, Ph: 852-9310.
J. Roth/Bookseller, Inc., 9020 W Olympic Blvd, Ph: 276-9414.
Solomon's Books and Gifts, 447 N Fairfax, Ph: 653-9045.

San Fernando Valley Area—Area Code (818)

Synagogues

Adat Ari El (C-US), 12020 Burbank Blvd, **North Hollywood**, Ph: 766-9426. Rabbi M. Rothblum. Services: Daily
Temple Ahavat Shalom (R-UAHC), 18200 Rinaldi Pl, **Northridge**, Ph: 360-2258. Rabbi J. Brown. Services: Shabbat
Aish Hatorah Institute (O), 12422 Chandler Blvd, **North Hollywood**, Ph: 980-6934. Rabbi Z. Block. Services: Shabbat
Temple Aliyah (C-US), 6025 Valley Circle, **Woodland Hills**, Ph: 346-3545. Rabbi M. Goldstine. Services: Shabbat
Beit Hamidrash of Woodland Hills (O), 22733 Oxnard, **Woodland Hills**, Ph: 884-3388. Rabbi Z. D. Rauch. Services: Shabbat
Temple Beth Ami (C-US), 18449 Kittridge St, **Reseda**, Ph: 343-4624. Rabbi D. Vorspan. Services: Shabbat
Temple Beth Emet (R), 600 N Buena Vista, **Burbank**, Ph: 843-9444. Rabbi W. Kramer. Services: Friday

Synagogues cont.

Temple Beth Hillel (R-UAHC), 12326 Riverside Dr, **North Hollywood**, Ph: 763-9148. Rabbi J. Kaufman. Services: Call for schedule.

Congregation Beth Kodesh (C-US), 7401 Shoup Ave, **West Hills**, Ph: 346-0811. Rabbi E. Schochet. Services: Daily

Congregation Beth Meier (C), 11725 Moorpark St, **Studio City**, Ph: 845-0515. Rabbi M. Schimmel. Services: Shabbat

Temple Beth Solomon of the Deaf (R-UAHC), 13580 Osborne St, **Arleta**, Ph: 899-2202—voice, 896-6721—TTD. Rabbi A. Berk. Services: Call for schedule.

Temple Beth Torah (R-UAHC), 16651 Rinaldi St, **Granada Hills**, Ph: 831-0835. Rabbi H. Essrig. Services: Friday

Blauner Youth Center (O-Lubav), 18211 Burbank Blvd, **Tarzana**, Ph: 784-9985. Rabbi M. Einbinder. Services: Shabbat

Temple B'nai Hayim (C-US), 4302 Van Nuys Blvd, **Sherman Oaks**, Ph: 788-4664. Rabbi S. Weltman. Services: Shabbat

Burbank Temple Emanu-El (C-US), 1302 N Glenoaks Blvd, **Burbank**, Ph: 845-1734. Rabbi M. Tomsky. Services: Shabbat

Chabad of Agoura (O-Lubav), 368 N Kanan Rd, **Agoura Hills**, Ph: 991-0991. Rabbi M. Bryski. Services: Shabbat and daily

Chabad of North Hollywood (O-Lubav), 13079 Chandler Blvd, **Van Nuys**, Ph: 989-9539. Rabbi A. Abend. Services: Daily

Chabad of Northridge (O-Lubav), 17142 Devonshire St, **Northridge**, Ph: 784-9985. Rabbi M. Bryski. Services: Shabbat

Chabad of Sherman Oaks (O-Lubav), 14615 Ventura Blvd #210, **Sherman Oaks**, Ph: 784-9985. Rabbi M. Weiss. Services: Shabbat

Chabad of Tarzana, (See Blauner Youth Center)

Chabad of the Valley (O-Lubav), 4915 Hayvenhurst Ave, **Encino**, Ph: 784-9985. Rabbi J. Gordon. Services: Daily

Em Habanim Sephardic Congregation (O), 5850 Laurel Canyon Blvd, **North Hollywood**, Ph: 762-7779/9868. Rabbi H. Louk. Services: Shabbat

Temple Emet (R), 20400 Ventura Blvd, **Woodland Hills**, Ph: 348-0670. Rabbi J. Sherwood. Services: Friday

Temple Judea (R-UAHC), 5422 Lindley Ave, **Tarzana,** Ph: 987-2616. Rabbi C. Akiva. Services: Shabbat

Temple Ner Maarav (C-US), 5180 Yarmouth Ave, **Encino,** Ph: 345-7833. Rabbi A. Kriegel. Services: Daily

Temple Ramat Zion (C-US), 17655 Devonshire St, **Northridge,** Ph: 360-1881. Rabbi S. Rothstein. Services: Daily

Sephardic Congregation Adat Yeshurun (O), 6348 Whitsett Ave, **North Hollywood,** Ph: 766-4682. Rabbi A. Gabay. Services: Call for schedule.

Shaarey Zedek Congregation (O-UOJC), 12800 Chandler Blvd, **North Hollywood,** Ph: 763-0560. Rabbi M. Sugarman. Services: Daily

Shir Chadash New Reform Congregation (R), 17000 Ventura Blvd #302, **Encino,** Ph: 988-6102. Rabbi S. Jacobs. Services: Friday

Temple Sinai of Glendale (R-UAHC), 1212 N Pacific Ave, **Glendale,** Ph: 246-8101. Rabbi C. Meyers. Services: Friday

Temple Solael (R), 6601 Valley Circle Blvd, **Canoga Park,** Ph: 348-3885. Rabbi B. Cohen. Services: Shabbat

Valley Beth Israel (C-US), 13060 Roscoe Blvd, **Sun Valley,** Ph: 782-2281. Rabbi M. Rubinstein. Services: Daily

Valley Beth Shalom (C-US), 15739 Ventura Blvd, **Encino,** Ph: 788-6000. Rabbi H. Schulweis. Services: Daily

Valley Mishkan Israel Congregation (O-UOJC), 6450 Bellingham Ave, **North Hollywood,** Ph: 769-8043. Rabbi N. Pauker. Services: Shabbat

Verdugo Hills Hebrew Center and Temple (C-US), 10275 Tujunga Canyon Blvd, **Tujunga,** Ph: 352-3171. Rabbi M. Goldstein. Services: Shabbat

Young Israel of Northridge (O-NCYI), 17511 Devonshire, **Northridge,** Ph: 368-2221. Rabbi A. Simkin. Services: Shabbat

Eating Out

B'nai B'rith Hillel of Northridge, 17729 Plummer St, **Northridge.** Friday evening service and dinner during the school year. RS: Young Israel of Northridge, (Rabbi A. Simkin). Call for reservations, Ph: 886-5101.

Eating Out cont.

Drexler's, 12519 1/2 Burbank Blvd, **North Hollywood,** Ph: 761-6405. Meals: b,l,d. Menu: Eastern European and deli. RS: Rabbinical Council of CA. Closed Shabbat.

Flora Falafel, 12450 Burbank Blvd, **North Hollywood,** Ph: 766-6567. Meals: l,d. Menu: Falafel, shwarma, Mideastern. RS: Rabbinical Council of CA. Closed Shabbat.

Golan, 6365 Woodman Ave, **Van Nuys,** Ph: 989-5423. Meals: l,d. Menu: (Glatt meat) Fish and Israeli cuisine. RS: Rabbinical Council of CA. Closed Shabbat.

Golan Woodland Hills, 21036 Victory Blvd, **Woodland Hills,** Ph: 887-9593. Meals: l,d. Menu: (Glatt meat) Mideastern, European, Chinese. Salad bar. RS: Rabbi Y. Bukspan. Closed Shabbat.

Hadar I, 12514 Burbank Blvd, **North Hollywood,** Ph: 762-1155. Meals: b,l,d. Menu: (Glatt meat) Chinese, Israeli & European. RS: Rabbi Y. Bukspan. Closed Shabbat.

Kibbutz, 6365 Woodman Ave, **Van Nuys,** Ph: 989-5175. Meals: b,l,d. Menu: (Dairy; cholov Yisroel) Borekas, omelettes, bagels, Italian dishes. RS: Rabbinical Council of CA. Credit cards. Closed Shabbat.

La Pizza, 12515 Burbank Blvd, **North Hollywood,** Ph: 760-8190. Meals, l,d. Menu: (Dairy; cholov Yisroel) Italian cuisine. RS: Rabbi S. Furst. Credit cards. Closed Shabbat.

Tiberias, 18046 Ventura Blvd, **Encino,** Ph: 343-3705. Meals: l,d. Menu: (Glatt meat) Mideastern. Order ahead Shabbat take-out. RS: Rabbinical Council of CA. Credit cards. Closed Shabbat.

Food

Bon Bon Kosher Sweets, 15030 Ventura Blvd, **Sherman Oaks,** Ph: 981-5426. Candy store. RS: Rabbinical Souncil of CA. Closed Shabbat.

Continental Kosher Bakery, 12419 Burbank Blvd, **North Hollywood,** Ph: 762-5005. (Pareve). RS: Rabbi S. Furst, Orthodox Union and Vaad Ha-ir.

Drexler's, 12519 1/2 Burbank Blvd, **North Hollywood,** Ph: 761-6405. Traditional dishes for take-out, wines and frozen foods. RS: Rabbinical Council of CA. Closed Shabbat.

Hughes, Balboa & Devonshire, Ph: 363-3173. Carries kosher hard cheeses and glatt kosher deli.

Le Market, 12516 Burbank Blvd, **North Hollywood**, Ph: 763-5223. Complete kosher grocery. Frozen meats and poultry. RS: Rabbi S. Furst. Closed Shabbat.

Little Israel, 18038 Ventura Blvd, **Encino**, Ph: 609-1001. Kosher grocery. Many Israeli products. Closed Shabbat.

Miller's Butcher Store in Miller's Market, 17261 Van Owen St, **Van Nuys**, Ph: 345-9222. Meats and poultry. Complete kosher grocery. RS: Rabbinical Council of CA. Closed Shabbat.

Mr. Kosher, 17922 Ventura Blvd, **Encino**, Ph: 345-5100. Meat, poultry, fish, groceries. RS: Rabbinical Council of CA. Closed Shabbat.

Roz. Kosher Meats, 12422 Burbank Blvd, **North Hollywood**, Ph: 760-7694. Meat, poultry, fish, deli, sandwiches for take-out, complete kosher grocery and kosher wines. RS: Rabbi Y. Bukspan and Rabbinical Council of CA. Closed Shabbat.

Sammy's Kosher Bakery, 12450 Burbank Blvd, **North Hollywood**, Ph: 769-8352. Pareve breads and cakes, dairy donuts and sandwiches. RS: Rabbi Y. Bukspan. Closed Shabbat.

Ventura Kosher Meats, 18357 Ventura Blvd, **Tarzana**, Ph: 881-3777/6800. Complete kosher grocery and meat market. RS: Rabbinical Council of CA. Closed Shabbat.

Accommodations

Mikado, 12600 Riverside Dr, **North Hollywood**, Ph: 763-9141. Walk to Shaarey Zedek Congregation. A few kitchenettes.

Private accommodations; Contact Chabad of the Valley, Ph: 907-7491; or Rabbi M. Sugarman at Shaarey Zedek Congregation, Ph: 763-0560.

Mikvah

Valley Mikvah Society, 12800 Chandler Blvd, **North Hollywood**. Call two days in advance, Ph: 506-0996 (evenings only).

Day Schools

Adat Ari El Day School (C), 5540 Laurel Canyon Blvd, **North Hollywood**, Ph: 766-4992.

33

Day Schools cont.

Kadima Hebrew Academy (C), 5724 Oso Ave, **Woodland Hills,** Ph: 346-0849.

West Valley Hebrew Institute, 5850 Fallbrook Ave, **Woodland Hills,** Ph: 884-3388.

Bookstores

House of David, 12826 Victory Blvd, **North Hollywood,** Ph: 763-2070.

Jerusalem Fair, 14245 Ventura Blvd, **Sherman Oaks,** Ph: 995-0116.

Shalom House, 8363 Reseda, **Northridge,** Ph: 701-9200.

Other Parts of Greater Los Angeles

Synagogues

Temple Beth Ami (C-US), 3508 E Temple Way, **West Covina,** Ph: (818) 331-0515. Services: Shabbat

Temple Beth David (R-UAHC), 9677 E Longden Ave, **Temple City,** Ph: (818) 287-9994. Rabbi A. Lachtman. Services: Friday

Temple Beth Ohr (R-UAHC), 15721 Rosecrans Ave, **La Mirada,** Ph: (714) 521-6765. Rabbi L. Goldmark. Services: Friday

Beth Shalom of Whittier (C-US), 14564 E Hawes St, **Whittier,** Ph: (213) 941-8744. Rabbi S. Podwol. Services: Shabbat, Sunday, Monday and Thursday

Temple Beth Torah of West San Gabriel Valley (C-US), 225 S Atlantic Blvd, **Alhambra,** Ph: (818) 284-0296 or (213) 283-2035. Rabbi W. Gordon. Services: Shabbat, Sunday, Monday and Thursday

Temple B'nai Emet (C-US), 482 N Garfield Ave, **Montebello,** Ph: (213) 721-7064. Rabbi A. Green. Services: Shabbat, Sunday, Monday and Thursday

Temple Ner Tamid (R-UAHC), 10629 Lakewood Blvd, **Downey,** Ph: (213) 861-9276. Services: Friday

Temple Shaarei Tikvah (C-US), 550 S 2nd Ave, **Arcadia,** Ph: (818) 445-0810. Rabbi D. Barnett. Services: Shabbat

Temple Shalom - West Covina (R), 1912 W Merced Ave, **West Covina,** Ph: (818) 337-6500. Rabbi E. Nattiv. Services: Friday

Southwest Temple Beth Torah (C), 14725 S Gramercy Pl, **Gardena**, Ph: (213) 327-8734. Services: Shabbat

LOS GATOS (See San Jose)

MALIBU (See GREATER LOS ANGELES)

MANHATTAN BEACH   Area Code (213)

Synagogues

Congregation Tifereth Jacob (C-US), 2617 Bell Ave, Ph: 546-3667. Rabbi M. Hyman. Services: Friday

MENDOCINO   Area Code (707)

Synagogues

Mendocino Coast Jewish Community (unaffiliated), P.O. Box 291, **Little River**, 95456, Ph: 937-1635. Rabbi M. Holub. Services: Call. Meets at Mendocino Presbyterian Church.

MISSION VIEJO   Area Code (714)

Synagogues

Temple Eilat (C-US, R-UAHC), 22081 Hidalgo, Ph: 770-9606. Rabbi B. Artson. Services: Shabbat, Monday and Thursday.

MODESTO   Area Code (209)   J-pop. 450

Synagogues

Congregation Beth Shalom (C-US), 1705 Sherwood Ave, Ph: 522-5613. Rabbi S. Gravdenz. Services: Shabbat

MONTEBELLO (See GREATER LOS ANGELES)

MURRIETTA   Area Code (714)   J-pop. 400

Synagogues

Congregation B'nai Chaim & Community Centre (C), 29500 Via Princesa, Ph: 677-7350. Rabbi D. Kane. Services: Shabbat

NAPA   Area Code (707)   J-pop. 450

Synagogues

Congregation Beth Sholom (Independent), 1455 Elm St,
Ph: 224-3291. Rabbi D. Kopstein. Services: Friday

NEWHALL   Area Code (805)

Synagogues

Congregation Beth Shalom of San Clarita Valley (C-US), 23045
Lyons Ave, Ph: 254-2411. Rabbi R. Hauss. Services: Shabbat

NEWPORT BEACH (See also LONG BEACH)
Area Code (714)

Synagogues

Temple Bat Yahm (R), 1011 Camelback Rd, Ph: 644-1999. Rabbi
M. Miler. Services: Friday

Temple Isaiah (C-US), 2401 Irvine St, Ph: 548-6900. Services:
Friday

Shir Ha-Ma'Alot-Harbor Reform Temple (R-UAHC), 2100 Mar
Vista, Ph: 644-7203. Rabbi B. King. Services: Friday

NORTH HOLLYWOOD (See GREATER LOS ANGELES)

NORTHRIDGE (See GREATER LOS ANGELES)

OAKLAND   Area Code (415)

Synagogues

Temple Beth Abraham (C-US), 327 MacArthur Blvd,
Ph: 832-0936. Rabbi J. Schonwald. Services: Shabbat, Monday
and Thursday

Beth Jacob Congregation (O-UOJC), 3778 Park Blvd,
Ph: 482-1147. Rabbi H. Zack. Services: Daily

Temple Beth Torah (R-UAHC), 42000 Paseo Padre Pkwy,
Fremont, Ph: 656-7141. Rabbi S. Kaplan. Services: Friday

Temple Israel (R-UAHC), 3183 McCartney Rd, **Alameda**,
Ph: 522-9355. Rabbi Biatch. Services: Friday

Temple Sinai (R-UAHC), 2808 Summit St, Ph: 451-3263. Rabbi S.
Chester. Services: Shabbat

Eating Out

The Grand Bakery, 3264 Grand Ave, Ph: 465-1110. Pastries, coffee
and beverages. RS: East Bay Vaad Hakashrut. Closed Shabbat.
Holyland Restaurant, 677 Rand, Ph: 272-0535. Meals: l,d. Menu:
Mideastern & European. RS: Rabbi H. Zack. Closed Shabbat.

Food

The Grand Bakery, 3264 Grand Ave, Ph: 465-1110. Breads, pastries, coffee, beverages. RS: East Bay Vaad Hakashrut. Closed
Shabbat, Monday.
Oakland Kosher Foods, 3256 Grand Ave, Ph: 451-3883. Fresh
meats, poultry deli foods, frozen foods, groceries and kosher
wines. Shabbat take-out. RS: East Bay Vaad Hakashrut. Closed
Shabbat.

Mikvah (See **Berkeley)**

ONTARIO   Area Code (714)

Synagogues

Temple Sholom of Ontario (C-US), 963 W 6th St, Ph: 983-9661.
Rabbi Dr. H. Brooks. Services: Shabbat and Sunday

PACIFIC PALISADES (See **GREATER LOS ANGELES**)

PALM DESERT (See **PALM SPRINGS**)

PALM SPRINGS   Area Code (619)   J-pop. 9,600

Synagogues

JCC of Palm Springs/Temple Isaiah (O,C,R), 332 W Alejo Rd,
Ph: 325-2281. Rabbi J. Hurwitz. Services: Daily
Chabad of Palm Springs (O-Lubav), 425 Avenida Ortega,
Ph: 325-0774. Rabbi Y. Denebeim. Services: Daily, in winter;
Shabbat, in summer. Call for candle-lighting time (20-30
minutes earlier than L.A.).

Synagogues cont.

The Desert Synagogue (Kehillat Hamidbar) (O-UOJC), 1068 N Palm Canyon, Ph: 327-4848. Rabbi M. Lamm. Services: Shabbat (Call for information July and August).

Temple Ne've Shalom (C-US), 66-777 E Pierson Blvd, **Desert Hot Springs**, Ph: 329-5168. Rabbi E. Gottesman. Services: Shabbat

Temple Sinai (R), 43435 Monterey Ave, **Palm Desert**, Ph: 568-9699. Rabbi Y. Liebowitz. Services: Shabbat

Food

Catarelli's, 196 S Indian Ave, Ph: 325-0177. Separate section for kosher fish.

L & H Kosher Market, 618 E Sunny Dunes Rd, Ph: 325-0139. Only packaged goods are kosher. Closed Shabbat.

Mikvah

Chabad House, 425 Avenida Ortega. Call to make appointment, 325-0774.

Day School

Desert Torah Academy-Lubavitch, P.O. Box 8218, 96623, Ph: 325-3212.

PALO ALTO (See also SAN FRANCISCO)   Area Code (415)

Synagogues

Congregation Ahavas Yisroel - Lubavitch (O-Lubav), 3070 Louis Rd, Ph: 424-9800. Rabbi Y. Levin. Services: Daily

Congregation Kol Emeth (C-US), 4175 Manuel Ave, Ph: 948-7498. Rabbi S. Lewis. Services: Daily

Palo Alto Orthodox Minyan (O-UOJC), 453 Sherman Ave, Ph: 326-5001. Rabbi Y. Young. Services: Daily

Food (See also San Jose)

Mollie Stone's Supermarket, 164 California Ave, Ph: 323-8361. Large selection of kosher items. Frozen meat, poultry, cheeses, cholov Yisroel products.

Accommodations

Shabbat hospitality; call:
Rabbi Y. Levin at Chabad, Ph: 424-9800;
Palo Alto Orthodox Minyan, Ph: 326-5001.

Bookstore

Bob and Bob, 151 Forest Ave, Ph: 329-9050.

PASADENA (See also GREATER LOS ANGELES)
Area Code (818)

Synagogues

Pasadena Jewish Temple and Center (C-US), 1434 N Altadena Dr,
Ph: 798-1161. Rabbi G. Kollin. Services: Shabbat

PETALUMA   Area Code (707)

Synagogues

Congregation B'nai Israel (C-US), 740 Western Ave, Ph: 762-0340.
Rabbi M. Ballonoff. Services: Saturday, 1st and 3rd Fridays

POMONA   Area Code (714)

Synagogues

Temple Beth Israel (R-UAHC), 3033 N Towne Ave, Ph: 626-1277.
Rabbi E. Kaplan. Services: Shabbat

POWAY   Area Code (619)

Synagogues

Temple Adat Shalom (R-UAHC), 15905 Pomerado Rd,
Ph: 451-1200. Rabbi D. Prinz. Services: Shabbat.
Congregation Chabad of Rancho Bernardo (O-Lubav), 16934 Old
Espola Rd, Ph: 451-0455. Rabbi Y. Goldstein. Services: Daily

Accommodations

Best Western Hotel, 17065 W Bernardo Dr, **Rancho Bernardo**,
Ph: 485-6530. Some kitchens. Walk to Chabad.

RANCHO BERNARDO   Area Code (619)

Synagogues

Ner Tamid (C), 16981 Via Tazon #G, Ph: 592-9141. Rabbi S. Kligfeld. Services: Shabbat

RANCHO CUCAMONGA   Area Code (714)

Synagogues

Chabad of the Inland Empire, 8710 Baker Ave, Ph: 946-9224. Rabbi Y. Harlig. Services: Shabbat. Call first.

RANCHO PALOS VERDES (See also **GREATER LOS ANGELES**)   Area Code (213)

Synagogues

Chabad of Palos Verdes (O-Lubav), 28041 Hawthorne Blvd, Ph: 544-5544. Rabbi N. Gross. Services: Shabbat and Holidays
Congregation Ner Tamid of South Bay (C-US), 5721 Crestridge Rd, Ph: 377-6986. Rabbi R. Shulman. Services: Shabbat

REDONDO BEACH (See also **GREATER LOS ANGELES**) Area Code (213)

Synagogues

Temple Menorah (R-UAHC), 1101 Camino Real, Ph: 316-8444. Rabbi S. Silver. Services: Friday, 1st and 3rd Saturdays

REDWAY   Area Code (707)

Synagogues

B'nai Ha-aretz (Independent), P.O. Box 1835, 95560. Marilyn Andrews, secretary, Ph: 923-3377. Services: Call for information.

REDWOOD CITY (See also **SAN FRANCISCO**) Area Code (415)

Synagogues

Temple Beth Jacob (C-US), 1550 Alameda de las Pulgas,
Ph: 366-8481. Rabbi H. Teitelbaum. Services: Shabbat

Eating Out

Temple Beth Jacob, 1550 Alameda de las Pulgas, Ph: 366-8481.
RS: Rabbi D. Teitelbaum. Shabbat dinner is served the first
Friday of every month. The fee is $13.00. For reservations call
the Temple two days in advance.

Food (See **San Jose**)

RESEDA (See **GREATER LOS ANGELES**)

RICHMOND (See also **BERKELEY**)   Area Code (415)

Synagogues

Temple Beth Hillel (R-UAHC), 801 Park Central, Ph: 223-2560.
Rabbi J. Shanks. Services: Friday

RIVERSIDE   Area Code (714)   J-pop. 1,620

Synagogues

Temple Beth El (R-UAHC), 2675 Central Ave, Ph: 684-4511.
Rabbi P. Posner. Services: Friday

ROHNERT PARK (See also **SANTA ROSA**)   Area Code (707)

Synagogues

Sonoma County Synagogue Center (Recon), Rohnert Park
Community Center, Snyder Lane & Rohnert Park Expressway,
Ph: 664-8622. Patti Philo, Rabbinic Consultant. Services: 1st
and 3rd Fridays

SACRAMENTO   Area Code (916)   J-pop. 12,000

Synagogues

Congregation Beth Shalom (R-UAHC), 4746 El Camino Ave,
Ph: 485-4478. Rabbi J. Melamed. Services: Call for schedule.

Synagogues cont.

Congregation B'nai Israel (R-UAHC), 3600 Riverside Blvd,
    Ph: 446-4861. Rabbi L. Frazin. Services: Shabbat

Knesseth Israel Torah Center (O-UOJC), 1024 Morse Ave,
    Ph: 481-1159. Rabbi S. Rosen. Services: Daily

Mosaic Law Congregation (C-US), 2300 Sierra Blvd,
    Ph: 488-1122. Rabbi L. Moses. Services: Shabbat

Sunrise Jewish Congregation (R), P.O. Box 405, **Citrus Heights**,
    95621, Ph: 965-8322.

Food

Bob's Butcher Block & Deli, 6436 Fair Oaks Blvd, Ph: 482-6884.
    Take-out (meat): sandwiches, soups, salads, chili, side dishes.
    Baked goods. Also complete kosher grocery; refrigerated and
    frozen items. Fresh baked challahs and cakes by order. Will
    prepare complete meals for travelers to take along. (week's
    notice preferred). RS: Rabbi S. Rosen. Closed Shabbat.

Farah's Catering, 2319 El Camino Ave, Ph: 971-9500. Kosher
    grocery, frozen section. Closed Shabbat. (Deli not supervised.)
    RS: Rabbi S. Rosen (challahs only).

Mikvah

Knesseth Israel Torah Center, Ph: 481-1159.

SALINAS   Area Code (408)   J-pop. 500

Synagogues

Temple Beth El (R-UAHC), 1212 Riker St, Ph: 424-9151.
    Rabbi B. Kadden. Services: Friday

SAN BERNARDINO   Area Code (714)

Synagogues

Temple Emanu El (R-UAHC), 3512 N "E" St, Ph: 886-4818. Rabbi
    H. Cohn. Services: Shabbat

SAN DIEGO   Area Code (619)   J-pop. 70,000

Synagogues

Adat Ami (C), 1233 Camino del Rio S #275, Ph: 260-0626. Rabbi A. Kopikis. Services: Shabbat

Congregation Beth Israel (R-UAHC), 2512 3rd Ave, Ph: 239-0149. Rabbi M. Sternfield. Services: Friday

Beth Jacob Congregation (O-UOJC), 4855 College Ave, Ph: 287-9890. Rabbi E. Langer. Services: Daily

Congregation Beth Tefilah (C-US), 4967 69th St, Ph: 463-0391. Rabbi M. Manson. Services: Daily

Chabad House (O-Lubav), 6115 Montezuma Rd, (near San Diego State University), Ph: 265-7700. Rabbi Y. Fradkin. Services: Daily

Congregation Dor Hadash (Recon-FRCH), Office: 5790 Miramar Rd #205, Ph: 587-1270. Rabbi R. Herstik. Services: Call for schedule.

Temple Emanu-El (R-UAHC), 6299 Capri Dr, Ph: 286-2555. Rabbi M. Lawson. Services: Shabbat

Tifereth Israel Synagogue (C-US), 6660 Cowles Mountain Blvd, Ph: 697-6001. Rabbi L. Rosenthal. Services: Daily

Young Israel of San Diego (O-NCYI), 7424 Jackson Dr #5, Ph: 226-5762. Rabbi D. Korobkin. Services: Saturday.

Eating Out

Lang's Loaf, 6165 El Cajon Blvd, Suite F, Ph: 287-7306. Pareve bakery, side dishes for take-out. Meals: b,l,d. Menu: (Dairy: cholov Yisroel) Fish, vegetarian. RS: Vaad Horabonim of San Diego. Closed Shabbat.

Mosserella's Pizza, 6663 El Cajon Blvd, Ph: 668-0643. Meals: l,d. Menu: (Dairy: cholov Yisroel) Pizza, lasagna, salads. RS: Vaad Horabonim of San Diego. Closed Shabbat.

San Diego State University—Chabad House (cafeteria), 6115 Montezuma Rd, Ph: 582-7719. RS: Rabbi Y. Fradkin. Shabbat dinner and lunch are served weekly. Contact Rabbi Fradkin for further information.

Food

Alpha Beta, 7910 El Cajon Blvd, **La Mesa**, Ph: 464-3318. Large selection of kosher products.

Food cont.

Stump's Market, 6386 Del Cerro Blvd, Ph: 582-9905. Large
selection of kosher products.

Accommodations

Chabad House, 6115 Montezuma Rd. Accommodations for single
men. Also Shabbat hospitality. Call Rabbi Fradkin, 582-7719.
Hitching Post, 4949 Guava St, Ph: 464-4262. All rooms have
kitchens. Walk to Beth Jacob and Beth Tefilah Congregations.
The Lamplighter, 6474 El Cajon Blvd, Ph: 582-3088. Walk to Beth
Jacob and Beth Tefilah Congregations. Kitchenettes available.

Mikvah

Mikvah Israel, 5170 La Dorna, Ph: 287-6411.

Day Schools

Chabad Day School, 4905 Catoctin, Ph: 582-1784.
San Diego Hebrew Day School, 6365 Lake Atlin Ave,
Ph: 460-3300.
San Diego Jewish Academy, 6660 Cowles Mountain Blvd,
Ph: 697-2246; 457-5155.
Temple Beth Israel Day School (R), 2512 3rd Ave at Laurel,
Ph: 239-2157.

SAN FRANCISCO   Area Code (415)   J-pop. 45,500

Jewish Community Information & Referral: Ph: 777-4545
Monday-Friday 9:30 a.m.-1:30 p.m.

Synagogues

Congregation Adath Israel (O-UOJC), 1851 Noriega St,
Ph: 564-5665. Rabbi J. Traub. Services: Daily
Congregation Anshey S'fard (O-UOJC), 1500 Clement St,
Ph: 752-4979. Rabbi A. Hecht. Services: Daily
Congregation Beth Israel—Judea (C-US, R-UAHC), 625
Brotherhood Way, Ph: 586-8833. Rabbi H. Morris. Services:
Shabbat

Congregation Beth Sholom (C-US), 14th Ave and Clement St, Ph: 221-8736. Rabbi A. Graubert. Services: Daily

Congregation B'nai Emunah (C-US), 3595 Taraval St, Ph: 664-7373. Rabbi T. Alexander. Services: Daily

Chabad of San Francisco (O-Lubav), 11 Tillman Pl, Ph: 956-8644. Rabbi Y. Langer. Services: Sunday - Thursday p.m.; Shabbat services at Rabbi Langer's home, 2950 Anza. Open house and Shabbat meal.

Congregation Chevra Tehilim (O-UOJC), 751 25th Ave, Ph: 752-2866. Rabbi S. Krasner. Services: Daily

Congregation Emanu-El (R-UAHC), Arguello Blvd & Lake St, Ph: 751-2535. Rabbi G. Pomerantz. Services: Shabbat

Congregation Knesseth Israel (O), 1255 Post St, Ph: 771-3420. Services: Shabbat

Congregation Magain David Sephardim (O-UOJC), 351 4th Ave, Ph: 752-9095. Services: Shabbat, Sunday, Monday and Thursday

Congregation Ner Tamid (C-US), 1250 Quintara St, Ph: 661-3383. Rabbi Y. Nadler. Services: Daily

Congregation Sha'ar Zahav (R-UAHC), 220 Danvers Dr, Ph: 861-6932. Rabbi Y. Kahn. Services: Shabbat

Congregation Sherith Israel (R-UAHC), 2266 California St, Ph: 346-1720. Rabbi M. Weiner. Services: Shabbat

Congregation Torath Emeth (O), 768 27th Ave, Ph: 386-1830. Services: Shabbat and Sunday

Young Israel of San Francisco (O-NCYI), 1806-A Noriega St, Ph: 752-7333. Rabbi D. Goodman, Rabbi M. Rindenow. Services: Call for schedule.

Eating Out

Lotus Garden, 532 Grant Ave, Ph: 397-0707. Meals: l,d. Menu: Chinese vegetarian. RS: Rabbi L. Chiswell of Congregation Adath Israel. Amex, MC, Visa.

Natan's, 420 Geary, Ph: 776-2683. Meals: b,l,d. Menu: (Meat) Israeli, Middle Eastern. RS: Rabbi S. Krasner. Closed Shabbat.

Food

Israel's Kosher Market, 5621 Geary Blvd, Ph: 752-3064 or 386-9722. Complete kosher grocery. RS: Orthodox Rabbinical Council of San Francisco. Closed Shabbat.

Jacob's Kosher Meats, 2435 Noriega St, Ph: 564-7482. Kosher grocery. RS: Orthodox Rabbinical Council of San Francisco. Closed Shabbat.

Tel Aviv Strictly Kosher Market, 1301 Noriega St, Ph: 661-7588. Kosher grocery. Empire barbecued chickens on Thursday and Friday. RS: Orthodox Rabbinical Council of San Francisco. Closed Shabbat.

Wedermeyer's Bakery, Ph: 873-1000. Pareve breads. Available at supermarkets. RS: Rabbi M. Shick.

Accommodations

Shabbat hospitality:

Chabad Lubavitch of San Francisco, Rabbi Y. Langer, Ph: 956-8644.

Rabbi S. Krasner of Congregation Chevra Tehilim, Ph: 668-5871.

Rabbi B. Pil of Jewish Educational Center of San Francisco, 538 29th Ave, Ph: 221-7045.

Mikvah

Mikvah Israel B'nai David, 3355 Sacramento St. Call for recorded information, Ph: 921-4070.

Day School

Hebrew Academy of San Francisco, 645 14th Ave, Ph: 752-9583.

SAN JACINTO   Area Code (714)

Synagogues

Temple Beth Am (C), 20520 Hwy 79, Ph: 654-1414. Services: Friday

SAN JOSE   Area Code (408)   J-pop. 32,000

Synagogues

Congregation Am Echad (O-UOJC), 1504 Meridian Ave, Ph: 267-2591 or 264-3138. Rabbi A. H. Lapin. Services: Daily

Congregation Beth David (C-US), 19700 Prospect Rd, **Saratoga**, Ph: 257-3333. Rabbi D. Pressman. Services: Shabbat

Temple Beth Sholom (R), 2270 Canoas Garden Rd #A, Ph: 978-5566. Services: Friday

Temple Emanu-El (R-UAHC), 1010 University Ave, Ph: 292-0939. Rabbi J. Plaut. Services: Friday

Congregation Shir Hadash (R), 16555 Shannon Rd, **Los Gatos**, Ph: 358-1751. Rabbi A. Ward. Services: Friday; call for information.

Congregation Sinai of San Jose (Trad), 1532 Willowbrae Ave, Ph: 264-8542. Rabbi A. Berkowitz. Services: Saturday

Food

Willow Glen Kosher Market, 1185 Lincoln Ave, Ph: 297-6604. Meat, deli, breads and complete kosher grocery. Cholov Yisroel available. RS: Beth Din of San Jose. Closed Shabbat and Monday.

Accommodations

Shabbat hospitality - Call Congregation Am Echad, Ph: 267-2591 or 264-3138.

Day Schools

South Peninsula Hebrew Day School, 1030 Astoria Dr, **Sunnyvale**, Ph: 738-3060 or (415) 965-8390.

Yavneh Day School (C), 14855 Oka Rd, **Los Gatos**, Ph: 358-3413.

SAN LEANDRO (See also **OAKLAND**)   Area Code (415)

Synagogues

Temple Beth Sholom (C-US), 642 Dolores Ave, Ph: 357-8505. Rabbi I. Book. Services: Shabbat

SAN MATEO (See also **SAN FRANCISCO**)   Area Code (415)

Synagogues

Peninsula Temple Beth El (R-UAHC), 1700 Alameda de las
Pulgas, Ph: 341-7701. Rabbi P. Rubinstein. Services: Shabbat

SAN PEDRO (See **GREATER LOS ANGELES**)

SAN RAFAEL   Area Code (415)

Synagogues

Chabad of Marin, 1150 Idylberry Rd #B-122, Ph: 492-1666. Rabbi
C. Dalfin. Services: Daily

Congregation Rodef Sholom of Marin (R-UAHC), 170 N San
Pedro Rd, Ph: 479-3441. Rabbi M. Barenbaum. Services:
Shabbat

Accommodations

Private accommodations for Shabbat - call Chabad of Marin,
Rabbi C. Dalfin, Ph: 492-1666.

SANTA ANA (See also **GREATER LOS ANGELES**)
Area Code (714)

Synagogues

Temple Beth Sholom (R-UAHC), 2625 N Tustin Ave,
Ph: 532-6724. Rabbi F. Stern. Services: Friday

Food (See **Los Alamitos**)

SANTA BARBARA   Area Code (805)   J-pop. 3,800

Synagogues

Chabad of Santa Barbara (O-Lubav), 487 N Turnpike Rd,
Ph: 683-1544. Rabbi Y. Loshak. Services: Shabbat, Monday and
Thursday

Temple B'nai B'rith (R-UAHC), 900 San Antonio Creek Rd,
Ph: 964-7869. Rabbi A. Schaefer. Services: Shabbat

Young Israel of Santa Barbara, 1826C Cliff Dr, Ph: 966-4565.
   Rabbi A. Gelman. Services: Call for schedule.

SANTA CRUZ   Area Code (408)   J-pop. 1,200

Synagogues

Temple Beth El (R-UAHC), 920 Bay St, Ph: 423-3012. Rabbi R.
   Litvak. Services: Friday

SANTA MONICA (See also LOS ANGELES)
   Area Code (213)   J-pop. 8,000

Synagogues

Beth Sholom Temple (R-UAHC), 1827 California Ave,
   Ph: 453-3361. Rabbi M. Berk. Services: Friday
Bais Chabad (O-Lubav), 1428 17th St, Ph: 829-5620; 453-3011.
   Rabbi A. Levitansky. Services: Daily
Young Israel of Santa Monica (O-NCYI), 201 Hampton,
   Ph: 396-4777. Rabbi Y. Eichenblatt. Services: Shabbat

Accommodations

Daily, weekly or monthly apartment rentals are available through
   the Chabad House. Minutes' walk to Chabad. Call Rabbi S.
   Menkes, Ph: 829-5620.

Mikvah

Chabad Mikvah, (near Chabad of Simcha Monica), Ph: 829-3613.
   Call for information, Ph: 829-5620.

SANTA ROSA   Area Code (707)

Synagogues

Temple Beth Ami (C-US), 4676 Mayette Ave, Ph: 545-4334. Rabbi
   J. Slater. Services: Shabbat
Congregation Shomrei Torah (C), 1717 Yulupa Way, Ph: 578-5519.
   Rabbi M. Robinson. Services: Call for schedule.

SANTEE (See SAN DIEGO)

SARATOGA (See **SAN JOSE**)

SEPULVEDA (See **GREATER LOS ANGELES**)

SHERMAN OAKS (See **GREATER LOS ANGELES**)

SIMI VALLEY (See **GREATER LOS ANGELES**)

SOLANA BEACH (See also **SAN DIEGO**)   Area Code (619)

Synagogues

Congregation Beth Am (C), 525 Stevens Ave, Ph: 481-8454.
   Services: Shabbat.

STANFORD   Area Code (415)

Synagogues

Hillel Foundation at Stanford (Independent), Old Union
   Clubhouse, Ph: 723-1602. Rabbi A. Cartun. Services: Friday

STOCKTON   Area Code (209)   J-pop. 1,600

Synagogues

Temple Israel (R-UAHC), 5105 N El Dorado St, Ph: 477-9306.
   Rabbi S. Chester. Services: Friday

STUDIO CITY (See **GREATER LOS ANGELES**)

SUN VALLEY (See **GREATER LOS ANGELES**)

SUNNYVALE (See **SAN JOSE**)

TARZANA (See **GREATER LOS ANGELES**)

TEMPLE CITY (See **GREATER LOS ANGELES**)

THOUSAND OAKS   Area Code (805)

Synagogues

Temple Adat Elohim (R-UAHC), 2420 E Hillcrest Dr, Ph: 497-7101. Rabbi A. Greenbaum. Services: Shabbat

Temple Etz Chaim (C-US, R-UAHC), 1080 Janss Rd, Ph: 497-6891. Rabbi S. Paskow. Services: Shabbat, Sunday, Monday and Wednesday

TIBURON (See also SAN FRANCISCO)   Area Code (415)

Synagogues

Congregation Kol Shofar (C-US), 215 Blackfield Dr, Ph: 388-1818. Rabbi D. White. Services: Shabbat

TORRANCE (See LOMITA)

TUJUNGA (See GREATER LOS ANGELES)

TUSTIN (See also LONG BEACH)   Area Code (714)

Synagogues

Congregation B'nai Israel (C-US), 655 S "B" St, Ph: 730-9693. Rabbi E. Spitz. Services: Shabbat

Food (See **Los Alamitos**)

UKIAH   Area Code (707)

Synagogues

Mendocino County Jewish Community Inland Family (Unaffiliated), P.O. Box 416, **Redwood Valley**. Contact Judy Corwin, Ph: 468-0280. Services: Friday, once a month

VALLEJO   Area Code (707)

Synagogues

Congregation B'nai Israel (C), 1256 Nebraska St, Ph: 642-6526. Rabbi D. Kopstein. Services: 1st and 3rd Fridays

VAN NUYS (See GREATER LOS ANGELES)

VENICE (See also GREATER LOS ANGELES)   Area Code (213)

Synagogues

Temple Mishkon Tephilo (C), 206 Main St, Ph: 392-3029. Rabbi
N. Levy. Services: Shabbat

Pacific Jewish Center - Bay Cities Synagogue (Trad), 505 Ocean
Front Walk, Ph: 392-8749. Rabbi D. Lapin. Services: Daily

Day School

Emanuel Streisand School, 720 Rose Ave, Ph: 399-0303.

VENTURA   Area Code (805)

Synagogues

Chabad of Ventura (O-Lubav), 5850 Thille #101, Ph: (818)
658-7441. Rabbi Y. Ladowicz. Services: Shabbat and Holidays

Ventura Jewish Council - Temple Beth Torah (R-UAHC), 7620
Foothill Rd, Ph: 647-4181. Services: Shabbat

VISTA   Area Code (619)

Synagogues

Temple Judea (C-US), 1930 Sunset Dr, Ph: 724-8318. Rabbi M.
Gottlieb. Services: Shabbat

WALNUT CREEK (See also BERKELEY)   Area Code (415)

Synagogues

Congregation Beth Chaim (C), 2071 Tice Valley Blvd,
Ph: 930-9335. Meets at Contra Costa JCC. Rabbi G. Tishkoff.
Services: Friday

Congregation B'nai Israel Rossmoor (Independent), c/o Robert Bell,
3288 Granada #2B, Ph: 939-7190. Services: Call for
information.

Congregation B'nai Sholom (C-US), 74 Eckley Lane, Ph: 934-9446. Rabbi G. Freeman. Services: Shabbat

Congregation B'nai Tikvah (R), 25 Hillcroft Way, Ph: 933-5397. Rabbi R. Asher. Services: Friday

Food

Bagel King, 1686 Locust St, Ph: 938-5464; 1701A Willow Pass Rd, **Concord**, Ph: 938-5464. Complete kosher grocery; Empire, Sinai, other frozen items, some cholov Yisroel products. RS: Rabbi M. Schick (bagels only).

WEST COVINA (See GREATER LOS ANGELES)

WEST HOLLYWOOD (See GREATER LOS ANGELES)

WESTLAKE VILLAGE (See GREATER LOS ANGELES)

WESTMINSTER   Area Code (714)

Synagogues

Temple Beth David (R), 6100 Hefley St, Ph: 892-6623. Services: Friday.

Day School

Hebrew Academy - Lubavitch of Orange County, 14401 Willow Lane, Ph: 898-0051 or (213) 596-1681.

WHITTIER (See GREATER LOS ANGELES)

WOODLAND HILLS (See GREATER LOS ANGELES)

YORBA LINDA   Area Code (714)

Synagogues

Beth Meir HaCohen Congregation, North County Chabad Center (O-Lubav), 19045 Yorba Linda Blvd, Ph: 693-0770. Rabbi D. Eliezri. Services: Shabbat

Colorado

BOULDER (See also DENVER)   Area Code (303)

Synagogues

Congregation Bonai Shalom (C-US), 1527 Cherryvale Rd,
   Ph: 442-6605. Services: Shabbat

Congregation Har-Hashem (R-UAHC), 3950 Baseline Rd,
   Ph: 499-7077. Rabbi H. Rose. Services: Friday

Accommodations

Shabbat hospitality; call Bonai Shalom, Ph: 442-6605.

COLORADO SPRINGS   Area Code (719)   J-pop. 1,500

Synagogues

The Cadet Chapel (R), US Air Force Academy, Ph: 472-2636.
   Rabbi I. Ehrlich. Services: Friday

Chabad of Colorado Springs (O-Lubav), 3465 Nonchalant Circle,
   Ph: 596-7330. Rabbi M. Teitlebaum. Services: Saturday and
   Wednesday

Temple Shalom (C-US,R-UAHC), 1523 E Monument St,
   Ph: 634-5311. Rabbi H. J. Hirsch. Services: Friday (R) and
   Saturday morning (C)

Accommodations

Shabbat hospitality; contact Chabad, Ph: 596-7330.

Mikvah

Chabad Mikvah. Call Mrs. M. Teitlebaum, Ph: 596-7330.

DENVER   Area Code (303)   J-pop. 45,000

Kosher travelers' hotline: Rabbi M. Heisler, Vaad Hakashrus of
   Denver, Ph: 595-9349.

Synagogues

Congregation Adat Sholom (R-UAHC), 1379 E Rice Pl, **Aurora,**

Ph: 690-4108. Rabbi D. Zucker. Services: Meets at 1092 S Nome, Friday

Bais Medrash Kehillas Yaakov (O), 295 S Locust, Ph: 377-1200 or 333-5030. Rabbi M. Twerski. Services: Daily

Congregation Beth Hamedrosh Hagadol (Trad, O-UOJC), 560 S Monaco Pkwy, Ph: 388-4203. Rabbi S. Wagner. Services: Daily

Beth Joseph Congregation (Trad), 825 Ivanhoe St, **Littleton**, Ph: 355-7321. Rabbi C. Seiger. Services: Daily

Congregation Beth Shalom (C-US), 2280 E Noble Pl, **Littleton**, Ph: 794-6643. Rabbi F. Greenspahn. Services: Friday

Colorado Jewish Reconstructionist Fed. (Recon-FRCH), 6645 E Ohio Ave #600, Ph: 388-3441. Rabbi S. Kaye. Services: Call for information.

East Denver Orthodox Synagogue (O-UOJC), 198 S Holly, Ph: 322-7943. Services: Daily

Temple Emanuel (R-UAHC), 51 Grape St, Ph: 388-4013. Rabbi S. Foster. Services: Shabbat

Hebrew Educational Alliance (Trad-UOJC), 1555 Stuart St, Ph: 629-0410. Rabbi D. Goldberger. Services: Daily

Temple Micah (R), 2600 Leyden St, Ph: 388-4239. Rabbi R. Sonnenfeld. Services: Friday

Congregation Rodef Shalom (C-US), 450 S Kearney St, Ph: 399-0035. Rabbi J. Newman. Services: Shabbat

Temple Sinai (R-UAHC), 3509 S Glencoe St, Ph: 759-1827. Rabbi R. Zwerin. Services: Friday

Yeshivah Toras Chayim (O), 1400 Quitman St, Ph: 629-8200. Rabbi I. Kagan. Services: Daily

Congregation Zera Abraham (O), 1560 Winona Ct, Ph: 825-7517. Rabbi Y. Hopfer. Services: Daily

Congregation Zera Israel (O), 3934 W 14th Ave, Ph: 893-6777. Rabbi A. L. Fine. Services: Daily

Eating Out

Beth Israel Hospital (cafeteria), 1601 Lowell Blvd, Ph: 825-2190. RS: Rabbi M. Twerski. The hospital cafeteria is open to the public.

Eating Out cont.

East Side Kosher Deli, 5600 E Cedar, Ph: 322-9862. Meals: l,d. Menu: Deli, traditional, fish, salads. Also take-out. RS: Vaad Hakashrus of Denver. Closed Shabbat.

Mediterranean Health Cafe, 2817 E 3rd Ave, Ph: 399-2940. Meals: l,d. Menu: (Dairy vegetarian) Falafel, pita pizza, fish, soup, salads, vegetarian burgers, cholov Yisroel available. RS: Vaad Hakashrus of Denver. Closed Shabbat.

Food

B & J's Utica Grocery, 4500 W Colfax Ave, Ph: 534-2253. Deli-style dishes to go, and complete grocery including meat, fish and cheeses prepared for take-out. RS: Vaad Hakashrus of Denver. Closed Shabbat.

The Bagel Store, 942 S Monaco, Ph: 388-2648. Breads and pastries. RS: Vaad Hakashrus of Denver

Cub Foods, 20th & Sheridan, Ph: 232-8972. Large selection of kosher products.

King Sooper's, 890 S Monaco at Leetsdale, Ph: 333-1535. Large selection of kosher products.

New York Bagel Boys, 6449 E Hamden (at Monaco), Ph: 759-2212. Breads, bagels, pastries (pareve); cookies (dairy). RS: Rabbi M. Twerski.

Pete's Fruits & Vegetables, 5600 E Cedar. Large selection of kosher products. Also cholov Yisroel milk.

Rainbow Grocery (Health food store), 12131 E Iliff Ave, **Aurora**, Ph: 695-8008. Many kosher packaged products including dairy, tofu etc. Ask for their list, "Healthy and Kosher."

Rudi's Bakery. Breads under the supervision of Rabbi M. Twerski are available at King Sooper and Safeway supermarkets in the area.

Steinberg's Kosher Grocery & Delicatessen, 4017 W Colfax, Ph: 534-0314. Complete kosher grocery and full deli. Eat-in or take-out. RS: Vaad Hakashrus of Denver. Closed Shabbat.

Accommodations

Aristocrat Motor Hotel, 4855 W Colfax, Ph: 825-2755. Rooms

with kitchens are available. Located three blocks from Congregation Zera Abraham.

Bar-X Best Budget Bar & Motel, 5000 W Colfax, Ph: 534-7191. A few blocks from Congregation Zera Abraham.

Best Western Landmark Inn Hotel, 455 S Colorado Blvd, Ph: 388-5561. A mile and a half from Bais Medrash Kehillas Yaakov.

Shabbat hospitality; call Congregation Bais Medrash Kehillas Yaakov, Ph: 377-1200 or 333-5030.

Chabad Lubavitch of Colorado, 400 S Holly St, Ph: 329-0211. Rabbi Y. M. Popack will be happy to assist the Jewish traveler with further information on the Rocky Mountain Region and/or Shabbat hospitality.

Shabbat hospitality - call Rabbi M. Heisler, Ph: 893-9026.

Mikvah

Mikvah of Denver, 1404 Quitman St. Contact Mrs. I. Raiss, Ph: 893-5315.

Day School

Hillel Academy of Denver, 450 S Hudson St, Ph: 333-1511.

Bookstore

Boutique Judaica, 5078 E Hampden, Ph: 757-1317.

FORT COLLINS Area Code (303)   J-pop. 1,000

Synagogues

Congregation Har Shalom (R-UAHC), 725 W Drake, Ph: 223-5191. Rabbi E. Baskin. Services: Friday

LITTLETON (See **DENVER**)

PUEBLO Area Code (719)   J-pop. 250

Synagogues

Temple Emanuel (R), 1325 Grand Ave, Ph: 544-6448. Services: Call for information.

Synagogues cont.

United Hebrew Center (C-US), 106 W 15th St, Ph: 544-9897.
   Services: Shabbat

TRINIDAD   Area Code (303)

Synagogues

Temple Aaron (R), 305 Maple St, Mrs. G. Sanders, Ph: 846-2685.
   Services: Friday

Connecticut

BLOOMFIELD (See WEST HARTFORD)

BRIDGEPORT   Area Code (203)   J-pop. 18,000

Synagogues

Congregation Agudas Achim (O-UOJC), 85 Arlington St,
   Ph: 335-6353. Rabbi M. Epstein. Services: Daily
Temple Beth Shalom (C-US), 275 Huntington Rd, **Stratford**,
   Ph: 378-6175. Rabbi G. Yaffe. Services: Shabbat
Congregation Bikur Cholim (O), 2365 Park Ave, Ph: 336-2272.
   Rabbi J. Mendelson.
Congregation B'nai Israel (R-UAHC), 2710 Park Ave,
   Ph: 336-1858. Rabbi J. Prosnit. Services: Shabbat
Congregation Rodeph Sholom (C-US), Corner of Park and Capital
   Aves, Ph: 334-0159. Rabbi I. Stein. Services: Daily
Congregation Shaare Torah-Adath Israel (O-UOJC), 3050 Main
   St, Ph: 372-6513. Rabbi M. Ackerson. Services: Daily
Congregation Shirei Shalom (Recon), P.O. Box 372, **Monroe**,
   06468, Ph: 452-9851. Rabbi A. Winokur.

Eating Out

The Café, Bridgeport J.C.C., 4200 Park Ave, Ph: 372-7429. Meals:
   l,d. Menu: (Meat) Fast food - hot dogs, hamburgers. RS: Rabbi
   J. Epstein. Closed Shabbat. Closed Sundays in summer.

Food

Carry-Away Gourmet Bakery, 35 Stonybrook Rd, **Stratford,**
  Ph: 375-1181. Baked goods. (Pareve and dairy). RS: Rabbi J.
  Epstein.
State Kosher Meat Market, 1147 Madison Ave, Ph: 579-1699.
  Meat, poultry, baked products, hot take-out. Complete kosher
  grocery. RS: Rabbi J. Epstein. Closed Shabbat.

BRISTOL   Area Code (203)   J-pop. 200

Synagogues

Beth Israel (C-US), 339 West St, Ph: 585-7005. Rabbi S. Rothstein.
  Services: Shabbat

CHESHIRE (See MERIDEN)

COLCHESTER   Area Code (203)   J-pop. 575

Synagogues

Congregation Ahavath Achim (C-US), Lebanon Ave,
  Ph: 537-2809. Rabbi G. Freidlin. Services: Shabbat

DANBURY   Area Code (203)   J-pop. 3,500

Synagogues

Congregation B'nai Israel (C-US), 193 Clapboard Ridge Rd,
  Ph: 792-6161. Rabbi J. Davidson. Services: Daily
United Jewish Center (R-UAHC), 141 Deer Hill Ave,
  Ph: 748-3355. Rabbi J. Malino (Emeritus). Services: Shabbat

DERBY (See also NEW HAVEN)   Area Code (203)

Synagogues

Beth Israel Synagogue (C-US), 300 Elizabeth St, Ph: 777-1264.
  Rabbi J. Kohn. Services: Daily

EAST HARTFORD (See WEST HARTFORD)

ENFIELD   Area Code (203)

Food

Dianna's Bakery, 35 Pearl St, Ph: 741-3781. Pareve and dairy baked
  goods. RS: Springfield Vaad Hakashrut

FAIRFIELD (See also BRIDGEPORT)   Area Code (203)

Synagogues

Congregation Ahavath Achim (O-UOJC), 1571 Stratfield Rd,
  Ph: 372-6529. Rabbi J. Epstein. Services: Daily
Congregation Beth El (C-US), 1200 Fairfield Woods Rd,
  Ph: 374-5544. Rabbi L. Waldman. Services: Daily

Food

Moishe's Deli & Bakery, 2081 Blackrock Tpke, Ph: 333-3059.
  (Deli, baked goods). Take-out. RS: Rabbi J. Epstein.

Accomodations

Shabbat hospitality; call Rabbi J. Epstein, Ph: 372-6529.

Mikvah

Mikveh Israel, 1326 Stratfield Rd, call Dr. Nikki Levy,
  Ph: 374-2191.

Day School

Hillel Academy, 1571 Stratfield Rd, Ph: 374-6147/8.

GLASTONBURY   Area Code (203)

Synagogues

Congregation Kol Haverim (R-UAHC), 1079 Hebron Ave,
  Ph: 633-3966. Rabbi J. Plaut. Services: Fridays, except third;
  first and third Saturdays

GREENWICH   Area Code (203)   J-pop. 3,800

Synagogues

Chavurat Deevray Torah (R-UAHC), call Ken Asher,

Ph: 637-9478. Rabbi M. Golub. Services: every other Friday
Greenwich Reform Synagogue, 200 Riverside Ave, **Riverside**,
  Ph: 637-4463. Rabbi R. Lennick. Services: Friday
Temple Sholom (C-US), 300 E Putnam Ave, Ph: 869-7191. Rabbi
  H. Silverman. Services: Shabbat

HAMDEN (See NEW HAVEN)

HARTFORD (See WEST HARTFORD)

MADISON (See also NEW HAVEN)   Area Code (203)

Synagogues

Temple Beth Tikvah (R-UAHC), 196 Durham Rd, Ph: 245-7028,
  453-0826. Rabbi H. Sommer. Services: Friday

MANCHESTER (See also WEST HARTFORD)
  Area Code (203)

Synagogues

Temple Beth Sholom (C-US), 400 E Middle Tpke, Ph: 643-9563.
  Rabbi R. Plavin. Services: Daily

Food

Marc Baking Co., 846 Main St, Ph: 649-5380. Breads, cakes, pies.
  (Dairy and pareve). RS: Kashrut Commission of Greater
  Hartford.

MERIDEN   Area Code (203)   J-pop. 3,000

Synagogues

Temple Beth David (R-UAHC), 3 Main St, **Cheshire**, Ph:
  272-0037. Rabbi S. Steinberg. Services: Friday
Temple B'nai Abraham (C-US), 127 E Main St, Ph: 235-2581.
  Rabbi J. Goldstein. Services: Daily

MIDDLETOWN   Area Code (203)   J-pop. 1,300

Synagogues

Congregation Adath Israel (C-US), P.O. Box 337, 06457, Ph: 346-4709. Rabbi K. Leitner. Services: Daily

NEW BRITAIN (See also WEST HARTFORD)
Area Code (203)

Synagogues

Temple B'nai Israel (C-US), 265 W Main St, Ph: 224-0479. Rabbi N. Hershfield. Services: Shabbat and Sunday

Congregation Tiphereth Israel (O-UOJC), 76 Winter St, Ph: 229-1485. Rabbi H. Okolica. Services: Daily

Food

Finast, 60 E Main St, Ph: 229-4728. Some kosher products.

Shoshie Baking Co., 224 Allen St, Ph: 229-0099. Breads and pastries. RS: Kashrut Commission of Greater Hartford.

NEW HAVEN   Area Code (203)   J-pop. 28,000

Synagogues

Congregation Beth El-Keser Israel (C-US), 85 Harrison St, Ph: 389-2108. Rabbi S. Kane. Services: Daily

Beth Hamedrosh Hogodol B'nai Israel - Westville Synagogue (O-UOJC), 74 W Prospect St, Ph: 389-9513. Rabbi A. Feldman. Services: Daily

Congregation Beth Israel (O-UOJC), 232 Orchard St, Ph: 776-1468. Rabbi M. Hecht. Services: Daily

Temple Beth Sholom (C-US), 1809 Whitney Ave, **Hamden**, Ph: 288-7748. Rabbi B. Scolnic. Services: Daily

Bikur Cholim Shevet Achim Synagogue (O-UOJC), 278 Winthrop Ave, Ph: 776-4997. Rabbi D. Avigdor. Services: Daily

Congregation B'nai Jacob (C-US), 75 Rimmon Rd, **Woodbridge**, Ph: 389-2111. Rabbi M. Menitoff. Services: Daily

Temple Emanuel of Greater New Haven (R-UAHC), 150 Derby Ave, **Orange,** Ph: 397-3000. Rabbi G. Brieger. Services: Friday

Congregation Mishkan Israel (R-UAHC), 785 Ridge Rd,
Hamden, Ph: 288-3877. Rabbi H. Brockman. Services: Friday

Congregation Or Shalom (C-US), 205 Old Grassy Hill Rd,
Orange, Ph: 799-2341. Rabbi A. Wainhaus. Services: Shabbat

Congregation Sinai (C), 426 Washington Ave, **West Haven,**
Ph: 931-7946. Rabbi L. Heimer. Services: Daily

Yale Hillel (C,R), B004 Bingham Hall, Ph: 432-1134. Rabbi J.
Ponet. Services: Friday (R), Shabbat (C)

Yale University Young Israel House (O), 305 Crown St (side
entrance), Ph: 432-1890. Services: Call for schedule.

Yeshiva Gedolah (O-Lubav), 300 Norton St, Ph: 789-9879. Rabbi
Y. Kalmanson. Services: Daily

Young Israel of New Haven (O-NCYI), 292 Norton St,
Ph: 776-4212. Rabbi M. Whitman. Services: Daily

Eating Out

Abel's Restaurant, 2100 Dixwell Ave, **Hamden**, Ph: 281-3434.
Meals: b,l,d. Menu: (Meat) Deli, entrees, salads, side dishes.
Also take-out. RS: Rabbi A. Feldman. Closed Shabbat.

Edge of the Woods, 379 Whalley Ave, Ph: 787-1055. Meals: l,d.
Menu: (Dairy) Health food. Pasta, tofu dishes, salad bar. Also
take-out. RS: Rabbi M. Whitman.

Yale University Young Israel House, 305 Crown St (side entrance),
Ph: 432-1890. Meals: l (dairy), d (meat), except Sunday. Pay
ahead for Shabbat meals. RS: Rabbi M. Whitman.

Food

Catering by Abel, 1088 Orange Ave, **West Haven**, Ph: 932-0080.
Deli, variety of take-out dishes. RS: Rabbi A. Feldman. Closed
Shabbat.

Edge of the Woods, 379 Whalley Ave, Ph: 787-1055. Health food,
some hot & cold foods, breads (pareve), cakes, cookies and pastries (dairy). RS: Rabbi M. Whitman.

Gran Central, 82 York St, Ph: 562-9217. Good selection of kosher
products.

Leon's Factory Outlet, 1000 Universal Dr, **North Haven,**
Ph: 239-4500. Frozen dough. RS: Rabbi A. Feldman.

Food cont.

New Haven Sea Food, 363 Whalley Ave, Ph: 495-1379. Fresh fish. RS: Rabbi M. Whitman. Closed Shabbat.

Pathmark, 57 Boston Post Rd, **Orange**, Ph: 795-1204. Full line of kosher products.

Stop & Shop, 154 Amity Rd, Ph: 387-2260. Full line of kosher products.

Westville Kosher Bakery, 1658 Litchfield Tpke, **Woodbridge**, Ph: 387-2214. All baked goods pareve. RS: O.K. Laboratories. Closed Shabbat.

Westville Kosher Meat Market, 1666 Litchfield Tpke, **Woodbridge**, Ph: 389-1166. Meat, poultry, deli, kosher groceries, frozen products. RS: Rabbi A. Feldman. Closed Shabbat.

Yeshiva Gedolah, 300 Norton St, Ph: 789-9879. Kosher products available Wednesdays (delivered by truck from Crown Heights, NY).

Accommodations

Holiday Inn, 30 Whalley Ave, Ph: 777-6221. Regular keys. About a mile to Young Israel.

Shabbat hospitality; Call Yeshiva Gedolah of New Haven, Ph: 865-8458 or Rabbi M. Whitman at Young Israel, Ph: 776-4212.

Mikvah

New Haven Mikvah, 86 Hubinger St. Call for recorded information, Ph: 387-2184.

Lubavitch Woman's Mikvah, 12 Colony Rd. Contact Mrs. H. Levitansky, Ph: 777-8966.

Day Schools

Ezra Academy (C), 75 Rimmon Rd, **Woodbridge**, Ph: 389-5500.

The Gan School, 765 Elm St, Ph: 777-2200.

New Haven Hebrew Day School, 261 Derby Ave, **Orange**, Ph: 795-5261.

Bookstore

Jewish Book Shop, 570 Whalley Ave, Ph: 387-1818.

NEW LONDON Area Code (203)   J-pop. 4,000

Synagogues

Congregation Ahavath Chesed (O-UOJC), 590 Montauk Ave,
Ph: 442-3234. Rabbi S. Bluming. Services: Daily
Congregation Beth El (C-US), 660 Ocean Ave, Ph: 442-0418.
Rabbi C. Astor. Services: Daily
Temple Emanu-El (R-UAHC), 29 Dayton Rd, **Waterford,**
Ph: 443-3005. Rabbi A. Rosenberg. Services: Friday

Day School

Solomon Schechter Academy (C), 660 Ocean Ave, Ph: 443-5589.

NEW MILFORD Area Code (203)

Synagogues

Temple Sholom (R-UAHC), 122 Kent Rd N, Ph: 354-0273. Rabbi
N. Koch. Services: Shabbat

NEWINGTON (See WEST HARTFORD)

NEWTOWN Area Code (203)

Synagogues

Congregation Adath Israel (C), Huntingtown Rd, Ph: 426-5188.
Rabbi M. Beton. Services: Friday, 2nd and 3rd Saturday

NORWALK (See also STAMFORD)
Area Code (203)   J-pop. 9,500

Synagogues

Congregation Beth El (C-US), 109 East Ave, Ph: 838-2710. Rabbi
W. Marder. Services: Daily
Beth Israel Synagogue (O-UOJC), 40 King St, Ph: 866-0534.
Rabbi Y. Hecht. Services: Daily
Temple Shalom (R-UAHC), 259 Richards Ave, Ph: 866-0148.
Rabbi M. Abraham. Services: Friday

NORWICH   Area Code (203)   J-pop. 1,800

Synagogues

Beth Jacob Synagogue (C-US), 400 New London Tpke,
Ph: 886-2459. Rabbi M. Friedman. Services: Daily
Brothers of Joseph (O-UOJC), 2 Broad St, Ph: 887-3777. Rabbi S.
Rosenbluth. Services: Daily

Food

Bagel Coffee Shop, 327 Central Ave, Ph: 889-0423. Bakery
(pareve and dairy). Also bagels. RS: Rabbi S. Rosenbluth (bakery goods only). Closed Shabbat.

Mikvah

Brothers of Joseph, 2 Broad St. Contact Janet Rudolf,
Ph: 887-9112.

Day School

Hebrew Day School of Eastern Connecticut, 2 Broad St,
Ph: 823-1857.

ORANGE (See NEW HAVEN)

RIDGEFIELD   Area Code (203)

Synagogues

Shearith Israel (R-UAHC), 46 Peaceable St, Ph: 438-6589. Rabbi
J. Haddon. Services: Friday

ROCKVILLE (See VERNON)

SIMSBURY (See also WEST HARTFORD)   Area Code (203)

Synagogues

Farmington Valley Jewish Congregation, 55 Bushy Hill Rd,
Ph: 658-1075. Rabbi H. Herman. Services: Friday

SOUTH WINDSOR   Area Code (203)

Synagogues

Temple Beth Hillel (R-UAHC), 1001 Foster St, Ph: 644-8466.
Rabbi S. Chatinover. Services: Friday

STAMFORD   Area Code (203)   J-pop. 11,100

Synagogues

Congregation Agudath Sholom (O-UOJC), 301 Strawberry Hill
Ave, Ph: 325-3501. Rabbi J. Ehrenkranz. Services: Daily
Temple Beth El (C-US), 350 Roxbury Rd, Ph: 322-6901. Rabbi A.
Goldman. Services: Daily
Chavurat Aytz Chayim (R-UAHC), Ph: 329-7371. Rabbi M.
Golub. Services: Every other Friday
Temple Sinai (R-UAHC), Lakeside Dr & Interlaken Rd,
Ph: 322-1649. Rabbi S. Pearce. Services: Friday
Young Israel of Stamford (O-NCYI), 69 Oaklawn Ave,
Ph: 325-9504. Rabbi A. Bush. Services: Daily

Eating Out

Nosherye, 1035 Newfield Ave (J.C.C.), Ph: 329-7862. Meals: b,l,d.
Menu: (Meat and pareve) Soups, salads, hot dishes, deli.
(Owner is Shomer Shabbat). RS: Rabbi A. Bush. Closed Shabbat.

Food

Cerbone Bakery, 605 Newfield Ave, Ph: 348-9029. Breads and
pastries (pareve and dairy). RS: Rabbi J. Ehrenkranz.
Deli-Land, 88 Washington St, Ph: 838-6492. Deli, appetizers.
Take-out. RS: Rabbi E. Adler.
Gran Central Market, Ridgeway Center on Summer St,
Ph: 323-3532. Good variety of kosher products.
The Hot Bagel, 2139 Summer St, Ph: 975-0244. RS: Rabbi E.
Adler (bagels only).
Liz Sue Bagelry, 63 High Ridge Rd, Ph: 323-4611. Bagels. RS:
Rabbi J. Ehrenkranz.

Accommodations

The following hotels are about one mile from Congregation Agudath Sholom:

Holiday Inn Crown Plaza, 700 Main St, Ph: 358-8400. Regular keys.

Radisson Tara Hotel, 2701 Summer St, Ph: 359-1300. Regular keys.

Mikvah

Congregation Agudath Sholom, 301 Strawberry Hill Ave. Call Ruth Brooks, Ph: 325-3501.

Day School

Bi-Cultural Day School, 2186 High Ridge Rd, Ph: 329-2186.

STORRS (See also WILLIMANTIC)   Area Code (203)

Synagogues

Beth El Congregation of Mansfield (R), 54 N Eagleville Rd, Ph: 487-1223. Rabbi H. Cohen. Services: First Friday

B'nai B'rith Hillel Foundation at the University of Connecticut, 54 N Eagleville Rd, Ph: 487-1223. Mr. D. Silver, Director. Services: (Trad): Friday. Dinner every other Friday.

STRATFORD (See BRIDGEPORT)

TORRINGTON   Area Code (203)   J-pop. 560

Synagogues

Beth El Synagogue (C-US), 124 Litchfield St, Ph: 482-8263. Rabbi S. Parnes. Services: Shabbat

TRUMBULL (See also BRIDGEPORT)   Area Code (203)

Synagogues

Congregation B'nai Torah (C-US), 5700 Main St, Ph: 268-6940. Rabbi J. Wallin. Services: Shabbat

VERNON   Area Code (203)

Synagogues

Congregation B'nai Israel (C-US), 54 Talcott Ave, **Rockville**,
Ph: 871-1818. Rabbi M. Press. Services: Shabbat, daily p.m.

Food

Jennie's, 435 Hartford Tpke, Ph: 871-0099. Pareve breads, rolls,
challahs. Dairy pastries, cookies and cakes. RS: Kashrut
Commission of Greater Hartford.

Accommodations

Private accommodations; call the office at Congregation B'nai
Israel, Ph: 871-1818.

WALLINGFORD (See also NEW HAVEN)   Area Code (203)

Synagogues

Beth Israel Synagogue (C), 22 N Orchard St, Ph: 269-5983.
Services: Shabbat

WATERBURY   Area Code (203)   J-pop. 2,700

Synagogues

Congregation Beth El (C-US), 359 Cooke St, Ph: 756-4659.
Rabbi B. Leftin. Services: Daily
B'nai Shalom Synagogue (O-UOJC), 135 Roseland Ave,
Ph: 754-4159. Rabbi N. Ben-Zev. Services: Daily
Temple Israel (R-UAHC), 100 Williamson Dr, Ph: 574-1916.
Rabbi A. Miller. Services: Friday

Food

The following supermarkets carry a good selection of kosher
products:
Pathmark, 155-65 Thomaston Ave, Ph: 753-7265.
Shop Rite, 650 Wolcott Ct, Ph: 756-5614.
Stop & Shop, 240 Chase Ave, Ph: 756-4678.

Accommodations

Little House-on-the-Hill, 92 Woodlawn Terr, Mrs. Marianne Vandenburgh, Ph: 757-9901. Fifteen-minute walk to Beth Shalom Synagogue.

Mikvah

B'nai Shalom Synagogue, 135 Roseland Ave. Contact the synagogue, Ph: 754-4159 or Mrs. Rivka Ben-Zev, Ph: 753-1206.

WATERFORD (See NEW LONDON)

WEST HARTFORD   Area Code (203)   J-pop. 28,000

Synagogues

Congregation Agudas Achim (O-UOJC), 1244 N Main St, Ph: 233-6241. Rabbi E. Kaye. Services: Daily

Beth Ahm (C-US), 362 Palisade Ave, **Windsor**, Ph: 688-9989. Rabbi L. Kaplan. Services: Shabbat

Beth David Synagogue (O-UOJC), 20 Dover Rd, Ph: 236-1241. Rabbi W. Cohen. Services: Daily

Temple Beth El (C-US), 2626 Albany Ave, Ph: 233-9696. Rabbi S. Kessler. Services: Daily

Beth Hillel (C-US), 160 Wintonbury Ave, **Bloomfield**, Ph: 242-5561. Rabbi P. Lazowski. Services: Daily

Congregation Beth Israel (R-UAHC), 701 Farmington Ave, Ph: 233-8215. Rabbi H. Silver. Services: Shabbat

Temple Beth Tefilah (C-US), 465 Oak St, **East Hartford**, Ph: 569-0670. Services: Friday

Temple Beth Torah (C-US), 130 Main St, **Wethersfield**, Ph: 529-2410. Services: Friday and one Saturday

B'nai Shalom (C-US), 26 Church St, **Newington**, Ph: 667-0826. Rabbi J. Prouser. Services: Daily

Chabad House (O-Lubav), 2352 Albany Ave, Ph: 232-1116. Rabbi Y. Gopin. Services: Daily

Emanuel Synagogue (C-US), 160 Mohegan Dr, Ph: 236-1275. Rabbi J. Zelermyer. Services: Daily

Temple Sinai (R-UAHC), 41 W Hartford Rd, **Newington**, Ph: 561-1055. Rabbi J. Bennett. Services: Friday

Congregation Tiferes Israel (O-UOJC), 27 Brown St, **Bloomfield**, Ph: 243-1719. Rabbi H. Lindenthal. Services: Daily

Congregation Tikvoh Chadoshoh (C-US), 180 Still Rd, **Bloomfield**, Ph: 242-9099. Rabbi H. Bodenheimer. Services: Daily

United Synagogues of Greater Hartford (O-UOJC), 840 N Main St, Ph: 236-3338. Rabbi I. Avigdor. Services: Daily

Young Israel of Hartford (O-NCYI), 1137 Trout Brook Dr, Ph: 523-7804. Services: Shabbat

Young Israel of West Hartford (O-NCYI), 2240 Albany Ave, Ph: 233-0103. Rabbi M. Rosenfeld. Services: Daily

Food

Bloomfield Donut Shop, 715 Park Ave, **Bloomfield**, Ph: 242-6555. Dairy donuts, pastries, muffins. RS: Kashrut Commission of Greater Hartford. Open 24 hours daily.

Bostonian Fishery Inc., 21 Park St, **Hartford**, Ph: 247-4786/4798. Large selection of kosher fresh fish. RS: Kashrut Commission of Greater Hartford.

Crown Supermarket, 2471 Albany Ave, Ph: 236-1965. Prepared foods for take-out. Complete kosher supermarket. Shoshie bakery products and the fish department are under the supervision of the Kashrut Commission of Greater Hartford. Closed Shabbat.

Finast Superstore, Bishops Corner, Ph: 232-0451. Appetizer counter, side dishes, vacuum-packed meats, pareve baked goods, deli and dairy; cholov Yisroel products. RS: Kashrut Commission of Greater Hartford.

Fran's Candy Castle, 36 Whetten Rd, Ph: 232-2320. Candies, chocolates, gums, kosher candy, and fruit baskets made to order. Call in advance. RS: Kashrut Commission of Greater Hartford.

Waldbaum's, 335 Cottagegrove Rd, **Bloomfield**, Ph: 242-0135. RS: Rabbi I. Avigdor. (kosher meat department only). Closed Shabbat.

Mikvah

Mikvah of Greater Hartford, 61 N Main St. Contact Ms. M. Weinstein, Ph: 521-9446.

Day Schools

The Bess and Paul Sigel Hebrew Academy of Greater Hartford, 53 Gabb Rd, **Bloomfield**, Ph: 243-8333/4.

Solomon Schechter Day School of Greater Hartford (C), 26 Buena Vista Rd, Ph: 561-0700.

Bookstore

Judaica Store, 262 S Whitney, Ph: 236-9956.

WEST HAVEN (See NEW HAVEN)

WESTPORT (See also FAIRFIELD)   Area Code (203)

Synagogues

Beit Chaverim - Young Israel of Westport, 21 Charles St, Ph: 454-6664.

Temple B'nai Chaim, 170 Portland Ave, **Redding**, Ph: 544-1895.

Conservative Synagogue (C), 180 Post Rd E, Ph: 454-4673. Rabbi M. Pasternak. Services: first and third Friday; Saturday, Tuesday a.m.

Temple Israel (R-UAHC), 14 Coleytown Rd, Ph: 227-1293. Rabbi R. Orkand. Services: Shabbat

WETHERSFIELD (See WEST HARTFORD)

WILLIMANTIC   Area Code (203)   J-pop. 700

Synagogues

Temple B'nai Israel (C-US), 345 Jackson St, Ph: 423-3743. Rabbi M. Samuels. Services: Shabbat

Food

Waldbaum's Food Mart, Rte 195, **Mansfield**, Ph: 456-9954. Good selection of kosher products.

WINDSOR (See WEST HARTFORD)

WOODBRIDGE (See NEW HAVEN)

Delaware

DOVER   Area Code (302)   J-pop. 650

Synagogues

Congregation Beth Sholom (C-US), Queen & Clara Sts,
   Ph: 734-5578. Rabbi M. Goldblum. Services: Shabbat

NEWARK   Area Code (302)

Synagogues

Temple Beth-El (R-Recon-FRCH), 301 Possum Park Rd,
   Ph: 366-8330. Rabbi D. Kaplan. Services: Shabbat

WILMINGTON   Area Code (302)   J-pop. 9,500

Synagogues

Adas Kadesh Shel Emeth (Trad), Washington Blvd & Torah Way,
   Ph: 762-2705. Rabbi N. Schorr. Services: Daily
Congregation Beth Emeth (R-UAHC), 300 W Lea Blvd,
   Ph: 764-2393. Rabbi P. Grumbacher. Services: Shabbat
Congregation Beth Shalom (C-US), 18th & Baynard Blvd,
   Ph: 654-4462. Rabbi H. Yoskowitz. Services: Daily
Chabad of Delaware (O-Lubav), 1306 Grinnell Rd, Ph: 478-4400.
   Rabbi C. Vogel. Services: Call for information

Food

Bagels & Donuts, Silverside & Marsh Rd, Ph: 478-9016; 1901
   Penna Ave, Ph: 652-7960. RS: Vaad Hakashruth of Wilmington.
   (Bread, bagels, danishes, and muffins only).
Brandywine Pastry Bakery, 913 Brandywine Blvd, Ph: 762-6000.
   Pareve breads and pastries. RS: Vaad Hakashruth of
   Wilmington.
Shop Rite, 1600 W Newport Pike, **Newport,** Ph: 999-1227. Large
   selection of kosher products.

Food

Shabbat hospitality - call Chabad, Ph: 478-4400.

District of Columbia

Jewish Information & Referral Services: (301) 770-4848

WASHINGTON, D.C. (See also **SILVER SPRING, MD**)
Area Code (202)   J-pop. 25,400

Synagogues

Adas Israel Congregation (C-US), 2850 Quebec St NW,
Ph: 362-4433. Rabbi J. Wohlberg. Services: Shabbat

Congregation Beth Sholom (O-UOJC), 13th St & Eastern Ave NW,
Ph: 726-3869. Rabbi J. Tessler. Services: Daily

Kesher Israel Congregation (O), 2801 N St NW, **Georgetown**,
Ph: 333-4808. Rabbi B. Freundel. Services: Daily

Temple Micah (R-UAHC), 600 M St SW, Ph: 554-3099. Rabbi D.
Zemel. Services: Friday

Ohev Sholom (O-UOJC), 1600 Jonquil St NW, Ph: 882-7225.
Rabbi H. Klavan. Services: Daily

Temple Sinai (R-UAHC), 3100 Military Road NW, Ph: 363-6394.
Rabbi F. Reiner. Services: Friday

Congregation Tifereth Israel (C-US), 7701 16th St NW,
Ph: 882-1605. Rabbi A. Abramowitz. Services: Shabbat and
Sunday

Washington Hebrew Congregation (R-UAHC), 3935 Macomb St
NW, Ph: 362-7100. Rabbi J. Jospe. Services: Friday

Eating Out

B'nai B'rith Hillel Foundation of George Washington University,
"The Garden of Eat'n", 2300 H St NW, Ph: 296-8873. Lunch:
Mon-Fri. Dinner: Wed. only. Menu: Mon, Wed, Fri: Deli; Tue,
Thur: Dairy. RS: Rabbinical Council of Greater Washington.
Closed August through Labor Day.

Accommodations

Shabbat hospitality; call Rabbi B. Freundel at Kesher Israel
Congregation, Ph: 333-2337.

Florida

BELLE GLADE   Area Code (407)

Synagogues

Temple Beth Sholom (C), 224 NW Avenue G, Ph: 996-3886.

BOCA RATON
Area Code (407)   J-pop. Boca Raton - Delray Beach 55,000

Synagogues

Congregation Beth Ami of Palm Beach County (C), 1401 NW 4th
    Ave, Ph: 347-0031. Rabbi N. Zelizer. Services: Shabbat
Temple Beth El of Boca Raton (R-UAHC), 333 SW 4th Ave,
    Ph: 391-8900. Rabbi M. Singer. Services: Friday
Temple Beth Shalom (C-US), 19140 Lyons Rd, **Century Village
    West**, Ph: 483-5557. Rabbi D. Crain. Services: Daily
Congregation B'nai Israel (R-UAHC), 220 Yamato Rd, meets at
    Center for Group Counseling, 22445 Boca Rio Road,
    Ph: 241-8118. Rabbi R. Agler. Services: Shabbat
B'nai Torah Congregation (C), 6261 SW 18th St, Ph: 392-8566.
    Rabbi M. Ezring. Services: Daily
Boca Raton Synagogue (O), 22130 Belmar #1101, Ph: 394-5742.
    Services: Shabbat and Holidays
Congregation Kol Ami (Recon), 7040 W Palmetto Park Rd #184,
    Ph: 482-0445. Meets at 3200 N Military Trail. Services: Friday
Congregation Torah Ohr (O) 11946 Lyons Rd, Ph: 479-4049.
    Rabbi J. Biston. Services: Shabbat and daily a.m.
Young Israel of Boca Raton (O), 7955 Love Lane, Ph: 391-3235.
    Rabbi E. Rabovsky. Meets at Las Brisas Clubhouse, Montoya
    Circle. Services: Shabbat

Day School

Donna Klein Jewish Academy, 414 NW 35th St, Ph: 395-3212.

BONAVENTURE   Area Code (305)

Synagogues

B'nai Aviv (C-US), 16614 Saddle Club Rd, Ph: 384-8265. Meets at
  Another Generation Pre-School. Rabbi L. Fink. Services: Shabbat

BOYNTON BEACH   Area Code (407)

Synagogues

Congregation Beth Kodesh (C-US), 501 NE 26th Ave,
  Ph: 586-9428. Rabbi J. Chazin. Services: Shabbat, Monday and
  Thursday a.m.

Temple Torah (C), Lions Club, 3615 W Boynton Beach Blvd,
  Ph: 736-7687.

Eating Out (See **Delray Beach**)

BRADENTON   Area Code (813)

Synagogues

Temple Beth El (C-US), 2209 75th St W, Ph: 792-0870. Rabbi G.B.
  Weiss. Services: Shabbat, Monday and Thursday

CAPE CORAL   Area Code (813)

Synagogues

Temple Beth El (R-UAHC), 2721 Del Prado Blvd, Ph: 574-5115.
  Rabbi S. Agin. Services: Friday

Temple Beth Shalom (R), 702 SE 24th Ave, Ph: 772-4555. Rabbi
  Y. McDaniel. Services: Friday

CLEARWATER (See also **ST. PETERSBURG**)
  Area Code (813)

Synagogues

Congregation Beth Shalom (C-US), 1325 S Belcher Rd,
  Ph: 531-1418. Rabbi K. Brumberg. Services: Shabbat, Sunday,

Monday and Thursday a.m.

Temple B'nai Israel (R-UAHC), 1685 S Belcher Rd, Ph: 531-5829.
Rabbi A. Baseman. Services: Shabbat

Young Israel of Clearwater, (O-NCYI), 570 Kirkland Circle,
Dunedin, Ph: 733-6811. Rabbi S. Adler. Services: Shabbat and
Sunday

Accommodations:

Ramada Inn Countryside, 2560 U.S. 19 N, Ph: 796-1234. About a
mile from Young Israel.

COCONUT CREEK   Area Code (305)

Synagogues

Congregation Beth Shalom (C-US), 1447 Lyons Rd, Ph: 975-4666.
Rabbi L. Rosenblum. Services: Daily

Liberal Jewish Temple of Coconut Creek (R), Meets at 3950
Coconut Creek Pkwy, Ph: 973-7494. Rabbi B. Warshal.
Services: Call for schedule.

CORAL GABLES (See also **MIAMI** and **MIAMI BEACH**)
Area Code (305)

Synagogues

Temple Judea (R-UAHC), 5500 Granada Blvd, Ph: 667-5657.
Rabbi M. Eisenstat. Services: Friday

Temple Zamora (C), 44 Zamora Ave, Ph: 448-7132. Rabbi A.
Brilliant. Services: Shabbat

CORAL SPRINGS   Area Code (305)

Synagogues

Temple Beth Orr (R-UAHC), 2151 Riverside Dr, Ph: 753-3232.
Rabbi S. J. Levy, Rabbi M. Gross. Services: Shabbat

Synagogues cont.

Chabad Lubavitch Community Center (O-Lubav), 8803 Sample Rd, Ph: 345-0550. Rabbi Y. Biston. Services: Daily

Accommodations

Holiday Inn, 3701 University Dr, Ph: 753-9000. Around the corner from Chabad.

DAVIE (See FORT LAUDERDALE)

DAYTONA BEACH   Area Code (904)   J-pop. 2,000

Synagogues

Temple Israel of Daytona (C-US), 1400 S Peninsula Dr, Ph: 252-3097. Rabbi I. Barzak. Services: Shabbat

DEERFIELD BEACH   Area Code (305)

Synagogues

Temple Beth Israel of Deerfield Beach (C-US), 200 S Century Blvd, Ph: 421-7060. Rabbi S. April. Services: Daily

Temple B'nai Shalom of Deerfield Beach (R), 3501 West Dr, Ph: 428-1408. Rabbi A. Winters. Services: Friday

Young Israel of Deerfield Beach (O-NCYI), 1880H W Hillsboro Blvd, Ph: 421-1367. Services: Daily

Food

Star of David, 1806 W Hillsboro Blvd, Ph: 427-6400. Kosher supermarket. RS: Rabbi Malavsky of Beth Shalom, Hollywood. Closed Shabbat.

DELAND   Area Code (904)

Synagogues

Temple Israel (C-US), 1001 E New York Ave, Ph: 736-1646. Services: Friday

DELRAY BEACH   Area Code (407)

Synagogues

Congregation Anshei Emunah (O-UOJC), 16189 Carter Rd, Ph: 499-9229. Rabbi L. Sacks. Services: Daily

Congregation Anshei Shalom of West Delray (C-US), 7099 W Atlantic Ave, Ph: 495-1300, Rabbi I. Jacobs. Services: Daily

Temple Emeth (C-US), 5780 W Atlantic Ave, Ph: 498-3536. Rabbi L. Hering. Services: Daily

Temple Sinai (R-UAHC), 2475 W Atlantic Ave, Ph: 276-6161. Rabbi S. Silver. Services: Shabbat

Eating Out

Mahzon Tov Mandarin Kosher Restaurant, 5046 W Atlantic Ave, Ph: 496-6278. Meals: l,d. Menu: (Glatt meat) Chinese and American. RS: O.K. Laboratories. Closed Shabbat.

Food

Oriole Kosher Meat, 7351 W Atlantic Ave, Ph: 495-1144. Kosher grocery and fresh meat. RS: Rabbi L. Sacks. Closed Shabbat.

Accommodations

Private accommodations; contact Rabbi L. Sacks at Congregation Anshei Emunah, Ph: 499-9229.

DELTONA   Area Code (904)

Synagogues

Temple Shalom (R), 1785 Elkcam Blvd, Ph: 789-2202. Services: Friday

FORT LAUDERDALE   Area Code (305)   J-pop. 116,000

Synagogues

Temple Bat Yam (R-UAHC), 5151 NE 14th Terr, Ph: 928-0410. Rabbi L. Littman.

Temple Beth Israel (C-US), 7100 W Oakland Park Blvd, Ph: 742-4040. Rabbi H. Addison. Services: Daily

Temple Emanu-El (R-UAHC), 3245 W Oakland Park Blvd, Ph: 731-2310. Rabbi E. M. Maline. Services: Friday

Synagogues cont.

Temple Ohel B'nai Raphael (O-UOJC), 4351 W. Oakland Park Blvd, Ph: 733-7684. Services: Daily

Eating Out

Ilana Kosher Kitchen (in The J.C.C.), 5850 Stirling Rd, **Davie**, Ph: 434-0499 X357. Meals: b,l,d. Menu: (Meat) Continental. Also take-out. RS: Rabbi E. Davis. Closed Shabbat.

Mikvah (See **Hollywood**)

Bookstore

Judaica Treasures, 2325 S University Dr, **Davie**, Ph: 473-1444.

FORT MYERS   Area Code (813)   J-pop. Lee County 3,500

Synagogues

Temple Judea (C-US), 14486 A & W Bulb Rd, Ph: 433-0201. Rabbi T. August. Services: Shabbat, Monday and Thursday a.m.

FORT PIERCE   Area Code (407)   J-pop. 500

Synagogues

Temple Beth El (R), 4600 Oleander Ave W, Ph: 461-7428. Services: Friday

GAINESVILLE   Area Code (904)   J-pop. 1,200

Synagogues

B'nai B'rith Hillel Foundation at the University of Florida, 16 NW 18th St, Ph: 372-2900. Rabbi G. Friedman. Services: Friday (C,R), Saturday (C), Occasional Saturdays (O). Closed first three weeks in August.

Temple B'nai Israel (C-US), 3830 NW 16th Blvd, Ph: 376-1508. Rabbi A. Lehmann. Services: Shabbat

Temple Shir Shalom (R), 3855 NW 8th Ave, Ph: 371-6399. Services: Second and fourth Fridays

Eating Out

B'nai B'rith Hillel Foundation at the University of Florida, 16 NW
18th St, Ph: 372-2900. Tuesday and Sunday dinners. For Friday
evening dinner and Shabbat lunch, pay by Friday noon. Passover
store and meals. Closed first three weeks in August.

GULFPORT Area Code (813)

Synagogues

Congregation Beth Shalom (C-US), 1844 54th St S, Ph: 321-3380.
Rabbi S. Kaplan. Services: Shabbat

HALLANDALE (See also HOLLYWOOD or NORTH MIAMI BEACH) Area Code (305)

Synagogues

Hallandale Jewish Center (C-US), 416 NE 8th Ave, Ph: 454-9100.
Rabbi Dr. C. Klein. Services: Daily
Congregation Levi Yitzchok (O-Lubav), 1295 E Hallandale Beach
Blvd, Ph: 458-1877. Rabbi R. Tennenhaus. Services: Daily

Eating Out

Mayer's Embassy Kosher Steak House, 1025 E Hallandale Beach
Blvd, Ph: 456-7550. Meals: d. Menu: Steaks, American cuisine.
RS: Star-K. All major credit cards. Closed Shabbat.

Food

Kezreh Inc., 1025 E Hallandale Beach Blvd, Ph: 454-5776. Fresh
meats, deli, prepared foods, kosher groceries. RS: Orthodox
Rabbinical Board of Broward and Palm Beach Counties. Closed
Shabbat.

HIALEAH (See also MIAMI BEACH) Area Code (305)

Synagogues

Temple Tifereth Jacob (C), 951 E 4th Ave, Ph: 887-9595. Rabbi N.
Zwitman. Services: Shabbat

HOLLYWOOD (See also **NORTH MIAMI BEACH** and **MIAMI BEACH**) Area Code (305) J-pop. 60,000

For kosher food information, call Rabbi E. Davis at Young Israel of Hollywood, Ph: 966-7877.

Synagogues

American European Congregation (O), 315 Madison St, Ph: 922-4544. Services: Call for information.

Temple Beth Ahm (C-US), 9730 Stirling Rd, Ph: 431-5100. Rabbi A. Kapnek. Services: Shabbat

Temple Beth El (R-UAHC), 1351 S 14 Ave, Ph: 920-8225. Rabbi N. S. Lipson. Services: Shabbat

Temple Beth Shalom (C-US), 1400 N 46 Ave, Ph: 981-6111. Rabbi M. Malavsky. Services: Daily

B'nai Sephardim (O-Sephardic), 3670 Stirling Rd, Ph: 983-9981. Rabbi Y. Benhamu. Services: Daily

Temple Sinai (C-US), 1201 Johnson St, Ph: 920-1577. Rabbi R. Konigsburg. Services: Daily

Temple Solel (R-UAHC), 5100 Sheridan St, Ph: 989-0205. Rabbi R. Frazin. Services: Shabbat

Young Israel of Hollywood (O-NCYI), 3291 Stirling Rd, Ph: 966-7877. Rabbi E. Davis. Services: Daily

Eating Out

Jerusalem Pizza II, 5650 Stirling Rd, Ph: 964-6811. Meals: l,d. Menu: (Dairy: cholov Yisroel) Pizza, Israeli. RS: Orthodox Rabbinical Board of Broward and Palm Beach Counties. Closed Shabbat.

Maccabi Gardens, 4101 North Hills Dr, Ph: 981-7994. Meals: l,d. Menu: Jewish continental and Israeli. RS: Orthodox Rabbinical Board of Broward and Palm Beach Counties. All major credit cards. Prepaid Shabbat meals served during the season.

Food

Shigaoff, 3294 Stirling Rd, Ph: 989-0887. Butcher and take-out. Glatt meat. RS: Orthodox Rabbinical Board of Broward and Palm Beach Counties. Closed Shabbat.

West Hollywood Kosher Meats Inc, 142 S State Rd 7, Ph: 962-5018. Fresh and frozen meats. RS: Rabbi M. Malavsky of Beth Shalom. Closed Shabbat.

Mikvah

Young Israel of Hollywood, 3291 Stirling Rd. Contact Ms. C. Hirsch, Ph: 989-2387 (evenings only) or synagogue office, Ph: 966-7877.

HOMESTEAD   Area Code (305)

Synagogues

Homestead Jewish Center (C), 183 NE 8th St, Ph: 248-5724. Services: Shabbat

JACKSONVILLE   Area Code (904)   J-pop. 7,300

Synagogues

Congregation Ahavath Chesed (R), 8727 San Jose Blvd, Ph: 733-7078. Rabbi H. Greenstein. Services: Shabbat
Beth Shalom Synagogue (C-US), 4072 Sunbeam Rd, Ph: 268-0404. Rabbi G. R. Perras. Services: Shabbat
Etz Chaim Synagogue (O-UOJC), 10167 San José Blvd, Ph: 262-3565. Rabbi Y. Adler. Services: Daily
Jacksonville Jewish Center (C-US), 3662 Crown Point Rd, Ph: 268-6736. Rabbi D. Gaffney. Services: Shabbat and Sunday

Eating Out

Kosher Nutrition Center (cafeteria), 5846 Mount Carmel Terr, Ph: 737-9057. RS: Rabbi Y. Adler. Lunch is served Monday through Friday at noon. Contact the center for further information.

Food

Dunkin' Donuts, 4930 University Blvd N, Ph: 737-7244. Dairy. RS: Rabbi Y. Adler (baked goods only).
Kosher Kuts, 10501 San José Blvd, Ph: 260-MEAT. Butcher. Glatt meat. Full line of kosher cheeses and grocery products. RS: Rabbi Y. Adler. Closed Shabbat.

Food cont.

Waldz Bakery, 779 University Blvd, Ph: 743-2922. Breads and
cakes (dairy and pareve). RS: Rabbi Y. Adler.

Worman's Bakery, 204 Broad St, Ph: 354-5702; 1712 San Marco
Blvd, Ph: 396-0393. Breads and pastries. RS: Rabbi Y. Adler
(bakery goods only).

Accommodations

Private accommodations; contact Rabbi Y. Adler at Etz Chaim
Synagogue, Ph: 262-3565.

Ramada Inn, Mandarin Conference Center, 3130 Hartley Rd,
Ph: 268-8080. A mile to Etz Chaim Synagogue.

Mikvah

Etz Chaim Synagogue, 10167 San José Blvd. Call synagogue
office, Ph: 262-3565 or 737-7966.

Day Schools

Etz Chaim School, 10167 San Jose Blvd, Ph: 262-3565.

Solomon Schechter Day School (C), Jacksonville Jewish Center,
3662 Crown Point Rd, Ph: 292-1000.

JUPITER   Area Code (407)

Synagogues

Temple Beth Am (R), 759 Parkway St, Ph: 747-1109. Services:
Friday

KEY WEST   Area Code (305)   J-pop. 170

Synagogues

Congregation B'nai Zion (C), 750 United St, Ph: 294-3437. Rabbi
L. Dimpson. Services: Shabbat

KISSIMMEE (See ORLANDO)

LAKE WORTH (See also WEST PALM BEACH)
Area Code (407)

Synagogues

Lake Worth Jewish Center (C), 4550 Jog Rd, Ph: 967-3600. Rabbi K. Rocklin. Services: Shabbat

Temple Beth Sholom (C), 315 N "A" St, Ph: 585-5020. Rabbi E. Eisenberg. Services: Shabbat

LAKELAND Area Code (813)   J-pop. 800

Synagogues

Temple Emanuel (C-US), 730 Lake Hollingsworth Dr, Ph: 682-8616. Rabbi M. Levy. Services: Shabbat, Monday and Thursday a.m.

LAUDERHILL (See also FORT LAUDERDALE and SUNRISE) Area Code (305)

Synagogues

Hebrew Congregation of Lauderhill (C-US), 2048 NW 49th Ave, Ph: 733-9560. Rabbi I. Halpern. Services: Daily

LONGBOAT KEY Area Code (813)

Synagogues

Temple Beth Israel (R), 567 Bay Isles Rd, Ph: 383-3428. Rabbi S. Saperstein. Services: Friday

LONGWOOD (See also ORLANDO) Area Code (407)

Synagogues

Congregation Beth Am (C-US), 3899 Sand Lake Rd, Ph: 862-3505. Rabbi M. Baer. Services: Shabbat

MAITLAND (See ORLANDO)

MARGATE Area Code (305)

Synagogues

Temple Beth Am - Margate Jewish Center (C-US), 7205 Royal Palm Blvd, Ph: 974-8650. Rabbi P. Plotkin. Services: Daily

Synagogues cont.

Congregation Beth Hillel of Margate (C-US), 7638 Margate Blvd,
   Ph: 974-3090. Rabbi A. Drazin. Services: Daily

Eating Out

East Side Deli & Kosher Restaurant, 6846 W Atlantic Blvd,
   Ph: 971-8340. Meals: l,d. Menu: Deli and traditional. RS: Rabbi
   M. Malavsky of Beth Shalom in Hollywood. Closed Shabbat.

MERRIT ISLAND   Area Code (407)

Synagogues

Temple Israel (R-UAHC), 1900 S Tropical Trail, Ph: 453-5144.
   Rabbi A. Hillman. Services: Shabbat

MIAMI (See also MIAMI BEACH and NORTH MIAMI BEACH)
Area Code (305)   Dade County J-pop. 226,000

Synagogues

Ahavat Shalom Congregation (Trad), 985 SW 67th Ave,
   Ph: 261-5479. Services: Shabbat
Anshe Emes Congregation (C), 2533 SW 19th Ave, Ph: 854-7623.
Congregation Bet Breira (R-UAHC), 9400 SW 87th Ave,
   Ph: 595-1500. Rabbi B. Tabachnikoff. Services: Friday
Temple Beth Am (R-UAHC), 5950 N Kendall Dr, Ph: 667-6667.
   Rabbi J. Kendall. Services: Shabbat
Beth David Congregation (C-US), 2625 SW 3rd Ave,
   Ph: 854-3911. Rabbi J. Riemer. Services: Daily
Beth Kodesh (C-US), 1101 SW 12th Ave, Ph: 858-6334. Rabbi M.
   Shapiro. Services: Daily
Temple Beth Or (Recon-FRCH), 11715 SW 87th Ave,
   Ph: 235-1419. Rabbi R. Shapiro. Services: Friday
Bet Shira Congregation (C-US), 7500 SW 120th St, Ph: 238-2601.
   Rabbi D. Auerbach. Services: Daily
Temple Beth Tov (C), 6438 SW 8th St, Ph: 261-9821. Rabbi N.
   Bryn. Services: Daily
B'nai B'rith Hillel Foundation (R), University of Miami, 1100
   Stanford Dr, Ph: 665-6948. Rabbi L. Feldstein. Services: Friday

B'nai Israel & Greater Miami Youth Synagogue (O), 16260 SW 288th St, **Naranja**, Ph: 264-6488 or 245-8594. Rabbi Z. Glixman. Services: Shabbat

Havurah of South Florida (Recon.), 9315 SW 61st Ct, Ph: 666-7349. Rabbi M. Chefitz. Services: Saturday

Temple Israel of Greater Miami (R-UAHC), 137 NE 19th St, Ph: 573-5900. Rabbi R. Perlmeter. Services: Friday. Kendall branch: 9990 N Kendall Dr, Ph: 595-5055. Services: Friday

Temple Judea (R), 5500 Granada Blvd, Ph: 667-5657. Rabbi M. Eisenstat.

Temple Samu-El Or Olam (C-US), 9353 SW 152nd Ave, Ph: 382-3668. Rabbi E. Farber and Rabbi S. Rudy. Services: Daily

Shaare Tefillah Torah Center of Kendall (O-UOJC), 7880 SW 112th St, Ph: 232-6833. Rabbi H. Becker. Services: Shabbat

Temple Shir Ami (R), 9920 SW 131st St, Ph: 253-9666. Rabbi B. Goldstein.

Temple Zion-Israelite Center (C-US), 8000 Miller Rd, Ph: 271-2311. Rabbi M. Laxmeter. Services: Daily

Eating Out

My Chosen Delight Deli Restaurant, 7118 SW 117th Ave, Ph: 596-5223. Meals: l,d, Sunday: brunch. Menu: Deli, complete dinners. Also pareve bakery and take-out. RS: Rabbi R. Glixman. Closed Shabbat

Food

Weberman's Traditional Foods, 3301 NE 59th St, Ph: 751-7100. Take-out, deli, meats, fish, bakery. RS: National Kashruth. Closed Shabbat.

Accommodations

Private accommodations; B'nai Israel & Greater Miami Youth Synagogue holds a weekly Shabbaton. This includes lodging and meals. For fees and further information contact Rabbi R. Glixman, Ph: 264-6488 or 245-8594.

Mikvah

Mikvah, 16260 SW 288th St. Contact Rabbi R. Glixman,
    Ph: 264-6488 or the B'nai Israel office, Ph: 245-8594.

Day Schools

Bet Shira Solomon Schechter Day School (C), 7500 SW 120th St,
    Ph: 238-2606.
Goldstein Hebrew Academy, 12401 SW 102nd Ave, Ph: 253-2300.
Temple Beth Am Day School (R), 5950 N Kendall Dr,
    Ph: 665-6228.

Bookstore

The Chosen Gift, 7146 SW 117th Ave, Ph: 596-3639.

MIAMI BEACH   Area Code (305)

Synagogues

Congregation Adas Dej, 225 37th St, Ph: 673-9428. Rabbi J.
    Paneth. Services: Daily
Agudath Israel Hebrew Institute (O), 7801 Carlyle Ave,
    Ph: 866-5226. Rabbi S. Ever. Services: Daily
Beth El Congregation of the Hebrew Academy (O), 2400 Pinetree
    Dr, Ph: 532-6421. Rabbi S. Schiff. Services: Daily
Temple Beth El of North Bay Village (C-US), 7800 Hispanola Ave,
    Ph: 861-4005. Rabbi Dr. N. Shapiro. Services: Shabbat,
    Monday and Thursday mornings.
Beth Israel Congregation (O-UOJC), 770 40th St, Ph: 538-1251.
    Rabbi M. Shapiro. Services: Daily
Beth Jacob Congregation (Trad), 311 Washington Ave,
    Ph: 672-1882/6150. Rabbi S. Swirsky. Services: Daily
Temple Beth Raphael (C), 1545 Jefferson Ave, Ph: 538-4112.
    Rabbi R. Carmi. Services: Daily
Temple Beth Sholom (R-UAHC), 4144 Chase Ave, Ph: 538-7231.
    Rabbi G. Glickstein. Services: Shabbat
Beth Tfilah Congregation (O), 935 Euclid Ave, Ph: 538-1521.
    Rabbi I. Tropper. Services: Daily
Beth Yoseph Chaim Congregation (O), 843 Meridian Ave,
    Ph: 531-2150. Rabbi D. Rozencwaig. Services: Daily

Temple B'nai Zion (C), 200 178th St, **Sunny Isles**, Ph: 932-2159. Rabbi S. Burstein. Services: Daily

Cuban Hebrew Congregation-Temple Beth Shmuel (C), 1700 Michigan Ave, Ph: 534-7213. Rabbi B. Konovitch. Services: Shabbat, afternoons

Temple Emanu-El (C-US), 1701 Washington Ave, Ph: 538-2503. Dr. I. Lehrman. Services: Daily

Knesseth Israel Congregation (O), 1415 Euclid Ave, Ph: 538-2741. Rabbi J. Melber. Services: Daily

Congregation Lubavitch Russian Center (O-Lubav), 1120 Collins Ave, Ph: 673-5755. Rabbi S. Blank. Services: Daily

Temple Menorah (C-US), 620 75th St, Ph: 866-0221. Rabbi E. Pearlson. Services: Shabbat

Mogen David Congregation (O), 9348 Harding Ave, Ph: 865-9714. Services: Shabbat and mornings

Temple Moses (O-UOJC), 1200 Normandy Dr, Ph: 861-6308. Rabbi A. Amselem. Services: Daily

Temple Ner Tamid (C-US), 7902 Carlyle Ave, Ph: 866-8345. Rabbi E. Labovitz. Services: Daily

Ohev Shalom Congregation (O), 7055 Bonita Dr, Ph: 865-9851. Rabbi P. Weberman. Services: Daily

Ohr Hachaim Congregation (O), 317 47th St, Ph: 674-1326. Rabbi A. Feuer. Services: Daily

Pavillion Hebrew Study Group (C), 5601 Collins Ave, Ph: 865-6511. Rabbi B. Silver. Services: Saturday

Sephardic Jewish Center of Greater Miami (Trad), 645 Collins Ave, Ph: 534-4092. Rabbi S. Nahmias. Services: Saturday

Shul of Bal Harbour (O), Sheraton Bal Harbour, 9540 Collins Ave, Ph: 868-1411. Rabbi S. Lipskar. Services: Shabbat

Talmudic University of Florida Congregation (O), 1910 Alton Rd, Ph: 534-7050. Rabbi Y. Zweig. Services: Daily

West Avenue Jewish Center (O), 1140 Alton Rd, Ph: 534-3444. Rabbi D. Golowinski. Services: Daily

Young Israel of Sunny Isles (O-NCYI), 17395 N Bay Rd, Ph: 935-9095. Rabbi R. Sufrin. Services: Daily

Eating Out

Benjamin's, 5101 Collins Ave, (Sea Coast Towers South), Ph: 865-2001. Meals: l,d. Menu: (Meat) Continental. RS: National Kashruth. Major credit cards. Closed Shabbat.

Embassy 41 Delicate-Essen, 534 41st St, Rd, Ph: 534-7550. Meals: l,d. Menu: Deli-style dishes. Also take-out. RS: National Kashruth. Closed Shabbat.

Embassy Peking, 4101 Pinetree Dr, Ph: 538-7550. Meals: d. Menu: American and Chinese. Pre-paid reservations for Shabbat. RS: National Kashruth.

Guiseppe Goldberg, Sans Souci Hotel, 31st St & Collins, Ph: 531-8261. Meals: d. Menu: (Glatt meat) Italian. RS: National Kashruth. Closed Shabbat.

King David Kosher Foods Inc, 1339 Washington Ave, Ph: 534-0197. Meals: l,d, Menu: (Glatt meat) Deli-style dishes. RS: National Kashruth. Closed Shabbat.

Pita Pita, 1448 Washington Ave, Ph: 532-1411. Meals: l,d. Menu: (Glatt meat) Israeli. RS: O.K. Laboratories. Closed Shabbat.

Royal Hungarian, Cadillac Hotel, 3925 Collins Ave, Ph: 532-8566 Meals: d. Menu (Meat): Hungarian/Traditional. RS: National Kashruth. Open during season. Prior payment for Shabbat.

Sea View Dining Restaurant, in the Casablanca Hotel, 6345 Collins Ave, Ph: 866-8851. Meals: b,l,d. Menu: Traditional. RS: National Kashruth. Pre-pay Shabbat meals.

Yo Si Peking, Eden Roc Hotel, 4525 Collins Ave, Ph: 532-9060. Meals: l,d, Menu: Chinese. RS: National Kashruth. Pre-pay for Shabbat meals during season.

Zelig's International Cuisine, Carriage Club, 5005 Collins Ave, Ph: 861-9444. Meals: d. Menu: Entrees, salads, soups. RS: Star-K. Open for pre-paid Shabbat reservations during the season.

Food

Abraham's Bakery, 7423 Collins Ave, Ph: 861-0291. Pareve baked goods. RS: Orthodox Rabbinical Council. Closed Shabbat.

Adam's Meat Market, 1405 Washington Ave, Ph: 532-0103 RS: Rabbi A. Safra. Closed Shabbat.

B. E. Kosher, 1436 Alton Rd, Ph: 531-7060. Meats, groceries and dairy products. RS: Lubavitch, Margareten. Closed Shabbat.

Goldstein's Butcher Shop, 7443 Collins, Ph: 865-4981 RS: Rabbi Safra. Closed Shabbat.

Goren's Vienna Bakery, 1233 Lincoln, Ph: 672-3928. Breads and pastries. RS: O.K. Laboratories. Closed Shabbat.

National Hebrew Glatt, 736 41st St, Ph: 532-2210. Complete kosher grocery. Cholov Yisroel. Closed Shabbat.

Pastry Lane, 4022 Royal Palm, Ph: 674-9523. Breads and pastries (pareve) RS: National Kashruth. Closed Shabbat.

Patio Bake Shop, 7440 Collins, Ph: 861-4810. Breads & pastries (pareve). RS: National Kashruth. Closed Shabbat.

Shmuel's Bakery/41st Glatt Mart, 765 Arthur Godfrey Rd, Ph: 538-4528. Bakery (pareve), kosher grocery, cholov Yisroel products. RS: OK Laboratories. Closed Shabbat.

Hotels

The following hotels serve kosher food only and hold synagogue services daily:

Caribbean Hotel, 3737 Collins Ave, Ph: 531-0061. Glatt meat. RS: Orthodox Union. Shomer Shabbat. Dairy coffee shop and restaurant open to public. Open summers.

Continental Hotel, 4000 Collins Ave, Ph: 538-6721. Glatt meat. Shomer Shabbat. RS: National Kashruth.

Crown Hotel, 4041 Collins Ave, Ph: 531-5771. Glatt meat. RS: Orthodox Union. Shomer Shabbat. Dairy coffee shop and restaurant open to public. November - April. Not kosher in summer.

Sans Souci Hotel, 3101 Collins Ave, Ph: 531-8261. Shomer Shabbat. Glatt meat. RS: National Kasruth. Dairy coffee shop and restaurant open to public. Open all year.

Saxony Hotel, 3201 Collins Ave, Ph: 538-6811. RS: National Kashruth. Shomer Shabbat. Glatt meat. Dairy coffee shop and restaurant open to public. Open November through April.

Shore Club, 1901 Collins Ave, Ph: 538-7811. Glatt meat. RS: Rabbi Z. Glixman. Shomer Shabbat.

Tarleton Hotel, 2469 Collins Ave, Ph: 538-5721. RS: Rabbi J. Kaufman. Shomer Shabbat.

Mikvah

Congregation Adas Dej, 225 37th St, Ph: 674-8204, or Mrs. Chanah Schwartz, Ph: 531-6810.

Daughters of Israel, 151 Michigan Ave. Contact Mrs. Hassia Moredokh, Ph: 672-3500.

Day Schools

Hebrew Academy of Greater Miami, 2400 Pine Tree Dr, Ph: 532-6421.

Lehrman Day School (C), 727 Lehrman Dr, Ph: 866-2771.

Lubavitch Educational Center, 1140 Alton Rd, Ph: 673-5664.

Toras Emes Academy, 7902 Carlyle Ave, Ph: 868-1388.

Yeshiva Elementary School of Greater Miami, 1965 Alton Rd, Ph: 673-0710.

Bookstores

National Hebrew Israeli Gift Center, 736 41st St, Ph: 532-2210.

Torah Treasures, 1309 Washington Ave, Ph: 673-6095.

NAPLES   Area Code (813)   J-pop. 750

Synagogues

Temple Shalom (R-UAHC), 1575 Pine Ridge Rd, Ph: 597-8158. Rabbi S. Phillips. Services: Shabbat and Sunday

NORTH BAY VILLAGE (See also MIAMI BEACH)
Area Code (305)

Synagogues

Temple Beth El of North Bay Village (C-US), 7800 Hispanola Ave, Ph: 861-4005. Rabbi N. Shapiro. Services: Shabbat, Monday and Thursday

NORTH MIAMI   Area Code (305)

Synagogues

Temple Beth Moshe (C-US), 2225 NE 121st St, Ph: 891-5508. Rabbi J. Lang. Services: Daily

Eating Out

Sara's Dairy Restaurant, 2214 NE 123rd St, Ph: 891-3312. Meals:
b,l.d. Menu: Pizza/vegetarian. RS: Star-K. Closed Shabbat.

NORTH MIAMI BEACH Area Code (305)

Synagogues

Temple Adath Yeshurun (C-US), 1025 NE Miami Gardens Dr,
Ph: 947-1435. Rabbi S. Freedman. Services: Daily

Congregation Agudath Achim-Third Avenue Hebrew Religious
Community Center (O), 19255 NE 3rd Ave, Ph: 651-5392.
Services: Daily

Congregation Ahavas Yisroel-Chabad (O), 20910 W Dixie Hwy,
Ph: 933-0770. Rabbi C. Brusowankin. Services: Call for
schedule.

Aventura-Turnberry Jewish Center-Beth El (C-US), 20400 30th
Ave, **Aventura**, Ph: 935-0666. Rabbi D. Satzman. Services:
Daily

Beth Moshe Congregation (C), 2225 NE 121st St, Ph: 891-5508.
Rabbi J. Lang.

Beth Torah (C-US), 1051 N Miami Beach Blvd, Ph: 947-7528.
Rabbi M. Lipschitz. Services: Daily

B'nai Sephardim (O), 17495 NE 6th Ave, Ph: 653-9562. Services:
Daily

Congregation Magen David of the Sephardic Jewish Center of
North Miami Beach (Trad), 17100 NE 6th Ave, Ph: 652-2099.
Rabbi M. Melamed. Services: Shabbat

Shaarey Tefilah (O-UOJC), 991 NE 172nd St, Ph: 651-1562. Rabbi
Y. Sprung. Services: Daily

Temple Sinai of North Dade (R-UAHC), 18801 NE 22nd Ave,
Ph: 932-9010. Rabbi R. Kingsley. Services: Shabbat

Congregation Torah Ve'Emunah, 1000 NE 175th St, Ph: 653-6996.
Rabbi Y. Bensinger. Services: Daily

Young Israel of Greater Miami (O-NCYI), 990 NE 171st St,
Ph: 651-3591. Rabbi D. Lehrfield. Services: Daily

Young Israel of Sky Lake (O-NCYI), 1850 NE 183rd St,
Ph: 945-8712. Rabbi A. Groner. Services: Daily

Eating Out

Famous Pita Hut, 175 Sunny Isles Blvd, Ph: 354-3989. Meals: l,d. Menu: (Glatt meat) Kabobs, hamburgers, shwarma, falafel. RS: O.K. Laboratories. Closed Shabbat.

Hamifgash Restaurant, 17044 W Dixie Hwy, Ph: 947-4946, Meals: l, d. Menu: Middle Eastern. RS: Star-K of Baltimore. Closed Shabbat.

Jerusalem Kosher Pizza & Falafel, 761 NE 167th St, Ph: 653-6662. Meals: l,d. Menu: Israeli. RS: Star-K. Closed Shabbat.

Kaifeng, 18117 NE 19th Ave, Ph: 940-6500. Meals: l,d. Menu: Chinese. Eat-in, take-out or delivery. RS: National Kashruth.

Sara's Dairy Restaurant, 1127 NE 163rd St, Ph: 948-7777. Meals, b,l,d. Menu: Pizza/vegetarian, cholov Yisroel. RS: Star-K. Closed Shabbat.

Wing Wan II, 1640 NE 164th St, Ph: 945-3585. A few tables. Meals: l,d. Menu: Chinese/Szechuan. RS: Star-K of Baltimore. Closed Shabbat.

Food

Abraham's Bakery, 757 NE 167th, Ph: 652-1363. Pareve breads and pastries. RS: Orthodox Rabbinical Council. Closed Shabbat.

Glatt Kosher Meat Market, 1123 NE 163rd St, Ph: 944-7726. Fresh meat, poultry, kosher groceries. RS: Rabbi P. Weberman. Closed Shabbat.

Isaac's Kosher Kitchen/Blintzes N' Things, 16460 NE 16th Ave, Ph: 944-5222. Prepared meat and dairy dishes to go. Separate kitchens on premises. RS: Rabbi R. Glixman. Closed Shabbat.

Kosher Magic Caterers, 1839 NE 183rd St, Ph: 932-6687. Deli & take-out. RS: Star-K. Closed Shabbat.

Kosher Treats, 1682 NE 164th St, Ph: 947-1800. Prepared meat, poultry, side dishes and groceries. RS: National Kashruth. Closed Shabbat.

Mendelson's Butcher Shop, 1354 NE 163rd St, Ph: 945-6451. Fresh meat and poultry, some frozen and packaged products. RS: Rabbi M. Lipschitz of Beth Torah. Closed Shabbat.

New Deal Strictly Kosher Meat and Poultry Market, 1362 NE 163rd St, Ph: 945-2512. RS: Rabbi M. Lipschitz

Pastry Lane, 1692 NE 164th St, Ph: 944-5934. Breads and pastries. RS: National Kashruth. Closed Shabbat.

South Florida Meats, 1324 NE 163rd St, Ph: 949-6068. Butcher & complete kosher grocery. RS: Rabbi R. Glixman (fresh meat and poultry only). Closed Shabbat.

Wing Wan II, 1640 NE 164th St, Ph: 945-3585. Menu: Chinese/ Szechuan. Take-out. RS: Star K. Closed Shabbat.

Mikvah

Mikvas Blima of North Dade, 1054 NE Miami Gardens Dr. Call Mikva office, Ph: 949-9650.

Day Schools

Hillel Community Day School, 19000 NE 25th Ave, Ph: 931-2831.

Sinai Academy of the Temple Sinai (R), 18801 NE 22nd Ave, Ph: 932-9010.

Bookstore

Judaica Enterprises, Inc., 1125 NE 163rd St, Ph: 945-5091.

NORTH PORT   Area Code (813)

Synagogues

North Port Temple Beth El (C), 3840 S Biscayne Dr, Ph: 426-3341. Services: Shabbat

Jewish Center (C-US), Biscayne Blvd, Ph: 426-9048. Services: Shabbat

OCALA   Area Code (904)   J-pop. 100

Synagogues

Temple Beth Shalom (R-UAHC), 1109 NE 8th Ave, Ph: 629-3587. Rabbi M. D. Bial. Services: Friday

Temple B'nai Darom (R-UAHC), Corner Banyan Rd & Banyan Course, Ph: 687-1733. Rabbi H. Jaye. Services: Friday

ODESSA   Area Code (813)

Synagogues

Congregation Beth Am (R), 16553 Hutchenson Rd, Ph: 968-8511.

ORLANDO   Area Code (407)   J-pop. 18,000

Synagogues

Chabad of Greater Orlando (O-Lubav), 642 Greenmeadow Ave, **Maitland**, Ph: 740-8770. Rabbi S. Dubov. Services: Call for information.

Temple Israel (C-US), 4917 Eli St, Ph: 647-3055. Rabbi A. Londy. Services: Daily

Congregation of Liberal Judaism (R-UAHC), 928 Malone Dr, Ph: 645-0444. Rabbi L. Halpern. Services: Shabbat

Ohev Shalom (C-US), 5015 Goddard Ave, Ph: 298-4650. Rabbi R. Adler. Services: Shabbat, Monday and Thursday a.m.

Eating Out

(Some Disney World restaurants stock frozen kosher meals, and some of the larger hotels will order them on request.)

Elaine's Café and Catering, 3716 Howell Branch Rd, **Winter Park**, Ph: 679-9000. Meals: l,d. Menu: (Meat) Deli sandwiches, salads, soups, entrees. RS: Orlando Rabbinical Council, Rabbi M. Shapiro of Beth Am, Longwood. Closed Shabbat.

Kinneret Kitchens, 517 South Delaney, Ph: 422-7205. Senior citizens' dining room. Meals: d, Mon.-Fri. at 5 p.m. Call at least 24 hrs. in advance to reserve a meal. RS: Rabbi R. Adler.

Palm Terrace Resturant, Hyatt Orlando Hotel, 6375 W Irlo Bronson Hwy, (U.S. 192) **Kissimmee**, Ph: 396-1234. Meals: b,d. Menu: Traditional-Continental. RS: Orthodox Union

Food

Amira's Catering and Specialty, 1351 East Altamont, **Altamont Springs**, Ph: 767-7577. Cold cuts, side dishes, frozen meals, groceries. RS: Orlando Rabbinical Council, Rabbi M. Shapiro of Beth Am, Longwood. Closed Shabbat.

Kosher Korner, 1035 Semoran Blvd, **Casselberry**, Ph: 834-4335. Complete kosher grocery and take-out. Packaged frozen Glatt meat. Will deliver to hotels. RS: Lubavitch. Closed Shabbat.

Market Place Deli, Hyatt Orlando, 6375 W Irlo Bronson Hwy, (U.S. 192) **Kissimmee**, Ph: 396-1234. Menu: Deli sandwiches, kosher groceries and packaged goods. RS: Orthodox Union. Open Nov.1-Mar.23/June 15-Sept. 5.

Accommodations

Days Suites, 5820 W Irlo Bronson Hwy, (U.S. 192) **Kissimme**, Ph: 396-7900. Suites with kitchens. Sells Wilton frozen dinners. (RS: Orthodox Union).

Hyatt Orlando Hotel, 6375 W Irlo Bronson Hwy, (U.S. 192), Exit 25A on I4, **Kissimmee**, Ph: 396-1234. Synagogue on premises.

Private accommodations; call Chabad, Ph: 740-8770.

Residence Inn, 7610 Canada Ave, Ph: 345-0117; 4786 U.S. Hwy 192, **Kissimmee**, Ph: 396-2056. Studios and suites with kitchens.

Vistana Resort, 8800 Vistana Center Dr, Ph: 239-3100. Two-bedroom suites with kitchens.

Day School

Hebrew Day School of Central Florida, 851 N Maitland Ave, **Maitland**, Ph: 647-0713.

Bookstore

The Source, 110 Longwood Ave, **Altamonte Springs**, Ph: 830-1948.

ORMOND BEACH   Area Code (904)

Synagogues

Temple Beth El (R-UAHC), 579 N Nova Rd, Ph: 677-2484. Rabbi B. Altman. Services: Friday, Sunday and Holidays

Day School

Bet Sefer Heritage School, 55 N Washington, Ph: 676-0539.

PALM BEACH (See also WEST PALM BEACH)
Area Code (407)

Synagogues

Temple Emanu-El (C-US), 190 N County Rd, Ph: 832-0804. Rabbi
L. Feldman. Services: Shabbat

PALM BEACH GARDENS (See also WEST PALM BEACH)
Area Code (407)

Synagogues

Temple Beth David (C-US), 4657 Hood Rd, Ph: 694-2350. Rabbi
D. Goldstein. Services: Shabbat

PALM CITY   Area Code (407)

Synagogues

Treasure Coast Jewish Center - Congregation Beth Abraham
(C-US), 3998 SW Leighton Farms Rd, Ph: 287-8833, Rabbi E.
Schwartz. Services: Friday

PALM COAST   Area Code (904)

Synagogues

Temple Beth Shalom (C), 44 Wellington Dr, Ph: 445-3006.
Services: Shabbat

PALM HARBOR   Area Code (813)

Synagogues

Ahavat Shalom (R), 1575 Curlew Rd, Ph: 785-8811. Rabbi G.
Klein. Services: Friday

PEMBROKE PINES (See also NORTH MIAMI BEACH or
MIAMI BEACH)   Area Code (305)

Synagogues

Temple Beth Emet (R-UAHC), 10801 Pembroke Rd, Ph: 431-3638.
Rabbi B. Greenspon. Services: Friday

Century Pines Jewish Center (C), Century Village, 13400 SW 10th
    St, Ph: 431-3300. Rabbi Z. Friedman. Services: Shabbat and
    High Holidays
Young Israel of Pembroke Pines, Century Village, 13460 SW 10th
    St, Ph: 435-2432. Services: Daily

PENSACOLA   Area Code (904)   J-pop. 775

Synagogues

Temple Beth-El (R-UAHC), 800 North Palafox, Ph: 438-3321.
    Rabbi D. Ostrich. Services: Friday
B'nai Israel (C-US), 1829 N 9th Ave, Ph: 433-7311. Rabbi E.
    Halpern. Services: Shabbat

Food

Premier Bakery, 1124 W Garden St, Ph: 438-1263. Breads and pas-
    tries. RS: Rabbi E. Halpern.

PLANTATION (See also NORTH MIAMI BEACH or MIAMI

BEACH)   Area Code (305)

Synagogues

Temple Kol Ami (R-UAHC), 8200 Peters Rd, Ph: 472-1988. Rabbi
    S. Harr. Services: Shabbat
Ramat Shalom (Recon-FRCH), 11301 W Broward Blvd,
    Ph: 472-3600. Rabbi E. Skiddell. Services: Shabbat

POMPANO BEACH   Area Code (305)

Synagogues

Temple Sholom (C-US), 132 SE 11th Ave, Ph: 942-6410. Rabbi S.
    April. Services: Daily

PORT CHARLOTTE   Area Code (813)   J-pop. 400

Synagogues

Temple Shalom (R-UAHC), 23190 Utica Ave, Ph: 625-3116. Rabbi
    L. Bogage. Services: Shabbat

PORT ST. LUCIE   Area Code (407)
J-pop. Stuart; Port St. Lucie 3,000

Synagogues

Congregation Beth Israel (R), 1390 SW Dorcester St, Ph: 879-1879. Services: Shabbat

ROYAL PALM BEACH   Area Code (407)

Synagogues

Temple Beth Zion (C-US), 129 Sparrow Dr, Ph: 798-8888. Rabbi S.J. Weinberg. Services: Shabbat

ST. AUGUSTINE   Area Code (904)

Synagogues

Congregation Sons of Israel (C), 161 Cordova St, Ph: 829-9532. Services: Friday

ST. PETERSBURG   Area Code (813)   J-pop. 9,500

Synagogues

Temple Beth El (R-UAHC), 400 S Pasadena Ave, Ph· 347-6136. Rabbi I. Youdovin. Services: Shabbat

Congregation B'nai Israel (C-US), 301 59th St N, Ph: 381-4900. Rabbi J. Luski. Services: Daily

Eating Out

Jo-El's Specialty Foods, 2619 23rd Ave, Ph: 321-3847. Some tables. Meals: l. Menu: Deli. RS: Rabbi J. Luski. Closed Shabbat.

Food

Jo-el's Specialty Foods, 2619 23rd Ave N, Ph: 321-3847. Complete kosher grocery, including frozen Empire poultry, TV dinners, and frozen meats. Closed Shabbat.

Day School

Pinellas County Jewish Day School (C), 301 59th St N,
Ph: 381-8111.

SARASOTA   Area Code (813)   J-pop. 9,500

Synagogues

Temple Beth Shalom (C-US), 1050 S Tuttle Ave, Ph: 955-8121.
Rabbi M. Roth. Services: Shabbat, Monday, Wednesday and
' Thursday

Congregation B'nai Torah (C), 2054 Hawthorne St, Ph: 957-3187.
Services: Shabbat and Sunday

Chabad Lubavitch of Sarasota and Manatee Counties (O-Lubav),
2457 Oak Dr, Ph: 371-5537. Rabbi S. Steinmetz. Services:
Shabbat. (Yarzeit minyan can be arranged.)

Temple Emanu-El (R-UAHC), 151 S McIntosh Rd, Ph: 371-2788.
Rabbi C. Arfa. Services: Shabbat

Venice-Jewish Community Center (R, C), 600 Auburn Rd, **Venice**,
Ph: 484-2022. Services: Friday. Call for schedule.

Food

Chabad Lubavitch has a kosher co-op which imports food from
Miami, Ph: 371-5537. Order three weeks in advance.

SATELLITE BEACH   Area Code (407)

Synagogues

Temple Beth Shalom (C-US), NE 3rd St, Ph: 773-3039. Rabbi P.
Grob. Services: Shabbat

SEMINOLE   Area Code (813)

Synagogues

Congregation Beth Chai (C-US), 8400 125th St N, Ph: 393-5525.
Rabbi S. Hoffman. Services: Shabbat

SUNRISE (See also FORT LAUDERDALE)   Area Code (305)

Synagogues

Congregation Bet Chaverim (C), 3003 N University Dr, Ph: 476-9071. Rabbi K. Stone. Services: Shabbat

Temple Bet Tikvah (R), 3000 N University Dr, Ph: 741-8088. Rabbi A. Friedman. Services: Friday

Temple Beth Israel (C-US), 7100 W Oakland Park Blvd, Ph: 742-4040. Rabbi H. Addison. Services: Daily

Temple Sha'aray Tzedek (C-US), 4099 Pine Island Rd, Ph: 741-0295. Rabbi B. Presler. Services: Daily

Synagogue of Inverrary Chabad (O-Lubav), 4561 N University Dr, Ph: 748-1777. Rabbi A. Lieberman. Services: Daily

Eating Out

Falafel King, 8336 W Oakland Park Blvd, Ph: 742-2725. Meals: l,d. Menu: Israeli and Mid-eastern cuisine (meat and pareve). RS: Kosher Supervision of Broward, Rabbi M. Malavsky of Beth Shalom, Hollywood. Closed Shabbat.

Food

Pita Pan, 8602 NW 44th St, Ph: 741-0171. Pita bread, falafel. Middle Eastern kosher grocery and bakery. RS: Orthodox Rabbinical Board of Broward and Palm Beach Counties. Closed Shabbat.

Stern's Bakery, 1775 Sunrise Blvd, Ph: 472-8082. Pareve and dairy. RS: Kosher Supervision of Broward, Rabbi M. Malavsky of Beth Shalom, Hollywood.

Sunrise Kosher Meat Market, 8330 W Oakland Park Blvd, Ph: 741-0855. Complete kosher grocery. RS: Kosher Supervision of Broward, Rabbi M. Malavsky of Beth Shalom, Hollywood. Closed Shabbat.

Bookstore

Little Israel, 7828 NW 44th St, Ph: 749-7674.

SURFSIDE (See also NORTH MIAMI BEACH and MIAMI BEACH) Area Code (305)

Synagogues

Congregation Mogen David of Surfside (O), 9348 Harding Ave, Ph: 865-9714. Services: Daily

Food

Surfside Kosher Meat Market, 9517 Harding Ave, Ph: 868-0559. Meat & poultry. Also take-out: Sandwiches, meat dishes. RS: Kosher Supervision of Broward, Rabbi M. Malavsky of Beth Shalom, Hollywood. Closed Shabbat.

TALLAHASSEE Area Code (904) J-pop. 1,500

Synagogues

Temple Israel (R-UAHC), 2215 Mahan Dr, Ph: 877-3517. Rabbi S. Garfein. Services: Friday

Congregation Shomrai Torah (C), 4858 Forest Pkwy, Ph: 893-9674. Services: Shabbat

TAMARAC (See also FORT LAUDERDALE) Area Code (305)

Synagogues

Congregation Beth Tefilah (C), 6435 W Commercial Blvd, Ph: 726-7756 or 722-7607. Services: Daily

Temple Beth Torah - Tamarac Jewish Center (C-US), 9101 NW 57th St, Ph: 721-7660. Rabbi M. Gold. Services: Daily

Congregation Migdal David (O-UOJC), 8575 West McNab Rd, Ph: 726-3583. Rabbi C. Snyder. Services: Daily

Food

Kosher Mart, 7051 NW 88th St, Ph: 726-9500. Complete kosher grocery, bakery, meat and dairy depts. RS: Rabbi P. Plotkin.

TAMPA   Area Code (813)   J-pop. 12,500

Synagogues

Bais Tefilah Congregation (O), 14908 Pennington Rd, Ph: 963-2317. Rabbi Y. Dubrowski. Services: Shabbat and Sunday

Congregation Beth Am (R), 12440 N Dale Mabry Hwy, Building E, #4, Ph: 968-8511. Rabbi E. Jordan. Services: Friday

Temple David (C), 2001 W Swann Ave, Ph: 254-1771. Rabbi S. Mallinger. Services: Shabbat. Call for further information.

Jewish Congregation of Sun City Center (C), 1115 E Delwebb Blvd, Ph: 634-9507. Services: Shabbat

Congregation Kol Ami (C-US), 3919 Moran Rd, Ph: 962-6338. Rabbi B. Shull. Services: Shabbat

Rodeph Shalom Congregation (C-US), 2713 Bayshore Blvd, Ph: 837-1911. Rabbi A. Lavinsky. Services: Daily

Schaarai Zedek (R-UAHC), 3303 Swann Ave, Ph: 876-2377. Rabbi R. Birnholz. Services: Shabbat

Young Israel of Tampa (O-NCYI), 3721 Tacon St, Ph: 832-3018 or 254-2907. Rabbi E. Rivkin. Services: Daily

Food

Tampa Kosher Meat, 2305 Morrison Ave, Ph: 253-5993. Small kosher grocery and meat market. RS: Rabbi S. Mallinger of Temple David. Closed Shabbat.

Accommodations

Private accommodations; call Rabbi Y. Dubrowski of Chabad, Ph: 962-2375.

For Shabbat hospitality; call Virginia Gordemir of Young Israel, Ph: 286-0522.

American Motel, 3314 S Dale Mabry Hwy, Ph: 837-9510. One block to Young Israel.

Mikvah

Mikvah Israel of Tampa Bay, 3600 E Fletcher Ave. Call Mrs. Sulha Dubrowski of Chabad, Ph: 962-2375.

Day School

Hebrew Academy, 14908 Pennington Rd, Ph: 963-0706.

VERO BEACH   Area Code (407)   J-pop. 300

Synagogues

Temple Beth Shalom (R-UAHC), 365 43rd Ave, Ph: 569-4700. Rabbi J. R. Davis. Services: Shabbat

WEST PALM BEACH   Area Code (407)   J-pop. 55,000

Synagogues

Congregation Aitz Chaim (O), Century Village, 2518 N Haverhill Rd, Ph: 686-5055. Rabbi O. Werner. Services: Daily

Congregation Anshei Sholom (C-US), 5348 Grove St, Ph: 684-3212. Rabbi I. Vander Walde. Services: Daily

Temple Beth El (C-US), 2815 N Flagler Dr, Ph: 833-0339. Rabbi S. Levine. Services: Daily

Temple Beth Torah (R-UAHC), 900 Big Blue Trace, Ph: 793-2700. Rabbi S. Westman. Services: Friday

Chabad House-Lubvatch (O-Lubav), 5335 N Military Trail, Ph: 640-8111. Rabbi S. Ezagui. Services: Shabbat

Golden Lakes Temple (C), 1470 Golden Lakes Blvd, Ph: 689-9430. Rabbi J. Speiser. Services: Daily

Temple Israel (R-UAHC), 1901 N Flagler Dr, Ph: 833-8421. Rabbi H. Shapiro. Services: Friday

Temple Judea (R-UAHC), 100 N Chillingworth Dr, Ph: 471-1526. Rabbi J. Levine. Services: Friday

Food

Chiffon Bakery, 6076 Okeechobee Blvd, Ph: 683-7703. Pareve & dairy. RS: Orthodox Rabbinical Board of Broward and Palm Beach Counties. Closed Shabbat.

Palm Beach Kosher Market, 5085 Okeechobee Blvd, Ph: 686-2066. Complete kosher grocery store: Meats, groceries, dairy. RS: Palm Beach County Board of Rabbis. Closed Shabbat.

Accommodations

Days Inn, 6255 Okeechobee Blvd, Ph: 686-6000. This motel is within walking distance of Congregation Aitz Chaim.

Day School

Jewish Community Day School of Palm Beach County, 5801 Parker Ave, Ph: 585-2227.

Georgia

ALBANY   Area Code (912)   J-pop. 400

Synagogues

Albany Hebrew Congregation (R-UAHC), 200 S Jefferson St, Ph: 432-6536. Rabbi E. Palnick. Services: Friday

ATHENS   Area Code (404)   J-pop. 300

Synagogues

Congregation Children of Israel (R-UAHC), 115 Dudley Dr, Ph: 549-4192. Rabbi R. D. Gerson. Services: Friday

ATLANTA   Area Code (404)   J-pop. 60,000

Synagogues

Congregation Ahavath Achim (C-US), 600 Peachtree Battle Ave NW, Ph: 355-5222. Rabbi A. Goodman. Services: Daily

Congregation Anshe S'fard (O), 1324 N Highland Ave NE, Ph: 874-4513. Rabbi N. Katz. Services: Shabbat

Bet Haverim (Recon - Gay and Lesbian), P.O. Box 54947, 30308-0947, Ph: 642-3467. Meets at Interfaith Network, 1053 Juniper St. Services: Friday, third Saturday

Congregation Beth Jacob (O-UOJC), 1855 LaVista Rd, Ph: 633-0551. Rabbi E. Feldman. Services: Daily

Congregation Beth Shalom (C-US), 5303 Winters Chapel Rd, Ph: 399-5300. Rabbi M. Zimmerman. Services: Shabbat

Congregation Beth Tefillah (O-Lubav), 5065 High Point Rd, Ph: 843-2464. Rabbi Y. New. Services: Shabbat

Congregation B'nai Torah (Trad), 700 Mount Vernon Hwy, Ph: 257-0537. Rabbi J. Mintz. Services: Daily

Temple Emanu-El (R-UAHC), 1580 Spalding Dr, Ph: 395-1340. Rabbi B. Friedman. Services: Shabbat

Congregation Kehillat Chaim (R-UAHC), 10200 Woodstock Rd, Ph: 641-8630. Rabbi H. Winokur. Services: Friday

Ner Hamizrach (Iranian), Meets at Congregation Beth Jacob, 1855 LaVista Rd, Ph: 636-2473. Rabbi S. Khoshkerman. Services: Daily

Congregation Or Veshalom (Trad-Sephardic), 1681 N Druid Hills Rd NE, Ph: 633-1737. Rabbi R. Ichay. Services: Shabbat

Congregation Shearith Israel (Trad), 1180 University Dr NE, Ph: 873-1743 Rabbi M. Kunis. Services: Daily

Temple Sinai (R-UAHC), 5645 Dupree Dr NW, Ph: 252-3073. Rabbi P. Kranz. Services: Shabbat

The Temple (R-UAHC), 1589 Peachtree Rd, Ph: 873-1731. Rabbi S. Wasserman. Services: Shabbat

Eating Out

Arthur's Deli, 2166 Briarcliff Rd, NE, Ph: 634-6881. Meals: l,d. Sunday: l. Menu: Sandwiches, hamburgers, hot dogs, variety of hot dishes. Also take-out. RS: Atlanta Kashruth Commission. Closed Shabbat.

Quality Kosher Meats & Deli, 2161 Briarcliff Rd, Ph: 636-1114. Meals: b,l. Menu: (Meat) Soup, meat and chicken entrees. Also take-out. RS: Atlanta Kashruth Commission. Closed Shabbat.

Wall Street Pizza, 2470 Briarcliff Rd, Ph: 633-2111. Meals: l,d. Menu: (Dairy: cholov Yisroel) Pizza, Italian dishes, salad, sandwiches, desserts. Also take-out and delivery. RS: Atlanta Kashruth Commission. Closed Shabbat.

Food

Arthur's Kosher Meat Market, 2166 Briarcliff Rd NE, Ph: 634-6881. Also at 120 Copeland Rd, Ph: 252-4396. Complete kosher grocery, including fresh meat and poultry, deli, fish and cheeses. Also take-out. (Only sandwiches at Copeland Rd location). RS: Atlanta Kashruth Commission. Closed Shabbat.

Quality Kosher Meats & Deli, 2161 Briarcliff Rd, Ph: 636-1114. Take-out deli, fish, cheeses as well as fresh meat and groceries. RS: Atlanta Kashruth Commission. Closed Shabbat.

Superior Baking, 3015 W Druid Hills Rd, Ph: 633-1986. Breads, cakes and pastries (pareve). RS: Atlanta Kashruth Commission. Closed Shabbat.

Accommodations

Private accommodations - Bed and Breakfast Atlanta is an agency that reserves rooms in private homes. Shomer Shabbat homes available. Rates from $48.00 to $72.00 for a room with a bath, within walking distance of synagogues. 1801 Piedmont Ave #208, 30324. Paula Gris, Ph: 875-0525.

Shabbat hospitality; call Mr. Fred Glusman at Congregation Beth Jacob, Ph: 633-0551.

Courtyard Marriott, 5601 Peachtree Dunwoody Rd, Ph: 843-2300. Half-hour walk to Chabad House.

Marriott Courtyard - Executive Park, 1236 Executive Park Dr, Ph: 728-0708. Half-hour walk to Congregation Beth Jacob.

Sheraton Emory Inn, 1641 Clifton NE, Ph: 633-4111. Half-hour walk to Congregation Beth Jacob.

Squire Inn, 5750 Roswell Rd, Ph: 252-5782. Thirty-five-minute walk to Chabad House.

Mikvah

Congregation Beth Jacob, 1855 LaVista Rd. Call Synagogue office, Ph: 633-0551. Evenings, call Mrs. Debbie Dubin, Ph: 325-4479.

Day Schools

The Epstein School (C), 335 Colewood Way, Ph: 843-0111.
Greenfield Hebrew Academy, 5200 Northland Dr, Ph: 843-9900.
Torah Day School of Atlanta, 3130 Raymond Dr, Ph: 457-1962.

Bookstore

Judaica Corner, 2183 Briarcliff Rd, Ph: 636-2473.

AUGUSTA   Area Code (404)   J-pop. 1,400

Synagogues

Adas Yeshurun (Trad-UOJC), 935 Johns Rd, Ph: 733-9491. Rabbi
    M. Hyman. Services: Daily
Congregation Children of Israel-Walton Way Temple (R-UAHC),
    3005 Walton Way, Ph: 736-3140. Rabbi J. Parr. Services: Friday

Food

Kroger's, 2801 Washington, Ph: 736-1414. Frozen Empire
    products.

Mikvah

Congregation Adas Yeshurun, 935 Johns Rd. Call Synagogue
    office, Ph: 733-9491.

BAINBRIDGE   Area Code (912)

Synagogues

Temple Beth El (R-UAHC), Broad & Evans, Ph: 432-6536.
    Services: Call Mr. Kres for schedule, Ph: 246-1842.

COLUMBUS   Area Code (404)   J-pop. 1,000

Synagogues

Temple Israel (R-UAHC), 1617 Wildwood Ave, Ph: 323-1617.
    Rabbi L. Schlesinger. Services: Shabbat
Shearith Israel Synagogue (C-US), 2550 Wynnton Rd,
    Ph: 323-1443. Rabbi L. Schwartz. Services: Daily

DALTON   Area Code (404)   J-pop. 225

Synagogues

Temple Beth El (C-US), 501 Valley Dr, Ph: 278-6798. Rabbi Z. Ettinger. Services: Shabbat and Holidays

DUNWOODY   Area Code (404)

Synagogues

Emanu-El (R), 1580 Spalding Dr, Ph: 395-1340. Rabbi B. Friedman.

MACON   Area Code (912)   J-pop. 900

Synagogues

Temple Beth Israel (R-UAHC), 892 Cherry St, Ph: 745-6727. Rabbi J. Heyman III. Services: Friday

Sherah Israel (C-US), 611 First St, Ph: 745-4571. Rabbi D. Edelstein. Services: Shabbat

MARIETTA   (See also **ATLANTA**)   Area Code (404)

Synagogues

Congregation Etz Chaim (C-US), 1190 Indian Hills Pkwy, Ph: 973-0137. Rabbi S. Lewis. Services: Shabbat

Kol Emeth (R), Suite 225 Merchants Walk, Ph: 973-3533. Rabbi S. Lebow.

RIVERDALE   (See also **ATLANTA**)   Area Code (404)

Synagogues

Congregation B'nai Israel (R-UAHC), 2165 Hwy 138, Ph: 471-3586. Rabbi F. Davidson. Services: Daily

ROME   Area Code (404)

Synagogues

Rodeph Sholom Congregation (R), 406 E First St, B. Wachsteter, President, Ph: 291-0678. Services: Call for information.

ROSWELL   Area Code (404)

Synagogues

Beth Tikvah (R), P.O. Box 1425, 30077-1425, Ph: 642-0434.
   Rabbi D. Tam.
Kehillat Chaim (R), 10200 Woodstock Rd, Ph: 641-8630. Rabbi H.
   Winokur.

SAVANNAH   Area Code (912)   J-pop. 2,750

Synagogues

Congregation Agudath Achim (C-US), 9 Lee Blvd, Ph: 352-4737.
   Rabbi S. Grundfast. Services: Daily
Congregation B'nai B'rith Jacob (O-UOJC), 5444 Abercorn St,
   Ph: 354-7721. Rabbi A. Slatus. Services: Daily
Temple Mickve Israel (R-UAHC), 20 E Gordon St, Ph: 233-1547.
   Rabbi A. Belzer. Services: Shabbat

Eating Out

Alan Gottlieb's Deli Restaurant, Twelve Oaks DuMarche Shopping
   Center, 5500 Abercorn St, Ph: 355-1765. Meals: l,d. Menu:
   (Meat) Hot dishes, salads, sandwiches, desserts. RS: Rabbi A.
   Slatus. Closed Shabbat.

Food

Alan Gottlieb's Deli Restaurant, Twelve Oaks DuMarche Shopping
   Center, 5500 Abercorn St, Ph: 355-1765. Kosher groceries and
   take-out. Two days' notice for advance orders. RS: Rabbi A.
   Slatus. Closed Shabbat.

Accommodations

The following hotels are fifteen to twenty minutes' walk from
   Congregation B'nai B'rith Jacob:
Courtyard by Marriott, 6703 Abercorn, Ph: 354-7878.
Fairfield Inn, 2 Lee Blvd, Ph: 353-7100.
Homewood Suites, 5820 Whitebluff Rd, Ph: 353-8500. Suites with
   kitchens.
Laquinta, 6805 Abercorn St, Ph: 355-3004.

Mikvah

B'nai B'rith Jacob, 108 Atlas St. Call Mrs. Lisa Garfunkel,
Ph: 354-9619.

Day Schools

Rambam Day School, 100 Atlas St, Ph: 354-0653; 5111 Abercorn,
Ph: 352-7994.

SNELLVILLE (See also **ATLANTA**)   Area Code (404)

Synagogues

Temple Beth David (R-UAHC), Meets at Button Gwinnett United
Church of Christ, 869 Cole Dr, **Lilburn**, Ph: 662-4373. Rabbi
R. M. Baroff. Services: Friday

VIDALIA   Area Code (912)

Synagogues

Beth Israel Congregation (O), Aimwell Rd, Ph: 537-4536.
Services: Friday and Holidays

Hawaii

HAWAII   Area Code (808)   J-pop. 280

Synagogues

Temple Beth Aloha (R), P.O. Box 1538, **Hilo**, 96720. President:
Mr. F. Horwitz, Ph: 969-4153. Services: Call for schedule.
Kona Beth Shalom (R), P.O. Box 3122, **Kamuela**, 96743.
Contact Helen Rabin, Ph: 883-9514 or Rosalyn Silver,
Ph: 322-9144.

KAUAI   Area Code (808)

Synagogues

Jewish Community of Kauai, P.O. Box 3749, **Lihue**, 96766. Evelyn
Prybutok, Ph: 826-9418. Services: Once a month and Holidays

MAUI   Area Code (808)

Synagogues

Congregation Gan Eden (R), P.O. Box 555, **Kihei**, 96753. Meets at St. Anthony High School Library, 1618 Lower Main, **Wailuku**. Mr. R. Matassarin, President, Ph: 669-6529. Services: Second and fourth Friday

Jewish Congregation of Maui. Contact Deborah Zeleznik, Ph: 669-7695 or Pauline Kristel, Ph: 879-2767. Services: Every third Friday

OAHU   Area Code (808)   J-pop. 6,400

Synagogues

Aloha Jewish Chapel (Military), Makalapa Gate, **Pearl Harbor**, Ph: 471-3971. Services: Friday

Chabad of Hawaii (O-Lubav), 4218 Waialae Ave, **Honolulu**, Ph: 735-8161. Rabbi I. Krasnjansky. Services: Shabbat

Temple Emanu-El (R-UAHC, Trad), 2550 Pali Hwy, **Honolulu**, Ph: 595-7521. Rabbi S. Barack. Services: Call for schedule.

Congregation of Sof Ma'arav (C), P.O. Box 11154, **Honolulu**, 96828. Meets at 2500 Pali Hwy,. President: J. Popper, Ph: 595-3678. Services: First three Saturdays

Food

For kosher food information, call Harvey Elkins, Ph: 377-5545.

Frozen kosher meals available at Kahala Hilton and Hilton Hawaiian Village Hotels. Order in advance.

Foodland, 1460 S Beretania St, **Honolulu**, Ph: 946-4654. Frozen packaged kosher Empire and Sinai meat and chicken.

Accommodations

Kahala Hilton Hotel, 5000 Kahala Ave, Ph: 734-2211. Walk to Chabad House.

Mikvah

Call Mrs. Pearl Krasnjansky, Ph: 735-8161.

Idaho

BOISE   Area Code (208)   J-pop. 220

Synagogues

Congregation Ahavath Israel Synagogue-Beth Israel (C, R-UAHC), 1102 State St, Ph: 343-6601; 342-7247. Services: Friday

POCATELLO   Area Code (208)

Synagogues

Temple Emanuel, 306 N 18th Ave, Ph: 232-4758. Services: Call for schedule.

Illinois

AURORA (See also **CHICAGO**)   Area Code (708)   J-pop. 500

Synagogues

Temple B'nai Israel (C-US), 400 N Edgelawn Dr, Ph: 892-2450. Rabbi H. Agress. Services: Shabbat

BELLEVILLE (See also **ST. LOUIS, MO**)   Area Code (618)

Synagogues

Beth Israel/Agudas Achim Temple (C), "C" and High Sts, Ph: 233-3602. Rabbi A. Rubin. Services: Friday

BENTON   Area Code (618)

Synagogues

United Hebrew Temple (R), E Park Ave, Ph: 439-9090. Services: Call for schedule.

114

BLOOMINGTON   Area Code (309)

Synagogues

Moses Montefiore Temple (R-UAHC), 102 Robinhood Lane,
   Ph: 662-3182. Rabbi C. Librach. Services: Friday

BUFFALO GROVE (See also CHICAGO, HIGHLAND PARK and SKOKIE)   Area Code (708)

Synagogues

Congregation B'nai Shalom (Trad), 701 W Aptakisic, Ph:
   541-1460. Rabbi M. Urkowitz. Services: Shabbat and Holidays.
Chabad of Buffalo Grove (O-Lubav), 16296 Aptakisic Rd, **Prairie
   View**, Ph: 808-7770. Rabbi Skatz. Services: Shabbat
Mishpaha-Our Family (C), 760 Checker Dr, Ph: 459-3279. Rabbi
   M. Rosen. Services: Call for information.
Temple Shir Shalom (R-UAHC), Meets at Stevenson High School,
   Rte 22, **Prairie View**, Ph: 948-7224. Rabbi M. Levenson.
   Services: Friday

CARBONDALE   Area Code (618)   J-pop. 100

Synagogues

Congregation Beth Jacob (C,R-UAHC), R.R. 7, P.O. Box 3336,
   Ph: 529-1409. Rabbi R. Sternberg. Services: Twice a month.

CENTRALIA   Area Code (618)

Synagogues

Temple Solomon (R), 104 N Pine St, Ph: 532-2822. Services: Call
   for schedule.

CHAMPAIGN-URBANA   Area Code (217)   J-pop. 2,000

Synagogues

B'nai B'rith Hillel Foundation at the University of Illinois (O,R,C),
   Jewish Student Union, 503 E John St, Ph: 344-1328. Rabbi J.
   Falick. Services: Shabbat

Synagogues cont.

Sinai Temple (R, C), 3104 W Windsor Rd, Ph: 352-8140. Rabbi B. Bloom. Services: Friday, Saturday (C) once a month.

Eating Out

B'nai B'rith Hillel Foundation at the University of Illinois - Jewish Student Union, 503 E John St, Ph: 344-1328. Dinner is served Monday, Wednesday and Friday. RS: Rabbi J. Falick, Director. Call for reservations.

CHICAGO(See also SKOKIE and HIGHLAND PARK)
Area Code (312)   J-pop. 248,000

Synagogues

Adas Bnai Israel (O), 6200 N Kimball, Ph: 583-8141. Rabbi J. Nayman. Services: Daily

Adas Yeshurun Anshe Kanesses Israel (O), 2949 W Touhy, Ph: 465-2288. Rabbi Z. Cohen. Services: Daily

A. G. Beth Israel (O), 3635 W Devon Ave, Ph: 539-9060. Rabbi I. Glickman. Services: Daily

Agudath Achim - Bikur Cholem (O), 89 S Houston, Ph: 768-7685. Rabbi D. Bateman. Services: Saturday and Sunday

Anshe Emet Synagogue (C-US), 3760 N Pine Grove Ave, Ph: 281-1423. Rabbi M. Siegel. Services: Daily

Congregation Anshe Mizrach (O), 627 W Patterson Ave, Ph: 525-4034. Rabbi S. Rockove. Services: Call for schedule.

Anshe Motele (O), 6520 N California Ave, Ph: 743-9452; 743-2420. Rabbi A. Abramson. Services: Daily

Anshe Sholom B'nai Israel Congregation (O), 540 W Melrose Ave, Ph: 248-9200. Rabbi J. Deitcher. Services: Daily

Temple Beth-El of Chicago (R-UAHC), 3050 W Touhy St, Ph: 274-0341. Rabbi J. Sagarin. Services: Daily

Beth Itzchok (O-UOJC), 6716 N Whipple St, Ph: 973-2522. Rabbi L. Matanky. Services: Call for schedule

Beth Itzchok of Albany Park (O), 4645 N Drake, Ph: 478-6416. Rabbi L. Matanky. Services: Daily

Beth Sholom Ahavas Achim (O, Trad), 5665 N Jersey, Ph: 267-9055. Rabbi M. Soloveichik. Services: Daily

Beth Sholom of Rogers Park (Trad), 1233 W Pratt Blvd, Ph: 743-4160. Rabbi H. Wachsmann. Services: Daily

B'nai Jacob of West Rogers Park (C), 6200 N Artesian Ave, Ph: 274-1586. Rabbi E. Einhorn. Services: Saturday

B'nai Zion (C-US), 6759 N Greenview Ave, Ph: 465-2161. Rabbi N. Kleinman. Services: Daily

Congregation B'nei Ruven (O-UOJC), 6350 N Whipple St, Ph: 743-5434. Rabbi H. Shusterman. Services: Daily

Central Synagogue of South Side Hebrew Congregation (C-US), 30 E Cedar St, Ph: 787-0450. Rabbi S. Rosenbaum. Services: Shabbat

Chabad (F.R.E.E. - Friends of Refugees of Eastern Europe) (O-Lubav), 6335 N California Ave, Ph: 274-5123. Rabbi S. Notik. Services: Shabbat, daily a.m.

Chabad House of Lincoln Park (O-Lubav), 515 W Grant Pl, Ph: 281-7770. Rabbi M. Benhayoun. Services: Shabbat

Chabad of the Loop (O-Lubav), 401 S LaSalle St #9, Ph: 427-7770. Rabbi M. Benhayoun. Services: Weekdays

Chesed L'Avrohom Nachlas David (O), 6342 N Troy, Ph: 973-5161. Rabbi Y. Eichenstein. Services: Daily

Chevro Kadish Machzikai Hadas (O), 2040 W Devon, Ph: 764-8760. Rabbi Y. Goldman. Services: Shabbat and daily

Chicago Loop Synagogue (Trad), 16 S Clark St, Ph: 346-7370. Rabbi S. Kroll. Services: Daily

Chicago Sinai Congregation (R-UAHC), 5350 S Shore Dr, Ph: (708) 288-1600. Rabbi H. Berman. Services: Shabbat and Sunday

Emanuel Congregation (R-UAHC), 5959 N Sheridan Rd, Ph: (708) 288-1600. Rabbi J. Edelheit. Services: Shabbat

Congregation Ezra Habonim (C-US), 2620 W Touhy Ave, Ph: 743-0154. Rabbi J. Padorr. Services: Shabbat and Sunday

Congregation Ezras Israel (Trad), 7001 N California Ave, Ph: 764-8320. Rabbi B. Kaganoff. Services: Daily

Congregation K.I.N.S. of West Rogers Park (Trad), 2800 W North Shore Ave, Ph: 761-4000. Rabbi P. Greenman. Services: Daily

KAM-Isaiah Israel (R-UAHC), 1100 Hyde Park Blvd, Ph: 924-1234. Rabbi A. Wolf. Services: Shabbat

Synagogues cont.

Congregation Kehilath Jacob Beth Samuel (O), 3701 W Devon Ave, Ph: 539-7779. Rabbi J. Frank. Services: Call for schedule.

Congregation Kol Ami - the Near North Temple (R-UAHC), 845 North Michigan #909E, Ph: 644-4775. Rabbi A. Kaiman. Services: Friday

Lake Shore Drive Synagogue (Trad), 70 E Elm, Ph: 337-6811. Services: Shabbat and Sunday

Lawn Manor - Beth Jacob Congregation (C-US), 6601 S Kedzie Ave, Ph: 476-2924. Rabbi E. H. Prombaum. Services: Shabbat and Sunday

Lev Someach (O-UOJC), 5555 N Bernard St, Ph: 267-4390. Rabbi E. Twersky. Services: Daily

Temple Menorah (R-UAHC), 2800 W Sherwin Ave, Ph: 761-5700. Rabbi D. Weiss. Services: Shabbat

Mikro Kodesh Anshe Tiktin (Trad), 2832 W Foster Ave, Ph: 784-1010. Rabbi I. Miller. Services: Daily

Ner Tamid Congregation of North Town (C-US), 2754 W Rosemont Ave, Ph: 465-6090. Rabbi S. Klein. Services: Daily

Or Chadash (R), 656 W Barry, Ph: 248-9456. Services: Call for schedule.

Poalie Zedek (O), 2801 W Albion, Ph: 752-2770. Rabbi M. Small. Services: Daily

Congregation Rodfei Zedek (C-US), 5200 S Hyde Park Blvd, Ph: 752-2770. Services: Daily

Congregation Shaare Tikvah (C-US), 5800 N Kimball Ave, Ph: 539-2202. Rabbi G. Haber. Services: Daily

Shaarei Torah Anshei Maariv (O), 2756 W Morse Ave, Ph: 262-0430. Rabbi B. Rosenthal. Services: Daily

Shearith Yisrael (O), 2938 W Arthur, Ph: 262-0666. Rabbi M. Unger. Services: Daily

Temple Sholom (R-UAHC), 3480 Lake Shore Dr, Ph: 525-4707. Rabbi F. Schwartz. Services: Daily

Congregation Tifereth Moshe (O), 6308 N Francisco Ave, Ph: 764-5322. Rabbi C. Goldzweig. Services: Shabbat

Warsaw Bickur Cholim Congregation (O), 3541 W Peterson Ave, Ph: 588-0021. Services: Daily

Eating Out

Dog-On-It, 2748 W Devon, Ph: 338-2493/2494. Meals: Mon-Thurs: l,d; Fri: l; Sun: b. Menu: (Glatt meat) Hot dogs, hamburgers, french fries; Sunday: omelettes. RS: Chicago Rabbinical Council. Closed Shabbat.

Dunkin' Donuts, 3132 W Devon, Ph: 262-4560. Meals: b,l,d. Menu: (Dairy) donuts, cookies, soups. RS: Chicago Rabbinical Council.

Jerusalem Pizza Shop, 3014 W Devon, Ph: 262-0515. Meals: l,d. Menu: (Dairy: cholov Yisroel) Pizza and vegetarian dishes. RS: O.K. Laboratories. Closed Shabbat.

La Misada, 151 E Wacker Dr, at Hyatt Regency, Ph: 565-1234. Meals: l,d. Menu: (Glatt meat) Continental cuisine. RS: Chicago Rabbinical Council. Closed Shabbat.

Mi Tsu Yun Restaurant, 3010 W Devon, Ph: 743-4843. Meals: l,d. Menu: (Glatt meat) Chinese-American cuisine. Also take-out. RS: O.K. Laboratories. Closed Friday and Shabbat.

North Shore Deli and Restaurant, 2919 W Touhy, Ph: 743-3354. Meals: b,l,d. Menu (Glatt meat) American-Israeli. Soup, salads, sandwiches, entrees, vegetarian. Also take-out. RS: Chicago Rabbinical Council. Closed Shabbat.

Tel-Aviv Kosher Pizza & Dairy Restaurant, 6349 N California St, Ph: 764-3776. Meals: l,d. Menu: Dairy dishes (cholov Yisroel) and Mexican. RS: Chicago Rabbinical Council. Closed Shabbat.

Yossi's Chinese Restaurant, 2712 W Pratt Blvd, Ph: 764-3563. Meals: l,d. Lunch menu: Deli. Dinner menu: Chinese. Glatt meat. RS: Rabbi Y. Richter, Crown-K. Closed Shabbat.

Food

Gitel's Bakery, 2745 W Devon, Ph: 262-3701. Breads and pastries (pareve). RS: Chicago Rabbinical Council. Closed Shabbat.

Illinois Nut Outlet, 6218 N Lincoln Ave, Ph: 463-5777. Nuts, candy, dried fruit and chocolates. RS: Chicago Rabbinical Council. Closed Shabbat.

Kosher Karry, 2828 W Devon, Ph: 973-4355. Glatt meat. Traditional dishes prepared for take-out and complete kosher grocery. RS: Chicago Rabbinical Council. Closed Shabbat.

119

Food cont.

Kosher Zion Sausage Company of Chicago, 5511 N Kedzie, Ph: 463-3351. Sausages, fresh meats and poultry. Glatt available. RS: Rabbinical Council of Chicago. Closed Shabbat.

Moshe's New York Kosher, 2900 W Devon, Ph: 338-3354. Complete kosher grocery and deli department. RS: Chicago Rabbinical Council. Closed Shabbat.

North Shore Kosher Bakery, 2919 W Touhy Ave, Ph: 262-0600. Breads and pastries (pareve). RS: Chicago Rabbinical Council. Closed Shabbat.

Tel-Aviv Kosher Bakery, 2944 W Devon, Ph: 764-8877. Breads and pastries. RS: Orthodox Union. Closed Shabbat.

Accommodations

Hyde Park Hilton, 4900 S Lakeshore Dr, Ph: 288-5800. Walk to Congregation Rodfe Zedek.

Private accommodations; contact Bnei Akiva of Chicago, 6500 N California, 60645. Ph: 338-6569.

Shabbat hospitality; call Chabad of Illinois, Ph: 262-2770.

Mikvah

Daughters of Israel, 3110 W Touhy Ave. Contact Mrs. Debbie Peikes, Ph: 479-9238.

Day Schools

Akiba Schechter Jewish Day School (C), 5200 S Hyde Park Blvd, Ph: 493-8880.

Bais Yaakov Hebrew Parochial School, 2447 W Granville Ave, Ph: 465-3770; Boys Division: Yeshiva Tiferes Tzvi, 6122 N California Ave, Ph: 973-5690.

Hillel Torah North Suburban Day School, 4008 W Rosemont, Ph: 777-2406.

The Rosenwald School (R), 5959 N Sheridan Rd, Ph: 878-5828.

Yeshiva Sheiris Yisroel-The Veitzener Cheder, 6526 N California Ave, Ph: 262-0885

Bookstores

Chicago Hebrew Bookstore, 2942 W Devon, Ph: 973-6636.

Rosenblum's Hebrew Book Store, 2906 W Devon, Ph: 262-1700.

DANVILLE   Area Code (217)

Synagogues

Congregation Israel (C-US), 949 N Walnut, Ph: 442-6643. Rabbi
S. Switkin. Services: Call for schedule.

DECATUR   Area Code (217)

Synagogues

Temple B'nai Abraham (R-UAHC), 1326 W Eldorado,
Ph: 429-5740. Rabbi J. Pine. Services: Shabbat

DEERFIELD (See also CHICAGO)   Area Code (708)

Synagogues

Congregation Beth Or (Humanistic, R), P.O. Box 234, 60015,
Ph: 945-0477. Rabbi D. Friedman. Services: Friday
B'nai Tikvah (C-US), 795 Wilmot Rd, Ph: 945-0470. Rabbi R.
Frankel. Services: Shabbat and Sunday
Moriah (C-US), 200 Taub Dr, Ph: 948-5340. Rabbi S. Fraint.
Services: Shabbat, Sunday, Monday and Thursday

DES PLAINES (See also CHICAGO)   Area Code (708)

Synagogues

Chabad (F.R.E.E.) of Niles (O-Lubav), 9401 Margail, Ph:
297-2976. Rabbi B. Scheiman. Services: Shabbat, Sunday,
Monday and Thursday a.m.
Maine Township Jewish Congregation (C-US), 8800 Ballard Rd,
Ph: 297-2006. Rabbi E. Winter. Services: Daily

Mikvah (See **Chicago**)

ELGIN (See also CHICAGO)   Area Code (708)   J-pop. 600

Synagogues

Congregation Kneseth Israel (C), 330 Division St, Ph: 741-5656.
Rabbi M. Scharf. Services: Shabbat

121

EVANSTON (See also CHICAGO)   Area Code (708)

Synagogues

Beth Emet - The Free Synagogue (R-UAHC), 1224 Dempster, Ph: 869-4230. Rabbi P. Knobel. Services: Friday

B'nai B'rith Hillel Foundation at Northwestern University (Trad, R), 1935 Sherman Ave, Ph: 328-0650. Rabbi N. Balinsky. Services: Trad: Shabbat; R: every other Friday

Jewish Reconstructionist Congregation (Recon-FRCH), 303 Dodge Ave, Ph: 328-7678. Rabbi A. Rachlis. Services: Shabbat

Mikdosh El Hagro Hebrew Center (C-US), 303 Dodge St, Ph: 328-9677. Rabbi Y. Eckstein. Services: Daily

Sephardic Congregation (Israelite Portuguese Fraternity) (O-UOJC), 1819 W Howard St, Ph: 475-7707. Rabbi M. Azose. Services: Shabbat, Sunday and Thursday

Tennenbaum Chabad House (O-Lubav), 2014 Orrington Ave (near Northwestern University), Ph: 869-8060. Rabbi D. Klein. Services: Shabbat and Sunday

Eating Out

B'nai B'rith Hillel Foundation at Northwestern University, 1935 Sherman Ave, Ph: 328-0650. Meals: d, Wednesday, Friday; l,d, Shabbat (during school year). RS: Rabbi M. Balinsky (O). Call a day in advance for reservations.

Accommodations

Holiday Inn, 1501 Sherman Ave, Ph: 491-6400. Walk to Hillel.

Orrington Hotel, 1710 Orrington Ave, Ph: 866-8700. Short walk to Hillel or Chabad House.

For Shabbat hospitality and/or sleeping accommodations, call Chabad House, Ph: 869-8060.

Mikvah (See Chicago)

GALESBURG   Area Code (309)   J-pop. 100

Synagogues

Temple Sholom (R), corner North & Monroe Sts, Ph: 343-3323. Services: Friday

GLENCOE (See also CHICAGO)   Area Code (708)

Synagogues

Am Shalom (R-UAHC), 840 Vernon Ave, Ph: 835-4800. Rabbi H.
   Kudan. Services: Shabbat
North Shore Congregation Israel (R-UAHC), 1185 Sheridan Rd,
   Ph: 835-0724. Rabbi H. Bronstein. Services: Shabbat

GLENVIEW (See also CHICAGO)   Area Code (708)

Synagogues

B'nai Jehoshua Beth Elohim (R-UAHC), 901 Milwaukee Ave, Ph:
   729-7575. Rabbi M. Shapiro, Rabbi D. Fine. Services: Friday

GODFREY (See also ST. LOUIS, MO)   Area Code (618)

Synagogues

Temple Israel (C), 1414 W Delmar Ave, Ph: 466-4641. Rabbi M.
   Saperstein. Services: Friday

HIGHLAND PARK (See also CHICAGO)   Area Code (708)

Synagogues

B'nai Torah (R-UAHC), 2789 Oak St, Ph: 433-7100. Rabbi J.
   Magidovitch. Services: Friday
Chabad of Highland Park (O-Lubav), 1871 Sheahen Ct,
   Ph: 433-1567. Rabbi Y. Schanowitz. Services: Shabbat
Lakeside Congregation (R-UAHC), 1221 County Line Rd,
   Ph: 432-7950. Rabbi C. Levi. Services: Sunday
North Suburban Synagogue Beth El (C-US), 1175 Sheridan Rd,
   Ph: 432-8900. Rabbi V. Kurtz. Services: Daily
Congregation Solel (R-UAHC), 1301 Clavey Rd, Ph: 433-3555.
   Rabbi E. M. Romirowsky. Services: Shabbat

Eating Out

Selig's Kosher Delicatessen, 209 Skokie Valley Rd, Ph: 831-5560.
   Meals: b,l,d. Menu: Deli-style dishes. RS: Chicago Rabbinical
   Council. Closed Shabbat.

Food

Highland Park Kosher Market, 1813 St. John Ave, Ph: 432-0748.
Fresh meat and poultry. RS: Rabbi H. Gross. Closed Shabbat.
Selig's Kosher Delicatessen, 209 Skokie Valley Rd, Ph: 831-5560.
Kosher grocery and take-out. RS: Chicago Rabbinical Council.
Closed Shabbat.
Shaevitz Kosher Meats, 712 Central Ave, Ph: 432-8334. Fresh meat
and poultry, deli, some dairy products. RS: Rabbi H. Gross.
Closed Shabbat.

Mikvah (See Chicago)

HOFFMAN ESTATES (See also CHICAGO)   Area Code (708)

Synagogues

Beth Tikvah Congregation (R-UAHC), 300 Hillcrest Blvd,
Ph: 885-4545. Rabbi H. Gamoran. Services: Friday

HOMEWOOD (See also CHICAGO)   Area Code (708)

Synagogues

Temple B'nai Yehuda (R-UAHC), 1424 W 183rd St, Ph: 799-4110.
Rabbi L. Wolkow. Services: Shabbat

JOLIET (See also CHICAGO)   Area Code (815)   J-pop. 850

Synagogues

Joliet Jewish Congregation (Trad), 250 N Midland Ave,
Ph: 741-4600. Rabbi M. Hershman. Services: Shabbat

KANKAKEE   Area Code (815)   J-pop. 200

Synagogues

B'nai Israel (R), 600 S Harrison Ave, Ph: 935-1174. Rabbi A.
Yanow. Services: Call for information.

LINCOLNWOOD (See also **CHICAGO**)   Area Code (708)

Synagogues

Lincolnwood Jewish Congregation (Trad), 7117 N Crawford,
   Ph: 676-0491. Rabbi J. Lehrfield. Services: Daily
Congregation Yehuda Moshe (O), 4721 W Touhy, Ph: 673-5870;
   674-6918. Rabbi O. Fasman. Services: Shabbat

Food

The Milk Pail, 3320 W Devon Ave, Ph: 673-3459. Full kosher
   store; cholov Yisroel products. Glatt meat available. RS:
   Chicago Rabbinical Council. Closed Shabbat.

Mikvah

Congregation Yehuda Moshe, 4721 W Touhy, Ph: 673-5870 or
   674-6918.

LOMBARD (See also **CHICAGO**)   Area Code (708)

Synagogues

Etz Chaim (R-UAHC), 1710 S Highland Ave, Ph: 627-3912. Rabbi
   S. Bob. Services: Shabbat

LONG GROVE (See also **CHICAGO**)   Area Code (708)

Synagogues

Congregation Beth Judea (C-US), Box 5304 R.F.D., 60047,
   Ph: 634-0777. Rabbi H. Lifshitz. Services: Shabbat and Sunday
Temple Chai (R-UAHC), Box 1670 R.F.D., 60047, Ph: 537-1771.
   Rabbi H. Caminker. Services: Shabbat

MORTON GROVE (See also **CHICAGO**)   Area Code (708)

Synagogues

Northwest Suburban Jewish Congregation (C-US), 7800 W Lyons,
   Ph: 965-0900. Rabbi E. Feldheim. Services: Daily

NAPERVILLE (See also **CHICAGO**)   Area Code (708)

Synagogues

Congregation Beth Shalom (Recon-FRCH), 1433 N Main St,
    Ph: 961-1818. Rabbi M. Remson. Services: Shabbat

NORTHBROOK (See also **HIGHLAND PARK**)
Area Code (708)

Synagogues

Congregation Beth Shalom (C-US), 3433 Walters Ave,
    Ph: 498-4100. Rabbi C. Wolkin. Services: Daily
Northbrook Congregation Ezra Habonim (C-US), 2095 Landwehr
    Rd, Ph: 480-1690. Rabbi D. Sherbill. Services: Daily
Young Israel of Northbrook (O-NCYI), 3545 W Walters Rd,
    Ph: 480-9462. Rabbi H. Berger. Services: Shabbat and
    Holidays.

Accommodations

Shabbat hospitality; Call Rabbi H. Berger of Young Israel of
    Northbrook, Ph: 274-4455.

Day School

Sager Solomon Schechter Day School (C), 350 Maxine Cohen
    Memorial Dr, Ph: 498-2100.

NORTHFIELD (See also **CHICAGO**)   Area Code (708)

Synagogues

Am Yisrael (C-US), 4 Happ Rd, Ph: 446-7215. Rabbi W. Frankel.
    Services: Shabbat and Sunday
Temple Jeremiah (R-UAHC), 937 Happ Rd, Ph: 441-5760. Rabbi
    R. Schreibman. Services: Friday

OAK PARK (See also **CHICAGO**)   Area Code (708)

Synagogues

Oak Park Temple - B'nai Abraham Zion (R-UAHC), 1235 N
    Harlem Ave, Ph: 386-3937. Rabbi G. Gerson. Services: Shabbat

Shir Ami (C-Chavurah), meets at 124 N Kenilworth, Ph: 386-5860.
Services: Saturday and Holidays.

OLYMPIA FIELDS (See also **CHICAGO**)   Area Code (708)

Synagogues

Temple Anshe Sholom - Beth Torah (R-UAHC), 20820 Western
Ave, Ph: 748-6010. Rabbi D. Gluckman. Services: Friday

PARK FOREST   Area Code (708)

Synagogues

Congregation Am Echad (C-US), 160 Westwood Dr,
Ph: 747-9513; 748-5722. Rabbi S. Tores. Services: Daily
Congregation Beth Sholom (R-UAHC), 1 Dogwood, Ph: 747-3040.
Rabbi E. Dreyfus. Services: Friday

PEORIA   Area Code (309)   J-pop. 1,000

Synagogues

Congregation Agudas Achim (Trad), 3616 N Sheridan Rd,
Ph: 688-4800. Rabbi J. Cohen. Services: Daily
Congregation Anshai Emeth (R), 5614 N University St,
Ph: 691-3323. Rabbi M. Arsers. Services: Friday

Mikvah

Congregation Agudas Achim, 3616 N Sheridan Rd, Ph: 688-4800.

Day School

Peoria Hebrew Day School, 3616 N Sheridan Rd, Ph: 688-2821.

QUINCY   Area Code (217)

Synagogues

Temple B'nai Sholom (R), 427 N 9th, Ph: 222-8537. Services: Call
for schedule and location.

RIVER FOREST (See also **CHICAGO**)   Area Code (708)

Synagogues

West Suburban Temple Har Zion (C-US), 1040 N Harlem Ave,
   Ph: 366-9000. Rabbi Dr. V. Mirelman. Services: Daily

ROCK ISLAND   Area Code (309)

Synagogues

Tri-City Jewish Center (C-US), 2715 30th St, Ph: 788-3426. Rabbi
   S. Herman. Services: Daily

ROCKFORD   Area Code (815)   J-pop. 1,000

Synagogues

Temple Beth El (R-UAHC), 1203 Comanche Dr, Ph: 398-5020.
   Rabbi J. Zahn. Services: Shabbat
Ohave Sholom Synagogue (C-US), 3730 Guilford Rd,
   Ph: 226-4900. Services: Shabbat, Sunday & Monday

SKOKIE (See also **CHICAGO**)   Area Code (708)

Synagogues

Bene Shalom of the Deaf (R), 4435 Oakton, Ph: 677-3330. Rabbi
   D. Goldhamer. Services: Friday
Beth Israel (R), 3601 W Dempster, Ph: 675-0951. Rabbi M.
   Weinberg. Services: Shabbat
Congregation B'nai Emunah (C-US), 9131 Niles Center Rd,
   Ph: 674-9292. Rabbi H. Stern. Services: Shabbat
Chabad of Skokie (O-Lubav), 4059 Dempster St, Ph: 677-1770.
   Rabbi Y. Posner. Services: Shabbat
Hebrew Theological College, 7135 N Carpenter Rd, Ph: 674-7750.
   Services: Daily
Temple Judea Mizpah (R-UAHC), 8610 Niles Center Rd,
   Ph: 676-1566. Rabbi M. Berkson. Services: Shabbat, daily
Congregation Kol Emeth (C-US), 5130 W Touhy Ave,
   Ph: 673-3370. Rabbi B. Mussman. Services: Daily

Niles Township Jewish Congregation (Recon-FRCH), 4500
Dempster St, Ph: 675-4141. Rabbi N. Brief. Services: Daily

Congregation Or Torah (O), 3740 Dempster St, Ph: 679-3645.
Rabbi M. Yeres. Services: Shabbat

Persian (Iran) Hebrew Congregation (O), 3820 Main St,
Ph: 674-5444. Rabbi N. Weiss. Services: Shabbat

Skokie Central Traditional Congregation (Trad), 4040 Main St,
Ph: 674-4117. Rabbi L. Montrose. Services: Daily

Skokie Valley Traditional Synagogue (O, Trad), 8825 E Prairie,
Ph: 674-3473. Rabbi L. Tuchman. Services: Parallel traditional
and orthodox services on Shabbat and Holidays. Daily services
are orthodox.

Eating Out

Falafel King, 4507 Oakton, Ph: 677-6020. Meals: l,d. Menu: (Glatt
meat) Israeli cuisine. RS: Chicago Rabbinical Council. Closed
Shabbat.

Kosher City, 3353 Dempster, Ph: 679-2850. Meals: l,d. Menu:
(Glatt meat) Hamburgers, hot dogs, steak sandwiches, deli sand-
wiches, soups. RS: Chicago Rabbinical Council. Closed
Shabbat.

Slice of Life, 4120 W Dempster, Ph: 674-2021. Meals: b (Sun
only), l,d. Menu: (Dairy) Italian (pasta, fish, salads). RS:
Chicago Rabbinical Council. Closed Shabbat.

Food

Chaim's Kosher Bakery, 4956 W Dempster, Ph: 675-1005. RS:
Chicago Rabbinical Council. Closed Shabbat.

Good Morgan Kosher Fish Market, 4020 Oakton St, Ph: 679-5533.
Fresh fish. RS: Chicago Rabbinical Council. Closed Shabbat.

Hungarian Kosher Foods, 4020 W Oakton, Ph: 674-8008. Meat
market, deli, take-out. Glatt available. Complete kosher supermarket. RS: Chicago Rabbinical Council. Closed Shabbat.

King David Kosher Bakery, 3309 Dempster St, Ph: 677-4355.
Breads and pastries (pareve). RS: Chicago Rabbinical Council.
Closed Shabbat.

129

Kosher Gourmet, 3552 Dempster St, Ph: 679-0432. Glatt meat. Continental and Chinese dishes prepared for take-out and packaged kosher foods. RS: Chicago Rabbinical Council. Closed Shabbat.

Tel-Aviv Kosher Shopping Plaza, 4956 W Dempster St, Ph: 675-1005. Complete kosher grocery including deli meats and baked goods. RS: Chicago Rabbinical Council. Closed Shabbat.

Accommodations

Private accommodations; contact Congregation Or Torah Hospitality Committee, Ph: 679-3645.

Mikvah (See **Chicago**)

Day Schools

Arie Crown Hebrew Day School, 4600 Main St, Ph: 982-9191.

Cheder Lubavitch Hebrew Day School, Boy's Division: 5201 W Howard, Ph: 675-6777; Girl's Division: 3635 W Devon Ave, Ph: 463-0663.

Hillel Torah North Suburban Day School, 7120 N Laramie Ave, Ph: 674-6533.

Skokie Solomon Schechter Day School (C), 9301 Gross Point Rd, Ph: 679-6270.

Bookstore

Hamakor Judaica-The Gallery, 4150 Dempster, Ph: 677-4150.

SPRINGFIELD   Area Code (217)   J-pop. 1,000

Synagogues

Temple B'rith Sholom (R-UAHC), 1008 S Fourth St, Ph: 525-1360. Rabbi S. Moch. Services: Friday

Temple Israel, 1140 W Governor St, Ph: 546-2841. Rabbi B. Marks. Services: Shabbat

VERNON HILLS   Area Code (708)

Synagogues

Or Shalom of Lake County (R-UAHC), 21 Hawthorne Pkwy,
Ph: 362-1948. Rabbi S. Gordon. Services: Friday

WAUKEGAN   Area Code (708)   J-pop. 500

Synagogues

Am Echad (C), 1500 Sunset, Ph: 336-9110. Rabbi W. Fertig.
Services: Call for schedule.

WESTCHESTER (See also **CHICAGO**)   Area Code (708)

Synagogues

B'nai Israel of Proviso (O), 10216 Kitchner St, Ph: 343-0288.
Rabbi L. Lieberworth. Services: Shabbat and holidays.

WHEELING   Area Code (708)

Synagogues

Beth Am (R), 850 Jenkins Ct, Ph: 459-1677. Rabbi R. Goodman.
Services: Friday

WILMETTE (See also **CHICAGO**)   Area Code (708)

Synagogues

Beth Hillel Congregation (C-US), 3220 Big Tree Lane,
Ph: 256-1213. Rabbi G. Botnick. Services: Daily

Mikvah (See **Chicago**)

Indiana

BLOOMINGTON   Area Code (812)   J-pop. 1,000

Synagogues

Congregation Beth Sholom (R,C), 3750 E 3rd St, Ph: 334-2440.
Rabbi J. Friedman. Services: Shabbat

B'nai B'rith Hillel Foundation (Recon), 730 E 3rd St,
Ph: 336-3824. Rabbi S. Shifron. Services: Shabbat

Chabad House Jewish Student Center (Lubav), 518 E 7th St,
Ph: 332-4511. Emergency number, 334-7719. Rabbi D. Kaye.
Services: Shabbat

Eating Out

Shabbat meals served at Chabad House, 518 E 7th St. Call for res-
ervation, Ph: 332-4511. Reasonable charge.

Food

Kroger, Jackson Creek Plaza, Ph: 333-5766. Carries kosher hard
cheeses and Empire poultry products.

Take-out meals available from Chabad House on advance notice.
Call Rabbi D. Kaye, Ph: 332-4511.

Accommodations

Indiana Memorial Union Hotel, E 7th St, (on campus),
Ph: 855-2536. Short walk to Chabad House.

EAST CHICAGO   Area Code (219)

Synagogues

B'nai Sholom Congregation (Trad), 4508 Baring Ave,
Ph: 397-3106. Rabbi J. Shuback. Services: Saturday

ELKHART (See also SOUTH BEND)   Area Code (219)

Synagogues

Temple Israel (C), 430 N 2nd St, Ph: 294-2031. Call for schedule.

132

EVANSVILLE   Area Code (812)   J-pop. 520

Synagogues

Temple Adath B'nai Israel (R-UAHC), 3600 Washington Ave, Ph: 477-1577. Rabbi A. Abrams. Services: Friday

Accommodations

Private accommodations; call Ms. Vicki May at Temple Adath B'nai Israel, Ph: 477-1577.

FORT WAYNE   Area Code (219)   J-pop. 1,125

Synagogues

Congregation Achduth Vesholom (R-UAHC), 5200 Old Mill Rd, Ph: 744-4245. Rabbi R. Safran. Services: Shabbat

Congregation B'nai Jacob (C), 2340 Fairfield Ave, Ph: 744-2183. Rabbi P. Aloof. Services: Shabbat

Food

Kroger, Southgate Mall, Ph: 745-7800. Frozen Empire poultry products.

Super Roger's, 6316 Covington Plaza, Ph: 432-2511. Frozen Empire poultry products.

GARY   Area Code (219)   J-pop. 2,300

Synagogues

Temple Israel (R-UAHC), 601 N Montgomery St, Ph: 938-5232. Rabbi S. Halpern. Services: Friday

HAMMOND   Area Code (219)

Synagogues

Temple Beth-El (R-UAHC), 6947 Hohman Ave, Ph: 932-3754. Rabbi M. N. Stevens. Services: Friday

Congregation Beth Israel (C-US), 7105 Hohman Ave, Ph: 931-1312. Rabbi R. Ostrovsky. Services: Shabbat

INDIANAPOLIS   Area Code (317)   J-pop. 10,000

Synagogues

Congregation Beth El Zedeck (C-US, Recon-FRCH), 600 W 70th St, Ph: 253-3441. Rabbi D. Sasso. Services: Daily

Congregation B'nai Torah (O-UOJC), 6510 Hoover Rd, Ph: 253-5253. Rabbi R. Shechter. Services: Daily

Indianapolis Hebrew Congregation (R-UAHC), 6501 N Meridian St, Ph: 255-6647. Rabbi B. Boxman. Services: Shabbat

United Orthodox Hebrew Congregation (O), 5879 Central Ave, Ph: 253-4591. Services: Daily

Food

Atlas Supermarket, 720 E 54th St, Ph: 255-6800. Large selection of kosher groceries, frozen foods and wines.

Reiswerg's Kosher Meat Market & Deli, 63-34 Guilford, Ph: 257-0422. Kosher grocery. No kosher supervision.

Accommodations

Shabbat hospitality:

Call Rabbi A. Grossbaum at Chabad House, Ph: 251-5573. Shabbat meals can be arranged. Please call ahead.

Call Rabbi R. Shechter at Congregation B'nai Torah, Ph: 253-5253.

Mikvah

Congregation B'nai Torah, 6510 Hoover Rd. Call the synagogue office, Ph: 253-5253.

Day School

Hebrew Academy of Indianapolis, 6602 Hoover Rd, Ph: 251-1261.

LAFAYETTE   Area Code (317)   J-pop. 500

Synagogues

Temple Israel (R-UAHC), 620 Cumberland Ave, **West Lafayette**, Ph: 463-3455. Rabbi S. Weingart. Services: Friday

Sons of Abraham (Trad), 661 N 7th St, Ph: 742-2113. Services: Shabbat (In case of need, special minyanim can be arranged. Call Dr. Edward Simon, Ph: 494-4991; 463-7871 or Rabbi Gedalyah Engel, Ph: 743-1716.)

Food

Home-baked kosher challahs available form Mrs. E. Simon, Ph: 463-7871.

Accommodations

For Shabbat hospitality, call Dr. and Mrs. Edward Simon, Ph: 463-7871 or Rabbi Gedalyah Engel, Ph: 743-1716.

MICHIGAN CITY   Area Code (219)   J-pop. 280

Synagogues

Sinai Temple (R-UAHC), 2800 Franklin St, Ph: 874-4477. Rabbi J. Weisblatt. Services: Friday

MUNCIE   Area Code (317)   J-pop. 160

Synagogues

Temple Beth-El (R-UAHC) 525 W Jackson St, Ph: 288-4662. Services: Friday

RICHMOND   Area Code (317)

Synagogues

Beth Boruk Temple (R-UAHC), 2810 Southeast Pkwy, Ph: 962-6501. Services: Friday

SOUTH BEND   Area Code (219)   J-pop. 1,800

Synagogues

Temple Beth-El (R-UAHC), 305 W Madison St, Ph: 234-4402. Rabbi M. Feinstein. Services: Shabbat

Hebrew Orthodox Congregation (O-UOJC), 3207 High St, Ph: 291-4239; 291-9014. Rabbi Y. Gettinger. Services: Daily

Sinai Synagogue (C), 1102 E LaSalle Ave, Ph: 234-8584. Rabbi H. Shub. Services: Daily

Eating Out

Meals available (b,l,d every day during the school year) in dining room of Rabbi Naftali Riff Yeshiva, 3207 High St, Ph: 291-4239; 291-9014. Please call in advance.

Food

Hebrew Orthodox Congregation, 3207 High St, Ph: 291-4239. The congregation runs a food co-op which maintains a full selection of kosher products. To order specific items call in advance.

Hot Dog House, 2419 Lincoln Way W, **Mishawaka**, Ph: 259-6484. Kosher groceries and packaged deli.

Kroger, 2330 Hickory Rd, **Mishawaka**, Ph: 255-4488. Kosher hard cheeses, Empire frozen poultry, soups, blintzes, etc.

Accommodations

Private accommodations; call Rabbi Y. Gettinger or Mr. Mike Lehrman c/o Steel Warehouse, Inc., Ph: 1-800-348-2529 X137 (toll free). A service of the Hebrew Orthodox Congregation.

Mikvah

Hebrew Orthodox Congregation, 3207 High St. Contact Mrs. Miriam Gettinger, Ph: 287-2600 or Mrs. Tsipi Lerman, Ph: 287-7147; 236-5127.

Day School

South Bend Hebrew Day School, 206 W 8th St, **Mishawaka**, Ph: 255-3351.

TERRE HAUTE   Area Code (812)   J-pop. 325

Synagogues

United Hebrew Congregation (R-UAHC), 540 S Sixth St, Ph: 232-5988. Rabbi J. Klein. Services: Friday

WHITING   Area Code (219)

Synagogues

Congregation B'nai Judah (C-US), 1549 Davis Ave, Ph: 659-0797. Services: Shabbat

136

Iowa

AMES   Area Code (515)   J-pop. 200

Synagogues

Ames Jewish Congregation (R), 3721 Calhoun Ave, Ph: 233-1347;
232-0448. Services: Friday

CEDAR RAPIDS   Area Code (319)   J-pop. 430

Synagogues

Temple Judah (R-UAHC), 3221 Lindsay Lane SE, Ph: 362-1261.
Rabbi E. Chesman. Services: Shabbat

COUNCIL BLUFFS (See also OMAHA, NE)   Area Code (712)

Synagogues

B'nai Israel Synagogue (C), 618 Mynster St, Ph: 322-4705.
Services: Call for information.

DAVENPORT (See also ROCK ISLAND, IL)   Area Code (319)

Synagogues

Temple Emanuel (R-UAHC), 1115 Mississippi Ave, Ph: 326-4419.
Rabbi H. Karp. Services: Friday

DES MOINES   Area code (515)   J-pop. 2,800

Synagogues

Congregation Beth El Jacob (O-UOJC), 954 Cummins Pkwy,
Ph: 274-1551. Rabbi M. Berg. Services: Daily
Temple B'nai Jeshurun (R-UAHC), 5101 Grand Ave, Ph: 274-4979.
Rabbi S. Fink. Services: Shabbat
Chabad of Iowa, 2932 University Ave, Ph: 279-7727. Rabbi M.
Kasowitz. Services: Call for information.
Tifereth Israel (C-US), 924 Polk Blvd, Ph: 255-1137. Rabbi N.
Sandler. Services: Shabbat

Food

The Nosh, 800 First St, **West Des Moines**, Ph: 255-4047. Kosher groceries, including Empire, Sinai and Best frozen meats. Meat section closed Shabbat.

Accommodations

Shabbat hospitality; Call Rabbi M. Kasowitz of Chabad House, Ph: 279-7727.

Mikvah

Congregation Beth El Jacob, 954 Cummins Pkwy. Contact Synagogue office, Ph: 274-1551.

Day School

Des Moines Jewish Academy, 924 Polk Blvd, Ph: 274-0453.

DUBUQUE   Area Code (319)

Synagogues

Temple Beth El (R), 475 W Locust St, Ph: 583-3473. Services: Call for information.

FAIRFIELD   Area Code (515)

Synagogues

Beth Shalom (Unaffiliated), 308 S "B" St, Ph: 472-6324. Services: Friday

FORT DODGE   Area Code (515)

Synagogues

Beth-El Synagogue (C-US), 501 N 12th St, Ph: 573-8925. Services: Call for information

IOWA CITY   Area Code (319)   J-pop. 1,200

Synagogues

Agudas Achim Synagogue (C-US), 602 E Washington St, Ph: 337-3813. Rabbi J. Portman. Services: Shabbat

B'nai B'rith Hillel Foundation at the University of Iowa, 122 E
Market St, Ph: 338-0778. Rabbi J. Portman. Services: Shabbat

Eating Out

B'nai B'rith Hillel Foundation at the University of Iowa,
Ph: 338-0778. RS: Rabbi J. Portman. Friday dinners twice a
month. Sunday dinner once a month. Call ahead for information
and reservations.

OTTUMWA   Area Code (515)

Synagogues

Congregation B'nai Jacob (C-US), 529 E Main St, Ph: 682-1623.
Services: Call for schedule.

SIOUX CITY   Area Code (712)   J-pop. 630

Synagogues

Mount Sinai Temple (R-UAHC), 815 38th St, Ph: 252-4265. Rabbi
T. Friedmann. Services: Friday
Shaare Zion Synagogue (C-US), 1522 Douglas St, Ph: 252-4057.
Services: Daily
United Orthodox Synagogue (O), 14th & Nebraska Sts,
Ph: 255-7559. Rabbi S. Bolotnikov. Services: Saturday and
Holidays

Food

Sam's Kosher Market, 1911 Grandview Ave, Ph: 258-6648.
Groceries, fresh meat and poultry. Also frozen packaged foods.
RS: Rabbi S. Bolotnikov.

Accommodations

All of the following are within walking distance of the United
Orthodox Synagogue.
Hilton, 707 4th St, Ph: 277-4101.
Imperial Motel, 110 Nebraska St, Ph: 277-3151.
Regency Executive, 2nd & Nebraska St, Ph: 277-1550.

Mikvah

Jewish Community Center of Sioux City, 14th & Nebraska St. Call
Center office, Ph: 258-0618.

WATERLOO   Area Code (319)   J-pop. 235

Synagogues

Congregation Sons of Jacob (C-US), 411 Mitchell Ave,
Ph: 233-9448. Rabbi S. Serber. Services: Shabbat

Kansas

KANSAS CITY (See also **KANSAS CITY, MO**)
Area Code (913)

Synagogues

Beth Israel Abraham and Voliner West, 8675 W 96th St #100,
Overland Park, Ph: (816) 444-5747. Services: Shabbat and
Holidays

Chabad of Kansas City (Lubav), 6201 Indian Creek Dr, **Overland
Park**, Ph: 649-4852. Rabbi S. Wineberg, Rabbi B. Friedman.
Services: Shabbat, Sunday and Holidays

Kehilath Israel Synagogue (Trad), 10501 Conser St., **Overland
Park**, Ph: 642-1880. Rabbi H. Mandl. Services: Daily

Ohev Shalom (C), 5311 W 75th St, **Prairie Village**, Ph: 642-6460.
Rabbi D. Horwitz. Services: Daily

Eating Out

Jacobson's, 5200 W 95th St, Ph: 648-3880. Meals: l,d. Menu: Deli,
chili, chicken dishes. RS: Rabbi D. Glicksman. Closed Shabbat.

Jewish Community Campus Cafe, 5801 W 115th St, Ph: 451-1660.
Meals: b,l,d. Menu: (Meat & dairy) Soups, sandwiches, salads,
fish. RS: Rabbi D. Glicksman. Closed Shabbat.

Food

The Bagel and You, 5313 W 94th Terrace, **Prairie Village,**
Ph: 381-4455. RS: Rabbi D. Glicksman (bagels only).

Foodland, 5441 W 95th St, **Overland Park,** Ph: 381-4714. Bakery
(pareve and dairy). RS: Rabbi H. Mandl and Rabbi D.
Glicksman. Store has large selection of kosher products.

Hy-Vee, 11552 W 95th St, **Overland Park,** Ph: 894-1983. Good
selection of kosher products.

Matthew's Bakery, 10400 W. 103rd St, **Overland Park,**
Ph: 492-3723. Breads (pareve) and pastries (dairy). RS: Rabbi
D. Glicksman.

Schnuck's, 91st St & Metcalf, Ph: 648-6663. Large selection of
kosher products.

Accommodations

Shabbat hospitality:
Young Israel of Overland Park, Ph: 341-1597.
Chabad of Kansas City, Ph: 649-4852.

Mikvah

Kehilath Israel Synagogue, 10501 Conser St, **Overland Park,**
Ph: 642-1880

Day School

Hyman Brand Hebrew Academy of Greater Kansas City (C), 5801
W 115th St #102, **Overland Park,** Ph: 491-4082.

LEAWOOD (See **KANSAS CITY**)

MANHATTAN   Area Code (913)   J-pop. 100

Synagogues

Manhattan Jewish Congregation (Unaffiliated), 1509 Wreath Ave,
Ph: 539-8462 or 539-5115. Services: Friday and Holidays

OVERLAND PARK (See **KANSAS CITY**)

PRAIRIE VILLAGE (See **KANSAS CITY**)

TOPEKA   Area Code (913)   J-pop. 500

Synagogues

Temple Beth Sholom (R-UAHC), 4200 Munson Ave, Ph: 272-6040. Rabbi L. Karol. Services: Friday

WICHITA   Area Code (316)   J-pop. 1,000

Synagogues

Ahavath Achim Hebrew Congregation (Trad), 1850 N Woodlawn, Ph: 685-1339. Services: Saturday, Monday and Thursday a.m.
Temple Emanu-el (R-UAHC), 7011 E Central St, Ph: 684-5148. Rabbi K. Emert. Services: Shabbat

Mikvah

Ahavath Achim Hebrew Congregation, 1850 N Woodlawn, Ph: 685-1339.

Kentucky

LEXINGTON   Area Code (606)   J-pop. 2,000

Synagogues

Temple Adath Israel (R-UAHC), 124 N Ashland Ave, Ph: 269-2979. Rabbi J. Adland. Services: Friday
Congregation Ohavay Zion (C-US), 2048 Edgewater Ct, Ph: 266-8050. Rabbi E. Slaton. Services: Call for information.

Food

Foodtown, Lansdowne Shopping Center, Ph: 266-0832. Some Empire products.

LOUISVILLE   Area Code (502)   J-pop. 9,200

Synagogues

Congregation Adath Jeshurun (C-US), 2401 Woodbourne Ave, Ph: 458-5359. Rabbi R. Slosberg. Services: Daily

Congregation Anshei Sfard (O), 3700 Dutchman's Lane,
Ph: 451-3122. Rabbi A. Litvin. Services: Daily

Knesseth Israel Congregation (Trad), 2531 Taylorsville Rd,
Ph: 459-2780. Rabbi M. Feigenbaum. Services: Daily

Temple Shalom (R-UAHC), 4220 Taylorsville Rd, Ph: 458-4739.
Rabbi S. Miles. Services: Friday

The Temple (R-UAHC), 5101 Brownsboro Rd, Ph: 423-1818.
Rabbi C. Diamond. Services: Shabbat

Eating Out

Jewish Community Center Snack Bar, 3600 Dutchman's Lane,
Ph: 459-0660. RS: Vaad Hakashrut of Louisville. Menu: Meat
and dairy dishes. Closed Shabbat.

Four Courts (cafeteria), 2100 Millvale Rd, Ph: 451-0990. RS: Vaad
Hakashrut of Louisville. Visitors to this nursing home can buy
breakfast, lunch or dinner. Call in advance.

Jewish Hospital, 217 E Chestnut, Diet office, Ph: 587-4292. Serves
kosher meals to visitors 7 days a week. RS: Vaad Hakashrut of
Louisville. Call in 24 hours in advance.

Food

Han's Pastries, 3089 Breckinridge Lane, Ph: 452-9164. Cakes and
breads (pareve and dairy). RS: Vaad Hakashrut of Louisville.

Strathmoor Market, 2733 Bardstown Rd, Ph: 458-2276. Packaged
kosher products, fresh and frozen meat. RS: Vaad Hakashrut of
Louisville. Closed Shabbat.

Accommodations

Breckinridge Inn, 2800 Breckinridge Lane, Ph: 456-5050. One
and one-half miles to Congregation Anshei Sfard.

Shabbat hospitality; call Congregation Anshei Sfard office,
Ph: 451-3122.

Mikvah

Anshei Sfard, 3700 Dutchman's Lane. Call synagogue office,
Ph: 451-3122 or Chabad, Ph: 459-1770.

Day School

Eliahu Academy, 3819 Bardstown Rd, Ph: 459-0797.

OWENSBORO   Area Code (502)

Synagogues

Temple Adath Israel (R-UAHC), 429 Daviess St, Ph: 683-9723.
Services: Friday, once a month

PADUCAH   Area Code (502)

Synagogues

Temple Israel (R-UAHC), 332 Joe Clifton Dr, Ph: 442-4104.
Rabbi L. Zoll. Services: Friday, twice a month

Louisiana

ALEXANDRIA   Area Code (318)   J-pop. 350

Synagogues

B'nai Israel Traditional Synagogue (C-US), 1907 Vance St,
President: Dr. B. Kaplan, Ph: 445-4586 or 445-9367. Services:
Shabbat, Holidays; Kaddish by special request
Congregation Gemiluth Chassodim (R-UAHC), 2021 Turner St,
Ph: 445-3655. Rabbi A. Task. Services: Shabbat

Accommodations

Private accommodations; for an invitation to a kosher meal, call
Dr. B. Kaplan of B'nai Israel Congregation, Ph: 445-4586.

BATON ROUGE   Area Code (504)   J-pop. 1,200

Synagogues

Congregation B'nai Israel (R-UAHC), 3354 Kleinert Ave,
Ph: 343-0111. Rabbi B. Weinstein. Services: Friday
Beth Shalom (R-UAHC), 9111 Jefferson Hwy, Ph: 924-6773.
Rabbi D. Caplan. Services: Friday

LAFAYETTE   Area Code (318)

Synagogues

Temple Rodeph Sholom (R-UAHC), 603 Lee St, Ph: 234-3760.
  Rabbi H. Sandman. Services: Friday

Yeshurun Synagogue (R), 1520 Kaliste Saloom Rd, Ph: 984-1775
  or 981-5292. Services: Friday

LAKE CHARLES   Area Code (318)   J-pop. 300

Synagogues

Temple Sinai (R-UAHC), 713 Hodges St, Ph: 439-2866. Rabbi S.
  Stein. Services: Friday

METAIRIE (See also NEW ORLEANS)   Area Code (504)

Synagogues

Congregation Gates of Prayer (R-UAHC), 4000 W Esplanade Ave,
  Ph: 885-2600. Rabbi R. Loewy. Services: Shabbat

Tikvat Shalom Conservative Congregation (C-US), 3737 W
  Esplanade Ave, Ph: 889-1144. Rabbi E. Cytryn. Services:
  Shabbat

Young Israel—Chabad of Metairie (O-NCYI), 4141 W Esplanade
  Ave, Ph: 887-6997. Rabbi Y. Nemes. Services: Daily

Eating Out

Kosher Kajun, 3520 N Hullen, Ph: 888-2010. Meals: b,l,d. Menu:
  Deli sandwiches and some side dishes. Also take-out. Will
  deliver to downtown hotels. RS: Rabbi G. Newman of Beth
  Israel Congregation, New Orleans. Closed Shabbat

Food

The Bagel Factory, 3113 Causeway Blvd, Ph: 837-8707. Bagels and
  breads. RS: Rabbi G. Newman of Beth Israel Congregation,
  New Orleans.

Dorignac Food Center, 710 Veterans Blvd, Ph: 834-8216. Kosher
  frozen foods and grocery items. Kosher bakery (pareve and
  dairy). RS: Rabbi G. Newman.

145

Food cont.

Food Cooperative - Lakeshore Hebrew Day School, 5210 W Esplanade Ave, Ph: 885-4532. Empire and Sinai products.

Kosher Kajun, 3520 N Hullen, Ph: 888-2010. Deli, large variety of kosher frozen products and kosher groceries; also meats, cheeses and cakes. RS: Rabbi G. Newman. Closed Shabbat.

Accommodations

Kosher Bed and Breakfast, room and bath for one person. $60.00 per night. Shabbat arrangements available. Ph: Carol, 831-2230 or 833-1352.

Day School

Lakeshore Hebrew Day School, 5210 W Esplanade Ave, Ph: 885-4532/4536.

MONROE   Area Code (318)   J-pop. 525

Synagogues

Congregation B'nai Israel (R-UAHC), 2400 Orell Pl, Ph: 387-0730. Rabbi D. L. Kline. Services: Friday

NEW ORLEANS (See also METAIRIE)
Area Code (504)   J-pop. 12,000

Synagogues

Anshe Sfard (O), 2230 Carondelet St, Ph: 522-4714. Services: Shabbat, Sunday morning and Holidays

Beth Israel Congregation (O-UOJC), 7000 Canal Blvd, Ph: 283-4366. Rabbi G. Newman. Services: Daily

Chabad House (O-Lubav), 7037 Freret St (at Tulane campus), Ph: 866-5164. Rabbi Z. Rivkin. Services: Shabbat and Holidays

Congregation Chevra Thilim (C-US), 4429 S Claiborne Ave, Ph: 895-7987. Services: Daily

Temple Sinai (R-UAHC), 6227 St. Charles Pl, Ph: 861-3693. Rabbi E. Cohn. Services: Shabbat

Touro Synagogue (R-UAHC), 1501 Gen. Pershing St, Ph: 895-4843. Rabbi D. Goldstein. Services: Shabbat

Eating Out

Hillel House, 912 Broadway, Ph: 866-7060. Visitors are welcome
to participate in Friday night services and dinner as well as
Sunday dinners. Contact Rabbi H. Wagman.

Accommodations

Private accommodations for Shabbat; call Chabad House,
Ph: 866-5164.

Mikvah

Beth Israel Congregation, 7000 Canal Blvd. Contact Marlene Lew,
Ph: 288-8943.

Chabad House Mikvah, 7037 Freret St, Ph: 866-5164 (days) or
Mrs. Jenny Kaufmann, Ph: 866-4217 (evenings) or Mrs. Bluma
Rivkin, Ph: 866-5342 (evenings).

SHREVEPORT   Area Code (318)   J-pop. 1,000

Synagogues

Congregation Agudath Achim (C-US), 9401 Village Green Dr,
Ph: 797-6401. Rabbi Dr. S. Moskowitz. Services: Shabbat

B'nai Zion Congregation (R-UAHC), 245 Southfield Rd,
Ph: 861-2122. Rabbi M. Matuson. Services: Shabbat

Maine

AUBURN   Area Code (207)

Synagogues

Congregation Beth Abraham (C), Main St & Laurel Ave, Ph: 783-
13-02. Rabbi N. Geller. Services: Daily

Temple Shalom Synagogue Center (C-US, R-UAHC), 74 Bradman
St, Ph: 786-4201. Rabbi S. Goodman. Services: Shabbat,
Sunday, Monday and Thursday a.m.

AUGUSTA   Area Code (207)

Synagogues

Temple Beth El (R), Woodlawn St, President Robert Katz,
   Ph: 623-1035. Services: One Friday a month and Holidays

BANGOR   Area Code (207)   J-pop. 1,250

Synagogues

Beth Abraham (O-UOJC), 145 York St, Ph: 947-0876; 945-5940.
   Rabbi H. Isaacs. Services: Daily
Congregation Beth El (R), Main & Union Ss, Ph: 945-9442,
   President: Dr. S. Block. Services: Friday
Congregation Beth Israel (C-US), 144 York St, Ph: 945-3433.
   Rabbi J. Schonberger. Services: Daily

Eating Out

The Bagel Shop, 1 Main St, Ph: 947-1654. Meals: b,l,d. Menu:
   American cuisine with separate service for meat and dairy. RS:
   Rabbi H. Isaacs. Closed Shabbat.

Mikvah

Bangor Mikvah, 133 Pine St. Contact Beth Abraham,
   Ph: 947-0876, or Rabbi H. Isaacs, Ph: 945-5940.

BATH   Area Code (207)

Synagogues

Beth Israel Congregation (C), 862 Washington St, Ph: 443-5181.
   Services: High Holidays.

OLD ORCHARD BEACH   (See Also PORTLAND)
   Area Code (207)

Synagogues

Congregation Beth Israel (O), 49 E Grand Ave, Ph: 934-2973.
   Services: Daily (summer only)

Food

Shop & Save, Rte 1, **Saco**, Ph: 282-4152. Empire frozen products.
   Shaw's Supermarket, 1375 Congress St, Westgate Mall,
   Ph: 774-7661. Empire frozen products.

Accommodations

Beau Rivage, 54 E Grand Ave, Ph: 934-4668. Located across the
   street from Congregation Beth Israel.
Green Dolphin, 62 E Grand Ave, Ph: 934-4764. Located across the
   street from Congregation Beth Israel. Rooms with kitchen facilities are available.

PORTLAND   Area Code (207)

Synagogues

Temple Beth El (C-US), 400 Deering Ave, Ph: 774-2649. Rabbi S.
   Frisch. Services: Daily
Etz Chaim (O), 267 Congress St, Ph: 773-2339. Services: Shabbat
   and daily p.m.
Portland Reform Congregation Bet Ha'am (R), 111 Wescott St,
   South Portland, Ph: 879-0028. Rabbi W. Berkowitz. Services:
   Friday
Congregation Shaarey Tphiloh (O-UOJC), 76 Noyes St,
   Ph: 773-0693. Rabbi J. Reifman. Services: Daily

Food

Penny-Wise Market, 182 Ocean Ave, Ph: 772-8808. Good selection
   of kosher groceries, deli, frozen foods and TV dinners. Also
   kosher butcher shop, which is closed Shabbat. RS: Rabbi J.
   Reifman (butcher shop only).

Accommodations

Private accommodations: For Shabbat meals - call Rabbi M.
   Wilansky, Chabad House, Ph: 871-8947.
Ramada Inn, 1230 Congress, Ph: 774-5611. Fifteen-minute walk to
   Congregation Shaarey Tphiloh. About a mile from Chabad
   House. Reserve well in advance.

Accommodations cont.

Susse Chalet, 340 Park Ave (Congress St. exit, 295), Ph: 871-0611.
Walk to Congregation Shaarey Tphiloh and Chabad House.
Reserve well in advance.

Mikvah

Shaarey Tphiloh Synagogue, 76 Noyes St. Contact synagogue
office, Ph: 773-0693 or Jennifer Kolko, Ph: 773-5099.

Day School

The Abraham S. and Fannie B. Levey Hebrew Day School, 76
Moyes St, Ph; 774-7676.

Maryland

ANNAPOLIS (See also BALTIMORE and SILVER SPRING)
Area Code (301)   J-pop. 2,000

Synagogues

Chapel at U.S. Naval Academy, Mitscher Hall, Ph: 267-2881.
Chaplain Rabbi A. Solomovitz (R). Services: Friday
Congregation Kneseth Israel (O-UOJC), Hilltop Lane & Spa Rd,
Ph: 269-0740. Rabbi S. Gordon. Services: Daily
Kol Ami Congregation, 1909 Hidden Meadow Lane,
Ph: 266-6006.
Lubavitch Jewish Center of Annapolis, 1240M Gemini Dr,
Ph: 263-8544. Rabbi D. Kugel. Services: Shabbat

Food

Magruder's, 2108 Solomons Island Rd, Ph: 266-0001. Empire
products.

ARNOLD   Area Code (301)

Synagogues

Temple Beth Sholom (R-UAHC), 1461 Baltimore-Annapolis Rd,
Ph: 974-0900. Rabbi R. Klensin. Services: Shabbat

BALTIMORE   Area Code (301)   J-pop. 93,000

Synagogues

Adath Yeshurun (O-UOJC), Old Court & Rolling Rds, Ph: 655-7818. Rabbi S. Shafran. Services: Daily

Agudath Israel (O), 6202 Park Heights Ave, Ph: 764-7778. Rabbi M. Heinemann. Services: Daily

Anshe Emunah - Aitz Chaim Liberty Jewish Center (O-UOJC), 8615 Church Lane, **Randallstown**, Ph: 922-1333. Rabbi J. Max. Services: Daily

Arugas Hobosem Congregation (O), 6615 Park Heights Ave, Ph: 358-4340. Rabbi A. Taub. Services: Daily

Baltimore Hebrew Congregation (R-UAHC), 7401 Park Heights Ave, Ph: 764-1587. Rabbi J. Katz. Services: Shabbat

Beth Abraham Congregation (O), 6208 Wallis Ave, Ph: 358-7456. Services: Daily

Beth Am Synagogue (Independent), 2501 Eutaw Pl, Ph: 523-2446. Rabbi I. Schiffer. Services: Saturday

Beth El (C-US), 8101 Park Heights Ave, Ph: 484-0411. Rabbi M. Loeb. Services: Daily

Beth Isaac Adath Israel (O), 4398 Crest Heights Rd, Ph: 486-8338. Rabbi M. Blitz. Services: Daily

Beth Israel (C-US), 9411 Liberty Rd, **Randallstown,** Ph: 922-6565. Rabbi S. Essrog. Services: Daily

Beth Jacob Congregation (O-UOJC), 5713 Park Heights Ave, Ph: 466-4266. Rabbi R. Schwartz. Services: Daily

Beth Tfiloh Congregation (O-UOJC), 3300 Old Court Rd, Ph: 486-1900. Rabbi M. Wohlberg. Services: Daily

B'nai Jacob (O-UOJC), 3615 Seven Mile Lane, Ph: 764-6781. Rabbi J. Baumgarten. Services: Daily

Bolton Street Synagogue (Independent), 1316 Park Ave, Ph: 225-3000. Services: Friday

Chizuk Amuno (C-US), 8100 Stevenson Rd, Ph: 486-6400. Rabbi J. Zaiman and Rabbi J. Rosen. Services: Daily

Temple Emanuel (R-UAHC), 3301 Milford Mill Rd, Ph: 922-3642. Rabbi G. Buchdahl. Services: Friday

Synagogues cont.

Garrison Forest Beth Keneseth (O-UOJC), 2 Tahoe Circle, **Owings Mills**, Ph: 363-6352. Rabbi M. Shuvalsky. Services: Shabbat

The Har Sinai Congregation (R-UAHC), 6300 Park Heights Ave, Ph: 764-2882. Rabbi D. Holtz, Rabbi F. Herman. Services: Shabbat

Lubavitch of Maryland (O-Lubav), 6509 Deancroft Rd and 6110 Park Heights Ave, Ph: 486-2666. Rabbi S. Kaplan. Services: Shabbat

Moses Montefiore Woodmoor Hebrew Congregation (O-UOJC), 3605 Coronado Rd, Ph: 655-4484. Rabbi E. Ackerman. Services: Daily

Ner Israel High School (O), 400 Mount Wilson Lane, Ph: 484-7200. Services: Daily

Ner Tamid—Greenspring Valley Synagogue (O-UOJC), 6214 Pimlico Rd, Ph: 358-6500. Rabbi C. Landau. Services: Daily

Temple Oheb Shalom (R-UAHC), 7310 Park Heights Ave, Ph: 358-0105. Rabbi D. Berlin. Services: Shabbat

Ohel Yaakov (O-UOJC), 3200 Glen Ave, Ph: 578-9336. Rabbi B. Dinovitz. Services: Daily

Ohr Knesseth Israel—Anshe Sfard, Rogers Ave Synagogue (O-UOJC), 3910 W Rogers Ave, Ph: 466-8800. Rabbi M. Shuvalsky. Services: Daily

Randallstown Synagogue Center - Ahvas Achim (O-UOJC), 8729 Church Lane, **Randallstown**, Ph: 655-6665. Rabbi L. Oberstein. Services: Daily

Shaarei Tfiloh (O-UOJC), 2001 Liberty Heights Ave, Ph: 523-4375 or 523-7912. Services: Shabbat and Sunday

Shaarei Zion (O-UOJC), 6602 Park Heights Ave, Ph: 466-3060. Rabbi J. Shapiro. Services: Daily

Shearith Israel (O), Glen & Park Heights Ave, Ph: 466-3060. Services: Daily

Shomrei Emunah (O-UOJC), 6221 Greenspring Ave, Ph: 358-8604. Rabbi B. Bak. Services: Daily

Suburban Orthodox (O-UOJC), 7504 Seven Mile Lane, Ph: 484-6114. Rabbi E. Preis. Services: Daily

Synagogue Center (O), 7124 Park Heights Ave, Ph: 764-0262 or 764-2735. Rabbi S. Vitsick. Services: Daily

Winands Road Synagogue Center (O-UOJC), 8701 Winands Rd, **Randallstown**, Ph: 655-1353. Rabbi S. Salfer. Services: Daily

Yeshivas Chofetz Chaim - Talmudical Academy (O), 4445 Old Court Rd, **Pikesville**, Ph: 484-5370. Services: Daily

Eating Out

Chapp's of Pomona, 1700 Reisterstown Rd #125-126, Ph: 653-3198/3199. Meals: l,d. Menu (Meat and vegetarian): Chinese and American. RS: Star-K of Baltimore. Closed Shabbat.

Johns Hopkins University/Young Israel, 34th & Charles Sts, Ph: 338-8000. Lunch and dinner are served daily during the school year. RS: Rabbi E. Preis. Call for reservations and information.

The Knish Shop, 508 Reisterstown Rd, Ph: 484-5850. Meals: l. Menu: Deli-style dishes and sandwiches, soups. RS: Rabbi L. Fischer. Closed Shabbat.

Kosher Bite Restaurant, 6309 Reisterstown Rd, Ph: 358-6349. Meals: l,d. Menu: Fast food: Hamburgers, hot dogs, sandwiches etc. RS: Star-K of Baltimore. Closed Shabbat.

Milk & Honey Bistro, 1777 Reisterstown Rd, Ph: 486-4344/4345. Meals: b,l,d. Menu: (Dairy) Bagels, spreads, omelettes, salads, etc. Also carry-out bakery (pareve). RS: Star-K of Baltimore. Closed Shabbat.

Royal Restaurant, 7006-A Reisterstown Rd, Ph: 484-3544. Meals: l,d. Menu: Meat and fish dishes. RS: Star-K of Baltimore. Closed Shabbat.

Tov Pizza, 6313 Reisterstown Rd, Ph: 358-5238. Meals: l,d. Menu: Pizza, falafel and dairy dishes. RS: Kof-K. Closed Shabbat.

Food

Danielle's Cuisine, 401 Reisterstown Rd, Ph: 486-1487. Prepared meat and poultry dishes, salads and side dishes for take-out. Also pareve baked goods. RS: Rabbi S. Bayarsky. Closed Shabbat.

Food cont.

Goldman's Kosher Bakery, 6848 Reisterstown Rd, Ph: 358-9625. Deli meats, breads and pastries. RS: Star-K of Baltimore. Closed Shabbat.

Ijac's Kosher Meat Market, 4030 Fallstaff Rd, Ph: 358-9633. RS: Star-K of Baltimore. Closed Shabbat.

The Knish Shop, 508 Reisterstown Rd, Ph: 484-5850. Take-out meat, poultry and side dishes. Dairy case with packaged cheeses and frozen foods. RS: Rabbi L. Fischer. Closed Shabbat.

Liebes' Kosher Delicatessen & Carry, 607 Reisterstown Rd, Ph: 653-1977. Take-out deli, fish platters and dairy dishes. RS: Owner supervised. Closed Shabbat.

O'Fishel's, 509 Reisterstown Rd, Ph: 764-FISH. Take-out: Chicken, side dishes, salads. RS: Star-K of Baltimore. Closed Shabbat

Pariser's, 6711 Reisterstown Rd, Ph: 764-1700. Breads and pastries. RS: Star-K of Baltimore. Closed Shabbat.

Schmell & Azman Kosher Bakery, 104 Reisterstown Rd, Ph: 484-7343. Breads and pastries. RS: Star-K of Baltimore. Closed Shabbat.

Seven Mile Market, 4000 Seven Mile Lane, Ph: 653-2000. Bakery, meat, fish, packaged food. RS: Star-K of Baltimore. Closed Shabbat.

Shlomo's Kosher Meat Market, 4030 Fallstaff Rd, Ph: 358-9633. Meats and poultry. RS: Star-K of Baltimore.

Village Market, Colonial Village Shopping Center, 7006 Reistertown Rd, Ph: 486-0979. Dried fruits and nuts. RS: Star-K of Baltimore.

Accommodations

Private accommodations; call: Rabbi S. Shafran of Adath Yeshurun, Ph: 655-7818 or 922-7356; Rabbi S. Salfer at Winands Road Synagogue Center, **Randallstown**, Ph: 655-1353; or Rabbi A. Taub of Kahal Arugas Habosem, Ph: 358-9722 or 358-4340.

Mikvah

Mikvah of Baltimore, 3500 W Rogers Ave. Call for recorded information, Ph: 664-5834.

Mikvah, 6615 Park Heights Ave. Contact Mrs. Perkel, Ph: 764-6122 or Mrs. Labovitz, Ph: 358-1928 for Shabbat or Yom Tov use.

Day Schools

Bais Yaakov for Girls, 11111 Park Heights Ave, **Owings Mill**, Ph: 363-3300.

Beth Tfiloh Community School, 3300 Old Court Rd, Ph: 486-1905 or 653-7223.

Solomon Schechter Day School of Chizuk Amuno (C), 8100 Stevenson Rd, Ph: 486-8640.

Yeshiva Chofetz Chaim, Talmudical Academy of Baltimore, 4445 Old Court Rd, Ph: 484-6600.

Yeshiva Kochav Yitzchak, Torah Institute of Baltimore, 2500 E Northern Pkwy, Ph: 426-3363.

Bookstores

Central Hebrew Bookstore, 228 Reisterstown Rd, Ph: 653-0550.

Pern's Hebrew Book & Gift Shop, 7012 Reisterstown Rd, Ph: 653-2450.

BETHESDA (See also SILVER SPRING)   Area Code (301)

Synagogues

Am Hatorah Orthodox Congregation (O-UOJC), Meets at Landon School (Banfield Center), 6101 Wilson Lane, Ph: 229-7017. Services: Saturday

Congregation Beth El (C-US), 8215 Old Georgetown Rd, Ph: 652-2606. Rabbi F. Maltzman. Services: Daily

Bethesda Jewish Congregation (Liberal), 6601 Bradley Blvd, Ph: 469-8636. Rabbi R. Brenner. Services: Friday

BOWIE (See also SILVER SPRING)   Area Code (301)

Synagogues

Nevey Shalom (C-US), 12218 Torah Lane, Ph: 262-4020;
262-9020. Rabbi P. Kerbel. Services: Daily

Temple Solel (R-UAHC), 2901 Mitchellville Rd, Ph: 249-CHAI.
Rabbi M. Kramer. Services: Friday

CHEVY CHASE (See also SILVER SPRING)   Area Code (301)

Synagogues

Congregation Ohr Kodesh (C-US), 8402 Freyman Dr,
Ph: 589-3880. Rabbi L. Fishman. Services: Daily

Temple Shalom (R-UAHC), 8401 Grubb Rd, Ph: 587-2273. Rabbi
B. Kahn. Services: Friday

COLLEGE PARK (See also SILVER SPRING)
Area Code (301)

Eating Out

University of Maryland - B'nai B'rith Hillel Foundation Kosher
Dining Room, 7612 Mowatt Lane, Ph: 422-6200. RS:
Rabbinical Council of Greater Washington. Lunch and dinner
are served daily during the school year. Call for reservations.

COLUMBIA   Area Code (301)

Synagogues

Beth Shalom of Howard County (C), Meets at Owen Brown
Interfaith Center, 7246 Cradlerock Way, Ph: 381-7883. Rabbi K.
L. Cohen. Services: Shabbat

Columbia Jewish Congregation (Independent), 5885 Robert Oliver
Pl, Ph: 730-6044. Rabbi M. Siegal. Services: Shabbat

Temple Isaiah (R-UAHC), 5885 Robert Oliver Pl, Ph: 730-8277.
Rabbi M. Panoff. Services: Shabbat

Lubavitch Center for Jewish Education (O-Lubav), 10126 Rodona
Dr, Ph: 740-2424. Rabbi H. Baron. Services: Shabbat

Accommodations

Columbia Inn, 10207 Wincopin Circle, Ph: 730-3900. One-half mile to Lubavitch Center.

Mikvah

Lubavitch Mikvah, 10126 Rodona Dr. To be completed September, 1991. Call Lubavitch Center, Ph: 740-2424.

EASTON   Area Code (301)

Synagogues

Temple B'nai Israel (C), Adkins Ave, Ph: 822-0553. Services: First Friday of the month

FREDERICK   Area Code (301)

Synagogues

Congregation Beth Shalom, 20 W 2nd St, Ph: 663-3437. Rabbi M. Kossman. Services: Shabbat

GAITHERSBURG (See also SILVER SPRING)
   Area Code (301)

Synagogues

Kehilat Shalom (C-US), 9915 Appleridge Rd, Ph: 869-7699. Rabbi S. Hyman. Services: Shabbat

Chabad of Gaithersburg, 18940 Montgomery Village Ave, Ph: 926-3632. Rabbi S. Raichik. Services: Saturday

GERMANTOWN   Area Code (301)

Synagogues

Ohr Chadash Organization (Synagogue), Box 508, (20874), Ph: 963-6423. Services: Bi-weekly Shabbat

GREENBELT (See also SILVER SPRING)   Area Code (301)

Synagogues

Congregation Mishkan Torah (C-US, Recon-FRCH), Ridge & Westway Rds, Ph: 474-4223. Rabbi S. Grife. Services: Shabbat

HAGERSTOWN   Area Code (301)   J-pop. 300

Synagogues

Congregation B'nai Abraham (R-UAHC), 53 Baltimore St, Ph: 733-5039. Rabbi J. Rabinowitz. Services: Friday

HAVRE DE GRACE   Area Code (301)

Synagogues

Harford Jewish Center (R), 8 N Earlton Rd, Ph: 939-3170. Rabbi K. Block. Services: Friday

HYATTSVILLE   Area Code (301)

Synagogues

Beth Torah Congregation (C), 6700 Adelphi Rd, Ph: 927-5525. Rabbi M. L. Abrams. Services: Shabbat.
Friends of Chabad at Hillel (O-Lubav), 6711 Wells Pkwy, Ph: 422-6200. Rabbi B. Chanowitz. Services: Shabbat. Call for additional information.

KENSINGTON (See also SILVER SPRING)   Area Code (301)

Synagogues

Temple Emanuel (R-UAHC), 10101 Connecticut Ave, Ph: 942-2000. Rabbi W. Stone. Services: Friday

LEXINGTON PARK   Area Code (301)

Synagogues

Beth Israel Synagogue (C), Bunker Hill Dr, Ph: 862-2052. Services: Once a month; call for schedule

OLNEY   Area Code (301)

Synagogues

Congregation B'nai Shalom of Olney (C), 18401 Burtfield Dr, Ph: 774-0879. Rabbi P. Pohl. Services: Daily, except Sunday

PIKESVILLE (See BALTIMORE)

POTOMAC   Area Code (301)

Synagogues

Beth Sholom Congregation (O), 11825 Seven Locks Rd, Ph: 279-7010. Rabbi J. Tessler. Services: Daily

Congregation B'nai Tzedek (C), 11315 Falls Rd, Ph: 299-4095. Meets at Harker School, 8411 Harker Dr. Rabbi S. Weinblatt. Services: Shabbat

Congregation Har Shalom (C-US), 11510 Falls Rd, Ph: 299-7087. Rabbi L. Cahan. Services: Daily

Eating Out

Hunan Gourmet, 350 Fortune Terr, Ph: 424-0191. Meals: l,d. Menu: (Meat and fish) American and Continental. Also take-out. RS: Rabbinical Council of Greater Washington. Closed Shabbat.

RANDALLSTOWN (See BALTIMORE)

REISTERSTOWN (See BALTIMORE)

ROCKVILLE (See also SILVER SPRING)   Area Code (301)

Synagogues

Temple Beth Ami (R-UAHC), 800 Hurley Ave, Ph: 340-6818. Rabbi J. Luxemburg. Services: Shabbat

Beth Tikvah (C-US), 2200 Baltimore Rd, Ph: 762-7338. Rabbi H. Gorin. Services: Daily

B'nai Israel (C-US), 6301 Montrose Rd, Ph: 881-6550. Rabbi M. Simon. Services: Daily

Synagogues cont.

Chabad House (O-Lubav), 311 W Montgomery Ave, Ph: 340-6858.
  Rabbi S. Kaplan. Services: Shabbat
Magen David Sephardic Congregation (O), 11418 Old Georgetown
  Rd, Ph: 770-6818. Rabbi C. Kassorla. Services: Daily

Day Schools

Charles E. Smith Jewish Day School (C), 1901 E Jefferson St,
  Ph: 881-1400.
Silver Spring Hebrew Day Institute, 11710 Hunters Lane, Ph:
  984-2111.

Eating Out

Royal Dragon, 4840 Boiling Brook Pkwy, Ph: 468-1922. Meals:
  l,d. Menu: (Meat) Chinese. RS: Rabbinical Council of
  Washington. Closed Shabbat.

Food

Katz's Supermarket, 4860 Boiling Brook Pkwy, Ph: 468-0400.
  Large selection of kosher products.

SALISBURY   Area Code (301)

Synagogues

Congregation Beth Israel (C-US), Camden & Wicomico,
  Ph: 742-2564. Rabbi I. Silber. Services: Shabbat

SILVER SPRING (See also WASHINGTON, D.C.)
  Area Code (301)

Jewish Information & Referral Service: 770-4848

Synagogues

Congregation Har Tzeon - Agudath Achim (C-US), 1840
  University Blvd W, Ph: 649-3800. Rabbi R. Landman.
  Services: Daily
Temple Israel (C-US), 420 University Blvd E, Ph: 439-3600. Rabbi
  D. Oler. Services: Daily

Congregation Shaare Tefila (C-US), 11120 Lockwood Dr,
Ph: 593-3410. Rabbi M. Halpern. Services: Daily
Silver Spring Jewish Center (O), 1401 Arcola Ave, Ph: 649-4425.
Rabbi H. Kranz. Services: Daily
Southeast Hebrew Congregation (O), 10900 Lockwood Ave,
Ph: 593-2120. Rabbi K. Winter. Services: Daily
Woodside Synagogue/Ahavas Torah (O), 9001 Georgia Ave,
Ph: 585-0671. Rabbi Y. Breitowitz. Services: Daily
Young Israel - Shomrai Emunah (O-NCYI), 1132 Arcola Blvd,
Ph: 593-4465. Rabbi G. Anemer. Services: Daily

Eating Out

The Nut House, 11419 Georgia Ave, **Wheaton**, Ph: 942-5900.
Meals: l,d. Menu: Pizza, sandwiches, dairy dishes. RS:
Rabbinical Council of Greater Washington. Closed Shabbat.

Food

De-Luxe Bakery, 11225 New Hampshire Ave, Ph: 593-6607.
Breads and pastries. RS: Rabbinical Council of Greater
Washington
Shalom Strictly Kosher Market, 2307 University Blvd W,
Wheaton, Ph: 946-6500. Fresh meat and poultry, deli-style
dishes, fresh fish and appetizers for take-out. Complete kosher
supermarket. RS: Rabbinical Council of Greater Washington.
Closed Shabbat.
Shaul's and Herzl's Kosher Market, 2503 Enals Ave, **Wheaton**,
Ph: 949-8477. Fresh meat, poultry and fish, sandwiches and side
dishes for take-out. RS: Rabbinical Council of Greater
Washington. Closed Shabbat.
The Wooden Shoe Pastry Shop, 11301 Georgia Ave, Ph: 942-9330.
Breads and pastries. RS: Rabbinical Council of Greater
Washington. Closed Shabbat.

Accommodations

Both of the following motels are across the street from
Congregation Beth Sholom in Washington, D.C.:
Days Inn, 8040 13th St, Ph: 588-4400.

Accommodations cont.

EconoLodge, 7990 Georgia Ave, Ph: 565-3444
Shabbat hospitality; Call Betty Kramer of Woodside Synagogue,
Ph: 585-8080.

Mikvah

Mikvah of Washington, 8901 Georgia Ave. Call for recorded information, Ph: 565-3737.
Silver Spring Jewish Center, 1401 Arcola Ave, Ph: 649-4425;
649-2799

Day Schools

Hebrew Academy of Greater Washington, 2010 Linden Lane,
Ph: 587-4100.
Hebrew Day Academy of Montgomery County, 1401 Arcola Ave,
Ph: 649-5400.

Bookstores

The Jewish Bookstore, 11250 Georgia Ave, **Wheaton**,
Ph: 942-2237.
Libson's Hebrew Books, 2305 University Blvd W, Ph: 933-1800.

TEMPLE HILLS   Area Code (301)

Synagogues

Congregation Shaare Tikvah (C-US), 5404 Old Temple Hills Rd,
Ph: 894-4303. Rabbi D. Bockman. Services: Shabbat

WHEATON (See SILVER SPRING)

DO YOU HAVE ANY
comments, additions or corrections to share with us?
PLEASE USE THE
convenient form at the back of this book.

Massachusetts

ACTON   Area Code (508)

Synagogues

Congregation Beth Elohim (Independent), Hennessey Dr, Ph: 263-3061. Rabbi L. Mintz.

AMHERST   Area Code (413)   J-pop. 750

Synagogues

B'nai B'rith Hillel Foundation at the University of Massachusetts, 388 N Pleasant St, Ph: 549-1710. Rabbi S. Perlmutter. Services: Shabbat and Holidays

Chabad House (O-Lubav), 30 N Hadley Rd, Ph: 549-4094. Rabbi C. Adelman. Services: Shabbat

Jewish Community of Amherst (Independent), 742 Main St, Ph: 256-0160. Rabbi S. Weinberg. Services: Friday

Eating Out

B'nai B'rith Hillel Foundation at the University of Massachusetts, 388 N Pleasant St, Ph: 549-1710. The kosher kitchen serves weeknight dinners cafeteria-style at Hampden Dining Commons. RS: Springfield Vaad Hakashruth. Visitors are welcome.

ANDOVER   Area Code (508)

Synagogues

Temple Emanuel (R-UAHC), 7 Haggett's Pond Rd, Ph: 470-1356. Rabbi R. Goldstein. Services: Shabbat

ARLINGTON   Area Code (617)

Eating Out

Dough-C-Donuts, 1360 Massachusetts Ave, Ph: 643-4550. Donuts, muffins, coffee. RS: Vaad Harabonim of Massachusetts.

ATHOL   Area Code (508)

Synagogues

Temple Israel (Independent), 107 Walnut St, Ph: 249-9481. Rabbi
Y. Zylberberg. Services: Shabbat

ATTLEBORO   Area Code (508)   J-pop. 200

Synagogues

Agudas Achim Congregation (Independent), Toner & Kelley Blvds,
Ph: 222-2243. Rabbi A. M. Gouze. Services: Saturday

BELMONT (See also **BOSTON**)   Area Code (617)

Synagogues

Beth El Temple Center (R-UAHC), 2 Concord Ave, Ph: 484-6668.
Rabbi F. Raj. Services: Daily

BEVERLY (See also **BOSTON**)   Area Code (508)

Synagogues

Temple B'nai Abraham (C-US), 200 E Lothrop St, Ph: 927-3211.
Rabbi D. Abramson. Services: Shabbat, Sunday, Monday and
Thursday

BOSTON (See also **BRIGHTON, BROOKLINE, CAMBRIDGE, LYNN, NEWTON** and **PEABODY**)
Area Code (617)   J-pop. Metropolitan Region - 228,000

Synagogues

Temple Adas Hadrath Israel (C-US), 28 Arlington St, **Hyde Park**,
Ph: 364-2661. Services: Shabbat and Sunday
The Boston Synagogue (O), 55 Martha Rd, Ph: 523-0453. Services:
Shabbat, Sunday, Monday and Thursday
Boston University Hillel (O,C,R), 233 Bay State Rd, Ph: 353-3633.
Services: Shabbat, when classes are in session.
Chabad House (O-Lubav), 491 Commonwealth Ave, Ph: 424-1190.
Rabbi C. Prus. Services: Daily

Georgetown Synagogue (O), 412 Georgetown Dr, **Hyde Park,**
Ph: 361-8212. Services: Call for schedule.

Temple Hillel B'nai Torah (C-US), 120 Corey St, **West Roxbury,**
Ph: 323-0486. Rabbi E. Somers. Services: Daily

Temple Israel (R-UAHC), Longwood Ave & Plymouth St,
Ph: 566-3960. Rabbi B. Mehlman. Services: Shabbat

Old Vilna Shul (O), 16 Phillips St, Ph: 227-0587. Services: Call for
schedule.

Eating Out

Boston University Hillel, 233 Bay State Rd, Ph: 266-3880. Lunch
and dinner served daily. (Saturdays: lunch only; Sundays: dinner
only.) Glatt meat. RS: Vaad Harabonim of Massachusetts. For
Shabbat meals, reserve three days in advance.

Milk Street Café, 50 Milk St, Ph: 542-3663. Meals: b,l. Menu:
Vegetarian and dairy dishes. RS: Rabbi D. Moskovitz. Closed
Shabbat and Sunday.

Milk Street Café, Park at Post Office Square, Ph: 350-7275. Outdoor
café. Meals: b,l,d. (Closes at 7:00) Menu: Vegetarian and dairy
dishes. Also noon-time Glatt deli cart. RS: Rabbi D. Moskovitz.
Closed Shabbat.

Food

Charles Gilbert and Davis, 1580 VFW Pkwy, **West Roxbury,**
Ph: 325-7750. Appetizers, specialty foods, breads and dairy
pastries. RS: Vaad Harabonim of Massachusetts. Closed Shabbat
and Sunday.

Parkway Kosher Meat Market, 1004 W Roxbury Pkwy, **West
Roxbury,** Ph: 469-9100. Fresh meat and poultry. RS: Rabbi M.
Savitsky and Rabbi M. Twersky. Closed Shabbat.

BRAINTREE (See also **BOSTON**)   Area Code (617)

Synagogues

Temple B'nai Shalom (C-US), 41 Storrs Ave, Ph: 843-3687. Rabbi
T. Silverberg. Services: Saturday

Food

Cookies Cook'n, South Shore Plaza, Ph: 843-8803. Cookies, muffins, etc. RS: Vaad Harabonim of Massachusetts

BRIGHTON (See also BOSTON)   Area Code (617)

Synagogues

Temple B'nai Moshe (Independent), 1845 Commonwealth Ave, Ph: 254-3620. Rabbi E. Greenberg. Services: Daily

Congregation Kadimah-Toras Moshe (O-UOJC), 113 Washington St, Ph: 254-1333. Rabbi A. Halbfinger. Services: Daily

Lubavitch Shul (O-Lubav), 239 Chestnut Hill Ave, Ph: 782-8340. Rabbi C. Prus. Services: Daily

Sephardic Community of Greater Boston (Sephardic), 74 Corey Rd, Ph: 739-9181. Rabbi A. Hamaoui. Services: Daily

Eating Out

Kosher Mart, 154 Chestnut Hill Ave, Ph: 254-9529. Meals: l,d. Menus: Both meat and dairy (Glatt meat and cholov Yisroel). Pareve, vegetarian and meat dishes; also pizza. RS: Rabbi Y. Zuber. Closed Shabbat.

Food

Bon Bon Donut Shop, 533 Washington St, Ph: 254-3228. Donuts and muffins. RS: Vaad Harabonim of Massachusetts.

Brighton Kosher Meat Market, 1620 Commonwealth Ave, Ph: 277-0786. Prepared chicken and cold cuts. RS: Rabbi M. Savitsky and Rabbi M. Twersky. Closed Shabbat.

Kosher Mart, 154 Chestnut Hill Ave, Ph: 254-9529. Glatt meat, cholov Yisroel. Also bakery and kosher grocery. Take-out dinners, appetizers and deli-style foods. RS: Rabbi Y. Zuber. Closed Shabbat.

Mikvah

Daughters of Israel, 101 Washington St, Ph: 782-9433.

Lubavitch Mikvah, 239 Chestnut Hill Ave. Call one day in advance, Ph: 782-8340.

BROCKTON   Area Code (508)   J-pop. 8,000

Synagogues

Congregation Agudas Achim (O-UOJC), 144 Belmont Ave, Ph: 583-0717. Rabbi S. Weiss. Services: Daily

Temple Beth Emunah (C-US), Torrey & Pearl Sts, Ph: 583-5810. Rabbi H. Werb. Services: Daily

Temple Israel (R-UAHC), 184 W Elm St, Ph: 587-4130. Rabbi R. Messing. Services: Shabbat

Food (See also **Canton**)

Mikvah (See **Sharon**)

BROOKLINE   (See also **BOSTON**)   Area Code (617)
J-pop. 26,000

Synagogues

Congregation Beth David (O), 64 Corey Rd, Ph: 232-2349. Rabbi I. Twersky. Services: Daily

Congregation Beth Pinchas-New England Chassidic Center (O), 1710 Beacon St, Ph: 734-5100. Grand Rabbi L. Horowitz, Rabbi N. Horowitz. Services: Daily

Temple Beth Zion (C-US), 1566 Beacon St, Ph: 566-8171. Rabbi D. Neiman. Services: Daily

Congregation Chai Odom (O-UOJC), 77 Englewood Ave, Ph: 734-5359. Rabbi S. Margolis. Services: Daily

Temple Emeth (C-US), 194 Grove St, Ph: 469-9400. Rabbi A. Turetz. Services: Daily

Congregation Kehillath Israel (C-US), 384 Harvard St, Ph: 277-9155. Rabbi S. Stern. Services: Daily

Congregation Lubavitch (O-Lubav), 100 Woodcliff Rd, **South Brookline**, Ph: 469-9007. Rabbi R. Liberman. Services: Shabbat

Maimonides School Minyan (O), Philbrick Rd & Boylston St, Ph: 232-4452. Services: Daily

Temple Ohabei Shalom (R-UAHC), 1187 Beacon St, Ph: 277-6610. Rabbi E. Lipoff. Services: Daily

Synagogues cont.

Sephardic Congregation of New England (O), 51 Salisbury Rd, Ph: 964-1526 Rabbi Dr. H. Mazor. Services: Saturday

Sephardic Congregation of Greater Boston (O), 62 Green St, Ph: 277-9429. Rabbi A. Hamaoui. Services: Shabbat and Sunday

Temple Sinai (R-UAHC), 50 Sewall Ave, Ph: 277-5888. Rabbi F. Waldorf. Services: Shabbat

Young Israel of Brookline (O-NCYI), 62 Green St, Ph: 734-0276. Rabbi G. Gewirtz. Services: Daily

Eating Out

Cafe Shalom, 404 Harvard St, Ph: 277-0698. Meals: l,d. Menu: Vegetarian, fish and Israeli dishes, also take-out. RS: Rabbi D. Moskovitz. Closed Shabbat.

Milk Street Cafe, Longwood Galleria, 350 Longwood Ave, Ph: 739-2233. Meals: b,l,d. Menu: Vegetarian and dairy dishes. RS: Rabbi D. Moskovitz. Closed Shabbat and Sunday.

Rubin's Restaurant, 500 Harvard St, Ph: 566-8761. Meals: b,l,d. Menu: Meat, poultry and fish dishes. RS: Vaad Harabonim of Massachusetts. Closed Shabbat.

Food

The Butcherie, 428 Harvard St, Ph: 731-9888. Prepared meat, poultry, fish, side dishes and a complete line of kosher groceries. Packaged Glatt meat available. RS: Rabbi M. Savitsky and Rabbi M. Twersky. Closed Shabbat.

Cookies Cook'n, 1940 Beacon St, Ph: 277-2492. Cookies, muffins, bagels. RS: Vaad Harabonim of Massachusetts. Closed Shabbat.

Eagerman's Bakery, 415 Harvard St, Ph: 566-8771. Smoked fish, breads and dairy pastries. RS: Vaad Harabonim of Massachusetts.

Kupel's Bake and Bagel, 421 Harvard St, Ph: 566-9528. Smoked fish, breads and dairy pastries. RS: Vaad Harabonim of Massachusetts.

Leaven and Earth Bakery, 406 Harvard St, Ph: 566-8798. (Pareve). RS: Vaad Harabonim of Massachusetts. Closed Shabbat.

Rubin's Restaurant, 500 Harvard St, Ph: 566-8761. Prepared meals and deli-style food to go. RS: Vaad Harabonim of Massachusetts. Closed Shabbat.

Ruth's Kitchen, 401 Harvard St, Ph: 734-9810. Take-out: Traditional, oriental, vegetarian. RS: Rabbi D. Moskovitz. Closed Shabbat.

Taam Tov Bakery, 305A Harvard St, Ph: 566-8136. Breads and pastries. RS: Vaad Harabonim of Massachusetts. Closed Shabbat

Accommodations

Beacon Plaza, 1459 Beacon St, Ph: 232-6550.

Holiday Inn, 1200 Beacon St, Ph: 277-1200. Located within walking distance of Young Israel of Brookline.

Terrace Motel, 1650 Commonwealth Ave, Ph: 566-6260. Kitchenettes. Within walking distance of Congregations Beth Pinchas, Chai Odom and Beth David in **Brookline**; Lubavitch, Kadimah-Toras Moshe and B'nai Moshe in **Brighton**.

Day Schools

Maimonides School, 34 Philbrick Rd, Ph: 232-4452.

New England Hebrew Academy-Lubavitch Yeshiva, 9 Prescott St, Ph: 731-5330.

Torah Academy, 11 Williston Rd, Ph: 731-3196.

Bookstores

Israel Book Shop, 410 Harvard St, Ph: 566-7113.

Kolbo, 435-437 Harvard St, Ph: 731-8743.

BURLINGTON   Area Code (617)

Synagogues

Temple Shalom Emeth (R-UAHC), 14-16 Lexington St,
  Ph: 272-2351. Rabbi S. Abramson. Services: Friday

CAMBRIDGE (See also BOSTON)   Area Code (617)

Synagogues

Temple Beth Shalom of Cambridge (Trad), 8 Tremont St,
  Ph: 864-6388. Rabbi M. Holcer. Services: Daily
Hillel House, Harvard University (O, C, Egalitarian), 74 Mount
  Auburn St, Ph: 495-4696. Rabbi S. Finestone, Director. Services:
  Daily

Eating Out

Harvard Hillel Dining Hall, 74 Mount Auburn St, Ph: 876-3535.
  Dinner is served daily. RS: Vaad Harabonim of Massachusetts. A
  three-day advance notice is required for Shabbat meals.
MIT Hillel (cafeteria), Walker Memorial Hall, 312 Memorial Dr, Ph:
  253-2982. Dinner is served weekdays. RS: Vaad Harabonim of
  Massachusetts. Reservations are required for Shabbat meals. Call
  for schedule and fees.

Accommodations

Harvard Motor House, 110 Mount Auburn St, Ph: 864-5200. Five-
  minute walk to the Harvard Hillel House.

CANTON   Area Code (617)

Synagogues

Temple Beth Abraham (C-US), 1301 Washington St, Ph: 828-5250.
  Rabbi W. Hamilton. Services: Daily
Temple Beth David of the South Shore (R-UAHC), 256 Randolph
  St, Ph: 828-2275. Rabbi E. Goldstein. Services: Friday

Food

The Butcherie, 110 Washington St, Ph: 828-3530. Fresh meat and
poultry; deli and groceries. Packaged Glatt meat available. RS:
Rabbi M. Savitzky and Rabbi M. Twersky. Closed Shabbat.

Town Lyne Bakery, 12 Washington St, Ph: 828-2260. Breads and
dairy pastries. RS: Vaad Harabonim of Massachusetts.

Mikvah (See **Sharon**)

CHELMSFORD   Area Code (508)

Synagogues

Congregation Shalom (R-UAHC), Richardson Rd, Ph: 251-8091.
Rabbi T. Bard. Services: Call for schedule.

CHELSEA (See also **BOSTON**)   Area Code (617)

Synagogues

Congregation Agudas Sholom (O-UOJC), 145 Walnut St,
Ph: 884-8668. Reverend A. Benkovitz. Services: Daily

Congregation Ahavas Achim Anshe Sfard (O), 57 Country Rd,
Ph: 889-2016. Rabbi N. Cywiak. Services: Daily

Temple Emanuel (C-US), 60 Tudor St, Ph: 889-1736. Rabbi B.
Rodwogin. Services: Daily

Congregation Shaare Zion (O), 76 Orange St, Ph: 884-0498.
Services: Daily

Congregation Shomrei Linas Hazadek (O), 140 Shurtleff St,
Ph: 884-9443. Rabbi H. Tennebaum. Services: Daily

CHESTNUT HILL (See also **BOSTON**)   Area Code (617)

Synagogues

Temple Emeth (C-US), 194 Grove St, Ph: 469-9400. Rabbi A.
Turetz. Services: Daily

Congregation Lubavitch (O), 100 Woodcliff Rd, Ph: 469-9007.
Rabbi R. Lieberman. Services: Daily

Congregation Mishkan Tefila (C-US), 300 Hammond Pond Pkwy,
Ph: 332-7770. Rabbi R. Yellin. Services: Daily

Food

Cheryl Ann's, 1010 W Roxbury Pkwy, Ph: 469-9241. Breads and
   dairy pastries. RS: Vaad Harabonim of Massachusetts.

CONCORD   Area Code (508)

Synagogues

Kerem Shalom (Independent), 659 Elm St, Ph: 369-1223. Rabbi M.
   Luckens. Services: Call for schedule.

DEDHAM   Area Code (617)

Food

Cookies Express, 252 Bussey St, **East Dedham**, Ph: 461-0044.
   Dairy. RS: Vaad Harabonim of Massachusetts. Closed Shabbat.

DOVER   Area Code (508)

Synagogues

B'nai Jacob Synagogue of Dover (Trad), 7 Donnelly Dr,
   Ph: 785-0990. Rabbi Dr. I. Korff. Services: Saturday

Food (See **Canton**)

Mikvah (See **Sharon**)

EASTON   Area Code (508)

Synagogues

Temple Chayai Shalom (Independent), 9 Mechanic St,
   Ph: 238-6385. Rabbi P. Levenson.

EVERETT (See also **BOSTON**)   Area Code (617)

Synagogues

Congregation Tifereth Israel (Trad), 34 Malden St, Ph: 387-0200.
   Rabbi N. Polen. Services: Daily

FALL RIVER   Area Code (508)   J-pop. 1,780

Synagogues

Congregation Adas Israel (O-UOJC), 1647 Robeson St,
   Ph: 674-9761. Rabbi N. Weinberg. Services: Daily
Temple Beth El (C-US), 385 High St, Ph: 674-3529. Rabbi W.
   Kaufman. Services: Daily

FALMOUTH   Area Code (508)

Synagogues

The Falmouth Jewish Congregation (R-UAHC), 7 Hatchville Rd,
   East Falmouth, Ph: 540-0602. Rabbi E. Lieberman. Services:
   Friday

FITCHBURG   Area Code (508)

Synagogues

Congregation Agudas Achim (Independent), 40 Boutelle St,
   Ph: 342-7704. Rabbi H. Roth. Services: Shabbat

FRAMINGHAM   Area Code (508)   J-pop. 10,800

Synagogues

Chabad House of Framingham (O-Lubav), 74 Joseph Rd,
   Ph: 877-5313. Rabbi Y. Lazaros. Services: Saturday and Sunday
Temple Beth Am (R-UAHC), 300 Pleasant St, Ph: 872-8300. Rabbi
   D. Splansky. Services: Shabbat
Temple Beth Shalom (C-US), Pamela Rd, Ph: 877-2540. Rabbi M.
   Levine. Services: Daily

Food (See also **Canton**)

Bread Basket, 151 Cochituate Rd, Ph: 875-9441. Breads and dairy
   pastries. RS: Vaad Harabonim of Massachusetts.
Cookies Cook'n, Framingham Mall, Rte 30, Ph: 872-1052. Cookies,
   etc. RS: Vaad Harabonim of Massachusetts
Vispy Bakery, 464 Waverly St, Ph: 820-9335. Breads & pastries
   (pareve). RS: Vaad Harabonim of Massachusetts.

Food cont.

Hurwitz Meat Market, 326 Concord, Ph: 875-0481. Meat, poultry, barbecued chicken, frozen foods. RS: Rabbi M. Twersky. Closed Shabbat.

Mikvah (See **Sharon**)

GLOUCESTER   Area Code (508)   J-pop. 450

Synagogues

Temple Ahavath Achim (C-US), 86 Middle St, Ph: 281-0739. Rabbi M. Geller. Services: Shabbat

GREENFIELD   Area Code (413)   J-pop. 900

Synagogues

Temple Israel (C-US), 27 Pierce St, Ph: 773-5884. Rabbi L. Rieser. Services: Shabbat

HAVERHILL   Area Code (508)   J-pop. 1,500

Synagogues

Congregation Anshe Shalom (O), 427 Main St, Ph: 372-2276. Services: Call for schedule

Temple Emanu-El (R-UAHC), 514 Main St, Ph: 373-3861. Rabbi I. Korinow. Services: Daily

Day School

Solomon Schechter Day School of the Merrimack Valley (C), 514 Main St, Ph: 372-4140.

HINGHAM   Area Code (617)

Synagogues

Congregation Sha'aray Shalom (R-UAHC), 1112 Main St, Ph: 749-8103. Rabbi S. Karol. Services: Friday

HOLBROOK   Area Code (617)

174

Synagogues

Temple Beth Shalom (Independent), 95 Plymouth St, Ph: 767-4922. Rabbi E. Hurvitz. Services: Friday

Food (See **Canton**)

HOLYOKE (See also SPRINGFIELD)
Area Code (413)   J-pop. 550

Synagogues

Congregation Rodphey Sholom (O-UOJC), 1800 Northampton St, Ph: 534-5262. Rabbi Y. Tsaidi. Services: Shabbat, Sunday, Monday and Thursday

Congregation Sons of Zion (C-US), 378 Maple St, Ph: 534-3369. Rabbi G. Mazer. Services: Daily

HULL   Area Code (617)

Synagogues

Temple Beth Sholom (C-US), 600 Nantasket Ave, Ph: 925-0091. Rabbi E. Somers. Services: Daily

Temple Israel of Nantasket (Independent), Hadassah Way, Ph: 925-4860. Services: Daily (summer only)

HYANNIS   Area Code (508)

Synagogues

Cape Cod Synagogue (R-UAHC), 145 Winter St, Ph: 775-2988, Rabbi H. Robinson. Services: Friday

HYDE PARK (See BOSTON)

LAWRENCE   Area Code (508)

Synagogues

Congregation Tifereth Anshe Sfard - Sons of Israel (C-US), 492 Lowell St, Ph: 686-0391. Services: Saturday

Congregation Anshai Sholum (O), 411 Hampshire St, Ph: 683-4544. Services: Shabbat

LEOMINSTER   Area Code (508)   J-pop. 700

Synagogues

Congregation Agudat Achim (C-US), 268 Washington St,
Ph: 534-6121. Rabbi J. Gutoff. Services: Shabbat

Food

Cookies Cook'n, Sears Town Mall, Ph: 537-6967. Cookies, muffins,
bagels. RS: Vaad Harabonim of Massachusetts.

LEXINGTON (See also BOSTON)   Area Code (617)

Synagogues

Chabad Center (O-Lubav), 9 Burlington St, Ph: 863-8656. Rabbi A.
Bukiet. Services: Saturday morning and Holidays

Temple Emunah (C-US), 9 Piper Rd, Ph: 861-0300. Rabbi B.
Eisenman. Services: Daily

Temple Isaiah (R-UAHC), 55 Lincoln St, Ph: 862-7160. Rabbi C.
Yales. Services: Shabbat

LONGMEADOW (See SPRINGFIELD)

LOWELL   Area Code (508)   J-pop. 2,000

Synagogues

Temple Beth El (C-US), 105 Princeton Blvd, Ph: 453-0073/7744.
Rabbi J. Layman. Services: Saturday

Temple Emanuel of Merrimack Valley (R-UAHC), 101 W Forest,
Ph: 454-1372. Rabbi E. Gendler. Services: Friday

Montefiore Synagogue (O-UOJC), 460 Westford St, Ph: 459-9400.
Rabbi A. Schwartz. Services: Daily

Food

Greater Lowell Kosher Meat Co-op, c/o Montefiore Synagogue, Ph:
459-9400. To order kosher meat or groceries, call at least two
weeks in advance.

Sun Food, 199 Plains St, Ph: 441-6900. Many kosher items,
including Empire products.

Accommodations

Private accommodations; call Montefiore Synagogue, Ph: 459-9400.

Day School

Merrimack Valley Hebrew Academy, 18 Academy Dr, Ph: 452-0499.

LYNN (See also **BOSTON**)
Area Code (617)   J-pop. North Shore Area - 25,000

Synagogues

Ahavat Sholom (O-UOJC), 151 Ocean St, Ph: 593-9255. Rabbi S. Zaitchik. Services: Daily

Congregation Anshai Sfard (O), 150 S Common St, Ph: 599-7131. Services: Daily

Congregation Chevra Tehillim (O-UOJC), 12 Breed St, Ph: 598-2964. Rabbi Dr. S. Fox. Services: Daily

Mikvah

Mikvat Bnot Yisrael, 151 Ocean St. Contact Mrs. B. Twersky, Ph: 599-7495; Mrs. S. Kaufman, Ph: 599-4902

MALDEN (See also **BOSTON**)   Area Code (617)

Synagogues

Congregation Agudas Achim (Trad), 160 Harvard St, Ph: 322-9380. Rabbi Y. Weinberg. Services: Daily

Congregation Beth Israel (O-UOJC), 10 Dexter St, Ph: 322-5686. Rabbi M. Geller. Services: Daily

Temple Ezrath Israel (C-US), 245 Bryant St, Ph: 322-7205. Rabbi H. Kummer. Services: Shabbat, Sunday, Monday and Thursday

Temple Tifereth Israel (R-UAHC), 539 Salem St, Ph: 322-2794. Rabbi S. Pollack. Services: Daily

Young Israel of Malden (O-NCYI), 45 Holyoke St, Ph: 322-9438. Services: Daily

Food

Joseph's Bakery, 237 Ferry St, Ph: 322-6170. RS: Vaad Harabonim of Massachusetts.

MARBLEHEAD (See also BOSTON)   Area Code (617)

Synagogues

Temple Emanu-El (R-UAHC), 393 Atlantic Ave, Ph: 631-9300.
  Rabbi R. Shapiro. Services: Shabbat and Holidays
Orthodox Congregation of the North Shore (O), 17 Seaview Ave,
  Ph: 631-4925. Services: Shabbat
Temple Sinai of Swampscott—Marblehead (C-US), 1 Community
  Rd, Ph: 631-2763/2244. Rabbi J. Goldberg. Services: Daily

Day School

Eli & Bessie Cohen Hillel Academy (C), 6 Community Rd,
  Ph: 639-2880.

MARLBOROUGH   Area Code (508)

Synagogues

Temple Emanuel (C-US), 150 Berlin Rd, Ph: 485-7565. Rabbi J. B.
  Ehrmann. Services: Call for schedule.

MEDFORD (See also BOSTON)   Area Code (617)

Synagogues

Temple Shalom of Medford (C-US), 475 Winthrop St,
  Ph: 396-3262. Rabbi Y. Wosk. Services: Daily

Food

Donuts With a Difference, 35 Riverside Ave, Ph: 396-1021. Donuts,
  muffins and coffee. RS: Vaad Harabonim of Massachusetts.

MEDWAY   Area Code (508)

Synagogues

Congregation Agudath Achim (C), 73 Village St, Ph: 533-8970.
  Services: second Friday

MELROSE (See also BOSTON)   Area Code (617)

Synagogues

Temple Beth Shalom (R-UAHC), 21 E Foster St, Ph: 665-4520.
Rabbi P. Cohen. Services: Friday

MILFORD   Area Code (508)

Synagogues

Temple Beth Shalom (Independent), 59 Pine St, Ph: 473-1590.
Rabbi H. Lazaros. Services: Shabbat

MILLIS (See also CANTON)   Area Code (508)

Synagogues

Congregation Ael Chunon (O), 334 Village St, Ph: 376-5894.
Services: Saturday

MILTON (See also BOSTON)   Area Code (617)

Synagogues

Congregation B'nai Jacob (O), 100 Blue Hill Pkwy, Ph: 698-9649.
Rabbi N. Korff. Services: Daily
Temple Shalom (C-US), 180 Blue Hill Ave, Ph: 698-3394. Rabbi J.
Weistrop. Services: Daily

NATICK (See also FRAMINGHAM)   Area Code (508)

Synagogues

Chabad Lubavitch (O), 2 Mill St, Ph: 650-1499. Rabbi L. Fogelman.
Services: Saturday
Temple Israel (C-US), 145 Hartford St, Ph: 650-3521. Services:
Daily

Food

Eagerman's Bakery, 810 Worcester Rd, Ph: 235-1092. Smoked fish,
breads and dairy pastries. RS: Vaad Harabonim of Massachusetts.
Roche Brothers, Rte 135, Ph: 655-5540. Some Empire products.
Stop & Shop, 829 Wooster St, Ph: 653-2270. Some Empire
products.

NEEDHAM   Area Code (617)

Synagogues

Temple Aliyah (C-US), 1664 Central Ave, Ph: 444-8522. Rabbi E.
Schoenberg. Services: Daily

Temple Beth Shalom (R-UAHC), 670 Highland Ave, **Needham
Heights,** Ph: 444-0077. Rabbi R. Sonsino. Services: Friday

NEW BEDFORD   Area Code (508)   J-pop. 3,000

Synagogues

Congregation Ahavath Achim (O-UOJC), 385 County St,
Ph: 994-1760. Rabbi B. Hartman. Services: Daily

Tifereth Israel Synagogue (C-US), 145 Brownell Ave,
Ph: 997-3171. Rabbi B. Glassman. Services: Daily

NEWBURYPORT   Area Code (508)   J-pop. 280

Synagogues

Ahavas Achim Congregation (Independent), Olive & Washington
Sts, Ph: 462-2461. Rabbi S. Kenner. Services: Shabbat

NEWTON (See also **BOSTON**)   Area Code (617)   J-pop. 34,000

Synagogues

Congregation Agudas Achim Anshei Sfard (O), 168 Adams St,
Ph: 244-7353. Cantor: Rev. B. Barron. Services: Shabbat and
Holidays

Temple Beth Avodah (R-UAHC), 45 Puddingstone Lane,
Ph: 527-0045. Rabbi R. Miller. Services: Shabbat

Congregation Beth El Atereth Israel (O-UOJC), 561 Ward St,
Newton Centre, Ph: 244-7233. Rabbi G. Segal. Services: Daily

Congregation Chevra Shas (O), 25 Sherbrook Rd, Ph: 969-0925.
Services: Shabbat

Temple Emanuel (C-US), 385 Ward St, Ph: 332-5770. Rabbi S.
Chiel. Services: Daily

Temple Reyim (C-US), 1860 Washington St, Ph: 527-2410. Rabbi
S. Rosenberg. Services: Daily

Congregation Shaarei Tefillah of Newton (O-UOJCA), 35 Morseland Ave, **Newton Centre**, Ph: 527-7637. Services: Daily

Temple Shalom of Newton (R-UAHC), 175 Temple St, Ph: 332-9550. Rabbi D. Whiman. Services: Friday

Shir Hadash (Recon), 1320 Centre St, Ph: 965-6862. Rabbi B. R. Penzner. Services: Call for information.

Eating Out

Jewish Community Center Campus (snack bar), 333 Nahanton St, Ph: 965-7410. Meals: b,l,d. Menu: Sandwiches, soups, salads and hot specials. RS: Vaad Harabonim of Massachusetts. Closed Shabbat.

Food

All You Knead, 316 Walnut St, **Newtonville**, Ph: 244-6252. Lox and cream cheese, breads and dairy pastries. RS: Vaad Harabonim of Massachusetts.

Gordon & Alperin Kosher Meat Market, 552 Commonwealth Ave, Ph: 332-4170. Fresh meat and poultry, deli, prepared foods and kosher groceries. RS: Rabbi M. Savitsky and Rabbi M. Twersky. Closed Shabbat.

Lederman's Bakery, 1223 Centre St, Ph: 527-7896. Breads, pastries and dairy products. RS: Vaad Harabonim of Massachusetts.

Tuler's Bakery, 551 Commonwealth Ave, Ph: 964-5653. Breads and pastries (pareve). RS: Vaad Harabonim of Massachusetts.

Day Schools

The Rashi School (R), The Bigelow Center, 42 Vernon St, Ph: 332-7599.

Solomon Schechter Day School of Greater Boston (C), 60 Stein Circle, **Newton Centre**, Ph: 964-7765.

NEWTON CENTRE (See NEWTON)

NORTH ADAMS   Area Code (413)

Synagogues

Congregation Beth Israel (Independent), 265 Church St, Ph: 663-5830. Rabbi M. Shrager. Services: Daily

NORTHAMPTON   Area Code (413)   J-pop. 700

Synagogues

Congregation B'nai Israel (C-US), 253 Prospect St, Ph: 584-3593.
   Services: Call for schedule.

NORWOOD   Area Code (617)

Synagogues

Temple Shaare Tefilah (C-US), 556 Nichols St, Ph: 762-8670. Rabbi
   P. Barmash. Services: Shabbat, Sunday, Monday and Thursday

ONSET   Area Code (508)

Synagogues

Congregation Beth Israel of Onset (O), Onset Ave and Locust St, Ph:
   295-9185. Services: Daily, July 4 to Labor Day; also High
   Holidays. Winter number: c/o Burt Parker, Ph: (407) 498-2761.

Accommodations

Bridgeview Hotel Apartments, 6 South Water, Ph: 295-9820. This
   hotel is open year-round and features apartments with complete
   kitchens. Packaged kosher food is available upon request.
Onset Pointe Inn, 9 Eagle Way, Ph: 295-8442. Two blocks from
   Congregation Beth Israel.

PEABODY (See also BOSTON)   Area Code (508)

Synagogues

Temple Beth Shalom (R-UAHC), 489 Lowell St, Ph: 535-2100.
   Rabbi A. Nemitoff. Services: Shabbat
Temple Ner Tamid (C-US), 368 Lowell St, Ph: 532-1293. Rabbi A.
   Morhaim. Services: Daily
Congregation Sons of Israel (Trad), Park & Spring Sts,
   Ph: 531-7576. Services: Saturday, Sunday and Holidays
Congregation Tifereth Israel (Sephardic), 8 Pierpont St,
   Ph: 531-8135. Rabbi D. Pikelny. Services: special observances
   and High Holidays

Food

Anthony's, 4 Lake St, **West Peabody**, Ph: 535-5335. Breads and
   dairy pastries. RS: Vaad Harabonim of Massachusetts.

PITTSFIELD   Area Code (413)   J-pop. Berkshire County 3,100

Synagogues

Ahavath Sholom Synagogue (O), 177 Robbins Ave, Ph: 442-6609/8852. Services: Saturday

Temple Anshe Amunim (R-UAHC), 26 Broad St, Ph: 442-5910. Rabbi A. Berg. Services: Shabbat

Congregation Knesset Israel (C-US), 16 Colt Rd, Ph: 445-4872. Rabbi A. Rulnick. Services: Daily

PLYMOUTH   Area Code (508)   J-pop. 500

Synagogues

Congregation Beth Jacob (R-UAHC), 8 Pleasant St, Ph: 746-1575. Rabbi L. Silverman. Services: Friday

QUINCY (See also **BOSTON**)   Area Code (617)

Synagogues

Congregation Adas Shalom (Independent), 435 Adams St, Ph: 471-1818. Rabbi T. Silverberg. Services: Shabbat

Temple Beth El (Independent), 1001 Hancock St, Ph: 479-4309. Rabbi D. Jacobs. Services: Daily

Beth Israel Synagogue (O-UOJC), 33 Grafton St, Ph: 472-6796. Rabbi J. Mann. Services: Daily

RANDOLPH   Area Code (617)

Synagogues

Temple Beth Am (C-US), 871 N Main St, Ph: 963-0440. Rabbi L. Weiss. Services: Daily

Young Israel Kehillath Jacob of Mattapan-Randolph (O-NCYI), 374 N Main St, Ph: 986-6461. Rabbi B. Shaffer. Services: Daily

Food (See also **Canton**)

Randolph Kosher Meat Market, 41 N Main St, Randolph Center, Ph: 961-2931. Fresh meats and poultry, a few frozen items. RS: Rabbi M. Savitsky and Rabbi M. Twersky. Closed Shabbat.

184

Zeppy's Bakery, 937 N Main St, Ph: 963-9837. Smoked fish, breads and dairy pastries. RS: Vaad Harabonim of Massachusetts.

Mikvah (See **Sharon**)

Bookstore

Davidson's Hebrew Book Store, 1106 N Main St, Ph: 961-4989.

REVERE (See also **BOSTON**)   Area Code (617)

Synagogues

Congregation Ahavas Achim Anshei Sfard (O), 89 Walnut Ave, Ph: 289-1026. Services: Daily

Temple B'nai Israel (Independent), 1 Wave Ave, Ph: 284-8388. Rabbi M. Sokoll. Services: Shabbat, Sunday, Monday and Thursday.

Congregation Tifereth Israel (O), 43 Nahant Ave, Ph: 284-9255. Rabbi A. Teitel. Services: Daily

Food

Liberman's Bake-ree, 107 Shirley Ave, Ph: 289-0041. Breads and dairy pastries. RS: Vaad Harabonim of Massachusetts.

Myer's Kosher Kitchen, 176 Shirley Ave, Ph: 289-2063. Prepared chicken and meat dishes, soups, side dishes and groceries. RS: Rabbi M. Twersky and Rabbi S. Zaitzchik. Closed Shabbat.

ROSLINDALE   Area Code (617)

Food

Gooches, 4140 Washington St, Ph: 325-3298. Bakery (pareve). RS: Vaad Harabonim of Massachusetts.

SALEM (See also **BOSTON**)   Area Code (508)

Synagogues

Temple Shalom of Salem (C-US), 287 Lafayette St, Ph: 741-4880. Rabbi S. Kenner. Services: Shabbat, Sunday, Monday and Thursday

SAUGUS   Area Code (617)

Synagogues

Congregation Ahavas Shalom (C), 343 Central Ave, Ph: 233-1357.
   Rabbi E. Goldstein. Services: High Holidays

SHARON   Area Code (617)

Synagogues

Congregation Adath Sharon (C-US), 18 Harding St, Ph: 784-2517.
   Rabbi L. Berkowitz. Services: Shabbat and Sunday
Chabad Center, (Lubav), 10 Worcester Rd, Ph: 784-8167. Rabbi C.
   Wolosow. Services: Daily
Temple Israel (C-US), 125 Pond St, Ph: 784-3986. Rabbi B. Starr.
   Services: Daily
Temple Sinai of Sharon (R-UAHC), 100 Ames St, Ph: 784-6081.
   Rabbi H. Kosovske. Services: Shabbat
Young Israel of Sharon (O-NCYI), 9 Dunbar St, Ph: 784-6112.
   Rabbi M. Sendor. Services: Daily

Mikvah

South Shore Area Mikvah, 9 Dunbar St, corner Bradford Ave,
   Ph: 784-7444.

Day School

Striar Hebrew Academy of Sharon, 162 N Main St, Ph: 784-8700.

SOMERVILLE (See also BOSTON)   Area Code (617)

Synagogues

Temple B'nai B'rith (Independent), 201 Central St, Ph: 625-0333.
   Services: Saturday
Havurat Shalom Community (Independent), 113 College Ave,
   Ph: 623-3376. Services: Shabbat

Food

Freedman's Baking Company, 65 Foley St, Ph: 623-5500. Breads

(pareve) and pastries (dairy). RS: Vaad Harabonim of
Massachusetts.

La Ronga, 599 Somerville Ave, Ph: 625-8600. Bakery (pareve). RS:
Vaad Harabonim of Massachusetts.

SOUTHBRIDGE   Area Code (508)

Synagogues

Congregation Ahavath Zion (Independent), 69 Eastford Rd,
Ph: 765-5797.

SPRINGFIELD (See also LONGMEADOW)
Area Code (413)   J-pop. 11,000

Synagogues

Temple Beth El (C-US), 979 Dickinson St, Ph: 733-4149. Rabbi H.
Schwartz. Services: Daily

Congregation Beth Israel (O-UOJC), 1280 Williams St,
Longmeadow, Ph: 567-3210/7354. Rabbi E. Slepoy. Services:
Daily

Congregation B'nai Jacob (C-US), 2 Eunice Dr, **Longmeadow**, Ph:
567-0058. Rabbi G. Greene. Services: Shabbat, Sunday, Monday
and Thursday

Congregation Kesser Israel (O), 19 Oakland St, Ph: 732-8492. Rabbi
I. Edelman. Services: Daily

Kodimoh Synagogue (O-UOJC), 124 Sumner Ave, Ph: 781-0171.
Rabbi E. Rosenzveig. Services: Daily

Synagogue of Lubavitcher Yeshiva (O-Lubav), 1148 Converse St,
Longmeadow, Ph: 567-8665. Rabbi D. Edelman. Services: Call
for schedule.

Temple Sinai (R-UAHC), 1100 Dickinson St, Ph: 736-3619. Rabbi
M. Shapiro. Services: Friday

Eating Out

Abe's, 907 Sumner Ave, Ph: 733-3504. Sandwiches to eat in or take-
out. RS: Springfield Vaad Hakashruth. Closed Shabbat.

Eating Out cont.

Harvest Tyme, 1312 Memorial Ave, **West Springfield**, Ph: 733-7375. Meals: l,d. Menu: (Vegetarian) Soups, salads, lasagna, shepherd's pie, sandwiches, desserts. RS: Springfield Vaad Hakashruth.

Food

Abe's Kosher Meat Market, 907 Sumner Ave, Ph: 733-3504. Packaged deli, fresh and frozen meat and poultry. RS: Springfield Vaad Hakashruth. Closed Shabbat.

Belmont Waldbaum's, 355 Belmont Ave, Ph: 732-3866. Bakery (pareve and dairy). RS: Springfield Vaad Hakashruth.

Berman's Bakery, 1500 Main St, Ph: 739-7556. RS: Springfield Vaad Hakashruth (baked goods only).

Chocolate Works, 503 Sumner Ave, Ph: 733-1201. Pareve and dairy candies. RS: Springfield Vaad Hakashruth (approved items only).

Gus & Paul Bakery, 1209 Sumner Ave, Ph: 782-5710. Pareve and dairy. RS: Springfield Vaad Hakashruth.

Harvest Tyme Natural Foods, 1312 Memorial Ave, **West Springfield**, Ph: 733-7375. Deli and bakery, take-out. RS: Springfield Vaad Hakashruth.

Kimmell's Bagel Shop, 786 Williams St, **Longmeadow**, Ph: 567-3304. Bagels. RS: Springfield Vaad Hakashruth.

Sweet Tooth Goodie Shop, 2341 Boston Rd, **Wilbraham**, Ph: 596-9239. Bakery. Cakes, cookies, breads. RS: Springfield Vaad Hakashruth.

Mikvah

Israel Mikvah, 1104 Converse St, **Longmeadow**. Call Esther Chaitovsky, Ph: 736-1009, or Mikvah, Ph: 567-1607.

Day Schools

Heritage Academy, 594 Converse St, **Longmeadow**, Ph: 567-1517.
Lubavitcher Yeshiva Academy, 1148 Converse St, **Longmeadow**, Ph: 567-8665/7001.

STONEHAM (See also **BOSTON**)   Area Code (617)

Synagogues

Temple Judea (C-US), 188 Franklin St, Ph: 665-5752. Rabbi J. Stern. Services: Call for schedule.

STOUGHTON   Area Code (617)

Synagogues

Congregation Ahavath Torah (C-US), 1179 Central St, Ph: 344-8733. Rabbi H. Schechter. Services: Daily

Congregation Klal Yisrael (Independent), 1819 Central St, Ph: 341-8440. Rabbi D. L. Kaplan.

Shaloh Torah (O), 50 Ethel Way, Ph: 344-6334. Rabbi M. Gurkov.

Eating Out

Catering by Dreams, Striar Jewish Community Center, 445 Central St, Ph: 341-2016. Meals: Mon.-Thur. b,l,d.; Fri.b,l. Sun. b,l. Menu (Dairy): Soup, sandwiches, salads, falafel etc. RS: Vaad Harabonim of Massachusetts. Closed Shabbat.

Food (See also Canton)

Ruth's Bake Shop, 987 Central St, Ph: 344-8993. Breads, pastries and dairy items. RS: Vaad Harabonim of Massachusetts. Closed Monday.

Mikvah (See Sharon)

Day School

South Area Solomon Schechter Day School (C), 1179 Central St, Ph: 341-8040.

SUDBURY   Area Code (508)

Synagogues

Congregation Beth El of the Sudbury River Valley (R-UAHC), Hudson Rd, Ph: 443-9622. Rabbi L. Kushner. Services: Shabbat

Congregation B'nai Torah (R), 80 Woodside Rd, Ph: 443-2082. Rabbi R. Firestone. Services: Friday

SWAMPSCOTT (See also **BOSTON**)   Area Code (617)

Synagogues

Temple Beth El (C-US), 55 Atlantic Ave, Ph: 599-8005. Rabbi E.
  Weinsberg. Services: Daily
Temple Israel (C-US), 837 Humphrey St, Ph: 595-6635. Rabbi S.
  Shanblatt. Services: Daily

Food

Newman's Bakery, 248 Humphrey St, Ph: 592-1550. Salads,
  quiches, pizza, cakes and dairy pastries. RS: Vaad Harabonim of
  Massachusetts.

TAUNTON   Area Code (508)   J-pop. 1,200

Synagogues

Congregation Agudath Achim (C-US), 36 Winthrop St,
  Ph: 822-3230. Rabbi B. Lefkowitz. Services: Shabbat

VINEYARD HAVEN   Area Code (508)

Synagogues

Martha's Vineyard Hebrew Center (R-UAHC), Centre St,
  Ph: 693-0745. Rabbi R. Helman. Services: Friday

WAKEFIELD (See also **BOSTON**)   Area Code (617)

Synagogues

Temple Emanuel (Independent), 120 Chestnut St, Ph: 245-1886.
  Rabbi B. Spielman. Services: Shabbat

WALTHAM (See also **BOSTON**)   Area Code (617)

Synagogues

Temple Beth Israel (Independent), 25 Harvard St, Ph: 894-5146.
  Rabbi R. Meirowitz. Services: Daily

Eating Out

Brandeis University, Sherman Cafeteria, Ph: 736-4350. The cafeteria is open weekdays for breakfast, lunch and dinner. RS: Rabbi J. Mann. For Friday night meals, call Hillel for reservations and fees, Ph: 736-3570.

WAYLAND   Area Code (508)

Synagogues

Temple Shir Tikvah (R-UAHC), 141 Boston Post Rd, Ph: 358-5312. Rabbi H. Blumberg. Services: Friday

WELLESLEY (See also BOSTON)   Area Code (617)

Synagogues

Temple Beth Elohim (R-UAHC), 10 Bethel Rd, **Wellesley Hills**, Ph: 235-8419. Rabbi R. Weiss. Services: Shabbat

WEST ROXBURY (See BOSTON)

WESTBORO   Area Code (508)

Synagogues

Congregation B'nai Shalom (R-UAHC), 117 E Main St, Ph: 366-7191. Rabbi D. Hachen. Services: Friday

WESTWOOD   Area Code (617)

Synagogues

Temple Beth David (R-UAHC), Clapboardtree & Pond Sts, Ph: 769-5270. Rabbi H. Zoob. Services: Friday

WINCHESTER   Area Code (617)

Synagogues

Temple Shir Tikvah (R-UAHC), 21 Church St, Ph: 729-1188 or 643-8282. Rabbi D. Kudan. Services: Friday

WINTHROP (See also BOSTON)   Area Code (617)

Synagogues

Congregation Tifereth Abraham (O), 283 Shirley St, Ph: 846-5063. Reverend A. Zippor. Services: Saturday

Temple Tifereth Israel (C-US), 93 Veterans Rd, Ph: 846-1390. Rabbi Dr. I. Schreier. Services: Daily

Food

Fabiano's Bakery, 7 Somerset Ave, Ph: 846-5946. Breads and dairy pastries. RS: Vaad Harabonim of Massachusetts.

WOBURN   Area Code (617)

Food

Cookies Cook'n, 300 Mishawum Rd, Woburn Mall, Ph: 935-8087. Cookies, muffins, bagels. RS: Vaad Harabonim of Massachusetts.

WORCESTER   Area Code (508)   J-pop. 10,100

Synagogues

Congregation Beth Israel (C-US), 15 Jamesbury, Ph: 756-6204. Rabbi J. Rosenbaum. Services: Daily

Congregation Beth Judah—Young Israel (O-NCYI), 889 Pleasant St, Ph: 754-3681. Services: Shabbat and Sunday

Temple Emanuel (R-UAHC), 280 May St, Ph: 755-1257. Rabbi S. Gershon. Services: Daily

Congregation Shaarai Torah East (O), 32 Providence St, Ph: 756-3276. Services: Daily

Congregation Shaarai Torah West (O-UOJC), 835 Pleasant St, Ph: 791-0013. Services: Daily

Temple Sinai (R-UAHC), 661 Salisbury St, Ph: 755-2519. Rabbi S. Bernstein. Services: Friday

Tifereth Israel—Sons of Jacob Chabad (O-Lubav), 22 Newton Ave, Ph: 752-0904. Rabbi H. Fogelman. Services: Daily

Eating Out

Clark University, Jewish Student Coalition (cafeteria), Dana

Commons, 950 Main St. Weekday and Shabbat meals are served
regularly. RS: Worcester Vaad Hakashrut, Rabbi H. Fogelman.
For more information call 793-7205.

Yeshiva Achei T'mimim (cafeteria), 22 Newton Ave, Ph: 752-0904.
Meals: b,l,d. Call for reservations.

Food

Cookies Cook'n, Auburn Mall, **Auburn**, Ph: 832-6046. Cookies,
muffins, bagels. RS: Vaad Harabonim of Massachusetts.

Accommodations

For Shabbat hospitality; call Chabad Lubavitch, Ph: 752-0904.

Mikvah

Worcester Mikvah, 4 Huntley St, Ph: 756-6483 or Tammy Witker,
Ph: 752-7749.

Day Schools

Solomon Schechter Day School (C), Jamesbury Dr, Ph: 799-7888.
Yeshiva Achei Tmimim Academy, 22 Newton Ave, Ph: 752-0904.

Michigan

ANN ARBOR   Area Code (313)   J-pop. 4,500

Synagogues

Temple Beth Emeth (R-UAHC), 2309 Packard Rd, Ph: 665-4744.
Rabbi R. Levy. Services: Friday

Beth Israel Congregation (C-US), 2000 Washtenaw, Ph: 665-9897.
Rabbi R. Dobrusin. Services: Daily

B'nai B'rith Hillel Foundation at the University of Michigan (R, C,
O), 1429 Hill St, Ph: 769-0500. Services: Shabbat. Call for
schedule.

Chabad House (O-Lubav), 715 Hill St, Ph: 99-LEARN. Rabbi A.
Goldstein. Services: Daily

Eating Out

Chabad House, 715 Hill St, Ph: 99-LEARN. Shabbat and holiday
    dinners are served following evening and morning services. For
    information and reservations contact Rabbi A. Goldstein.
B'nai B'rith Hillel Foundation at the University of Michigan, 1429
    Hill St, Ph: 769-0500. Kosher dinners are served Monday through
    Friday. For RS and other information contact Michael Brooks,
    Director.

Food

Bush's Value Land, 2240 S Main, Ph: 663-2960. Empire poultry.
Farmer Jack, 2103 W Stadium Blvd, Ph: 668-6653. Kosher cheeses
    and Empire poultry.

Accommodations

Private accommodations and for Shabbat hospitality; call Rabbi A.
    Goldstein at the Chabad House, Ph: 99-LEARN.

Mikvah

Mikvah Yisroel, 715 Hill St. Call Mrs. E. Goldstein, Ph: 769-3078.

Day School

Hebrew Day School of Ann Arbor (C), 2937 Birch Hollow Dr,
    Ph: 971-4633

BAY CITY   Area Code (517)   J-pop. 280

Synagogues

Temple Israel—Bay City (C-US), 2300 Center Ave, Ph: 893-7811.
    Rabbi R. Scott. Services: Shabbat

BENTON HARBOR   Area Code (616)

Synagogues

Temple B'nai Shalom (C-US), 2050 Broadway, Ph: 925-8021.
    Rabbi A. Levenson. Services: Friday

BIRMINGHAM (See also **OAK PARK**)   Area Code (313)

Synagogues

Temple Beth El (R-UAHC), 7400 Telegraph Rd, Ph: 851-1100.
Rabbi J. I. Cook. Services: Shabbat

Day School

Beth Jacob School for Girls, 32605 Bellvine Trail, Ph: 644-3113.

DETROIT (See also **OAK PARK** and **SOUTHFIELD**)

Area Code (313)   Greater Detroit J-pop. 70,000

Synagogues

Borman Hall Synagogue (O), 19100 W Seven Mile Rd,
Ph: 532-7112. Rabbi A. Gardin. Services: Weekdays

Downtown Synagogue (C), 1457 Griswold, Ph: 961-9328. Rabbi N.
Gamze. Services: Daily
T'chiya Congregation (Recon-FRCH), 1404 Nicolet Pl,
Ph: 963-5021. Services: Call for schedule.

Eating Out

B'nai B'rith Hillel Foundation - Wayne State University, Room 667,
Student Center Bldg., 5221 Gullen Mall, Ph: 577-3459. Lunch is
served Monday - Friday between 11:00 and 2:00 (meat and
pareve). Also take-out. RS: Rabbi L. Finkelman, Director.

EAST LANSING   Area Code (517)

Synagogues

Shaarey Zedek (C-US,R-UAHC), 1924 Coolidge Rd,
Ph: 351-3570. Rabbi M. Hoffman. Services: Friday

FARMINGTON HILLS (See also **OAK PARK**)
Area Code (313)

Synagogues

Adat Shalom (C-US), 29901 Middlebelt Rd, Ph: 851-5100. Rabbi
E. Spectre. Services: Daily

Synagogues cont.

The Birmingham Temple (Humanistic), 28611 W Twelve Mile Rd,
    Ph: 477-1410. Rabbi S. Wine. Services: Friday
Chabad House of Farmington Hills (O-Lubav), 32000 Middlebelt
    Rd, Ph: 855-2910. Rabbi C. Bergstein. Services: Shabbat

Accommodations

Private accommodations; call Rabbi C. Bergstein, Ph: 855-2910.

Day School

Hillel Day School of Metropolitan Detroit (C), 32200 Middlebelt
    Rd, Ph: 851-2394.

FLINT   Area Code (313)   J-pop. 2,000

Synagogues

Temple Beth El (R-UAHC), 501 S Ballenger Way, Ph: 232-3138.
    Rabbi P. Tuchman. Services: Friday
Congregation Beth Israel (C-US, R-UAHC), G-5240 Calkins Rd,
    Ph: 732-6310. Rabbi P. Reis. Services: Daily
Chabad House of Eastern Michigan, 5385 Calkins Rd,
    Ph: 733-3779. Rabbi Y. Weingarten. Services: Shabbat and
    Holidays

Acccommodations

Private accommodations; call Chabad House of Eastern Michigan,
    Rabbi Y. Weingarten, Ph: 733-3779 or 230-0770.

Mikvah

Chabad House; new mikvah, to be completed by summer 1991,
    Ph: 733-3779.

GRAND RAPIDS   Area Code (616)   J-pop. 1,500

Synagogues

Ahavas Israel Synagogue (C-US), 2727 Michigan St NE,
    Ph: 949-2840. Rabbi M. Rascoe. Services: Daily
Chabad House of Western Michigan (O-Lubav), 2615 Michigan

Ave. NE, Ph: 957-0770. Rabbi Y. Weingarten. Services: Shabbat
and Rosh Chodesh

Temple Emanuel (R-UAHC), 1715 Fulton St, Ph: 459-5976. Rabbi
A. Lewis. Services: Friday

Food

D & W, Breton & Burton SE, Ph: 957-0733. Empire poultry.

Accommodations

Private accommodations; call Chabad House of Western Michigan,
Ph: 957-0770.

Mikvah

Chabad House of Western Michigan. Call Mrs. Sarah Weingarten,
Ph: 949-6788.

JACKSON   Area Code (517)   J-pop. 325

Synagogues

Temple Beth Israel (R-UAHC), 801 W Michigan Ave,
Ph: 784-3862. Rabbi A. Ponn. Services: Friday

KALAMAZOO   Area Code (616)   J-pop. 1,000

Synagogues

Temple B'nai Israel (R), 2224 Ridge Rd, Ph: 343-1790. Services:
Call for schedule.

Congregation of Moses (C-US), 2501 Stadium Dr, Ph: 342-5463.
Rabbi H. Spivak. Services: Shabbat

LANSING   Area Code (517)   J-pop. 2,100

Synagogues

Congregation Kehillat Israel (C-US), 2014 Forest Rd,
Ph: 882-0049. Services: Saturday

LIVONIA   Area Code (313)

Synagogues

Livonia Jewish Congregation (C), 31840 W Seven Mile Rd, Ph: 477-8974. Rabbi M. Gordon. Services: Shabbat

MIDLAND   Area Code (517)   J-pop. 200

Synagogues

Temple Beth El (C-US), 2505 Bay City Rd, Ph: 496-3720. Rabbi R. Scott. Services: Friday

MOUNT PLEASANT   Area Code (517)   J-pop. 120

Synagogues

Temple Benjamin (C-US), 502 N Brown St, Ph: 773-7711. Services: Friday

MUSKEGON   Area Code (616)   J-pop. 235

Synagogues

Temple B'nai Israel (R-UAHC), 391 W Webster St, Ph: 722-2702. Rabbi A. Alpert. Services: Call for schedule

OAK PARK (See also SOUTHFIELD and WEST BLOOMFIELD) Area Code (313)

For kosher information in the Greater Detroit area, call the Council of Orthodox Rabbis, Ph: 559-5005; 5006.

Synagogues

Beth Shalom (C-US), 14601 W Lincoln Rd, Ph: 547-7970. Rabbi D. Nelson. Services: Daily

B'nai Israel—Beth Yehuda (O), 15400 W Ten Mile Rd, Ph: 967-3969. Rabbi Y. Sperka. Services: Daily

B'nai Zion (O), 15250 W Nine Mile Rd, Ph: 968-2414. Rabbi S. Gruskin. Services: Daily

Congregation Dovid Ben Nuchim (O), 14800 W Lincoln Rd, Ph: 968-9784. Rabbi C. Grubner. Services: Daily

Temple Emanu-El (R-UAHC), 14450 W Ten Mile Rd,
   Ph: 967-4026. Rabbi L. Steinger. Services: Shabbat
Kollel Institute of Greater Detroit - B'nai Jacob (O), 15230 Lincoln
   Rd, Ph: 968-0764. Rabbi M. Schwab. Services: Daily
Lubavitch Center Synagogue (O-Lubav), 14000 W Nine Mile Rd,
   Ph: 737-7000. Rabbi Y. Kagan. Services: Daily
Congregation Shaarey Shomayim (O), 15110 W Ten Mile Rd
   (Jewish Community Center), Ph: 547-8555. Rabbi L. Goldman.
   Services: Daily
Young Israel of Greenfield (O-NCYI), 15140 W Ten Mile Rd,
   Ph: 967-3655. Rabbi R. Drucker. Services: Daily
Young Israel of Oak Woods (O-NCYI), 24061 Coolidge Hwy,
   Ph: 398-1177. Rabbi E. Cohen. Services: Daily

Eating Out

Mertz "Café Katon", 23005 Coolidge Rd, Ph: 547-3581. Meals: l,d.
   Menu: Pizza and dairy dishes. RS: Council of Orthodox Rabbis
   of Greater Detroit. Closed Shabbat.

Sperber's "Karry-Out," 25250 Greenfield Rd, Ph: 967-1161. Some
   tables. Meals: l,d. Menu: (Glatt meat) Deli, soups, entrees. RS:
   Council of Orthodox Rabbis of Greater Detroit. Closed Shabbat.

Food

J. Cohen & Son Kosher Meat Market, 26035 Coolidge Rd,
   Ph: 547-4121. RS: Council of Orthodox Rabbis of Greater
   Detroit. Closed Shabbat.

Dexter Davison Kosher Meat Market, 13181 W Ten Mile Rd,
   Ph: 548-6800. RS: Council of Orthodox Rabbis of Greater
   Detroit. Closed Shabbat.

Farmer Jack, 13115 W Ten Mile Rd, Ph: 542-1920. Cholov Yisroel
   products and kosher packaged meats. Also houses Tel Aviv
   (Glatt) kosher meat market under RS: Council of Orthodox
   Rabbis of Greater Detroit.

Lakewood Specialty, 25250 Greenfield Rd, Ph: 967-2021. Complete
   kosher grocery including meat, fish and cheeses. RS: Council of
   Orthodox Rabbis of Greater Detroit. Closed Shabbat.

199

Mansour's Market, 22175 Coolidge Rd, Ph: 399-4771. Cholov Yisroel products.

Mertz "Café Katon," 23005 Coolidge Rd, Ph: 547-3581. Small dairy grocery. Cholov Yisroel products. RS: Council of Orthodox Rabbis of Greater Detroit. Closed Shabbat.

Sperber's "Karry Out," 25250 Greenfield Rd, Ph: 967-1161. Take-out (Glatt meat). RS: Council of Orthodox Rabbis of Greater Detroit. Closed Shabbat.

Strictly Kosher Meat Market, 26020 Greenfield Rd, Ph: 967-4222. RS: Council of Orthodox Rabbis of Greater Detroit. Closed Shabbat.

Superior Kosher Meat Market, 23057 Coolidge Rd, Ph 547-3900. RS: Council of Orthodox Rabbis of Greater Detroit. Closed Shabbat.

Zeman's New York Bakery, 25258 Greenfield Rd, Ph: 967-3905. Breads and pastries (pareve). RS: Council of Orthodox Rabbis of Greater Detroit. Closed Shabbat.

Accommodations

Private hospitality; call or write:

Rabbi C. Grubner, 14100 Sherwood St, 48237, Ph: 398-1017;

Rabbi S. Gruskin, 23600 Kenosha Ave, 48237, Ph: 548-3876;

Mrs. Y. Kagan, Chabad House, Ph: 542-5058.

Southfield Hilton, 17017 W Nine Mile Rd, **Southfield**, Ph: 557-4800. 1¼-mile walk to Lubavitch Center Synagogue.

Mikvah

Mikvah Israel, 15150 W Ten Mile Rd, Ph: 967-3655 or Mrs. Lang, Ph: 967-0289.

Bookstore

Borenstein's, 25242 Greenfield Rd, Ph: 967-3920.

PETOSKEY   Area Code (616)

Synagogues

Congregation B'nai Israel (R-UAHC), Waukazoo and Michigan, Ph:

347-8740. Rabbi D. Shafran. Services: Shabbat (summers)

PONTIAC (See also OAK PARK)   Area Code (313)

Synagogues

Temple Beth Jacob (R-UAHC), 79 Elizabeth Lake Rd, Ph: 332-3212. Rabbi R. Weiss. Services: Friday

SAGINAW   Area Code (517)   J-pop. 200

Synagogues

Congregation Beth El (R), 100 W Washington Ave #200, Ph: 754-5171. Services: Call for schedule.

Temple B'nai Israel (C-US), 1424 S Washington Ave, Ph: 753-5230. Rabbi R. Scott. Services: Friday

SOUTHFIELD (See also OAK PARK)   Area Code (313)

Synagogues

Beth Achim (C-US), 21100 W Twelve Mile Rd, Ph: 352-8670. Rabbi M. Arm. Services: Daily

Beth Jacob—Mogain Abraham (O), 15751 W Lincoln Dr, Ph: 557-6750. Rabbi D. Loketch. Services: Daily

Congregation Beth Tifilo Emanuel Tikvah (O-UOJC), 24225 Greenfield Rd, Ph: 559-5022. Rabbi L. Levin. Services: Daily

B'nai David (Trad), 24350 Southfield Rd, Ph: 557-8210. Rabbi M. Yolkut. Services: Daily

Congregation Shaarey Zedek (C-US), 27375 Bell Rd, Ph: 357-5544. Rabbi I. Groner. Services: Daily

Shomrey Emunah (O), 25451 Southfield Rd, Ph: 559-1533. Rabbi S. Zachariash. Services: Daily

Young Israel of Southfield (O-NCYI), 27705 Lahser Rd, Ph: 358-0154. Rabbi E. Goldberg. Services: Daily

Eating Out

Dunkin' Donuts, 28799 Northwestern Hwy, Ph: 354-1614. Menu: (Dairy) Donuts, soup, sandwiches. RS: Council of Orthodox Rabbis of Greater Detroit.

Eating Out cont.

Sara's Kosher Deli, 15600 W Ten Mile Rd, Ph: 443-2425. Meals: l,d. Menu: (Glatt meat) Deli and full dinners. Everything available for take-out. RS: Council of Orthodox Rabbis of Greater Detroit. Closed Shabbat.

Food

Farmer Jack, 29800 Southfield Rd, Ph: 559-6121. Kosher section including cholov Yisroel milk. Also houses Tel Aviv (Glatt) kosher meat market under RS: Council of Orthodox Rabbis of Greater Detroit

Farmer Jack, 27155 Greenfield Rd, Ph: 569-0202. Some kosher cheeses.

Harvard Row Kosher Meat Market, 21780 W Eleven Mile Rd, Ph: 356-5110. RS: Council of Orthodox Rabbis of Greater Detroit. Closed Shabbat.

Zeman's New York Bakery, 30760 Southfield Rd, Ph: 646-7159. Breads and pastries (pareve and dairy). RS: Council of Orthodox Rabbis of Greater Detroit. Closed Shabbat.

Day School

The Akiba Hebrew Day School, 27700 Southfield Rd, **Lathrup Village**, Ph: 552-9690.

Yeshiva Beth Yehuda, 15751 W. Lincoln Dr, Ph: 557-6750.

Bookstore

Spitzer's, 21770 W Eleven Mile Rd, Ph: 356-6080.

TRAVERSE CITY   Area Code (616)

Synagogues

Temple Beth El (C, R), 311 W Park St, Ph: 946-1913. Rabbi A. Sleutelberg. Services: Call for schedule.

Food

Foggeralli's, 424 W Front St, Ph: 941-7651. Some kosher products.

TRENTON (See also OAK PARK)   Area Code (313)

Synagogues

Beth Isaac Synagogue (C), 2730 Edsel Dr, Ph: 675-0355. Services:
Friday

TROY   Area Code (313)

Synagogues

Congregation Shir Tikvah (R), 3633 W. Big Beaver, Ph: 643-6520.
Rabbi A. Sleutelberg. Services: Call for schedule.

WEST BLOOMFIELD (See also OAK PARK)
Area Code (313)

Synagogues

Bais Chabad Torah Center of West Bloomfield (O-Lubav), 5595 W
Maple Rd, Ph: 855-6170. Rabbi M. Silberberg. Services: Daily

Beth Abraham Hillel Moses (C), 5075 W Maple, Ph: 851-6880.
Rabbi I. Schnipper. Services: Daily

B'nai Israel (C), 4200 Walnut Lake Rd, Ph: 681-5353 or 681-6430.
Rabbi S. Kirshner. Services: Call for schedule.

Congregation B'nai Moshe (C-US), 6800 Drake Rd, Ph: 788-0600.
Services: Daily

Temple Israel (R-UAHC), 5725 Walnut Lake Rd, Ph: 661-5700.
Rabbi M. Syme. Services: Shabbat

Temple Kol Ami (R-UAHC), 5085 Walnut Lake Rd, Ph: 661-0040.
Rabbi N. Roman. Services: Friday

Ohel Moed of Shomrey Emunah (O), 6191 Farmington Rd,
Ph: 737-2756. Rabbi E. Jundef. Services: Shabbat and Holidays

Temple Shir Shalom (R-UAHC), 5642 Maple Rd, Ph: 737-8700.
Rabbi D. Schwartz. Services: Shabbat

Eating Out

Sperber North at J.C.C., 6600 W Maple Rd, Ph: 661-5151. Meals:
l,d. Menu (Glatt meat) Soups, salad, entrees, desserts.
RS: Council of Orthodox Rabbis of Greater Detroit. Closed
Shabbat.

Food

Aviva's Specialty, 5848 Applewood #1409, Ph: 932-4161. Candies, nuts, fruit baskets. RS: Council of Orthodox Rabbis of Greater Detroit. Closed Shabbat.

Farmer Jack, 6565 Orchard Lake Rd, Ph: 851-3850. Kosher section including cholov Yisroel milk. Also houses Tel Aviv kosher (Glatt) meat market under RS: Council of Orthodox Rabbis of Greater Detroit.

Mikvah

Bais Chabad, 5595 W Maple Rd, Ph: 855-6170 or Rabbi M. Silberberg, Ph: 626-1807

Day School

Yavneh Academy (R), 6600 Maple Rd, Ph: 661-1000, ext. 275.

Minnesota

DULUTH   Area Code (218)   J-pop. 500

Travelers' Information: Jewish Community Relations Council, Ph: 724-8857

Synagogues

Adas Israel Congregation (O), 302 E 3rd St, Ph: 722-6459. Services: Shabbat

Temple Israel (C-US, R-UAHC), 1602 E 2nd St, Ph: 724-8857. Rabbi A. Holtz. Services: Friday (R), Saturday (C)

Food

European Bakery, 109 W 1st St, Ph: 722-2120. Breads and cakes (pareve and dairy); also kosher frozen packaged goods.

Sher Brothers, 25 E 1st St, Ph: 722-5563. Kosher grocery. Closed Shabbat

Accommodations

Voyageur, 333 E Superior, Ph: 722-3911. Short walk to Adas Israel.

204

MINNEAPOLIS (See also ST. PAUL)
Area Code (612)   J-pop. 22,000

For kosher food information in the Minneapolis-St.Paul area, call Shimon Perez, Ph: 926-3185.

Synagogues

Congregation Adath Jeshurun (C-US), 3400 Dupont Ave S, Ph: 824-2685. Rabbi B. Cytron. Services: Daily

Bais Yisroel Congregation (O), 4221 Sunset Blvd, Ph: 926-7867. Rabbi M. Lieff. Services: Daily

Beth El Synagogue (C-US), 5224 W 26th St, Ph: 920-3512. Rabbi K. Abelson. Services: Daily

Bet Shalom (R-UAHC), 201 9th Ave N, **Hopkins**, Ph: 933-8525. Rabbi N. Cohen. Services: Friday

B'nai Emet (C-US), 3115 Ottawa Ave S, **St. Louis Park**, Ph: 927-7309. Rabbi Siegel. Services: Daily

Hillel Congregation (B'nai B'rith, University of Minnesota) (R-UAHC), 1521 University Ave SE, Ph: 379-4026. Rabbi I. Wise. Services: Shabbat

Temple Israel (R-UAHC), 2324 Emerson Ave S, Ph: 377-8680. Rabbi S. Pinsky. Services: Daily

Congregation Kenesseth Israel (O-UOJC), 4330 W 28th St, Ph: 920-2183. Rabbi J. Herzog. Services: Daily

Sharei-Chesed Congregation (O), 2734 Rhode Island Ave S, Ph: 929-2595. Rabbi B. Woolf. Services: Daily

Eating Out

Knollwood Place Apartments, 3630 Phillips Pkwy, **St. Louis Park**, Ph: 933-1833. Kosher dining room. Meals: Monday-Friday d., Sunday brunch. Menu: Meat, fish or dairy, depending on the day. RS: Twin Cities Rabbinical Council, Rabbi J. Herzog, Chairman. Reserve before 1 p.m.

Seward Café at Hillel House, 1521 University Ave SE, Ph: 379-4026. Meals: l, Monday-Friday. Menu: Vegetarian. RS: Twin Cities Rabbinical Kashruth Council, Rabbi J. Herzog, Chairman. Open during the school year.

Food

Gelpe's Old World Bakery, 2447 Hennepin Ave, Ph: 377-1870.
   Breads and pastries, beverages, candles. RS: Rabbi J. Herzog.
   Closed Shabbat.
Kosher in the Park (located in Chi's Market), 4000 Minnetonka
   Blvd, **St. Louis Park**, Ph: 920-4144. Meats, poultry, deli,
   sandwich plates to order. RS: Twin Cities Rabbinical Kashruth
   Council, Rabbi J. Herzog, Chairman. Closed Shabbat.
Rainbow's End, 7115 Cedar Lake Rd, **St. Louis Park**,
   Ph: 544-2253. Cakes (pareve). RS: Rabbi J. Herzog
Wuollet's Bakery, 3608 W 50th St, Ph: 922-4341. Breads and
   pastries. (Pareve and dairy). RS: Rabbi J. Herzog.

Accommodations

Shabbat hospitality, Jewish Recovery Network (for people with
   addictive problems); call Joyce, Ph: 545-2675.
Lakeland Motel, 4025 Hwy 7, **St. Louis Park**, Ph: 926-6575.
   Located within five blocks of Kenesseth Israel.
Knollwood Place Apartments, 3630 Phillips Pkwy, Ph: 933-1833.
   Has some guest accommodations. (See Eating Out).

Mikvah

Ritualarium Society, 4330 W 28th St, Ph: 926-3829.

Day Schools

Minneapolis Jewish Day School, 4330 S Cedar Lake Rd,
   Ph: 374-5650.
Torah Academy, 2800 Joppa Ave S, **St.Louis Park**, Ph: 920-6630.
Talmud Torah Day School (C), 8200 W 33rd St, Ph: 935-0316.

Bookstores

Brochin's, 4813 Minnetonka Blvd, Ph: 926-1875.
Elijah's Cup, 4212 Minnetonka Blvd, Ph: 925-2446.

ROCHESTER   Area Code (507)   J-pop. 400

Synagogues

B'nai Israel Synagogue (R-UAHC), 621 2nd St SW, Ph: 288-5825.
Rabbi D. Freedman. Services: Friday

Food

Chabad House, 730 2nd St SW, Ph: 288-7500. Rabbi D. Greene.
Chabad Lubavitch of Rochester has a kosher food co-op.

Accommodations

For Shabbat meals, call Rabbi D. Greene at Chabad Lubavitch of
Rochester, Ph: 288-7500. Ask about the many hotels and motels
within walking distance of Chabad House.

ST. PAUL (See also MINNEAPOLIS)
Area Code (612)   J-pop. 7,500

Synagogues

Adath Israel Synagogue (O-UOJC), 2337 Edgcumbe Rd,
Ph: 698-8300. Rabbi A. Zeilingold. Services: Saturday
Beth Jacob (C-US), 1179 Victoria Curve, **Mendota Heights,**
Ph: 452-2226. Rabbi M. Allen. Services: Saturday
Lubavitch House, Regional Hdqt. (O-Lubav), 15 Montcalm Ct,
Ph: 698-3858. Rabbi M. Feller. Services: Call for schedule.
Mount Zion Hebrew Congregation (R-UAHC), 1300 Summit Ave,
Ph: 698-3881. Rabbi C. Rosenstein. Services: Shabbat
Shaare Shalom Congregation (C-US), 2490 Edgcumbe Rd,
President: S. Brod. Ph: 699-9956. Services: Friday
Shir Tikvah Congregation (R), 1671 Summit Ave, Ph: 642-0952.
Rabbi S. Offner. Services: Call for schedule.
Temple of Aaron (C-US), 616 S Mississippi River Blvd,
Ph: 698-8874. Rabbis B. Raskas. Services: Shabbat

Eating Out

Old City Café, 1571 Grand Ave, Ph: 699-5347. Meals: l,d. Menu:
(Dairy: cholov Yisroel) Israeli, vegetarian. RS: Rabbi A.
Zeilingold. Closed Shabbat.

Accommodations

Private accommodations; call Chabad House, 15 Montcalm Ct, Ph: 698-3858.

Mikvah

Mikvah Association, 1516½ Randolph Ave. Contact Mrs. Mindy Feller, Ph: 698-6163 or 698-1298.

Day School

Lubavitcher Cheder Day School, 1758 Ford Pkwy, Ph: 698-0556.

Mississippi

BILOXI   Area Code (601)   J-pop. 150

Synagogues

Congregation Beth Israel (C-US), Camelia & Southern Aves, Ph: 388-5574. Rabbi I. Flax (Chaplain at Keesler Air Force Base). Services: Friday

CLARKSDALE   Area Code (601)   J-pop. 100

Synagogues

Congregation Beth Israel (R), 401 Catalpa St, Ph: 624-5862. Services: Friday

CLEVELAND   Area Code (601)   J-pop. 120

Synagogues

Temple Adath Israel (R-UAHC), 201 S Bolivar Ave, Ph: 843-2005. Rabbi M. Landau. Services: Friday

GREENVILLE   Area Code (601)   J-pop. 480

Synagogues

Hebrew Union Temple (R-UAHC), 504 Main St, Ph: 332-4153. Rabbi S. Relkin. Services: Shabbat

GREENWOOD   Area Code (601)

Synagogues

Congregation Ahavath Rayim (O-UOJC), Market St, Ph: 453-7537.
  Services: Friday

HATTIESBURG   Area Code (601)   J-pop. 120

Synagogues

Congregation B'nai Israel (R), 901 Mamie St, Ph: 545-3871.
  Rabbi J. Bluestein. Services: Friday

JACKSON   Area Code (601)   J-pop. 700

Synagogues

Congregation Beth Israel (R-UAHC), 5315 Old Canton Rd,
  Ph: 956-6215. Rabbi E. Gurvis. Services: Friday

MERIDIAN   Area Code (601)

Synagogues

Congregation Beth Israel (R), 3641 46th St, Ph: 483-3193.
  Rabbi C. Golden. Services: Friday

NATCHEZ   Area Code (601)

Synagogues

Congregation B'nai Israel (R), 213 S Commerce St. Historic site.

TUPELO   Area Code (601)

Synagogues

Temple B'nai Israel (C), Marshall & Hamlin Sts, Ph: 842-9169.
  Services: Friday

VICKSBURG   Area Code (601)   J-pop. 105

Synagogues

Anshe Chesed (R-UAHC), 2414 Grove St, Ph: 636-1126. Services:
  Friday

Missouri

BALLWIN (See **ST. LOUIS**)

CHESTERFIELD (See **ST. LOUIS**)

COLUMBIA   Area Code (314)   J-pop. 350

Synagogues

B'nai B'rith Hillel (Unaffiliated), 1107 University Ave, Ph: 443-7460. Rabbi H. Rosenfeld. Services: Shabbat

CREVE COEUR (See **ST. LOUIS**)

KANSAS CITY (See also **KANSAS CITY, KS**)
    Area Code (816)   J-pop. 19,100

Synagogues

Congregation Beth Israel Abraham and Voliner (O-UOJC), 8310 Holmes Rd, Ph: 444-5747. Rabbi D. Glicksman. Services: Daily
Congregation Beth Shalom (C-US), 9400 Wornall Rd, Ph: 361-2990. Rabbi A. Cohen. Services: Daily
New Reform Temple (R-UAHC), 7100 Main St, Ph: 523-7809. Rabbi R. Goldstein. Services: Friday
The Temple-Congregation B'nai Jehudah (R-UAHC), 712 E 69th St, Ph: 363-1050. Rabbi M. Zedek. Services: Daily

Food

Great Harvest Bread Company, 1209 W 103rd St, Ph: 941-2299. Whole wheat breads and rolls. RS: Rabbi D. Glicksman.
New York Bakery, 70th & Troost, Ph: 523-0432. Baked goods (pareve, except cheesecake). RS: Rabbi D. Glicksman (bakery department only).
Price Chopper, 1003 W. 103rd St, Ph: 942-4200. Large selection of kosher products.

RICHMOND HEIGHTS (See **ST. LOUIS**)

ST. JOSEPH   Area Code (816)

Synagogues

Temple Adath Joseph (R), 17th & Felix Sts, Ph: 279-3179. Rabbi J. Glickman. Services: Friday

ST. LOUIS   Area Code (314)   J-pop. 53,500

Synagogues

Agudas Israel Congregation (O), 8202 Delmar, Ph: 863-8978. Rabbi M. Greenblatt. Services: Daily

Bais Abraham Congregation (O-UOJC), 6910 Delmar, Ph: 863-9639. Rabbi A. Magence. Services: Daily

Beth Hamedrosh Hagodol Congregation (O-UOJCA), 1217 North & South Rd, Ph: 721-1037. Services: Daily

B'nai Amoona Congregation (C-US), 324 S Mason Rd, Ph: 576-9990. Rabbi B. Lipnick. Services: Daily

Congregation B'nai El (R-UAHC), 11411 N Outer Forty, Ph: 432-6393. Rabbi B. Susman. Services: Shabbat

B'rith Sholom Kneseth Israel Congregation (C-US), 1107 Linden Ave, Ph: 725-6230. Rabbi M. Miller. Services: Daily

Central Reform (R-UAHC), First Unitarian Church, 5007 Waterman, Ph: 361-3919. Rabbi S. Talve. Services: Saturday, first and third Fridays

Chesed Shel Emeth Congregation (O-UOJC), 700 North & South Rd, Ph: 727-7585. Rabbi S. Rivkin. Services: Daily

Temple Emanuel (R-UAHC), 12166 Conway Rd, Ph: 432-5877. Rabbi J. Rosenbloom. Services: Friday and Sunday

Temple Israel (R-UAHC), 10675 Ladue Rd, Ph: 432-8050. Rabbi E. Bram. Services: Shabbat

Kol Am Congregation (R-UAHC), 14455 E Clayton Rd, **Ballwin,** Ph: 227-7574. Rabbi L. Goldstein. Services: Friday

Congregation Mishkan Israel Sherei Thillim (O-UOJC), 7205 Dorset St, Ph: 863-7753. Services: Daily

Neve Shalom (R-UAHC), 11145 Clayton Rd, **Ballwin,** Ph: 991-4687. Rabbi J. Goodman. Services: Call for schedule.

Synagogues cont.

Congregation Nusach H'Ari B'nai Zion (O-UOJC), 8630 Olive Blvd, Ph: 991-2100. Rabbi A. Borow. Services: Daily

Congregation Shaare Emeth (R-UAHC), 11645 Ladue Rd, Ph: 569-0010. Rabbi J. Stiffman. Services: Shabbat

Shaare Zedek Synagogue (C-US), 829 N Hanley Rd, Ph: 727-1747. Rabbi K. Greene. Services: Daily

Tpheris Israel Chevra Kadisha Congregation (O-UOJC), 14550 Ladue Rd, **Chesterfield**, Ph: 469-7060. Rabbi A. Winter. Services: Daily

Traditional Congregation of Creve Coeur (Trad), 12437 Ladue Rd, **Creve Coeur**, Ph: 576-5230. Rabbi E. Zimand. Services: Daily

United Hebrew Temple (R-UAHC), 13788 Conway Rd, Ph: 469-0700. Rabbi H. Kaplansky. Services: Shabbat

Young Israel of St. Louis (O-NCYI), 7800 Groby Rd, Ph: 991-5203. Rabbi J. Bienenfeld. Services: Shabbat

Eating Out

Diamant Meat Market, 618 North & South Rd, **University City**, Ph: 721-9624. Meals: l. Menu: (Meat) Sandwiches. RS: Vaad Hoeir. Closed Shabbat.

Isaac Kabob House, 8206 Delmar, Ph: 863-5557. Meals: l,d. Menu: (Meat) Mediterranean; sandwiches, some vegetarian dishes. RS: Vaad Hoeir. Closed Shabbat.

Kohn's, 10424 Old Olive St Rd, Ph: 569-0727. Meals: b,l, (till 5:30 p.m.). Menu: (Meat and fish) Sandwiches, side dishes, salads. RS: Vaad Hoeir. Closed Shabbat.

Kosher Hangar Restaurant at Airport Marriott, I-70 at Lambert International Airport, Ph: 423-9700. Dinner twice a month on Sunday. Call for dates. Menu: (Meat) Continental cuisine. RS: Vaad Hoeir.

No Bull Cafe, 10477 Old Olive St Rd, Ph: 991-9533. Meals: l,d. Menu: (Dairy) Pizza, pasta, salads, sandwiches. RS: Vaad Hoeir. Closed Shabbat.

Sol's, 8627 Olive St Rd, Ph: 993-9977. Meals: l,d. Menu: (Meat) Sandwiches, hamburgers, chicken, french fries. RS: Vaad Hoeir. Closed Shabbat.

Food

Diamant Meat Market, 618 North & South Rd, **University City**, Ph: 721-9624. Meat, poultry. RS: Vaad Hoeir. Closed Shabbat.

The Fudgery, Union Station, 18th & Market St, Ph: 231-1901. Fudge (except Rocky Road and Chocolate Pecan). Dairy. RS: Vaad Hoeir.

Galler's, 8502 Olive St Rd, Ph: 993-4535. Take-out meat and side dishes. RS: Vaad Hoeir. Closed Shabbat.

Incredible Yogurt, 642 Cresswood Plaza, Ph: 961-0023; 1202 St. Louis Galleria, Ph: 727-2272; 515 N 6th St, St. Louis Center, Ph: 621-4841. RS: Vaad Hoeir (frozen yogurt only).

Isaac Kabob House, 8206 Delmar, Ph: 863-5557. Sandwiches and vegetarian dishes for take-out. RS: Vaad Hoeir. Closed Shabbat.

Kohn's, 10424 Old Olive St Rd, Ph: 569-0727. Take-out deli, chicken, fish and side dishes. RS: Vaad Hoeir. Closed Shabbat.

Mr. Donut, 7758 Olive Rd, **University City**, Ph: 863-8005. (Dairy) Donuts, pastry and coffee. RS: Vaad Hoeir.

Layton's, 7950 Clayton Rd, Ph: 647-2512. RS: Vaad Hoeir (ice cream only).

Petrofsky's Bakery, 7649 Delmar, Ph: 725-1802. Breads and pastries (pareve and dairy). RS: Vaad Hoeir. Closed Shabbat.

Pratzel's Bakery, 727 N New Ballas, Ph: 567-9197; 928 N McKnight, Ph: 991-0708. Breads and pastries (pas Yisroel). RS: Vaad Hoeir.

Schnuck's 10650 Olive Blvd, Ph: 567-3838. Fresh bakery items under Vaad Hoeir. Breads (pareve) and cakes (dairy).

Sol's, 8627 Olive St Rd, Ph: 993-9977. Take-out meat, poultry, side dishes and complete kosher grocery. RS: Vaad Hoeir. Closed Shabbat.

Accommodations

All hotels listed below are within walking distance of Agudas Israel and Chesed Shel Emeth Congregations:

Daniele Hotel, 216 N Meramec, Ph: 721-0101.

Holiday Inn—Clayton Plaza, 7730 Bonhomme, Ph: 863-0400.

Radisson Hotel, 7750 Carondelet, Ph: 726-5400.

Mikvah

Taharath Israel of St. Louis, 4 Millstone Campus, Ph: 569-2774.

Day Schools

Rabbi H. F. Epstein Hebrew Academy, 1138 N Warson Rd,
    Ph: 994-7856.
Solomon Schechter Day School of St. Louis (C), 324 S Mason Rd,
    Ph: 576-6177.
Torah Prep, 8659 Olive Blvd, Ph: 569-2929.

Bookstores

Midwest Jewish Bookstore, 8318 Olive St Rd, Ph: 993-6300.
The Source, 11044 Olive St Rd, Ph: 567-1925.

SPRINGFIELD   Area Code (417)   J-pop. 285

Synagogues

United Hebrew Congregation (R-UAHC), 1250 E Belmont,
    Ph: 866-4760. Rabbi B. Diamond. Services: Friday

Food

Harter House Meat Market, 1029 S Campbell, Ph: 866-5576. Some
    kosher packaged deli, frozen Best meat and Empire poultry.

UNIVERSITY CITY (See ST. LOUIS)

Montana

BILLINGS   Area Code (406)

Synagogues

Beth Aaron (R-UAHC), 1148 N Broadway, Ph: 248-6412. Rabbi R.
    Ratner. Services: Friday

BUTTE   Area Code (406)

Synagogues

Congregation B'nai Israel (R-UAHC), 3425 Quincy. President R.
Rafish, Ph: 723-3228. Services: Call for schedule.

GREAT FALLS   Area Code (406)

Synagogues

Great Falls Hebrew Association (R-UAHC), P. O. Box 6192, 59406,
Ph: 452-9521. Services: Call for schedule.

Nebraska

LINCOLN   Area Code (402)   J-pop. 1,000

Synagogues

South Street Temple (R-UAHC), 20th & South Sts, Ph: 435-8004.
Services: Friday
Congregation Tifereth Israel (C-US), 3219 Sheridan Blvd, Ph: 423-
8569. Rabbi E. Seidel. Services: Shabbat

OMAHA   Area Code (402)   J-pop. 6,500

Synagogues

Beth El (C-US), 210 S 49th St, Ph: 553-3221. Rabbi P. Drazen.
Services: Daily
Beth Israel Synagogue (O-UOJC), 1502 N 52nd St, Ph: 556-6288.
Rabbi I. Nadoff (Emeritus). Services: Daily
Temple Israel (R-UAHC), 7023 Cass St, Ph: 556-6536. Rabbi A.
Azriel. Services: Shabbat
Lubavitch of Nebraska, 640 S 124th Ave, Ph: 330-7400. Rabbi M.
Katzman. Services: Shabbat

Eating Out

Bagel Bin, 1215 S 119th St, Ph: 334-2744. Meals: b,l. Bagels,
cheeses and coffee. RS: Vaad Hakashrus of Omaha.
Bagel Joe's Deli, 1215 S 119th St, Ph: 334-2744. Meals: b,l,d. Deli-
style dishes. RS: Vaad Hakashrus of Omaha

Food

No Frills Supermarket, 8005 Blondo, Ph: 399-8780. Frozen kosher meats and packaged goods.

Accommodations

The following hotels are a mile from Lubavitch of Nebraska:
Dillon Inn, 9720 W Dodge Rd, Ph: 391-5300.
Holiday Inn, 655 N 108th St, Ph: 496-0850.
Shabbat hospitality; call Lubavitch of Nebraska, Ph: 330-7400.

Mikvah

Jewish Community Center, 333 S 132nd St, Ph: 334-8200, or call Mrs. Shani Katzman, Ph: 330-7400, 24 hours in advance.

Day School

Friedel Jewish Academy, 12604 Pacific, Ph: 334-0517.

Nevada

LAS VEGAS   Area Code (702)   J-pop. 18,000

Synagogues

Temple Beth Am (R), 4180 S Pecos, 2nd floor (office), Ph: 456-7014. Rabbi M. Hecht. Services: Friday

Temple Beth Sholom (C-US), 1600 E Oakey Blvd, Ph: 384-5070. Rabbi Dr. L. Lederman. Services: Daily

Chabad House of Southern Nevada (O-Lubav), 1805 Ivanhoe Way, Ph: 386-6880. Rabbi Y. Harlig. Services: Shabbat and Sunday

Temple Emanu-El, (C-US), Meets at Phoenix Plaza III, 6370 W Flamingo #15, near Torey Pines, Ph: 645-2848 or 363-8722. Services: Friday

Congregation Ner Tamid (R), 2761 Emerson Ave, Ph: 733-6292. Rabbi S. Akselrad. Services: Friday

Congregation Ohr Bamidbar (O-Sephardic), 2959 Emerson, Ph: 369-1175. Services: Shabbat and daily a.m.

Shaarei Tefilla (O-UOJC), 1331 S Maryland Pkwy, Ph: 384-3565. President: J. Super. Services: Daily

216

Eating Out

Jerusalem Kosher Restaurant and Deli, 1305 Vegas Valley Dr #C, Ph: 735-2878. Meals: l,d. Menu: Deli and traditional. Also take-out. RS: Kosher Overseers Association of America, Inc., Rabbi H. Sharfman. Closed Shabbat.

Accommodations

The Golden Nugget, 129 E Fremont, Ph: 385-7111. Has regular keys. One and one-half miles from Shaarei Tefilla
Shabbat hospitality; call Rabbi Y. Harlig at Chabad House, Ph: 386-6880.

Mikvah

Call Shaarei Tefilla, 1331 S Maryland Pkwy, Ph: 384-3565 or Chabad House, Ph: 386-6880.

Bookstore

Las Vegas Jewish Books & Gifts, Inc., 4130 S Sandhill Rd #A18, Ph: 451-1808.

RENO   Area Code (702)   J-pop. 1,400

Synagogues

Temple Emanu-El (C-US), 1031 Manzanita Lane, Ph: 825-5600. Rabbi I. Cutler. Services: Shabbat
Temple Sinai (R-UAHC), 3405 Gulling Rd, Ph: 747-5508. Rabbi M. Soifer. Services: Friday

New Hampshire

BETHLEHEM   Area Code (603)   J-pop. 100

Synagogues

Bethlehem Hebrew Congregation (C), Strawberry Hill St, Ph: 869-5747. Rabbi D. Gold. Services: (summers only) Daily and High Holidays

Synagogues cont.

Machzikei Hadas (O), Lewis Hill Rd (New Arlington Hotel), Ph: 869-5737. Services: (summers only) Daily

Food

Village Grocery, Main St, Ph: 869-2201. Some kosher products.

Accommodations

A. M. Goldstone's rooming house, Main St, Ph: 869-5865. Reserve well in advance.

The Bells bed & breakfast, (not kosher) Strawberry Hill St, Bill Sims, Mgr. Ph: 869-2647. Reserve well in advance.

Hearthside Village Motel, Rte 302, Ph: 444-1000, Winter Ph: (508) 222-9255. Cabins, some with kitchenettes. Synagogue next door.

New Arlington Hotel, Main St, Ph: 869-3353. Kosher meals, Shomer Shabbat. RS: Chassidic. Synagogue services: Daily. Open summers. Reserve well in advance.

Pinewood Motel, Rte 302, Ph: 444-2075.Complete kitchen facilities. Synagogue services daily during the summer. Owner provides challahs, candles and Shreiber meals. Reserve well in advance.

Mikvah

Machzikei Hadas, corner of Lewis Hill Rd and Main St (in New Arlington Hotel). Call Mr. S. Cohen, Ph: 869-5737.

CONCORD   Area Code (603)   J-pop. 450

Synagogues

Temple Beth Jacob (R-UAHC), 67 Broadway, Ph: 228-8581. Rabbi R. Schenkerman. Services: Friday

DOVER   Area Code (603)   J-pop. 450

Synagogues

Temple Israel (R-UAHC), 47 1/2 4th St, Ph: 742-3976. Rabbi J. Gerard. Services: Friday

HANOVER   Area Code (603)   Hanover-Lebonon J-pop. 360

Synagogues

Upper Valley Jewish Community (Egalitarian, Eclectic), Hillel
House at Dartmouth College, 13 Summer St, Ph: 643-8378. Rabbi
D. Siegel. Services: Saturday, twice a month.

Eating Out

Hillel House, 13 Summer St, Ph: 646-3441 ext. 3359. Friday
dinner. RS: Rabbi D. Siegel (Recon). No reservations needed.

KEENE   Area Code (603)

Synagogues

Congregation Ahavas Achim (Unaffiliated), P.O. Box O, 03431, Ph:
352-6747. Rabbi B. Kreiger (Recon). Services: Call for schedule.

LACONIA   Area Code (603)

Synagogues

Temple B'nai Israel (R), 210 Court St, Ph: 524-7044. Services: Call
for schedule.

MANCHESTER   Area Code (603)   J-pop. 3,000

Synagogues

Temple Adath Yeshurun (R-UAHC), 152 Prospect St,
Ph: 669-5650. Rabbi A. Starr. Services: Friday
Chabad Lubavitch of New Hampshire, 7 Camelot Pl,
Ph: 647-0204. Rabbi L. Krinsky. Services: Sunday a.m. and
Holidays
Temple Israel (C-US), 66 Salmon St, Ph: 622-6171. Rabbi R.
Polirer. Services: Daily

Food

Alexander's Supermarket, Northside Plaza, **Hookset**, D.W. Hwy,
Ph: 644-2106. Large selection of kosher products.
Shaw's Supermarket, Granite State Market Place, **Hookset**,
Ph: 623-8846. Good selection of kosher products.

NASHUA   Area Code (603)   J-pop. 480

Synagogues

Congregation Betenu (R, Recon), 12 Briarwood Dr, Ph: 886-1633.
   Rabbi J. Segal. Services: Call for schedule.
Temple Beth Abraham (C-US), 4 Raymond St, Ph: 883-8184. Rabbi
   M. Finkel. Services: Shabbat, daily

PORTSMOUTH   Area Code (603)   J-pop. 1,100

Synagogues

Temple Israel (C-US), 200 State St, Rabbi D. Mark. Ph: 436-5301.
   Services: Shabbat, Monday - Thursday p.m., Sunday a.m.

New Jersey

ABERDEEN (See also **MATAWAN**)   Area Code (908)

Synagogues

Temple Beth Ahm (C-US), 550 Lloyd Rd, Ph: 583-1700. Rabbi N.
   Cooper. Services: Daily
Temple Shalom (R-UAHC), 5 Ayrmont Lane, Ph: 566-2621. Rabbi
   H. Weiner. Services: Shabbat

Day School

Bayshore Hebrew Academy, 479 Lloyd Rd, Ph: 583-1229.

ADELPHIA (See also **LAKEWOOD**)   Area Code (908)

Synagogues

Talmudical High School (O), Adelphia Rd, Ph: 431-1600. Services:
   Daily

ASBURY PARK (See **WANAMASSA**)

ATLANTIC CITY
   Area Code (609)   Atlantic County J-pop. 15,800

Synagogues

Chelsea Hebrew Congregation (C), 4001 Atlantic Ave, Ph: 345-0825. Rabbi M. Fox. Services: Shabbat, Sunday, Monday and Thursday

Community Synagogue Beth Kehillah (C-US), 901-3 Pacific Ave, Ph: 345-3282. Rabbi M. Berkowitz. Services: Saturday and Holidays

International Hotel Synagogue (O), Chelsea & Pacific Aves, Ph: 344-7071. Services: Shabbat, daily during the summer.

Congregation Rodef Shalom (O), 4609 Atlantic Ave, Ph: 345-4580. Rabbi A. Spacirer. Services: Daily

Eating Out

Coffee Shop in the International Hotel, Chelsea at Pacific Ave, Ph: 344-7071. Meals: b,l. Menu: (Dairy) Fish, omelettes, pasta, soups. RS: Vaad Harabonim of Atlantic County. Closed Shabbat.

Mandarin Dragon, International Hotel, Chelsea at Pacific Ave, Ph: 344-7071. Meals: l,d. Menu: (Meat) Chinese, deli. RS: Vaad Harabonim of Atlantic County. Closed Shabbat.

Penguin's Ice Cream, S Lo Shopping Center on Tilton Rd, Ph: 645-3663. Menu: Ice cream, cookies, nuts and candy. RS: Rabbi A. Krauss of Beth El Synagogue in Margate. (Ice cream only).

Zawid's Kosher Caterers, 119 S Kingston Ave, Ph: 347-4254. Meals: d. Daily in summer, some weekends in winter. Menu: Traditional. RS: Rabbi M. Fox of Chelsea Hebrew Congregation.

Food

Ginsberg Bakery, New York and Drexel Ave, Ph: 345-2265. Breads, cakes and pastries (pareve). RS: Vaad Harabonim of Atlantic County.

Accommodations

International Hotel, Chelsea at Pacific Ave, Ph: 344-7071. This Shomer Shabbat resort hotel serves three meals daily and is open all year round. RS: Vaad Harabonim of Atlantic County

BAYONNE   Area Code (201)   J-pop. 2,500

Synagogues

Temple Beth Am (R-UAHC), 111 Ave B, Ph: 858-9052/2020. Rabbi
    G. Gladstone. Services: Shabbat
Temple Emanu-El (C-US), 735 Kennedy Blvd, Ph: 436-4499. Rabbi
    Z. Heller. Services: Daily
Congregation Ohav Shalom Uptown Synagogue (O-UOJC), 1022
    Ave C, Ph: 436-9762. Services: Daily
Congregation Ohav Zedek (O), 42nd St & Ave C, Ph: 437-1488.
    Services: Daily

Eating Out

Reitner's, 908 Broadway, Ph: 437-1594. Meals: l,d. Menu: (Glatt
    meat) Continental and International cuisine. RS: Vaad Ho'ir of
    Bayonne. Closed Shabbat.

Food

Pride Bakery, 460 Broadway, Ph: 436-7557. Breads and pastries
    (pareve). RS: Vaad Ho'ir of Bayonne.
Reitner's, 908 Broadway, Ph: 437-1594. Glatt meat, poultry, take-
    out delicatessen, kosher grocery and bakery. RS: Vaad Ho'ir of
    Bayonne. Closed Shabbat.

Mikvah (See Elizabeth)

BELLE MEAD (See also PRINCETON and SOMERVILLE)
    Area Code (201)

Synagogues

Jewish Community Center of Belle Mead (Recon), 253 Griggstown
    Rd, Ph: 359-0420. Rabbi S. Margolin. Services: Friday.

BELLEVILLE   Area Code (201)

Synagogues

Aahavath Achim (C), 122-39 Academy St, Ph: 759-9394. Rabbi K.
    M. Simkes. Services: Call for schedule.

BELMAR (See also LONG BRANCH)   Area Code (908)

Synagogues

Congregation Sons of Israel (O), 505 11th Ave, Ph: 681-3200. Rabbi
M. Greebel. Services: Daily

BERGENFIELD (See also TEANECK)   Area Code (201)

Synagogues

Bergenfield-Dumont Jewish Center (C-US), 165 N Washington Ave,
Ph: 384-3911. Rabbi J. Blass. Services: Daily

Congregation Beth Abraham (O), 396 New Bridge Rd,
Ph: 384-3114. Rabbi Y. Euburger. Services: Shabbat and Sunday

BLOOMFIELD (See also WEST ORANGE)   Area Code (201)

Synagogues

Temple Ner Tamid (C-US,R-UAHC), 936 Broad St, Ph: 338-6482.
Rabbi S. Kushner. Services: Shabbat, Monday and Thursday

BOONTON   Area Code (201)

Synagogues

Congregation Adat Israel (C), 200 Overlook Ave, Ph: 334-6044.
Rabbi G. Chirnomas. Services: Shabbat

Temple Beth Shalom (C-US), 110 Harrison St, Ph: 334-2714. Rabbi
B. Dollin. Services: Shabbat

BOUND BROOK   Area Code (908)

Synagogues

Congregation Knesseth Israel (C), 229 Mountain Ave,
Ph: 356-1634. Rabbi A. Decter. Services: Shabbat

BRADLEY BEACH (See also DEAL and OAKHURST)
Area Code (908)

Synagogues

Congregation Agudath Achim (O-UOJC), 301 McCabe Ave,
Ph: 774-2495. Rabbi H. Bialik. Services: Daily

Food

Epstein's Glatt Kosher Butcher Shop, 221 Newark Ave,
Ph: 774-4804. Meat and poultry. RS: Jersey Shore Orthodox
Rabbinate. Closed Shabbat.

Mikvah (See **Ocean**)

BRICKTOWN (See also LAKEWOOD)   Area Code (908)

Synagogues

Temple Beth Or (C-US), Van Zile Rd, Ph: 458-4700. Rabbi R.
Fierstien. Services: Daily

BRIDGETON   Area Code (609)

Synagogues

Congregation Beth Abraham (C-US,R-UAHC), Fayette St &
Belmont Ave, Ph: 451-7652. Rabbi I. Silverman. Services: Daily

BRIDGEWATER   Area Code (908)

Synagogues

Temple Sholom (C), Upper N Bridge St, Ph: 722-1339. Rabbi R.
Isaacs. Services: Daily

BURLINGTON   Area Code (609)

Synagogues

Congregation B'nai Israel, 212 High St, Ph: 386-0406. Rabbi H.
Fields. Services: Shabbat

CALDWELL (See also WEST ORANGE)   Area Code (201)

Synagogues

Congregation Agudath Israel of West Essex (C-US), 20 Academy
Rd, Ph: 226-3600. Rabbi A. Silverstein. Services: Shabbat

CARMEL   Area Code (609)

Synagogues

Temple Beth Hillel (R), Sherman Ave, Ph: 451-7764. Services:
Every other Friday

CARTERET   Area Code (908)

Synagogues

Carteret Jewish Community Center (C), 44 Noe St, Ph: 541-5500.
Rabbi H. Lieberman. Services: Shabbat

CEDAR GROVE   Area Code (201)

Synagogues

Temple Sholom of West Essex (R-UAHC), 760 Pompton Ave,
Ph: 239-1321. Rabbi N. Patz. Services: Shabbat

CHERRY HILL   Area Code (609)   J-pop. 28,000

Synagogues

Congregation Beth El (C-US), 2901 W Chapel Ave, Ph: 667-1302.
Rabbi H. Kahn and Rabbi I. Furman. Services: Daily

Temple Beth Sholom (C-US), 1901 Kresson Rd at Cropwell,
Ph: 751-6663. Rabbi A. Lewis. Services: Daily

Temple Emanuel (R-UAHC), Cooper River Pkwy & Donahue,
Ph: 665-0888. Rabbi J. David. Services: Shabbat

Congregation M'kor Shalom (R-UAHC), 850 Evsham Rd,
Ph: 424-4220. Rabbi F. Neulander. Services: Shabbat.

Congregation Sons of Israel (O-UOJC), 720 Cooper Landing Rd,
Ph: 667-9700. Rabbi B. Rothman. Services: Daily

Food (See also **Haddonfield**)

Cherry Hill Kosher Market, 907 W Marlton Pike, Ph: 428-6663.
Sandwiches and traditional dishes for take-out. RS: Tri-County
Vaad Hakashrut. Closed Shabbat.

Pastry Palace, Rte 73 & Church Road, **Mt. Laurel**, Ph: 778-7403.
Breads and pastries (mostly pareve). RS: Tri-County Vaad
Hakashruth.

Food cont.

Talk-of-the-Town Supermarket, Rte 41 (Kings Hwy) & Chapel Ave, Ph: 667-5600. Good selection of kosher products.

Accommodations

Private accommodations; contact Rabbi B. Rothman at Congregation Sons of Israel, Ph: 667-9700.

Cherry Hill Inn, Rte 38 & Haddonfield Rd., Ph: 662-7200. Walk to Congregation Sons of Israel.

Mikvah

Congregation Sons of Israel, 720 Cooper Landing Rd. Call synagogue office for information, Ph: 667-9700.

Day School

Harry B. Kellman Academy (C), 2901 W. Chapel Ave, Ph: 667-1302.

Politz Foundation School, 720 Cooper Landing Rd, Ph: 667-1013.

CINNAMINSON (See also CHERRY HILL)   Area Code (609)

Synagogues

Temple Sinai (C-US), New Albany Rd & Rte 130, Ph: 829-0658. Rabbi S. Fineblum. Services: Shabbat

CLARK (See also LINDEN)   Area Code (908)

Synagogues

Temple Beth Or (C-US), 111 Valley Rd, Ph: 381-8403. Rabbi S. Zell. Services: Shabbat

CLAYTON   Area Code (609)

Synagogues

Congregation Sons of Israel (C), P.O. Box 727, 08312, Ph: 881-2267. Rabbi J. Roth. Services: Call for schedule.

CLIFFSIDE PARK   Area Code (201)

COLONIA

COLONIA New Jersey

Synagogues

Temple Israel Community Center (C), 207 Edgewater Rd, Ph: 945-7310. Rabbi H. Kaplan. Services: Shabbat and Sunday a.m.

CLIFTON (See also PASSAIC PARK) Area Code (201)

Synagogues

Beth Shalom (R-UAHC), 733 Passaic Ave, Ph: 773-0355. Rabbi S. Skolnik. Services: Shabbat

Clifton Jewish Center (C-US), 18 Delaware St, Ph: 772-3131. Rabbi E. Markovitz. Services: Daily

The Garfinkle Chapel-Daughters of Miriam (O), 155 Hazel St, Ph: 772-3700. Rabbi I. Kronenberg. Services: Daily

Eating Out

The Village II Kosher Deli, 389 Piaget Ave, Ph: 772-5387. Meals: l,d. Menu: Deli-style food. Also take-out. RS: Rabbi H. Kaplan of Temple Israel, Cliffside Park.

CLINTON Area Code (201)

Synagogues

Reform Temple of Hunterdon County (R-UAHC), P.O. Box 5095, 08809, Ph: 735-6984. Services: Call for information.

CLOSTER Area Code (201)

Synagogues

Temple Beth-El of Northern Valley (R-UAHC), 221 Schraalenburgh Rd, Ph: 768-5112. Rabbi F. Pomerantz. Services: Shabbat

COLONIA (See also LINDEN) Area Code (908)

Synagogues

Temple Ohev Shalom (C-US), 220 Temple Way, Ph: 388-7222. Rabbi A. Haselkorn. Services: Shabbat

CRANFORD (See also ELIZABETH)   Area Code (908)

Synagogues

Temple Beth-El (C-US), 338 Walnut Ave, Ph: 276-9231. Rabbi R.
Hoffberg. Services: Shabbat

Day School

Solomon Schechter Day School of Essex & Union (C), 721 Orange
Ave, Ph: 272-3400.

DEAL (See also BRADLEY BEACH and OAKHURST)
Area Code (908)

Synagogues

Synagogue of Deal (O), 128 Norwood Ave, Ph: 531-3200. Rabbi I.
Dwek. Services: Daily
Congregation Zvi Lazadeek (O), 258 Norwood Ave, Ph: 531-4872.
Rabbi I. Farhi. Services: Daily

Eating Out

The Brooklyn Deli, 276 Norwood Ave, Ph: 870-DELI. Meals: l,d.
Menu: Deli, sandwiches, burgers, barbecued chicken, soups,
salads. RS: Jersey Shore Orthodox Rabbinate. Closed Shabbat.
Dalia's Restaurant, 116 Norwood Ave, Ph: 531-1404. Meals: Menu:
Deli and Mideastern. RS: Jersey Shore Orthodox Rabbinate.
Seasonal. Closed Shabbat.
Jerusalem II Pizza, 106 Norwood, Ph: 531-7936. Meals: l,d. Menu:
Pizza and Mediterranean food. RS: Jersey Shore Orthodox
Rabbinate. Closed Shabbat.

Food

Deal Hot Bagels & Bialys, 294 Norwood Ave, Ph: 517-8500.
Bagels, bialys; salads for take-out. RS: Jersey Shore Orthodox
Rabbinate. Closed Shabbat.
Shalom Grocery, 104 Norwood Ave, Ph: 531-9837. Kosher
groceries. Closed Shabbat.

Mikvah (See Ocean)

Bookstore

Mitzvah Mart, 276 Norwood Ave, Ph: 581-2618.

DOVER   Area Code (201)

Synagogues

Adath Shalom (C-US), 18 Thompson Ave, Ph: 366-0179. Rabbi B.
Dollin. Services: Shabbat

EAST BRUNSWICK (See also HIGHLAND PARK)
Area Code (908)

Synagogues

Temple B'nai Shalom (R), Old Stage & Fern Rds, Ph: 251-4300.
Rabbi E. Milgrim. Services: Shabbat

East Brunswick Jewish Center (C-US), 511 Ryders Lane,
Ph: 257-7070. Rabbi C. Rogoff. Services: Daily

Young Israel of East Brunswick (O-NCYI), 195 Dunhams Corner
Rd, Ph: 254-1860. Rabbi Y. Wasser. Services: Daily

Food

Betty's Cakery, 312 Rues Lane, Ph: 257-6155. Breads and pastries,
(pareve and dairy). RS: Rabbi S. Ralbag.

Day School

Solomon Schechter Day School of the Raritan Valley (C), 511
Ryders Lane, Ph: 238-7971.

EAST WINDSOR (See also HIGHTSTOWN)   Area Code (609)

Synagogues

Beth El Synagogue (C-US), 50 Maple Stream Rd, Ph: 443-4454.
Rabbi S. Tucker. Services: Shabbat

Congregation Toras Emes (O), 639 Abington Dr, **Twin Rivers**,
Ph: 443-4877. Rabbi A. Gramen. Services: Daily

Day School

Morris Namias Shalom Torah Academy, 639 Abbington Dr, **Twin
Rivers**, Ph: 443-4877.

EDISON (See also HIGHLAND PARK)   Area Code (908)

Synagogues

Congregation Beth El—Edison Jewish Center (C-US), 91 Jefferson
   Blvd, Ph: 985-7272. Rabbi B. Rosenberg. Services: Call for
   schedule.
Chabad House (O-Lubav)), 527 Grove Ave, Ph: 549-5771. Rabbi
   M. Schmukler. Services: Shabbat
Temple Emanu-El (R-UAHC), 100 James St, Ph: 549-4442. Rabbi
   A. Landsberg. Services: Shabbat
Congregation Ohr Torah (O-UOJC), 2 Harrison St, Ph: 572-7181.
   Rabbi Y. Luban. Services: Daily

Food

M & M Bagels, 1791 Rte 27, Ph: 572-1145. Bagels, spreads, salads,
   coffee. RS: Vaad Harabbanim of Raritan Valley. Closed Shabbat.

Day School

Rabbi Pesach Raymon Yeshiva, 2 Harrison St, Ph: 572-5052/5053.

ELBERON (See LONG BRANCH)

ELIZABETH   Area Code (908)   Union County J-pop. 30,000

Synagogues

Congregation Adath Jeshurun (O), 200 Murray St, Ph: 355-6723.
   Rabbi E. Teitz. Services: Daily
Congregation Bais Yitzchok - Chevra Thillim (O), 153 Bellevue St,
   Ph: 354-4759. Rabbi P. Teitz. Services: Daily
Temple Beth El (R-UAHC), 737 N Broad St, Ph: 354-3021. Rabbi
   N. Landman. Services: Shabbat
Temple B'nai Israel (C-US), 1005 E Jersey St, Ph: 354-0400. Rabbi
   G. Chertoff. Services: Daily
Elmora Hebrew Center (O), 420 W End Ave, Ph: 353-1740. Rabbi
   S. Rosenberg. Services: Daily (evening only)
Jewish Educational Center Synagogue (O), 330 Elmora Ave,
   Ph: 353-4446. Rabbi P. Teitz. Services: Daily
Jewish Educational Center Synagogue (O), 1391 North Ave,
   Ph: 354-6058; 354-4446. Rabbi E. Teitz. Services: Shabbat

Eating Out

Dunkin' Donuts, 186 Elmora Ave, Ph: 289-9327. Meals: b,l,d.
Menu: (Dairy) Donuts, muffins, soups, croissants, sandwiches.
RS: Rabbi P. Teitz.

Jerusalem Pizza, 150 Elmora Ave, Ph: 289-0291. Meals: l,d. Menu:
Israeli dishes, pizza and pasta. RS: Rabbi P. Teitz. Closed Shabbat.

Superior Glatt Kosher Deli & Restaurant, 140 Elmora Ave,
Ph: 352-0355. Meals: b,l,d. Menu: Pareve and meat dishes served.
Dairy dishes are prepared for take-out only. Frozen meals
available. RS: Rabbi P. Teitz. Closed Shabbat.

Food

Elizabeth Kosher Meat, 149 Elmora Ave, Ph: 353-5448. Meat &
poultry. RS: Rabbi P. Teitz. Closed Shabbat.

Kosher Paradise, 155 Elmora, Ph: 354-0448. Glatt meat, chicken
and fish dishes prepared for take-out; also packaged frozen foods.
RS: Rabbi P. Teitz. Closed Shabbat.

Accommodations

Private accommodations; call Rabbi E. Teitz or Ms. S. Resnick at
the Jewish Educational Center, Ph: 353-4446.

Mikvah

Tamar Devorah, 35 North Ave. Contact Mikvah office,
Ph: 352-5048.

Day School

Jewish Educational Center, 330 Elmora Ave, Ph: 353-4446.

Bookstores

Sky Hebrew Book Store, 1923 Springfield Ave, **Maplewood,**
Ph: 763-4244.

ELMWOOD PARK (See also **PASSAIC**)   Area Code (201)

Synagogues

Elmwood Park Jewish Center (C-US), 100 Gilbert Ave,
Ph: 797-7320. Services: Shabbat

EMERSON   Area Code (201)

Synagogues

Congregation B'nai Israel (C), 53 Palisade Ave, Ph: 265-2272.
Rabbi M. Kiel. Services: Shabbat and Sunday

ENGLEWOOD (See also TEANECK)
Area Code (201)   Bergen County J-pop. 85,000

Synagogues

Congregation Ahavath Torah (O-UOJC), 240 Broad Ave,
Ph: 568-1315. Rabbi S. Goldin. Services: Daily
Temple Emanu-El (C-US), 147 Tenafly Rd, Ph: 567-1300. Rabbi S.
Listfield. Services: Shabbat
Congregation Shomrei Emunah (O), 89 Huguenot Ave,
Ph: 567-9420. Rabbi M. Genack. Services: Daily

Eating Out

Hunan Englewood, 22 N Van Brunt St, Ph: 568-7291. Meals: l,d.
Menu: (Meat) Chinese, American. RS: Rabbinical Council of
Bergen County. Closed Shabbat.

Food

Kosher By The Case & Less, 255 Van Nostrand Ave, Ph: 568-2281.
Butcher. Glatt meat, poultry, frozen items. RS: Rabbinical Council
of Bergen County. Closed Shabbat.
Menagerie Caterers, 10 S Dean St, Ph: 569-2704. Glatt meat & dairy
take-out; frozen foods, groceries and fresh-baked goods. RS:
Rabbinical Council of Bergen County. Closed Shabbat.

Mikvah

The Englewood Mikvah, Congregation Shomrei Emunah, 89
Huguenot Ave (side entrance); call Mrs. J. Davidowicz,
Ph: 569-0862.

Day Schools

Moriah School of Englewood, 53 S. Woodland St, Ph: 567-0208.

Solomon Schechter Day School of Bergen County (C), 153 Tenafly Rd, Ph: 871-1152.

Bookstore

The Judaica House, 19 Grand Avenue, Ph: 567-1199.

ENGLISHTOWN (See also HIGHTSTOWN, LAKEWOOD and PERTH AMBOY) Area Code (908)

Synagogues

Temple Shaari Emeth (R-UAHC), Craig Rd, Ph: 462-7744. Rabbi P. Schechter. Services: Friday

Congregation Sons of Israel (O-UOJC), Gordon's Corner Rd, Ph: 446-3000. Services: Daily

Union Hill Congregation (O), 364 Union Hill Rd, Ph: 972-0955. Rabbi J. Maza. Services: Daily

Day School

Shalom Torah Academy of Englishtown-Old Bridge, Englishtown Rd-Rte 527, **Old Bridge**, Ph: 446-2121.

FAIR LAWN Area Code (201)

Synagogues

Ahavat Achim (O-UOJC), 18-19 Saddle River Rd, Ph: 794-3927. Rabbi N. Turk. Services: Daily

Temple Avoda (R-UAHC), 10-10 Plaza Rd, Ph: 797-9716. Rabbi J. Woll. Services: Friday

Temple Beth Sholom (C-US), 40-25 Fair Lawn Ave, Ph: 797-9321. Rabbi G. Listokin. Services: Daily

Congregation B'nai Israel (C-US), Pine Ave & 30th St, Ph: 797-9735. Rabbi Y. Thompson. Services: Daily

Fair Lawn Jewish Center (C-US), 10-10 Norma Ave, Ph: 796-5040. Rabbi S. Glustrom. Services: Daily

Shomrei Torah (O-UOJC), 19-09 Morlot Ave, Ph: 791-7910. Rabbi B. Yudin. Services: Daily

Eating Out

Fair Lawn Kosher Deli, 14-20 Plaza Rd, Ph: 703-0088. Meals: l,d.
   Menu (Meat): Israeli, Continental, salads, sandwiches. RS:
   Rabbinical Council of Bergen County. Closed Shabbat.
Plaza Pizza, 14-26 Plaza Rd, Ph: 796-3113. Meals: l,d. Menu: Pizza,
   falafel, Italian dishes, salads. RS: Rabbinical Council of Bergen
   County. Closed Shabbat.

Food

Ben-David International Foods Emporium, 24-28 Fair Lawn Ave,
   Ph: 794-7740. Deli, appetizers, cheeses, meat, groceries, produce
   and frozen foods. RS: Rabbinical Council of Bergen County.
   Closed Shabbat.
Hot Bagels, 6-07 Saddle River Rd, Ph: 796-9625; 13-38 River Rd,
   Ph: 791-5646. Bagels (Dairy). RS: Rabbinical Council of Bergen
   County (Bagels only).
New Royal Bake Shop, 19-09 Fair Lawn Ave, Ph: 796-6565. Baked
   goods (pareve and dairy), milk and cheeses. RS: Rabbinical
   Council of Bergen County. Closed Shabbat.
River Road Hot Bagels, 13-38 River Road, Ph: 791-5646.
   Bagels (Dairy). RS: Rabbinical Council of Bergen County
   (Bagel's only).

Mikvah (See **TEANECK** or **ENGLEWOOD**)

FLANDERS   Area Code (201)

Synagogues

Temple Hatikvah - Mt. Olive Jewish Center (C-US), Pleasant Hill
   Rd, Ph: 584-7010. Rabbi H. Cohen. Services: Shabbat

FLEMINGTON   Area Code (908)

Synagogues

Congregation Bet Tikva (C), Sand Hill Rd, Ph: 782-7778. Rabbi M.
   Birnbaum. Services: Shabbat
Flemington Jewish Community Center (C-US), Hopewell & E Main
   St, Ph: 782-6410. Rabbi E. Jaffe. Services: Shabbat

FLORHAM PARK   Area Code (201)

Synagogues

The Suburban Jewish Center of Morris County (C), 165 Ridgedale
Ave, Ph: 377-6020. Rabbi D. Allen. Services: Friday

FORT LEE (See also TEANECK)   Area Code (201)

Synagogues

Jewish Community Center of Fort Lee (C-US), 1449 Anderson Ave,
Ph: 947-1735. Rabbi I. Spielman. Services: Daily
Sephardic Congregation of Fort Lee (O), 313 Tom Hunter Rd,
Ph: 944-1126. Rabbi S. Abergel. Services: Shabbat
Young Israel of Fort Lee (O-NCYI), 1610 Parker Ave,
Ph: 592-1518. Rabbi N. Winkler. Services: Daily

FRANKLIN   Area Code (201)

Synagogues

Temple Shalom of Sussex County (R), Oak St, Ph: 827-5655.
Services: Friday

FRANKLIN LAKES   Area Code (201)

Synagogues

B'nai Jeshurun-Barnert Temple (R-UAHC), 747 Rte 208 S,
Ph: 848-1800. Rabbi M. Freedman. Services: Friday

FREEHOLD (See also LAKEWOOD)   Area Code (908)

Synagogues

Agudath Achim (O), Broad & Stokes St, Ph: 462-0254. Rabbi E.
Fischman. Services: Daily

GLEN ROCK (See also FAIR LAWN)   Area Code (201)

Synagogues

Glen Rock Jewish Center (C-US), 682 Harristown Rd,
Ph: 652-6624. Rabbi H. Krantz. Services: Shabbat

GLENWOOD   Area Code (201)

Synagogues

Temple Beth El of Sussex County (R), Call for location, Ph: 875-6495. Services: Friday

HACKENSACK (See also **TEANECK**)   Area Code (201)

Synagogues

Temple Beth-El (C), 280 Summit Ave, Ph: 342-2045. Rabbi R. Schumeister. Services: Daily

HADDONFIELD (See also **CHERRY HILL**)   Area Code (609)

Food

Bennett's Kosher Meats, 63 Ellis St, Ph: 428-1393. Kosher grocery and meat market. RS: Tri-County Vaad. Closed Shabbat.

HIGHLAND PARK   Area Code (908)

Synagogues

Congregation Ahavas Achim (O), P.O. Box 4242, Ph: 247-0532. Rabbi R. Schwarzberg. Services: Shabbat.

Congregation Etz Ahaim (O), 230 Dennison St, Ph: 247-3839. Rabbi Y. Levy. Services: Shabbat and Sunday

Highland Park Conservative Temple and Center (C-US), S Third Ave & Benner St, Ph: 545-6482. Rabbi Y. Hilsenrath. Services: Daily

Congregation Ohav Emet (O-UOJC), 415 Raritan Ave, Ph: 247-3038. Rabbi E. Kaminetzky. Services: Daily

Eating Out

Deli King Delicatessen, 425 Raritan Ave, Ph: 545-8595. Meals: l,d. Menu: (Glatt meat) Deli sandwiches, full-course dinners. RS: Vaad Hakashruth of Raritan Valley. Closed Shabbat.

Jerusalem Pizza, 231 Raritan Ave, Ph: 828-9687. Meals: l,d. Menu: (Dairy: cholov Yisroel) Pizza, pasta, falafel and salads. RS: Vaad Hakashruth of Raritan Valley. Closed Shabbat.

Food

Berkley Bakery, 405 Raritan Ave, Ph: 220-1919. Breads, cakes, pastries. Everything baked on premises is pareve. RS: Vaad Hakashruth of Raritan Valley. Closed Shabbat.

Dairy Deluxe, 811 Raritan Ave, Ph: 572-4111. Take-out ice cream. RS: Vaad Hakashruth of Raritan Valley.

Dan's Glatt Kosher Meats, 515 Rte 27, Ph: 572-2626. Glatt meat, deli, Chinese, take-out. Complete selection of packaged kosher foods. RS: Vaad Hakashruth of Raritan Valley. Closed Shabbat.

Deli King, 425 Raritan Ave, Ph: 545-8595. (Glatt meat) Prepared food for take-out, frozen foods. RS: Vaad Hakashruth of Raritan Valley. Closed Shabbat.

Good N' Glatt, 76 Raritan Ave, Ph: 247-7070. Butcher. Glatt meat. Some take-out, kosher mini-market. RS: Vaad Hakashruth of Raritan Valley. Closed Shabbat.

Mikvah

Park Mikvah, 112 S First Ave, Ph: 249-2411.

Bookstore

Highland Park Judaica, 227 Raritan Ave, Ph: 246-1690.

HIGHTSTOWN   Area Code (609)

Synagogues

Congregation Beth Chaim (R), Village Rd, **West Windsor**, Ph: 799-9401. Rabbi E. Wisnia. Services: Shabbat

Beth El Synagogue (C), 50 Maple Stream Rd, Ph: 443-4454. Rabbi S. Tucker. Services: Shabbat

Food

Kosher Kitchen, 405 Mercer, Ph: 448-5222. Meat, poultry, deli; complete kosher grocery. RS: Rabbi D. Szmerla of Lakewood. Closed Shabbat.

HILLSIDE (See also ELIZABETH)   Area Code (908)

Synagogues

Hillside Jewish Center (O), 1538 Summit Ave, Ph: 923-6191
Congregation Shomrei Torah Ohel Yosef Yitzchok (O), 910 Salem
  Ave, Ph: 289-0770. Rabbi M. Kanelsky. Services: Shabbat
Congregation Sinai Toras Chaim (O-UOJC), 1531 Maple Ave,
  Ph: (201) 923-9500. Services: Daily

HOBOKEN   Area Code (201)

Synagogues

United Synagogue of Hoboken (C-US), 830 Hudson St,
  Ph: 659-2614. Rabbi S. Dickstein. Services: Shabbat

HOPATCONG   Area Code (201)

Synagogues

Lake Hopatcong Jewish Community Center (C), 15 Durban Rd, Ph:
  398-8700. Rabbi A. Zdanowitz. Services: Shabbat

HOWELL (See also LAKEWOOD)   Area Code (908)

Synagogues

Congregation Ahavat Achim (C-US), Windeler Rd, Ph: 367-1677;
  363-0093. Rabbi N. Schindler. Services: Shabbat

Day School

Solomon Schechter Academy of Ocean & Monmouth Counties (C),
  101 Kent Rd, Ph: 370-1767.

IRVINGTON (See also WEST ORANGE)   Area Code (201)

Synagogues

Congregation Agudath Israel (O), 1125 Stuyvesant Ave,
  Ph: 761-6977. Rabbi J. Zakheim. Services: Daily
Anshe Lubavitz (O), 74 Mill Rd, Ph: 399-1199. Rabbi S. Liebman.
  Services: Daily

238

Temple B'nai Israel—Ahavas Achim (C), 706 Nye Ave,
Ph: 372-9656. Rabbi L. Yagod. Services: Daily

JERSEY CITY   Area Code (201)   J-pop. 5,500

Synagogues

Congregation Agudath Sholom (O), 2456 Kennedy Blvd, corner
Gifford Ave, Ph: 432-8379. Rabbi D. Wasserman. Services: Daily

Congregation Ahavas Achim (O), 79 Audubon Ave, Ph: 434-7604.
Rabbi Y. Steinberg. Services: Daily

Temple Beth-el (R), 2419 Kennedy Blvd, Ph: 333-4229. Rabbi K.
Brickman. Services: Shabbat

Congregation B'nai Jacob (C-US), 176 W Side Ave, Ph: 435-5725.
Rabbi J. B. Sacks. Services: Daily

Mount Sinai and Talmud Torah Synagogue (O), 128 Sherman Ave,
Ph: 659-4267. Rabbi C. Steinmetz. Services: Shabbat

Congregation Sons of Israel (O), 35 Cottage St, Ph: 798-0172. Rabbi
M. Kanelsky. Services: Daily

KEARNY (See also NEWARK)   Area Code (201)

Synagogues

Congregation B'nai Israel of Kearny & North Arlington (C-US),
780 Kearny Ave, Ph: 998-3813. Services: Shabbat

LAKE HIAWATHA   Area Code (201)

Synagogues

Lake Hiawatha Jewish Center (C-US), 140 Lincoln Ave,
Ph: 334-0959. Rabbi M. Kieffer. Services: Shabbat

Eating Out

Beck's Best Deli, 76 N Beverwyck Rd, Ph: 263-9515. Meals: b,l,d.
Menu: Deli-style Food. RS: Rabbi G. Chirnomas of Congregation
Adat Israel, Boonton.

Food

Singer's Kosher Meats, 59 N Beverwyck Rd, Ph: 263-3220. Side
dishes, fresh meat and poultry. RS: Rabbi A. Krief of Pinebrook
Jewish Center, Montville. Closed Shabbat.

LAKEWOOD   Area Code (908)   Ocean County J-pop. 9,500

Synagogues

Congregation Ahavat Shalom (C-US), Forest Ave & 11th St,
Ph: 363-5190. Rabbi L. Paskind. Services: Daily

Congregation Anshe Sfard (O), 1250 Madison Ave, Ph: 370-8782.
Rabbi S. Blech. Services: Daily

Temple Beth Am (R-UAHC), Madison & Carey St, Ph: 363-2800.
Rabbi S. Yedwab. Services: Friday

Congregation Dov "V" Schmuel (C), 1143 W County Line Rd,
Ph: 367-1999. Services: Shabbat

Lakewood Yeshivah—Beth Midrash (O-UOJC), 617 Private Way &
6th St, Ph: 363-1233. Services: Daily

Congregation Sons of Israel (O-UOJC), Madison Ave & 6th St,
Ph: 364-2230. Rabbi P. Levovitz. Services: Shabbat

Eating Out

Kosher Experience, in Shop Rite Supermarket, Rte 9 & Kennedy
Blvd, Ph: 370-0707. Meals: l,d. Menu: Deli, Chinese food, fish,
salads; also take-out. RS: Rabbi M. Chomsky. Closed Shabbat.

R & S Kosher Deli, 416 Clifton Ave, Ph: 363-6688. Meals: l,d.
Menu: (Glatt meat) Traditional. Also take-out. RS: Rabbi C.
Lesser. Closed Shabbat.

"TCBY", 183 Kennedy Blvd, Ph: 905-5035. Yogurt and frozen
yogurt. RS: Lakewood Kashruth Organization.

Food

Gelbstein's Bakery, 415 Clifton Ave, Ph: 363-3636. Breads and
pastries (pareve and dairy). RS: Rabbi I. Abadi. Closed Shabbat.

Gelbstein's Pizza Store, 415 Clifton Ave, (behind the bakery),
Ph: 905-4186. Take-out pizza, falafel, sandwiches etc. Cholov
Yisroel. RS: Rabbi I. Abadi. Closed Shabbat.

Joe's Olde Tyme Fish Store, 315 Cedar Bridge Ave, Ph: 367-FISH.
Fresh fish. RS: Lakewood Kashruth Organization

Kosher Experience, in Shop Rite Supermarket, Ph: 370-0707. Take-
out. RS: Rabbi M. Chomsky.

Lakewood Kosher Dairy, 241 4th St, Ph: 367-0711. Take-out pizza, falafel, knishes, salads, Italian dishes. Cholov Yisroel. RS: Owner-supervised. Closed Shabbat.

Lakewood Kosher Fish Market, 32 Clifton Ave, Ph: 363-0267. Fresh fish, frozen gefilte fish. RS: Rabbi B. Klein. Closed Shabbat.

Non-Profit Grocery, 231 Main St, Ph: 370-1934. Full line of kosher groceries. Closed Shabbat.

R & S Kosher Deli, 416 Clifton Ave, Ph: 363-6688. Take-out (Glatt meat); also frozen meats and poultry. RS: Rabbi C. Lesser. Closed Shabbat.

Shop Rite Supermarket, Kennedy Blvd near Rte 9, Ph: 363-8270. Large selection of kosher products.

Accommodations

Capitol Hotel and Motel, 325 7th St, Ph: 363-5000. Shomer Shabbat. Kosher meals, synagogue on premises. RS: Rabbi A. Wiesner.

Fox Lieberman Hotel, 814 Madison Ave, Ph: 367-9199. Shomer Shabbat. Kosher meals, synagogue on premises. RS: Rabbi J. Solomon.

Mikvah

Lakewood Mikvah, 705 Madison Ave. Ph: 370-8909.

Day Schools

Bezalel Hebrew Day School—Lakewood Hebrew Day School, 419 5th St, Ph: 363-1748.

Bnos Yisroel, 100 9th St, Ph: 367-4855.

Lakewood Cheder School, 901 Madison Ave, Ph: 364-1552. Girls' Division: Beis Faiga, 350 Courtney Rd, Ph: 363-5070.

Yeshiva Tiferes Torah, 75 E End Ave, Ph: 370-9889. Girls' Division: Ahavas Torah, 420 2nd St, Ph: 905-9319.

Yeshiva Yetev Lev Satmar, 405 Forest Ave, Ph: 363-9746.

Bookstore

Lakewood Judaica, 428 Clifton Ave, Ph: 364-8860.

LAWRENCEVILLE (See also TRENTON)   Area Code (609)

Synagogues

Adath Israel Congregation (C-US), 1958 Lawrenceville Rd, Ph: 896-4977. Rabbi D. Grossman. Services: Daily

Young Israel of Lawrenceville (O-UOJC), 4 Knox Ct, Ph: 883-8833. Rabbi J. Finkelstein. Services: Shabbat, Sunday, Monday and Thursday a.m.

LEONIA (See also ENGLEWOOD)   Area Code (201)

Synagogues

Congregation Adas Emuno (R-UAHC), 254 Broad Ave, Ph: 592-1712. Rabbi F. Dworkin. Services: Friday

Congregation Sons of Israel (C-US), 150 Grand Ave, Ph: 944-3477. Dr. Z. Block. Services: Shabbat (September-June)

LINDEN (See also ELIZABETH)   Area Code (908)

Synagogues

Congregation Anshe Chesed (O-UOJC), Orchard Terrace at St George Ave, Ph: 486-8616. Rabbi S. Dworken. Services: Daily

Temple Mekor Chayim-Suburban Jewish Center (C-US), Deerfield Rd & Academy Terrace, Ph: 925-2283. Rabbi R. Rubin. Services: Shabbat

Food

County Kosher, 1171 St. George Ave, Ph: 925-4050. Meat, poultry, deli, frozen foods, kosher groceries. RS: Rabbi H. Cohen. Closed Shabbat.

Accommodations

Private accommodations; call Rabbi S. Dworken, Ph: 925-2226.

LIVINGSTON (See also WEST ORANGE)
Area Code (201)   J-pop. 12,600

Synagogues

Temple Beth Shalom (C-US), 193 E Mt Pleasant Ave, Ph: 992-3600. Rabbi A. Fellner. Services: Daily

Temple B'nai Abraham (C-US, R-UAHC), 300 E Northfield Rd, Ph: 994-2290. Rabbi B. Friedman. Services: Shabbat

Temple Emanu-el (R-UAHC), 264 W Northfield Rd, Ph: 992-5560. Rabbi P. Kasdan. Services: Shabbat

Synagogue of the Suburban Torah Center (O-UOJC), 85 W Mt Pleasant Ave, Ph: 994-0122. Rabbi M. Kasinetz. Services: Daily

Eating Out

Delancey Street Deli, 515 S Livingston Ave, Ph: 992-9189. Meals: l,d. Menu: Deli sandwiches, soups, entrees. RS: Rabbi A. Marcus, Council of Orthodox Rabbis of Metro West. Closed Shabbat.

Jerusalem West Pizza, 16 E Mt Pleasant Ave, Ph: 533-1424. Meals: l,d. Menu: (Dairy) Pizza, falafel, Israeli dishes, soups, salads. RS: Rabbi A. Marcus, Council of Orthodox Rabbis of Metro West. Closed Shabbat.

Food

Metro Glatt, 515 S Livingston Ave, Ph: 992-9189. Butcher and take-out. RS: Rabbi A. Marcus, Council of Orthodox Rabbis of Metro West. Closed Shabbat.

Super-Duper Bagels, 498 S Livingston Ave, Ph: 533-1703. Bagels and spreads. RS: Rabbi A. Marcus, Council of Orthodox Rabbis of Metro West. Closed Shabbat.

LONG BRANCH (See also **DEAL**) Area Code (908)

Synagogues

Temple Beth Miriam (R-UAHC), 180 S Lincoln Ave, **Elberon**, Ph: 222-3754. Rabbi J. Goldman. Services: Friday

Congregation B'nai Shalom (C), 213 Lenox Ave, Ph: 229-2700. Rabbi J. Waxman. Services: Shabbat

Congregation Brothers of Israel (O-UOJC), 250 Park Ave, **Elberon**, Ph: 222-6666. Rabbi T. Roth. Services: Daily

Ohel Simha Congregation (O-Sephardic), 295 Park Ave, **Elberon**, Ph: 571-2711. Rabbi S. Choueka. Services: Daily

Synagogue of West Long Branch (O), 479 Monmouth Rd, **West Long Branch**, Ph: 870-9318. Rabbi R. Semah. Services: Daily

Food

Kosher International Supermarket, 169 Locust Ave, **West Long Branch**, Ph: 870-8777. Butcher and complete kosher supermarket. Also take-out. RS: Jersey Shore Orthodox Rabbinate. Closed Shabbat.

MAHWAH Area Code (201)

Synagogues

Temple Beth Haverim (R-UAHC), 59 Masonicus Rd, Ph: 529-1274. Rabbi M. Weinberg. Services: Friday

MANALAPAN Area Code (908)

Synagogues

Temple Beth Shalom of Western Monmouth County (C), 108 Freehold Rd, Ph: 446-1200. Rabbi I. Rothstein. Services: Shabbat

Congregation Sons of Israel (Trad), Gordon's Corner Rd, Ph: 446-3000. Services: Daily

Eating Out

Sabra Kosher Pizza, 339 Rte 9 S, Summerton Plaza, Ph: 577-1881. Meals: l,d. Menu: Pizza, falafel, Italian dishes, salad bar. RS: Star-K of Baltimore. Closed Shabbat.

Food

Salomon's Bake Shop, 700 Tennent Rd & Rte 9, Ph: 536-4500. Breads and pastries (pareve and dairy). RS: Rabbi I. Rothstein of Temple Beth Shalom.

MAPLEWOOD (See also WEST ORANGE)   Area Code (201)

Synagogues

Congregation Ahavath Zion (O), 421 Boyden Ave, Ph: 761-5444. Rabbi S. Gordon. Services: Daily

Beth Ephraim - B'nai Zion (O), 520 Prospect St, Ph: 762-5722. Rabbi O. Kline. Services: Shabbat

MARGATE (See also ATLANTIC CITY)   Area Code (609)

Synagogues

Beth El Synagogue (C-US), 500 N Jerome Ave, Ph: 823-2725 Rabbi A. Krauss. Services: Daily

Temple Emeth Shalom (R-UAHC), 8501 Ventnor Ave, Ph: 822-4343. Rabbi S. Rosen. Services: Friday

Congregation Zichron Moshe Yitzchok Trocki M'Vilna (O), 426 N Exeter, Ph: 822-9490. Rabbi M. Weiss. Services: Shabbat

Mikvah

Mikvah Israel, 8223 Fulton Ave, Ph: 822-9797.

Day School

Hebrew Academy of Atlantic County, 601 N Jerome Ave, Ph: 823-6681.

MARLBORO   Area Code (908)

Synagogues

Congregation Ohev Shalom (C), 103 School Rd W, Ph: 536-2300. Rabbi G. Schlesinger. Services: Shabbat, daily p.m.

Temple Rodeph Torah (R), Mohawk Dr, Ph: 308-0055. Rabbi D. Weber. Services: Shabbat

Day School

Solomon Schechter Day School of Marlboro (C), 22 School Rd E,
   Ph: 431-5525.

MARLTON (See also **CHERRY HILL**)   Area Code (609)

Synagogues

Congregation Beth Tikvah (C), Evesboro-Medford Rd,
   Ph: 983-8090. Rabbi G. Gans. Services: Shabbat

MATAWAN (See also **PERTH AMBOY**)   Area Code (908)

Synagogues

Temple Beth Ahm (C-US), 550 Lloyd Road, Ph: 583-1700. Rabbi
   N. Cooper. Services: Shabbat and Sunday
Congregation Beth Tefilah (O-UOJC), 479 Lloyd Rd,
   Ph: 583-6262. Rabbi S. Krupka. Services: Daily
Temple Shalom of Matawan (R-UAHC), 5 Ayrmont Lane,
   Ph: 566-2961. Rabbi H. Weiner. Services: Shabbat

Eating Out

Ken's Deli, Rte 34, Ph: 583-1111. Meals: b,l,d. Menu: Deli and fast
   food. RS: Rabbi N. Cooper of Temple Beth Ahm.

MAYWOOD   Area Code (201)

Synagogues

Temple Beth Israel (C-US), 34 W Magnolia Ave, Ph: 845-7550.
   Rabbi M. Panitz. Services: Shabbat

METUCHEN (See also **HIGHLAND PARK**)   Area Code (908)

Synagogues

Temple Neve Sholom (C-US), 250 Grove Ave, Ph: 548-2238. Rabbi
   G. Zelizer. Services: Shabbat

MILLBURN   Area Code (201)

Synagogues

Congregation B'nai Israel (C-US), 160 Millburn Ave, Ph: 379-3811. Rabbi S. Bayar. Services: Daily

Congregation Ohel Moshe (O). Call for location, Ph: 376-1763. Services: Saturday

MILLVILLE   Area Code (609)

Synagogues

Congregation Beth Hillel (C), 3rd & Oak Sts, Ph: 825-8672. Rabbi C. Gelernter. Services: Shabbat

MONTCLAIR (See also **PASSAIC**)   Area Code (201)

Synagogues

B'nai Keshet (Recon-FRCH, R-UAHC), Church St & Trinity Pl, Ph: 746-4889. Rabbi D. Ehrenkrantz. Services: Saturday

Congregation Shomrei Emunah (C-US), 67 Park St, Ph: 746-5031. Rabbi Dr. J. Chasan. Services: Shabbat

MONTVALE   Area Code (201)

Eating Out

Manhattan Deli, 26 B Chestnut Ridge Rd, Ph: 425-2690. Meals: b,l,d. Menu: (Meat) Deli sandwiches, entrees. Also take-out. RS: Rabbi D. Rosenzweig of the Jewish Community Center (C), Spring Valley.

MONTVILLE   Area Code (201)

Synagogues

Pine Brook Jewish Center (C-US), 174 Changebridge Rd, Ph: 227-3520. Dr. A. Krief. Services: Shabbat

MORRISTOWN
Area Code (201)   Morris County J-pop. 33,500

Synagogues

Congregation Ahavath Yisrael (O-UOJC), 9 Cutler St,
  Ph: 267-4184. Rabbi B. Goldfarb. Services: Shabbat and Sunday
Temple B'nai Or (R-UAHC), Overlook Rd, Ph: 539-4539. Rabbi Z.
  Levy. Services: Friday
Congregation Levi Yitzchok (O), 226 Sussex Ave,
  Ph: 984-6326/455-9031. Rabbi Z. Wilschanski. Services: Daily
Morristown Jewish Community Center (C-US), 177 Speedwell Ave,
  Ph: 538-9292. Rabbi D. J. Nesson. Services: Shabbat
Rabbinical College of America (O-Lubav), 226 Sussex Ave,
  Ph: 267-9404. Rabbi M. Herson. Services: Daily

Food

Kosher Food Service, Congregation Ahavath Yisroel, 9 Cutler St.
  This service provides kosher food for the community. For further
  information, contact Mrs. B. Mandel, Ph: 539-8693 or the
  synagogue office, Ph: 267-4184.

Accommodations

Private accommodations; contact Baruch Klar at the Rabbinical
  College of America, Ph: 267-9404.

Mikvah

Mikvah Bais Chana Lubavitch, 93 Lake Rd, Ph: 292-3932.

Day School

Cheder Lubavitch, 226 Sussex St, Ph 455-1367.

MOUNT FREEDOM (See RANDOLPH)

MOUNT HOLLY   Area Code (609)

Synagogues

Temple Har Zion (C), High & Ridgeway Sts, Ph: 267-0660. Rabbi
  R. Simon. Services: Shabbat

MOUNT LAUREL (See CHERRY HILL)

NEW BRUNSWICK (See also HIGHLAND PARK)
Area Code (908)   Middlesex County J-pop. 40,000

Synagogues

Anshe Emeth Memorial Temple (R-UAHC), 222 Livingston Ave,
Ph: 545-6484. Rabbi B. Miller. Services: Shabbat

Congregation B'nai Tikvah—Jewish Community Center of North
and South Brunswick (C-US), 1001 Finnegans Lane, **North
Brunswick,** Ph: 297-0696. Rabbi A. Warmflash. Services:
Shabbat

Chabad House (O-Lubav), 8 Sicard St (near Rutgers campus),
Ph: 828-9191. Rabbi Y. Carlebach. Services: Shabbat

Congregation Poile Zedek (O), 145 Neilson St, Ph: 545-6123. Rabbi
A. Mykoff.

Eating Out

B'nai Brith Hillel Foundation - Rutgers University (cafeteria),
Clifton Ave, Rutgers Lane, Ph: 545-2407. RS: Rabbi H. Weitzner.
Kosher dinners are served Monday through Friday evenings.
Travelers should call for further information.

Accommodations

Private accommodations; Contact Rabbi Y. Carlebach,
Ph: 828-9191.

NEW MILFORD   Area Code (201)

Synagogues

Beth Tikvah—New Milford Jewish Center (C-US), 435 River Rd,
Ph: 261-4847. Rabbi I. Reisner. Services: Daily

NEWARK (See also ELIZABETH)   Area Code (201)

Synagogues

Ahavas Sholom (O), 145 Broadway, Ph: 485-2609. Rabbi G.
Goldberg. Services: Shabbat

Mount Sinai Congregation (O), 250 Mt Vernon Pl, Ph: 763-1005.
Rabbi S. Bogomilsky. Services: Daily

NEWTON   Area Code (201)

Synagogues

Jewish Center of Sussex County (C), 13 Washington St, Ph: 383-4570. Rabbi P. Samuel-Sigel. Services: Shabbat

NORMA (See VINELAND)

NORTH BERGEN (See also TEANECK)   Area Code (201)

Synagogues

Temple Beth Abraham (O-UOJC), 8410 Fourth Ave, Ph: 869-2425. Rabbi A. Zigelman. Services: Daily
Temple Beth-El (C-US), 300 75th St and Hudson Ave, Ph: 869-9149. Rabbi M. Sofer. Services: Daily

Accommodations

Private hospitality; call Temple Beth Abraham, Ph: 869-2425.

NORTHFIELD   Area Code (609)

Synagogues

Beth Israel (R-UAHC), 2501 Shore Rd, Ph: 641-3600. Rabbi D. M. Weis. Services: Shabbat

NUTLEY (See also PASSAIC)   Area Code (201)

Synagogues

Temple B'nai Israel (C), 192 Centre St, Ph: 667-3713. Rabbi G. Kirschner. Services: Shabbat

OAKHURST (See also BRADLEY BEACH and DEAL)
Area Code (908)

Synagogues

Temple Beth El (C-US), 301 Monmouth Rd, Ph: 531-0300. Rabbi D. Silverman. Services: Daily
Congregation Magen David of West Deal (O), 395 Deal Rd, Ph: 531-3220. Rabbi E. Labaton. Services: Shabbat

Eating Out

Café Deal, 214 Roosevelt Ave, Ph: 531-8500. Meals: l, d. Menu: (Dairy) Italian. Pizza is cholov Yisroel. RS: Jersey Shore Orthodox Rabbinate. Closed Shabbat.

Deal Steak House, 214 Roosevelt Ave, Ph: 517-1331. Meals: l,d. Menu: Oriental, American. Hambugers, hot dogs, steak. RS: Jersey Shore Orthodox Rabbinate. Closed Shabbat.

Food

Hot Bagels, 67 Monmouth Rd, Ph: 870-6262. RS: Jersey Shore Orthodox Rabbinate (bagels only)

Netsach Israel Mini Market, 198 Monmouth Rd, Ph: 531-2100. Groceries, dairy products, frozen meat products. RS: Jersey Shore Orthodox Rabbinate. Closed Shabbat.

Scoops Ice Cream, 50 Monmouth Rd, Ph: 229-6269. Ice cream, tofutti, yogurt, cakes and pies. RS: Jersey Shore Orthodox Rabbinate.

Trecate's Pastry Shop, Cobblestone Village, West Park Ave, Ph: 493-4937.

Mikvah (See **Ocean**)

Day School

Deal Yeshiva, 301A Monmouth Rd, Ph: 531-3366.

OAKLAND   Area Code (201)

Synagogues

Jewish Community Center (C-US), 192 Ramapo Valley Rd, Ph: 337-5569. Rabbi A. Zdanowitz. Services: Shabbat

OCEAN (See also **BRADLEY BEACH, DEAL** and **OAKHURST**)
  Area Code (908)

Synagogues

Temple Beth Torah (C-US), 1200 Roseld, Ph: 531-4410. Rabbi J. Friedman. Services: Daily

Synagogues cont.

Congregation Sons of Israel (O-UOJC), 1025 Deal Rd; also meets
in **Wanamassa**, Ph: 775-1964. Rabbi Y. Carlbach. Services:
Shabbat

Mikvah

Shore Area Mikva, 201 Jerome Ave, Ph: 531-1712.

Day School

Hillel Yeshiva, 1025 Deal Rd, Ph: 493-9300.

OLD BRIDGE (See also HIGHLAND PARK)   Area Code (908)

Synagogues

Congregation Beth Ohr Jewish Community Center (C-US), 300 Rte
516, Ph: 257-9867. Rabbi R. Fagan. Services: Shabbat and
Sunday a.m.

Food

Goldberg's Kosher Meat, Rte 516, Ph: 679-2266. Meat, poultry and
kosher grocery. RS: Rabbi R. Port of Temple Ohav Shalom,
Parlin. Closed Shabbat.

PALISADES PARK   Area Code (201)

Eating Out

Jerusalem V Pizza, 446 Broad Ave, Ph: 947-7754. Meals: l,d.
Menu: Pizza, Mediterranean dishes. RS: Rabbinical Council of
Bergen County. Closed Shabbat.

PARAMUS (See also FAIR LAWN and TEANECK)
Area Code (201)

Synagogues

Congregation Beth Tefillah (O-UOJC), E 241 Midland Ave,
Ph: 265-4100. Rabbi B. Yasgur. Services: Daily
Jewish Community Center of Paramus (C-US), E 304 Midland
Ave, Ph: 262-7691. Rabbi A. Gotlieb. Services: Daily
K'hal Adath Jeshurun (O), 140 Arnot Pl, Ph: 967-9898 or call J.
Blumenthal, Ph: 967-0605. Rabbi M. Kuber. Services: Daily

Day School

Yavneh Academy, 155 Fairview Ave, Ph: 262-8494.

PARK RIDGE   Area Code (201)

Synagogues

Temple Beth Sholom of Pascack Valley (C-US), 32 Park Ave, Ph: 391-4620. Rabbi B. Mindick. Services: Shabbat

PARLIN (See also HIGHLAND PARK)   Area Code (908)

Synagogues

Temple Ohav Shalom—Sayreville Jewish Center (C-US), 3018 Bordentown Ave, Ph: 727-4334. Rabbi R. Port. Services: Shabbat

PARSIPPANY   Area Code (201)

Synagogues

Congregation Ahavat Torah of Parsippany (O-UOJC), 1180 Rte 46, Ph: 335-3636. Rabbi Z. D. Rauch. Services: Shabbat

Temple Beth Am, (R-UAHC), 879 S Beverwick Rd, Ph: 887-0046. Rabbi D. Franzel. Services: Friday

Eating Out

Arlington Deli, 744 Rte 46W, Ph: 335-9400. Meals: b,l,d. Menu: Continental dishes. RS: Rabbi H. Savitz (C) of West Caldwell.

Café Devorah Aspen Hotel, 808 Rte 46 W, Ph: 267-9404. Entertainment. Elegant kosher menu. RS: Rabbinical College of America. One Saturday night a month, during the winter.

Accommodations

Private accommodations; call Congregation Ahavat Torah, Ph: 335-3636.

Red Roof Inn, 855 Rte 46, Ph: 334-3737. One half mile to Congregation Ahavat Torah.

PASSAIC PARK (See also **CLIFTON**)
Area Code (201)   Passaic County J-pop. 18,700

Synagogues

Congregation Adas Israel (O-UOJC), 565 Broadway, Ph: 773-7272. Rabbi Dr. S. Rybak. Services: Daily

Ahavas Israel Passaic Park Jewish Community Center (O), 181 Van Houten Ave, Ph: 777-5929. Rabbi K. Poplack. Services: Daily

Bais Dovid (O), 72 Ascension St, Ph: 777-0649. Rabbi S. Isaacson. Services: Shabbat

Bais Torah U'Tiflah (O), Kent Court, Ph: 470-8888. Rabbi M. Zupnick. Services: Daily

Temple Emanuel (C), 181 Lafayette Ave, Ph: 777-9898. Rabbi J. Herman. Services: Call for schedule.

Congregation Tifereth Israel (O-UOJC), 180 Passaic Ave, Ph: 773-2552; 472-9855. Rabbi S. Weinberger. Services: Daily

Yeshiva Gedola of Passaic (O), 35 Ascension St, Ph: 472-6100. Rabbis M. Stern and C. Davis. Services: Daily

Young Israel of Passaic—Clifton (O-NCYI), 200 Brook Ave, Ph: 778-7117; 777-4422. Rabbi C. Wasserman. Services: Daily

Eating Out

Jerusalem II Pizza, 224 Brook Ave, Ph: 778-0960. Meals: l,d. Menu: Pizza, Mediterranean dishes. RS: Passaic Vaad. Closed Shabbat.

The Other Side, 209 Main Ave, Ph: 471-8443. Meals: l,d. Menu: (Glatt meat) Full grill, deli, chicken, salads, kugels. Also take-out.. RS: Kof-K and Passaic Vaad. Closed Shabbat.

Food

Makolet Plus, 200 Main Ave, Ph: 777-6969. Fresh meats and poultry. Complete kosher grocery. Cholov Yisroel products. RS: Kof-K. Closed Shabbat.

Passaic Park Bake Shop, 217 Main Ave, Ph: 471-3080. Breads and pastries (pareve). RS: Rabbi S. Isaacson.

Accommodations

Howard Johnson, 680 Rte 3, Ph: 471-3800. Walk to Adas Israel.

Mikvah

Mikvah Yisroel of Passaic-Clifton, 244 High St. Ph: 778-3596.

Day Schools

Hillel Academy (O), 565 Broadway, Ph: 777-0735.
Yeshiva K'tana of Passaic (O), 252 High St, Ph: 916-0666.

Bookstore

Kesser Gifts & Judaica, 216 Main Ave, Ph: 365-2218.

PATERSON (See also FAIR LAWN)   Area Code (201)

Synagogues

Community Synagogue (C), 660 14th Ave, Ph: 742-9345. Rabbi H.
   Bornstein. Services: Shabbat
Temple Emanuel of North Jersey (C-US), 151 E 33rd St,
   Ph: 684-5565. Rabbi J. Konheim. Services: Daily
Congregation United Brotherhood-Linath Hazedek (O), 6 Manor
   Rd, Ph: 794-7041. Rabbi M. Greenberg.

PERRINEVILLE (See also FREEHOLD and HIGHTSTOWN)
   Area Code (908)

Synagogues

Perrineville   Jewish   Center   (Trad),   Perrineville   Rd,
   Ph: 446-6018/1675. Rabbi S. Schevelowitz. Services: Shabbat

PERTH AMBOY (See also HIGHLAND PARK)
   Area Code (908)

Synagogues

Congregation Beth Mordecai (C-US), 224 High St, Ph: 442-2431.
   Rabbi H. Rudavsky. Services: Shabbat, Monday and Thursday
Congregation Shaarey Tefiloh (O-UOJC), 15 Market St,
   Ph: 826-2977. Rabbi A. Chomsky. Services: Daily

Mikvah

Congregation Shaarey Tefiloh, 15 Market St, Ph: 826-2977.

PISCATAWAY   Area Code (908)

Synagogues

Congregation B'nai Shalom (Recon), 25 Netherwood Ave,
  Ph: 885-9444. Rabbi R. Mark. Services: Call for schedule.

PLAINFIELD (See also LINDEN)   Area Code (908)

Synagogues

Temple Beth El (C-US), 225 E 7th St, Ph: 756-2333. Rabbi M.
  Samber. Services: Shabbat
Temple Sholom (R-UAHC), 815 W 7th St, Ph: 756-6447. Rabbi G.
  Goldman. Services: Friday
United Orthodox Synagogue (O), 526 W 7th St, Ph: 755-0043.
  Rabbi S. Katz. Services: Shabbat, Sunday, Monday & Thursday.

POMPTON LAKES   Area Code (201)

Synagogues

Congregation Beth Shalom (C-US), 21 Passaic Ave, Ph: 835-9785.
  Rabbi B. Schecter. Services: Daily

Day School

Solomon Schechter Day School of North Jersey (C), 21 Passaic
  Ave, Ph: 831-8000.

PRINCETON   Area Code (609)J-pop. 2,600

Synagogues

The Jewish Center (C), 435 Nassau St, Ph: 921-0100. Rabbi M.
  Glazer. Services: Shabbat

RAHWAY (See also LINDEN)   Area Code (908)

Synagogues

Temple Beth Torah - Rahway Hebrew Congregation (C-US), 1389
  Bryant St, Ph: 576-8432. Rabbi J. Rubenstein. Services:
  Shabbat, Sunday, Monday and Thursday

256

RANDOLPH   Area Code (201)

Synagogues

Mount Freedom Jewish Center (Trad), 1209 Sussex, **Mount Freedom,** Ph: 895-2100. Rabbi D. B. Bateman. Services: Daily

Day School

Nathan-Bohrer-Abraham Kaufman Hebrew Academy of Morris County (C), 146 Dover Chester Rd, Ph: 584-5530.

RED BANK (See also **LONG BRANCH**)   Area Code (908)

Synagogues

Congregation Beth Shalom (O-UOJC), 186 Maple Ave, Ph: 741-1657/431-4719. Rabbi J. Fischman. Services: Shabbat and Sunday

RIDGEFIELD PARK   Area Code (201)

Synagogues

Temple Emanuel (C-US, Trad.), 120 Park St, Ph: 440-0193. Rabbi S. Lerner. Services: Shabbat

Day School

Yeshiva of North Jersey, 712 Lincoln Ave, Ph: 807-1777.

RIDGEWOOD (See also **FAIR LAWN**)   Area Code (201)

Synagogues

Temple Israel & Jewish Community Center (C-US), 475 Grove St, Ph: 444-9320. Rabbi N. Marans. Services: Shabbat

RIVER EDGE (See also **FAIR LAWN**)   Area Code (201)

Synagogues

Temple Sholom (R-UAHC), 385 Howland Ave, Ph: 489-2463. Rabbi N. I. Borovitz. Services: Friday

ROCKAWAY Area Code (201)

Synagogues

Chabad Center of White Meadow Lake (O), 23 Pawnee Ave,
    Ph: 625-1525. Rabbi A. Herson. Services: Shabbat; Sunday,
    Monday, and Thursday a.m.
White Meadow Temple (C-US), 153 White Meadow Rd,
    Ph: 627-4500. Rabbi R. Dalin. Services: Daily

Food

Shop Rite, 279 Rte. 46, Ph: 625-4777. Kosher cheeses and Empire
    products.

Accommodations

Howard Johnson's Motel, Rte 80 & Greenpond Rd, Ph: 625-1200.
    One mile and a quarter from the Chabad Center.

ROOSEVELT (See also HIGHTSTOWN) Area Code (609)

Synagogues

Roosevelt Jewish Center (C), 20 Homestead Lane,
    Ph: 448-2526. Services: Shabbat

RUMSON (See also LONG BRANCH) Area Code (908)

Synagogues

Congregation B'nai Israel (C-US), Hance & Ridge Rds,
    Ph: 842-1800. Rabbi J. Rosoff. Services: Shabbat

RUTHERFORD (See also PASSAIC) Area Code (201)

Synagogues

Temple Beth-El (C-US), 185 Montross Ave, Ph: 438-4931. Rabbi
    A. Bergman. Services: Shabbat

SCOTCH PLAINS Area Code (908)

Synagogues

Temple Israel of Scotch Plains & Fanwood (C-US), 1920

Cliffwood St, Ph: 889-1830. Rabbi G. Nudell. Services: Shabbat

SHORT HILLS (See also NEWARK)   Area Code (201)

Synagogues

Congregation B'nai Jeshurun (R-UAHC), 1025 S Orange Ave,
Ph: 379-1555. Rabbi B. Greene. Services: Friday

SOMERVILLE   Area Code (908)

Synagogues

Temple Beth El (R-UAHC), 67 U.S. Hwy 206, Ph: 722-0674.
Rabbi W. Kraus. Services: Friday
Congregation Shaari Tefilah (Trad), 37 S. Bridge St, Ph: 685-0258.
Services: Call for schedule.

SOUTH ORANGE (See also WEST ORANGE)
Area Code (201)

Synagogues

Congregation Beth El of the Oranges & Maplewood (C-US), 222
Irvington Ave, Ph: 763-0111. Rabbi J. Orenstein. Services:
Shabbat
Congregation Oheb Shalom (C-US), 170 Scotland Rd,
Ph: 762-7067. Rabbi Dr. A. Shapiro. Services: Daily
Sharey Tefilo-Israel (R-UAHC), 432 Scotland Rd, Ph: 763-4116.
Rabbi H. Goldman. Services: Shabbat

Food

Zayda's, 309 Irvington Ave, Ph: 762-1812. Self-service butcher,
deli, kosher grocery; also take-out. RS: Rabbi S. Rosenberg of
Elmora Hebrew Center, Elizabeth. Closed Shabbat.

Accommodations

Private accommodations; call Rabbi J. Orenstein at Congregation
Beth El, Ph: 763-0111.

SOUTH RIVER (See also HIGHLAND PARK) Area Code (908)

Synagogues

Congregation Anshe Emeth (C), 88 Main St, Ph: 257-4190. Rabbi
  J. Maza. Services: Daily

SPARTA Area Code (201)

Synagogues

Congregation B'nai Emet (C), 134 W. Mountain Rd, Ph: 729-4621.
  Services: Call for schedule.

SPOTSWOOD Area Code (908)

Synagogues

Monroe Township Jewish Center (R-UAHC), 11 Cornell Ave,
  Ph: 251-1119. Rabbi S. Stern. Services: Friday

SPRAY BEACH Area Code (609)

Synagogues

Jewish Community Center of Long Beach Island (C), 15 E 24th St,
  Ph: 492-4090. Rabbi H. Rosenblum. Services: Shabbat (July and
  August only)

SPRINGFIELD (See also WEST ORANGE) Area Code (201)

Synagogues

Temple Beth Ahm (C-US), 60 Temple Dr, Ph: 376-0539. Rabbi P.
  Rank. Services: Daily
Congregation Israel of Springfield (O-UOJC), 339 Mountain Ave,
  Ph: 467-9666. Rabbi A. Yuter. Services: Daily
Temple Sha'arey Shalom (R-UAHC), 78 S Springfield Ave,
  Ph: 379-5387. Rabbi J. Goldstein. Services: Shabbat

Food

Bagels Supreme, 252 Mountain Ave, Ph: 376-9381. RS: Rabbi A.
  Yuter, Council of Orthodox Rabbis of Metro West.
Springfield Pastry Shop, 246 Mountain Ave, Ph: 376-6413. Breads

& pastries (pareve & dairy). RS: Rabbi A. Yuter, Council of Orthodox Rabbis of Metro West.

Accommodations

Private accommodations; contact the office at Congregation Israel of Springfield, Ph: 376-6806.

SUCCASUNNA Area Code (201)

Synagogues

Temple Shalom (R-UAHC), 215 S Hillside Ave, Ph: 584-5666. Rabbi J. Soffin. Services: Shabbat

SUMMIT Area Code (908)

Synagogues

Jewish Community Center (C-US), 67 Kent Place Blvd, Ph: 273-8130. Rabbi W. Horn. Services: Daily
Temple Sinai (R-UAHC), 208 Summit Ave, Ph: 273-4921. Rabbi E. Lewis. Services: Friday

TEANECK Area Code (201) Bergen County J-pop. 85,000

Synagogues

Beth Aaron (O-UOJC), 950 Queen Anne Rd, Ph: 836-6210. Rabbi E. Kanarfogel. Services: Daily
Congregation Beth Am (R-UAHC), 510 Claremont Ave, Ph: 836-5752. Rabbi A. Darnov. Services: Friday
Congregation Beth Sholom (C-US), Rugby Rd & Rutland Ave, Ph: 833-2620. Rabbi K. Berger. Services: Shabbat
Congregation B'nai Yeshurun (O-UOJC), 641 W Englewood Ave, Ph: 836-8916. Rabbi A. Weil. Services: Daily
Temple Emeth (R-UAHC), 1666 Windsor Rd, Ph: 833-1322. Rabbi L. Sigel. Services: Shabbat
Friends of Lubavitch (O-Lubav), 513 Kenwood Pl, Ph: 907-0686. Rabbi M. Weiss. Services: Shabbat and Sunday
Jewish Center of Teaneck (C), 70 Sterling Pl, Ph: 833-0515. Rabbi D. Feldman. Services: Daily

Synagogues cont.

Rinat Yisrael (O-UOJC), 389 W Englewood Ave, Ph: 837-2795.
  Rabbi Y. Adler. Services: Shabbat and Sunday

Eating Out

Grill Express, 540 Cedar Lane (to open July, 1991). Meals: l,d.
  Menu: (Glatt meat) Israeli, schwarma, shishlik, hamburgers,
  steak, salad. RS: Rabbinical Council of Bergen County. Closed
  Shabbat.
Hunan Teaneck, 515 Cedar Lane, Ph: 692-0099. Meals: l,d. Menu:
  (Glatt meat) Chinese. Take-out available. RS: Rabbinical
  Council of Bergen County. Closed Shabbat.
Jerusalem Pizza, 496 Cedar Lane, Ph: 836-2120. Meals: l,d. Menu:
  Mideastern and vegetarian dishes, fish, salads, knishes and ice
  cream. RS: Rabbinical Council of Bergen County. Closed
  Shabbat.
Noah's Ark, 482 Cedar Lane, Ph: 692-1200. Meals: l,d. Menu:
  (Glatt meat) Deli, soup, entrees, salads, desserts. Also take-out.
  RS: Rabbinical Council of Bergen County. Major credit cards.
  Closed Shabbat.
Santoro's 439 Cedar Lane, Ph: 836-9505. Meals: l,d. Menu:
  (Dairy: cholov Yisroel) Pasta and fish dishes. RS: Rabbinical
  Council of Bergen County. Reservations. Closed Shabbat.

Food

Bagel Palace, 402-404 Cedar Lane, Ph: 836-4660. Bagels (pareve)
  and spreads. RS: Rabbinical Council of Bergen County. Closed
  Shabbat.
Butterflake Bake Shop, 448 Cedar Lane, Ph: 836-3516. RS:
  Rabbinical Council of Bergen County.
Fancy Delights, 492A Cedar Lane, Ph: 487-4035. Candy, nuts,
  dried fruits, etc. RS: Rabbinical Council of Bergen County.
  Closed Shabbat.
Glatt Express, 1400 Queen Anne Rd, Ph: 837-8110. Butcher,
  kosher supermarket, appetizing dept. RS: Rabbinical Council of
  Bergen County. V, MC. Closed Shabbat.
Hot Bagels, 513 Cedar Lane, Ph: 836-9705. Pareve bagels. RS:
  Rabbinical Council of Bergen County (bagels only).

Ma'adan Caterers & Take Home Foods, 446 Cedar Lane,
Ph: 692-0192. Prepared chicken, meat dishes, side dishes and
packaged frozen foods. RS: Rabbinical Council of Bergen
County. Closed Shabbat.

Accommodations

Private accommodations; contact the office at Beth Aaron,
Ph: 692-9604.

Mikvah

Mikvah Association, 1726 Windsor Rd, Ph: Ph: 837-8220.

Bookstore

Balaban's Books, 506A Cedar Lane, Ph: 836-2894.

TENAFLY (See also TEANECK)   Area Code (201)

Synagogues

Congregation Beth Chavairuth (R-UAHC), 145 Stonehurst Dr,
Ph: 568-5189. Rabbi A. Fridkis. Services: Friday
Temple Sinai of Bergen County (R-UAHC), 1 Engle St,
Ph: 568-3035. Rabbi B. Block. Services: Shabbat

Eating Out

Temptations At The J.C.C., 411 E Clinton Ave, Ph: 871-2222. Meat
and poultry dishes, salads and sandwiches. RS: Rabbinical
Council of Bergen County. Closed Shabbat.

TINTON FALLS (See also LONG BRANCH)   Area Code (908)

Synagogues

Monmouth Reform Temple (R-UAHC), 332 Hance Ave,
Ph: 747-9365. Rabbi S. Priesand. Services: Friday

TOMS RIVER   Area Code (908)

Synagogues

Congregation B'nai Israel (C-US), Old Freehold Rd, Ph: 349-1244.
Rabbi R. Hammerman. Services: Daily

Synagogues cont.

Temple Beth Shalom (R), Old Freehold Rd, Ph: 349-3199. Rabbi
   B. Gottlieb. Services: Friday

TRENTON   Area Code (609) J-pop. 8,500

Synagogues

Congregation Ahavath Israel (C), 1130 Lower Ferry Rd,
   Ph: 882-3092. Rabbi B. Gerson. Services: Shabbat
Congregation Brothers of Israel (C-US), 499 Greenwood Ave,
   Ph: 695-3479. Rabbi H. Hersch. Services: Shabbat
Har Sinai Temple (R-UAHC), 491 Bellevue Ave, Ph: 392-7143.
   Rabbi D. Straus. Services: Friday

TURNERSVILLE   Area Code (609)

Synagogues

Congregation B'nai Tikvah (C), Fish Pond Rd and Spring Lake Dr,
   Ph: 589-6550. Rabbi L. Zucker. Services: Shabbat

TWIN RIVERS (See EAST WINDSOR)

UNION (See also ELIZABETH)   Area Code (908)

Synagogues

Congregation Beth Shalom (C-US), 2046 Vaux Hall Rd,
   Ph: 686-6773. Rabbi H. Morrison. Services: Shabbat
Temple Israel of Union (C), 2372 Morris Ave, Ph: 687-2120. Rabbi
   M. Korbman. Services: Shabbat

UNION CITY   Area Code (201)

Synagogues

Congregation Beth Jacob (O), 325 4th St, Ph: 863-3114. Rabbi A.
   Schiff. Services: Shabbat
Temple Israel Emanuel (O-UOJC), 314 33rd St, Ph: 866-6656.
   Rabbi A. Hirschman. Services: Shabbat

Day School

Mesivta Sanz of Hudson County, 3400 New York Ave,
Ph: 867-8690.

VENTNOR (See also ATLANTIC CITY)   Area Code (609)

Synagogues

Congregation Beth Judah (C-US), 6725 Ventnor Ave,
Ph: 822-7116. Rabbi A. Lucas. Services: Daily

VERONA (See also WEST ORANGE)   Area Code (201)

Synagogues

Congregation Beth Am (C), 56 Grove Ave, Ph: 239-0754. Rabbi R.
Mark. Services: Shabbat

VINELAND   Area Code (609) J-pop. 2,500

For information about kashruth or the Vineland Community, call
Rabbi Y. Rapoport of Chabad, Ph: 691-5656.

Synagogues

Agudath Achim Congregation (O), S Main Rd, corner of Iowa
Ave. Services: Saturday
Ahavas Achim (O), Plum St, Ph: 691-2218. Rabbi J. Loebenstein.
Services: Saturday and daily a.m.
Congregation Beth Israel (C-US), 1015 Park Ave, Ph: 691-0852.
Rabbi M. Kohn. Services: Daily
Norma Congregation Brotherhood (O), Wallace St & Almond Rd,
Norma, Ph: 691-4740. Rabbi A. Mayerfeld. Services: Shabbat
Sharith Haplaite Congregation (O), 1476 S Orchard Rd,
Ph: 691-1818. Services: Weekdays p.m.
Congregation Sons of Jacob (O), 321 Grape St, Ph: 692-4232.
Rabbi Y. Rapoport. Services: Saturday and daily

Food

Upper Krust Bakery, Main & Magnolia Rd, Ph: 691-6441. Breads
and pastries (mostly pareve). RS: Rabbi Y. Rapoport.

Accommodations

Days Inn, 100 W Landis Ave, Ph: 691-6685. Less than a mile from Congregation Sons of Jacob.

Private accommodations; for information call Mr. S. Mayerfeld, **Norma**, Ph: 692-1313.

Mikvah

Mikvah, Peach St, **Norma**. Contact Mrs. E. Mayerfeld, Ph: 691-7191.

WANAMASSA (See also OCEAN)   Area Code (908)

Synagogues

Congregation Sons of Israel (O-UOJC), Logan Rd & Park Blvd; also meets in **Ocean**, Ph: 775-1964. Rabbi Y. Carlbach. Services: Shabbat

WANAQUE   Area Code (201)

Synagogues

Lakeland Hills Jewish Center (C-US), 7 Conklintown Rd, Ph: 835-4786. Rabbi M. Mallach. Services: Friday

WARREN   Area Code (908)

Synagogues

Mountain Jewish Community Center (R), 104 Mt Horeb Rd, Ph: 356-8777. Rabbi H. Jaffe. Services: Friday

WASHINGTON   Area Code (908)

Synagogues

Jewish Center of Northwest Jersey (Unaffiliated), Youmans Ave, Ph: 689-0762. Rabbi J. Gelberman. Services: Call for information.

WASHINGTON TOWNSHIP   Area Code (201)

Synagogues

Temple Beth Or (R-UAHC), 56 Ridgewood Rd, Ph: 664-7422.
   Rabbi H. Berkowitz. Services: Friday

WAYNE   Area Code (201)

Synagogues

Temple Beth Tikvah (R-UAHC), 950 Preakness Ave,
   Ph: 595-6565. Rabbi I. Dresner. Services: Daily
Shomrei Torah-Wayne (C-US), 30 Hinchman Ave, Ph: 696-2500.
   Rabbi R. Eisenberg. Services: Shabbat

WEST CALDWELL (See also WEST ORANGE)
   Area Code (201)

Synagogues

Young Israel (O), 1 Henderson Dr, Ph: 575-1194. Rabbi Z. Segal.
   Services: Daily

Day School

Joseph Kushner Hebrew Academy, 1 Henderson Dr, Ph: 575-1194.

WESTFIELD (See also ELIZABETH)   Area Code (908)

Synagogues

Temple Emanu-El (R-UAHC), 756 E Broad St, Ph: 232-6770.
   Rabbi C. Kroloff and Rabbi M. Disick. Services: Shabbat and
   daily a.m.

WEST NEW YORK (See also TEANECK)   Area Code (201)

Synagogues

Congregation Shaare Zedek (O-UOJC), 5308 Palisade Ave,
   Ph: 867-6859. Rabbi L. Mozeson. Services: Daily

WEST ORANGE (See also LIVINGSTON)
Area Code (201)

Synagogues

Congregation Ahavas Achim B'nai Jacob and David (O-UOJC), 700 Pleasant Valley Way, Ph: 736-1407. Rabbi A. Marcus. Services: Daily

Daughters of Israel Geriatric Center (O), 1155 Pleasant Valley, Ph: 731-5100. Rabbi Z. Karpel. Services: Daily

Jewish Center of West Orange B'nai Sholom (C-US), 300 Pleasant Valley Way, Ph: 731-0160. Rabbi S. Asekoff. Services: Daily

Congregation Plaza (O), 750 Northfield Ave, Ph: 731-2186. Rabbi R. Rubin. Services: Saturday

Young Israel of West Orange (O-NCYI), 567-69 Pleasant Valley Way, Ph: 731-3383. Rabbi H. Horowitz. Services: Daily

Food

Gourmet Galaxy, 659 Eagle Rock Ave, Ph: 736-0060. Dairy appetizing store: cheeses, smoked fish, etc; frozen foods and kosher groceries. Some cholov Yisroel. RS: Rabbi A. Marcus, Council of Orthodox Rabbis of Metro West. Closed Shabbat.

Pleasandale Bakery, 480 Pleasant Valley Way, Ph: 736-3636. Breads and pastries (pareve and dairy). RS: Rabbi A. Marcus, Council of Orthodox Rabbis of Metro West. Closed Shabbat.

Reuben's Delite, 500 B Pleasant Valley Way, Ph: 731-6351. Take-out. Meat, poultry and fish, appetizers, side dishes, soups and breads. RS: Rabbi A. Marcus, Council of Orthodox Rabbis of Metro West. Closed Shabbat.

Accommodations

Private accommodations; call Rabbi A. Marcus at Congregation Ahavas Achim, Ph: 736-1407.

Mikvah

Essex County Ritualarium, 717 Pleasant Valley Way, Ph: 731-1427

Day School

Solomon Schechter Day School of Essex & Union (C), 122 Gregory Ave, Ph: 669-0790.

Bookstore

Sky Hebrew Book Store, 1923 Springfield Ave, **Maplewood,**
    Ph: 763-4244.

WESTWOOD   Area Code (201)

Synagogues

Temple Beth Or (R-UAHC), 56 Ridgewood Rd, Ph: 664-7422.
    Rabbi P. Berkowitz. Services: Shabbat

Eating Out

Bader's East Side Deli & Restaurant, 463 Broadway, Ph: 358-1200.
    Meals: b,l,d. Menu: Deli-style dishes. RS: Rabbi H. Lieberman
    of Carteret Jewish Community Center (C). Credit cards: Amex,
    V, MC, Diners. Closed Monday.

WILDWOOD   Area Code (609) J-pop. 425

Synagogues

Beth Judah Synagogue (C), Spencer & Pacific Aves, Ph: 522-7541.
    Rabbi J. Schechtman-Gabriel. Services: Saturday

WILLINGBORO (See also CHERRY HILL)   Area Code (609)

Synagogues

Congregation Beth Torah (C-US), Beverly Rancocas Rd,
    Ph: 877-4214. Rabbi B. Sendrow. Services: Shabbat
Temple Emanu-El (R-UAHC), John F. Kennedy Way,
    Ph: 871-1736/1797. Rabbi R. Levine. Services: Shabbat

WOODBRIDGE (See also HIGHLAND PARK)
    Area Code (908)

Synagogues

Congregation Adath Israel (C-US), 424 Amboy Ave,
    Ph: 634-9601. Rabbi M. Kula. Services: Shabbat, Monday and
    Thursday

WOODBURY HEIGHTS (See also **CHERRY HILL**)
Area Code (609)

Synagogues

Congregation Beth Israel (C-US), High & Warner Sts, Ph: 848-7272. Rabbi M. Kaplan. Services: Shabbat

WOODCLIFF LAKE   Area Code (201)

Synagogues

Temple Emanuel of The Pascack Valley (C-US), 87 Overlook Dr, Ph: 391-0801. Rabbi A. Ungar. Services: Daily

WYCKOFF   Area Code (201)

Synagogues

Temple Beth Rishon (C,R-UAHC), 585 Russell Ave, Ph: 891-4466. Rabbi A. Pearl. Services: Shabbat

New Mexico

ALBUQUERQUE   Area Code (505)   J-pop. 4,500

Synagogues

Temple Albert (R-UAHC), 3800 Louisiana Blvd NE, Ph: 883-1818. Rabbi P. Citrin. Services: Shabbat

Congregation B'nai Israel (C-US), 4401 Indian School Rd NE, Ph: 266-0155. Rabbi I. Celnik. Services: Shabbat, Monday and Thursday

Food

For kosher food information, call Eli or Ellen Follick, Ph: 828-2355.

The Kosher Food Store, 1619 San Pedro NE, Ph: 268-3740. Complete kosher grocery (all packaged): breads, cheeses, Glatt kosher meats, Sinai & Empire products, fish, challah and shelf goods. Closed Shabbat.

Accommodations

For a kosher meal or Shabbat accommodations, contact Eli and Ellen Follick, 7205 Chickadee Ave NE, 87109. Ph: 828-2355.

LAS CRUCES   Area Code (505)   J-pop. 525

Synagogues

Temple Beth-El (R-UAHC), 702 W Parker Rd, Ph: 524-3380. Rabbi C. Stanway. Services: Friday and first Saturday of month

ROSWELL   Area Code (505)

Synagogues

Congregation B'nai Israel (O,C,R), 712 N Washington Ave, Ph: 623-2073. Services: Friday and by arrangement

SANTA FE   Area Code (505)   J-pop. 900

Synagogues

Temple Beth Shalom (R-UAHC), 205 E Barcelona Rd, Ph: 982-1376. Rabbi P. Bentley. Services: Friday (R) and Saturday (C).

Kehillat Torah Bamidbar (O), 205 E Barcelona Rd, Ph: 989-9358. Rabbi S. Goldberg. Services: Daily

Food

Kaune's Food Town, 511 Old Santa Fe Trail, Ph: 982-2629. Large selection of kosher groceries, cheeses and frozen poultry.

Mrs. Arel Mishory will cater and deliver kosher meals to hotel guests. She can be reached at Kehillat Torah Bamidbar, Ph: 989-9358. RS: Rabbi S. Goldberg.

Accommodations

For visitors, one and two-bedroom apartments with kitchens for rent. 10141/2 Canyon Rd; mailing address: P.O. Box 1111, 87504. Frozen glatt kosher meat and poultry available. Contact Len Goodman, Ph: 982-2621. Half-hour walk to synagogue.

The following hotels (among others located at the "Plaza`") are within walking distance of the synagogue:

Budget Inn, 725 Cerrillos Rd, Ph: 982-5952

Residence Inn, 1698 Galisteo, Ph: 988-7300. All units have kitchenettes.

La Fonda Hotel, 100 E San Francisco St, Ph: 982-5511.

For Shabbat hospitality, call Kehillat Torah Bamidbar, Ph: 989-9358.

Mikvah

The Santa Fe community mikvah is in a private home. Contact Mrs. Arel Mishory at Kehillat Torah Bamidbar, Ph: 989-9358.

Day School

Torah Bamidbar Academy, 805 Early St, Ph: 984-2641.

New York

New York State information generally appears alphabetically under individual towns and cities. In New York City, the listings under each category heading are subdivided according to borough. Towns and cities in Nassau, Suffolk, Westchester and Rockland Counties are arranged under their county headings (see the table of contents).

ALBANY   Area Code (518)   J-pop. 12,000

For kosher information, call the Vaad Hakashruth of the Capital District, Ph: 489-1530.

Synagogues

Congregation Beth Abraham Jacob (O-UOJC), 340 Whitehall Rd,
Ph: 489-5819/5179. Rabbi M. Bomzer. Services: Daily

Congregation Beth Emeth (R-UAHC), 100 Academy Rd,
Ph: 436-9761. Rabbi M. Silverman. Services: Shabbat

Congregation B'nai Sholom (R-UAHC), 420 Whitehall Rd,
Ph: 482-5283. Rabbi D. Cashman. Services: Friday

Chabad Lubavitch Center of the Capital District (O-Lubav), 122 S
Main Ave, Ph: 482-5781. Rabbi I. Rubin. Services: Daily. Call
for location.

Daughters of Sarah Nursing Home, Washington Ave Exit,
Ph: 456-7831. Services: Friday (R), Saturday (Trad)

Temple Israel Kenesset Yisrael (C-US), 600 New Scotland Ave,
Ph: 438-7858. Rabbi P. Silton. Services: Daily

Congregation Ohav Sholom (C-US), New Krumkill Rd,
Ph: 489-4706. Rabbi B. Frydman-Kohl. Services: Daily

Congregation Shomray Torah (O), 463 New Scotland Ave,
Services: Daily

Eating Out

Dahlia's Vegetarian Bistro, 858 Madison Ave, Ph: 482-0931.
Meals: l,d. Menu: (Dairy, vegetarian) International cuisine;
entrees, soups, salads; homemade ice cream, sorbets, soft serve,
frozen yogurt. RS: Vaad Hakashruth of the Capital District.

Kosher dining at the State University of New York at Albany, 1400
Washington Ave (Dutch Quad Dining Hall), cafeteria style.
Meals: l,d. Sunday through Saturday (d). Glatt meat. To reserve
a meal, call the kitchen, Ph: 442-5947. For further information,
contact Rabbi Y. Kelman of the Vaad Hakashruth, Ph: 489-1530.
Open during academic year.

Food

Albany J.C.C., 340 Whitehall Rd, Ph: 438-6651. Sandwiches and
cold food to go. RS: Vaad Hakashruth of the Capital District.
Please call in advance.

Dahlia's Supreme Ice Cream, 858 Madison Ave, Ph: 482-0931. Ice
cream (43 flavors), sorbets, soft serve, frozen yogurt. RS: Vaad
Hakashruth of the Capital District.

Food cont.

Honest Weight Food Coop, 112 Quail St, Ph: 465-0383. Natural
foods. A list of products approved by the Vaad Hakashruth of
the Capital District is posted in the coop.

I Can't Believe It's Yogurt, Shop 'N Save Plaza, Ph: 438-1316.
Frozen yogurt. RS: Vaad Hakashruth of the Capital District.

Leo's Bakery, 28 Maple Ave, Ph: 482-7902. Breads and rolls
(pareve), cakes, cookies and other baked goods (dairy).

New Mt. Pleasant Bakery, 404 Delaware, Ph: 465-1499; 73 Wolf
Rd, **Colonie**, Ph: 459-7520. Breads and pastries (pareve and
dairy; Pas Yisroel (except donuts). RS: Vaad Hakashruth of the
Capital District.

Price Chopper Super Center, 1892 Central Ave, **Colonie**,
Ph: 456-9314. Full-service kosher department. Glatt meat, poul-
try, deli, dairy appetizers. RS: Vaad Hakashruth of the Capital
District. All products must have Vaad certification on label.
Store also carries large selection of kosher groceries.

Shop N' Save, 900 Central Ave, Ph: 438-7296; 98 Wolf Rd,
Colonie, Ph: 482-1085. Fresh kosher fish. RS: Vaad Hakashrut
of the Capital District. Also good selection of kosher products.

Mikvah

B'nos Israel of the Capital District, 190 Elm St. Contact
Congregation Beth Abraham Jacob, Ph: 489-5819 or Mrs. Laya
Levine, Ph: 438-1733.

Day Schools

Bet Shraga Hebrew Academy of the Capital District (C), 54 Sand
Creek Rd, Ph: 482-0464.

Maimonides Hebrew Day School of the Capital District, 420
Whitehall Rd, Ph: 482-3064.

AMENIA   Area Code (914)

Synagogues

Beth David (R-UAHC), P.O. Box 125, 12501, Ph: 373-8264. Rabbi
E. Stevens and Rabbi H. Rothstein. Services: Twice monthly.
Call for schedule.

AMHERST (See **BUFFALO**)

AMSTERDAM   Area Code (518)   J-pop. 450

Synagogues

Congregation Sons of Israel (C-US), 355 Guy Park Ave,
Ph: 842-8691. Rabbi G. Spector. Services: Shabbat

AUBURN   Area Code (315)   J-pop. 175

Synagogues

Congregation B'nai Israel (C-US), 8 John Smith Ave,
Ph: 253-6675. Services: Shabbat

BEACON   Area Code (914)

Synagogues

Beacon Hebrew Alliance (O), 55 Fishkill Ave, Ph: 831-2012.
Services: Shabbat

BINGHAMTON   Area Code (607)
Broome County J-pop. 3,000

Synagogues

Temple Beth El (Recon-FRCH), 117 Jefferson Ave, **Endicott**,
Ph: 797-0354. Rabbi L. Sussman. Services: Shabbat
Congregation Beth David (O-UOJC), 39 Riverside Dr,
Ph: 722-1793. Rabbi R. Weiss. Services: Daily
Chabad House of Binghamton (O-Lubav), 420 Murray Hill Rd,
Vestal, Ph: 797-0015. Rabbi A. Slonim. Services: Call for
schedule.
Temple Concord (R-UAHC), 9 Riverside Dr, Ph: 723-7355. Rabbi
A. Fertig. Services: Shabbat
Temple Israel (C-US), Deerfield Pl, Ph: 723-7461. Rabbi B. Starr.
Services: Daily

Eating Out

Kosher Kitchen at SUNY (cafeteria), Binghampton Campus, Vestal Pkwy E, University Union, Ph: 777-4980. Meals: l,d. Menu: (Meat and dairy) RS: Rabbi A. Skurowitz from Congregation Beth David.

Food

Baskin Robbins, Vestal Plaza, **Vestal**, Ph: 797-5154. All supervised products listed in letter on display. RS: Rabbi R. Weiss.

Binghamton Kosher Market, 14 Conklin Ave, Ph: 723-5331. Complete kosher grocery including prepared chicken and deli to go. RS: Rabbi R. Weiss. Closed Shabbat.

Butterflake Pastry Shop, 1159 Upper Front St, Ph: 724-7656. Challah, breads, pastry (dairy and pareve; list is posted). RS: Rabbi R. Weiss.

Carvel, 109 Riverside Dr, **Johnson City**, Ph: 798-7566; 526 Hooper Rd, **Endwell**, Ph: 748-0509. RS: Kof-K, by Rabbi R. Weiss.

Wagner's Cakes & Cookies, 46 Seminary Ave, Ph: 724-5550. Breads and pastries (pareve and dairy). RS: Rabbi R. Weiss.

Accommodations

Private accommodations; call Rabbi A. Slonim, Chabad, Ph: 797-0015.

Ramada Inn, 65 Front St, Ph: 724-2412. Five blocks to Congregation Beth David.

Mikvah

Beth David Mikvah, 39 Riverside Dr. Contact Mrs. Gella Weiss, Ph: 724-0599 or Mrs. Tzvia Staiman, Ph: 722-4131.

Day School

Hillel Academy of Broome County, 4737 Deerfield Pl, Ph: 722-9274.

BREWSTER   Area Code (914)

Synagogues

Temple Beth Elohim (R-UAHC), Rte 22, Ph: 279-4585.
  Rabbi S. Acrish. Services: Friday

BRONX (See NEW YORK CITY)

BROOKLYN (See NEW YORK CITY)

BUFFALO   Area Code (716)   J-pop. 18,500

For kosher food information; call the Va'ad Hakashrus of Buffalo,
  Rabbi Naphtali Burnstein, Administrator, Ph: 634-3990.

Synagogues

Congregation Beth Abraham (O), 1073 Elmwood Ave,
  Ph: 882-4362. Services: Shabbat and Holidays
Temple Beth Am (R-UAHC), 4660 Sheridan Dr, Ph: 633-8877.
  Rabbi S. Mason. Services: Shabbat and Holidays
Temple Beth El of Greater Buffalo (C-US), 2368 Eggert Rd,
  Tonawanda, Ph: 836-3762. Rabbi R. J. Eisen. Services: Daily
Temple Beth Shalom, (R), Bullis Rd, Elma, Ph: 681-5514.
  Services: Last Friday and Holidays
Temple Beth Zion (R-UAHC), 805 Delaware Ave, Ph: 886-7150.
  Rabbi Dr. M. Goldberg. Services: Shabbat
B'nai Sholom (Trad), 1675 N Forest Rd, **Williamsville,**
  Ph: 689-8203. Services: Shabbat and Sunday
Chabad House (O-Lubav) at State University of New York at
  Buffalo, 3292 Main St, Ph: 833-8334. Rabbi H. Greenberg.
  Services: Friday and Holidays
Chabad House (O-Lubav) at SUNY, Buffalo-Amherst Campus,
  2501 N Forest Rd, **Getzville**, Ph: 688-1642. Rabbi N. Gurary.
  Services: Shabbat and Holidays
Knesset Center (O-Lubav), 500 Starin Ave, Ph: 832-5063. Rabbi
  H. Greenberg. Services: Daily
Temple Shaarey Zedek (C-US), 621 Getzville Rd, Ph: 838-3232.
  Rabbi E. Marrus. Services: Daily

Synagogues cont.

Temple Sinai (Recon-FRCH), 50 Alberta Dr, Ph: 834-0708. Rabbi
J. Herzog. Services: Shabbat

Young Israel of Greater Buffalo (O-NCYI), 105 Maple Rd,
Williamsville, Ph: 634-0212. Rabbi N. Burnstein. Services:
Daily

Eating Out

Amherst Jewish Center, Glorious Foods Snack Bar, 2640 N Forest
Rd, **Getzville**, Ph: 636-0333. Meals: b,l. Menu: (Glatt meat)
Fast food, deli and pareve sandwiches, soups and pastries. RS:
Va'ad Hakashrus of Buffalo. Closed Shabbat.

Bakerman Fresh Coffee & Donut Shop, 2151 Delaware Ave,
Ph: 874-5420; 3381 Sheridan Dr, **Amherst**, Ph: 836-3810.
Coffee, tea, donuts, pastries. RS: Va'ad Hakashrus of Buffalo.

Chabad House, 3292 Main St and 2501 N Forest Rd, **Getzville**,
Ph: 688-1642. RS: Rabbi H. Greenberg. Shabbat meals are
served weekly. Call for reservations.

Kosher Deli at SUNY, Amherst Campus, Talbert Hall,
Ph: 636-3037. Meals: l. Menu: (Glatt meat) Deli. Monday -
Friday during semester. RS: Va'ad Hakashrus of Buffalo.

Food

Brown's Kosher Meats, 2111 Eggert Rd, **Amherst**, Ph: 836-3370.
RS: Rabbi H. Cassorla of Temple Beth Israel (C), Niagara Falls.
Closed Shabbat.

Cohen's Kosher Meats & Poultry Market, 340 Kenmore Ave,
Ph: 833-9400. RS: Va'ad Hakashrus of Buffalo. Closed Shabbat.

Glorious Foods, 338 Kenmore Ave, **Getzville**, Ph: 838-1040. Dairy
and Glatt meat take-out; fresh baked goods. Closed Shabbat.

Accommodations

Private accommodations; call Chabad House, Ph: 688-1642 or
Rabbi H. Greenberg, Ph: 837-2320.

Residence Inn, 100 Maple Rd, **Amherst**, Ph: 632-6622. Suites
with kitchens. Around the corner from Young Israel.

The following motels are a quarter mile from Young Israel:

Hampton Inn, 10 Flint Rd, **Amherst**, Ph: 689-4414.

278

Marriott, 1340 Millersport Hwy, **Amherst,** Ph: 689-6900.
Red Roof Inn, I290 & Millersport Hwy, **Amherst,** Ph: 689-7474.
Super 8, 1 Flint Rd, **Amherst,** Ph: 688-0817.

Mikvah

Buffalo Ritualarium, 1248 Kenmore Ave. Call Mrs. M. Stern,
Ph: 632-1531.

Day Schools

Kadimah School of Buffalo, 1 Cambridge Ave, Ph: 836-6903.
Torah Temimah School, 500 Starin Ave, Ph: 837-1164.

Bookstore

Mazel Tov Gift Shop, 1744 Hertel Ave, Ph: 838-5900.

CATSKILL REGION   Area Code (914)

Synagogues

Congregation Ezrath Israel (O-UOJC), Rabbi Eisner Sq,
Ellenville, Ph: 647-4450. Rabbi M. Frank. Services: Daily
Temple Israel of Catskill (R), Spring St, **Catskill,** Ph: 943-5758.
Rabbi P. Schlenker. Services: Friday (closed summers)
Temple Sholom (R-UAHC), Port Jervis & Dillon Rd, **Monticello,**
Ph: 794-8731. Rabbi L. Polonsky. Services: Friday
Congregation Tifereth Israel (O-UOJC), 18 Landfield Ave,
Monticello, Ph: 794-8470. Rabbi B. Leibowitz. Services: Daily

Eating Out

Please note: a number of kosher establishments open for the summer
months only. These may vary from year to year.

Moshe's Pizza, E Broadway & Waverly, **Monticello.** Menu: Pizza
and falafel. RS: Rabbi B. Leibowitz. Closed Shabbat. June-
Labor Day.
Jacob's Restaurant & Take-Out, Flalkoff's Bungalow Colony,
Monticello, Ph: 794-0008. Meals: l,d. Menu: Traditional. RS:
Rabbi G. Vinner. June-Labor Day.

Food

Madnick's Bakery, 121 Broadway, **Monticello**, Ph: 791-4063. RS: Star-K of Baltimore. Closed Shabbat.

Madnick's Bakery, Lake St, **South Fallsburg**, Ph: 434-7272. Breads and pastries. RS: Star-K. Closed Shabbat.

Resort Hotels (See also **Sharon Springs**)

Brown's, **Loch Sheldrake**, Ph: 434-5151. Synagogue on premises. RS: Rabbi J. Schlesinger. Open April-November.

Chalet Vim, **Woodbourne**, Ph: 434-5786. Shomer Shabbat. Cholov Yisroel available. Synagogue services daily. RS: Rabbi I. Isaacs. Open Passover through November.

Concord Hotel, **Kiamesha Lake**, Ph: 794-4000. Synagogue services daily. RS: Rabbi M. Gershon.

Golden Acres Farm and Ranch Resort, **Gilboa**, Ph: (607) 588-7329. Shomer Shabbat. Synagogue. RS: Vaad Hakashruth of the Capital District. Open Memorial-September 15.

Homowack Lodge, **Spring Glen**, Ph: 647-6800. Shomer Shabbat. Synagogue services daily. RS: Orthodox Union.

Hotel Lake House, Woodridge Rd, **Woodridge**, Ph: (718) 972-1306; (914) 434-7800. Cholov Yisroel. RS: Rabbi Y. Lebowitz. Open Passover through Succoth.

Kutsher's Country Club, **Monticello**, Ph: 794-6000. Synagogue services daily. RS: Rabbi S. Simpson.

New Life Health, Weight Control and Fitness Center, **Woodbourne** (at Chalet Vim), Ph: 434-5333. Cholov Yisroel Shomer Shabbat. RS: Rabbi I. Isaacs.

Oppenheimer's Regis Hotel, **Fleischmann's**, Ph: 254-5080. Shomer Shabbat. Cholov Yisroel. Synagogue services daily. RS: K'hal Adath Yeshurun of Washington Heights. Open Pesach through Succoth.

Zuckor's Glen Wild Hotel, **Glen Wild**, Ph: 434-7470. Shomer Shabbat. Cholov Yisroel. Synagogue. Open summers only.

Mikvah

Ellenville Mikvah, 312 Center St, **Ellenville**. Contact Mrs. Handler, Ph: 647-6846.

Mikvah of Monticello, 18 North St, **Monticello**. Contact Ms. C. Winzelberg, Ph: 794-6757.

Day School

Hebrew Day School of Sullivan and Ulster Counties, Rte 42, **Kiamesha Lake**, Ph: 794-7890/1.

Yeshiva K'Tana of Mountaindale, 35 Woodridge Rd, **Mountaindale**, Ph: 434-6140.

DEWITT (See SYRACUSE)

ELLENVILLE (See CATSKILL REGION)

ELMIRA   Area Code (607)   J-pop. 1,100

Synagogues

Congregation B'nai Israel (R-UAHC), 900 W Water St, Ph: 734-7735. Rabbi P. Aaronson. Services: Shabbat

Congregation Shomray Hadath (C-US), Cobbles Park E and W Water St, Ph: 732-7410. Rabbi J. Lapidus. Services: Saturday and Thursday

FLORIDA   Area Code (914)

Synagogues

Temple Beth Shalom (R), Roosevelt Ave, Ph: 651-7817. Rabbi S. Rheins. Services: Shabbat

GENEVA   Area Code (315)   J-pop. 300

Synagogues

Temple Beth El (R-UAHC), 755 S Main St, Ph: 789-2945. Rabbi D. Regenspan. Services: Friday

GLENS FALLS   Area Code (518)   J-pop. 800

Synagogues

Temple Beth El (R-UAHC), 3 Marion Ave, Ph: 792-4364. Rabbi R. Sobel. Services: Friday

Synagogues cont.

Congregation Shaaray Tefila (C-US), 68 Bay St, Ph: 792-4945.
Rabbi L. Alpern. Services: Shabbat and Sunday

GLOVERSVILLE   Area Code (518)   J-pop. 420

Synagogues

Knesseth Israel Synagogue (C-US), 34 E Fulton St, Ph: 725-0649.
Rabbi M. Feierstein. Services: Daily

GREENWOOD LAKE   Area Code (914)

Synagogues

Jewish Community Center of Greenwood Lake (Trad), Old Dutch
Hollow Rd, Ph: 477-2225. Rabbi M. Sarhi. Services: Shabbat

HENRIETTA   (See also ROCHESTER)   Area Code (716)

Synagogues

Temple Beth Am (C-US), 3249 E Henrietta Rd, Ph: 334-4855.
Rabbi S. Gulack. Services: Shabbat

HERKIMER   (See also UTICA)   Area Code (315)   J-pop. 180

Synagogues

Temple Beth Joseph (C-US), 327 N Prospect St, Ph: 866-4270.
Rabbi C. Leiffer. Services: Shabbat

HUDSON   Area Code (518)   J-pop. 470

Synagogues

Congregation Anshe Emeth (C), 240 Joslen Blvd, Ph: 828-6848.
Rabbi D. Fried. Services: Shabbat

ITHACA   Area Code (607)   J-pop. 1,250

For kosher food information, call Rabbi E. Silberstein,
Ph: 273-5394.

Synagogues

Temple Beth El (C-US), 402 N Tioga St, Ph: 273-5775. Rabbi S. Glass. Services: Shabbat

B'nai B'rith Hillel Congregation at Cornell University (O,C), 926 E State St, Anabel Taylor Hall, Ph: 256-4227. Rabbi L. Edwards. Services: Saturday

Center for Jewish Living at Cornell, Young Israel House (O-NCYI), 106 West Ave, Ph: 272-5810. Services: Daily. Saturday services at Anabel Taylor Hall.

Eating Out

Center for Jewish Living at Cornell (cafeteria), 106 West Ave, Ph: 272-5810. Meals: b,l,d. Menu: (Meat and dairy). Table service for Shabbat. RS: Rabbi A. Seiden (resident scholar for Young Israel House). Advance notice is required.

Accommodations

Shabbat hospitality; Chabad House of Ithaca (O-Lubav), 902 Triphammer Rd, Ph: 257-7379. Rabbi E. Silberstein.

Mikvah

Chabad Mikvah; contact Rabbi E. Silberstein, Ph: 257-7379 or Mr. J. Geldwerd, Ph: 273-5394.

KAUNEONGA LAKE   Area Code (914)

Synagogues

Temple Beth El (C), Ph: 583-4442. Rabbi A. Garmize. Services: Shabbat. Call for location.

KINGSTON   Area Code (914)   J-pop. 4,500

Synagogues

Congregation Agudas Achim (O-UOJC), 254 Lucas Ave, Ph: 331-1176. Rabbi Y. Seplowitz. Services: Saturday, Sunday, Monday and Thursday

Congregation Ahavath Achim (C), 8 Church St, **New Paltz**, Ph: 255-9817. Rabbi W. Strongin. Services: Shabbat

Synagogues cont.

Congregation Ahavath Israel (C-US), 100 Lucas Ave, Ph: 338-4409. Rabbi J. Fish. Services: Shabbat, Sunday, Monday and Thursday

Temple Emanuel (R-UAHC), 243 Albany Ave, Ph: 338-4271. Rabbi J. Eichhorn. Services: Friday

Food

Bread Alone, Rte 28, **Boiceville**, Ph: 657-3328. Bakery products with Vaad seal **only**. RS: Vaad Hakashruth of the Capital District.

Accommodations

The following hotels are less than a mile from Congregation Agudas Achim:

Holiday Inn Hotel, 503 Washington Ave, Ph: 338-0400. Frozen kosher dinners available - arrange with chef in advance.

Super 8 Motel, Washington Ave, Ph: 338-3078.

LAKE PLACID   Area Code (518)

Synagogues

Lake Placid Synagogue (C-US), 30 Saranac Ave, Ph: 523-3876. Rabbi S. Auerbach. Services: Shabbat

LAKE PEEKSKILL   Area Code (914)

Synagogues

Temple Israel (C), Lake Dr, Ph: 528-2305. Rabbi J. Goldberg. Services: Shabbat. Summers only.

LIBERTY   Area Code (914)   J-pop. 2,100

Synagogues

Congregation Ahavath Israel (C-US), 39 Chestnut St, Ph: 292-8843. Rabbi S. H. Dreifuss. Services: Daily

Mikvah

Liberty Mikvah, 37 Lincoln Pl, Ph: 292-6677. (Summers only).

LONG ISLAND (See NASSAU and SUFFOLK)

MAHOPAC   Area Code (914)

Synagogues

Temple Beth Shalom (C-US), 760 Rte 6, Ph: 628-6133.
Rabbi P. Fleischer. Services: Shabbat

MANHATTAN (See NEW YORK CITY)

MIDDLETOWN   Area Code (914)

Synagogues

Temple Sinai (C-US), 75 Highland Ave, Ph: 343-1861. Rabbi J.
Schwab. Services: Daily

Day School

Hebrew Day School of Orange County, 195 Watkins Ave,
Ph: 343-8588.

MONROE   Area Code (914)

Synagogues

Congregation Ahavas Torah (O), 26 Lincoln Rd, Ph: 783-7565.
Services: Saturday
Congregation Eitz Chaim (C), P.O. Box 183, 10950,
Ph: 783-7424. Rabbi A. Lew. Services: Shabbat
Monroe Temple of Liberal Judaism (R), 314 N Main St,
Ph: 783-2626. Rabbi G. Loeb. Services: Friday

Day School

United Talmudical Academy—Monroe Talmud Torah, 20 Getzel
Berger, Ph: 783-5845.

MONTICELLO (See CATSKILL REGION)

MOUNTAINDALE (See CATSKILL REGION)

NASSAU COUNTY   Area Code (516)   J-pop. 311,700

ATLANTIC BEACH (See also LONG BEACH)
Synagogues

Jewish Center of Atlantic Beach (O-UOJC), Nassau Ave & Park St,
   Ph: 371-0972. Rabbi B. Herring. Services: Daily

BALDWIN
Synagogues

Baldwin Jewish Centre (C-US), 885 E Seaman Ave, Ph: 223-5599.
   Rabbi M. Kroopnick. Services: Daily
South Baldwin Jewish Center (C-US), 2959 Grand Ave,
   Ph: 223-8688. Rabbi D. Arzt, Rabbi G. Pollack. Services: Daily

Eating Out

Ben's Delicatessen, 933 Atlantic Ave, **Baldwin Harbor**,
   Ph: 868-2072. Meals: l,d. Menu: Deli-style dishes. Also take-
   out. RS: Rabbi I. Steinberg.

BELLMORE
Synagogues

Bellmore Jewish Center (C-US), 2550 S Centre Ave, Ph: 781-3072.
   Rabbi J. Romm. Services: Daily
Temple Beth El (C-US), 1373 Bellmore Rd, **North Bellmore**,
   Ph: 781-2650. Rabbi H. Goldscheider. Services: Daily
Congregation Shaarei Shalom—East Bay Reform Temple (R),
   2569 E Merrick Rd, Ph: 781-5599. Rabbi P. Kushner. Services:
   Shabbat
Young Israel of North Bellmore (O-NCYI), 2428 Hamilton Rd,
   North Bellmore, Ph: 826-0048 or 826-1630. Rabbi M. Gorelik.
   Services: Shabbat and Sunday

Food

Jerusalem Harvest, 2645 Jerusalem Ave, **North Bellmore**,
   Ph: 781-0083. Meat and chicken entrees, salads, for take-out.
   RS: Vaad Harabonim of Long Island. Closed Shabbat.

286

BETHPAGE
Synagogues

Temple Beth Elohim (R-UAHC), 926 Round Swamp Rd, **Old Bethpage**, Ph: 694-4544. Rabbi L. Stein. Services: Shabbat

Bethpage Jewish Community Center (C-US), 600 Broadway, Ph: 938-7909. Rabbi B. Ginsberg. Services: Daily

CEDARHURST
Synagogues

Temple Beth El (C-US), 45 Locust Ave, Ph: 569-2700. Rabbi M. Edelman. Services: Daily

The Sephardic Temple (C-US), Branch Blvd at Halevy Dr, Ph: 295-4644. Rabbi A. Marans. Services: Daily

Young Israel of Lawrence—Cedarhurst (O-UOJC), Spruce St and Broadway, Ph: 569-3324. Rabbi M. Teitelbaum. Services: Daily

Eating Out

Burger Mayven, 530 Central Ave, Ph: 569-6183. Meals: l,d. Menu: Fast food. RS: Vaad Hakashrus of the Five Towns. Closed Shabbat.

Delicious Kosher Dairy Restaurant, 698 Central Ave, Ph: 569-6725. Meals: l,d. Menu: Fish and dairy dishes. Cholov Yisroel. RS: Vaad Hakashrus of the Five Towns. Closed Shabbat.

Jacob's Ladder, 83 Spruce St, Ph: 569-3373. Meals: l,d. Menu: Continental and Chinese cuisine. RS: Vaad Hakashrus of the Five Towns. All major cards. Closed Shabbat.

King David Restaurant, 550 Central Ave, Ph: 569-2920. Meal: l,d. Menu: Deli-style dishes. RS: Vaad Hakashrus of the Five Towns. Closed Shabbat.

Pockets, 588 Central Ave, Ph: 295-1710. Meals: l,d. Menu: (Glatt meat) Sephardic and Continental. Salad bar, shishkabob, entrees. Also take-out. RS: Vaad Hakashrus of the Five Towns. Closed Shabbat.

La Pasta Restaurant, 530 Central Ave, Ph: 569-8348. Meals: l,d. Menu: (Dairy: cholov Yisroel) Italian cuisine. RS: Vaad Hakashrus of the Five Towns. Credit cards. Closed Shabbat.

Eating Out cont.

Sabra Kosher Pizza, 560 Central Ave, Ph: 569-1563. Meals: l,d.
Menu: Dairy: cholov Yisroel. RS: Vaad Hakashrus of the Five
Towns. Closed Shabbat.

Food

Five Towns Bagels, 594 Central Ave, Ph: 569-7070. Bagels and
spreads. Some tables. RS: Vaad Hakashrus of the Five Towns.
Closed Shabbat.

Gourmet Glatt Emporium, 137 Spruce St, Ph: 569-2662. Kosher
grocery and self-service meat market. RS: Vaad Hakashrus of
the Five Towns. Closed Shabbat.

Moish's Bake Shop of Cedarhurst, 536 Central Ave, Ph: 374-2525.
Pareve, except cheesecake. RS: Vaad Hakashrus of the Five
Towns. Closed Shabbat.

Toddy's Appetizers, 115 Cedarhurst Ave, Ph: 295-1999. Take-out.
Pareve and dairy appetizers. RS: Vaad Hakashrus of the Five
Towns. Closed Shabbat.

Zomick's, 444 Central Ave, Ph: 569-5520. Breads and pastries.
RS: Vaad Hakashrus of the Five Towns. Closed Shabbat.

Bookstore

Elbaum Judaica, 694 Central Ave, Ph: 569-4577.

EAST MEADOW
Synagogues

East Meadow Jewish Center (C-US), 1400 Prospect Ave,
Ph: 483-4205. Rabbi R. Anorophy. Services: Daily

Temple Emanuel (R-UAHC), 123 Merrick Ave, Ph: 794-8911.
Rabbi J. Zion. Services: Shabbat

Suburban Park Jewish Center (C-US), 400 Old Westbury Rd,
Ph: 796-8833. Rabbi S. Davis. Services: Shabbat

Food

Nassau Kosher Meat, 495 Bellmore Ave, Ph: 333-1616. Fresh meat
and poultry, prepared foods for take-out, full line of kosher groceries (some cholov Yisroel products). RS: Vaad Harabonim of
Long Island. Closed Shabbat.

EAST ROCKAWAY (See HEWLETT)

ELMONT
Synagogues

Temple B'nai Israel (R-UAHC), Elmont Rd & Bayliss Ave, Ph: 354-1156. Rabbi S. Kehati. Services: Shabbat.

Elmont Jewish Center (C-US), 500 Elmont Rd, Ph: 488-1616. Rabbi J. Ozarowski. Services: Daily

FRANKLIN SQUARE
Synagogues

Franklin Square Jewish Center (C), Pacific & Lloyd St, Ph: 354-2322. Rabbi A. Shoulson. Services: Shabbat

FREEPORT
Synagogues

Congregation B'nai Israel (C-US), 91 N Bayview Ave, Ph: 623-4200. Rabbi S. J. Kane. Services: Daily

Union Reform Temple (R-UAHC), 475 N Brookside Ave, Ph: 623-1810. Rabbi L. Colton. Services: Shabbat

Food

Foodtown, 248 E Sunrise Hwy, Ph: 868-8400. Bakery (pareve and dairy) is under kosher supervision. RS: United Kosher Supervision, Rabbi Yaakov Spivak, Administrator.

GARDEN CITY
Synagogues

Garden City Jewish Center (R-UAHC), 168 Nassau Blvd, Ph: 248-9180. Rabbi S. Goodman. Services: Shabbat

GREAT NECK
Synagogues

Temple Beth El (R-UAHC), 5 Old Mill Rd, Ph: 487-0900. Rabbis M. Barzilai and J. Davidson. Services: Shabbat

Temple Emanuel of Great Neck (R-UAHC), 150 Hicks Lane, Ph: 482-5701. Rabbi R. Widom. Services: Shabbat

Synagogues cont.

Great Neck Synagogue (O-UOJC), 26 Old Mill Rd, Ph: 487-6100.
Rabbi D. Polakoff. Services: Daily

Temple Isaiah (R-UAHC), 35 Bond, Ph: 487-8709. Rabbi B.
Steinberg. Services: Friday

Temple Israel of Great Neck (C-US), 108 Old Mill Rd,
Ph: 482-7800. Rabbis M. Charry and C. Diamond. Services:
Daily

Young Israel of Great Neck (O-UOJC), 236 Middle Neck Rd, Ph:
829-6040. Rabbi Y. Lerner. Services: Daily

Eating Out

Colbeh, 75 N Station Place, Ph: 466-8181. Meals: l,d. Menu: (Glatt
meat) Persian. RS: Tablet-K. Closed Shabbat.

Darband, 158 Middleneck Rd, Ph: 829-0030. Meals: l,d. Menu:
(Glatt meat) Persian cuisine. RS: Vaad Harabonim of Queens.
Closed Shabbat.

Hunan Restaurant, 505/507 Middle Neck Rd, Ph: 482-7912. Meals:
l,d. Menu: (Glatt meat) Chinese and American. RS: Vaad
Harabonim of Queens. Closed Shabbat.

La Pizzeria, 114 Middle Neck Rd, Ph: 466-5114. Meals: l,d. Menu:
(Dairy: cholov Yisroel) Pizza, Italian dishes, Israeli salads, falafel.
RS: Vaad Harabonim of Queens. Closed Shabbat.

Nassiri, 33 N Station Plaza, Ph: 829-2222. Meals: l,d. Menu:
(Glatt meat) Persian cuisine. Shishkabob. RS: Tablet-K. Closed
Shabbat.

Shish Kabob Palace, 90 Middle Neck Rd, Ph: 487-2228. Meals: l,d.
Menu: (Glatt meat) Mideastern cuisine. Salads, kabobs.
RS: Vaad Harabonim of Queens. Closed Shabbat.

Food

Gel of Great Neck, 503 Middleneck Rd, Ph: 487-5886. Traditional
dishes prepared for take-out, kosher groceries. RS: Rabbi G.
Baras, Plainview. Closed Shabbat.

Accommodations

Private accommodations; call the office at Great Neck Synagogue,
Ph: 487-6100.

Mikvah

North Shore Mikvah, 26 Old Mill Rd, Ph: 487-2726.

Day School

North Shore Hebrew Academy, 16 Cherry Lane, Ph: 487-8964/8687.

GREENVALE
Eating Out

Ben's Delicatessen, 140 Wheatley Plaza, Ph: 621-3340. Meals: l,d. Menu: Deli, American cuisine. RS: Rabbi I. Steinberg

Food

Wheatley Bake Shop, 190 Wheatley Plaza, Ph: 621-7575. Dairy. RS: Vaad Harabonim of Long Island. Closed Shabbat.

HEMPSTEAD
Synagogues

Congregation Beth Israel (C), 141 Hilton Ave, Ph: 489-1818 Rabbi M. Green. Services: Shabbat

HEWLETT
Synagogues

Temple Beth Emeth (C-US), 30 Franklin Ave, Ph: 374-9220. Rabbi L. Levy. Services: Daily

Hewlett-East Rockaway Jewish Center (C-US), 295 Main St, **East Rockaway**, Ph: 599-2634. Rabbi S. Platek. Services: Saturday

Congregation Toras Chaim (O-UOJC), 1170 William St, Ph: 374-7363. Rabbi S. Lefkowitz. Services: Daily

Food

Simcha Glatt Kosher Take-Out, 1303 Broadway, Ph: 569-5411. Large variety of chicken, meat and side dishes. RS: Vaad Hakakshrus of the Five Towns. Closed Shabbat.

Accommodations

Private accommodations; call the office at Congregation Toras Chaim, Ph: 374-7363.

Mikvah

South Shore Mikvah, 1156 Peninsula Blvd, Ph: 569-5514.

Day School

Yeshiva Toras Chaim, 1170 William St, Ph: 374-7363.

HICKSVILLE
Synagogues

Hicksville Jewish Center (C-US), 6 Jerusalem Ave, Ph: 931-9323. Rabbi E. Goldstein. Services: Shabbat

Congregation Shaarei Zedek (O-UOJC), Old Country & New South Rd, Ph: 938-0420. Rabbis Y. Shuster and M. Sachs. Services: Daily

Bookstore

Theodore S. Cinnamon Ltd., 420 Jerusalem Ave, Ph: 935-7480.

JERICHO
Synagogues

Jericho Jewish Center (C-US) N Broadway-Jericho Rd, Ph: 938-2540. Rabbi S. Steinhart. Services: Daily.

Temple Or Elohim (R-UAHC), 18 Tobie Lane, Ph: 433-9888. Rabbi P. J. Bentley. Services: Shabbat

LAKE SUCCESS
Synagogues

Lake Success Jewish Center (C-US), 354 Lakeville Rd, Ph: 466-0569. Rabbi B. Stefansky. Services: Daily

LAWRENCE
Synagogues

Congregation Beth Sholom (O-UOJC), 390 Broadway, Ph: 569-3600. Rabbi K. Hain. Services: Daily

Temple Israel (R-UAHC), 140 Central Ave, Ph: 239-1140. Rabbis J. Bemporad and E. Wittstein. Services: Shabbat

Congregation Shaaray Tefila (O-UOJC), 25 Central Ave, Ph: 239-2444. Rabbi W. Wurzburger. Services: Daily

Temple Sinai of Long Island (R-UAHC), 131 Washington Ave, Ph: 569-0267. Rabbi R. Rozenberg. Services: Friday

Eating Out

Annie Chan's, 367 Central Ave, Ph: 374-1401. Meals: l,d. Menu: (Glatt meat) Chinese. RS: Vaad Hakashrus of the Five Towns. Closed Shabbat.

Jerusalem Pizza Plus, 344 Central Ave, Ph: 569-0074. Meals: l,d. Menu: (Dairy: cholov Yisroel) Pizza, pasta, falafel, fish, salads. RS: Vaad Hakashrus of the Five Towns. Closed Shabbat.

Food

Dunkin' Donuts, 299 Burnside Ave, Ph: 239-2052. Donuts, coffee, soup, eggs. RS: Vaad Hakashrut of the Five Towns.

Foodtown Supermarket, 603 Burnside Ave, Ph: 239-6617. Bakery (pareve and dairy) is under kosher supervision. RS: United Kosher Supervision, Rabbi Yaakov Spivak, Administrator.

Glatt Plus Kosher Meats, 290 Burnside Ave, Ph: 239-5458. Kosher groceries and fresh meats. RS: Vaad Hakashrus of the Five Towns. Closed Shabbat.

Mauzone of Lawrence, 341 Central Ave, Ph: 569-6411. Take-out (Glatt meat). Chicken, meat dishes and side dishes. RS: Vaad Hakashrus of the Five Towns. Closed Shabbat.

Super Sol, 330 Central Ave, Ph: 295-3300. Complete kosher super-market. RS: Vaad Hakashrus of the Five Towns.

Day School

The Brandeis School, 25 Frost Lane, Ph: 374-4747.

LEVITTOWN
Synagogues

Israel Community Center (C-US), 3235 Hempstead Tpke, Ph: 731-2580. Rabbi N. Valley. Services: Shabbat, Monday and Thursday

LIDO BEACH
Synagogues

Lido Beach Jewish Center (O-UOJC), 1 Fairway Rd, Ph: 889-9650. Rabbi D. Mehlman. Services: Daily

Accommodations

Private accommodations; contact Rabbi D. Mehlman, Ph: 889-9650 or 889-0382.

LONG BEACH
Synagogues

Congregation Bachurei Chemed (O), 210 Edwards Blvd, Ph: 432-0076. Rabbi Y. Frankel. Services: Shabbat, Sunday

Temple Beth El (O-UOJC), 570 Walnut St, Ph: 432-1678. Rabbi A. Kupchik. Services: Daily

East End Synagogue—Congregation Beth Sholom of Long Beach and Lido (C-US), 700 E Park Ave, Ph: 432-7464. Rabbi A. Miller. Services: Daily

Temple Emanu-El (R-UAHC), 455 Neptune Blvd, Ph: 431-4060. Rabbi H. Bernat. Services: Friday

Temple Israel of Long Beach (O-UOJC), 305 Riverside Blvd, Ph: 432-1410. Rabbi M. Alony. Services: Daily

Mesivta of Long Beach (C), 205 W Beach St, Ph: 431-7414. Rabbi Shayeh Kohn, Administrator. Services: Daily, during school year.

Sephardic Congregation of Long Beach (O), 161 Lafayette Blvd, Ph: 432-9224. Rabbi A. Abbitan. Services: Shabbat

Young Israel of Long Beach (O-NCYI), 158 Long Beach Blvd, Ph: 431-2404. Rabbi C. Wakslak. Services: Daily

Temple Zion (O-UOJC), 62 Maryland Ave, Ph: 432-5657. Rabbi I. Dropkin. Services: Shabbat and Sunday

Food

Country Boy Bakery, 256 E Park Ave, Ph: 889-7295. Pareve and dairy. Also cholov Yisroel products. RS: South Shore Vaad Hakashrus.

Long Beach Glatt, 172 E Park Ave, Ph: 889-2828. Traditional dishes to go, kosher groceries. RS: South Shore Vaad Hakashrus. Closed Shabbat.

Waldbaum's, 85 E Park Ave, Ph: 432-9077. Good selection of kosher products.

Accommodations

Jackson Hotel, 10 W Broadway, Ph: 431-3700. Shomer Shabbat. Synagogue services daily. RS: O.K. Laboratories. Open summers and Holidays.

Day School

Hebrew Academy of Long Beach, 530 W Broadway, Ph: 432-8285.

LYNBROOK
Synagogues

Congregation Beth David (C-US), 188 Vincent Ave, Ph: 599-9464. Rabbi L. Diamet. Services: Daily

Temple Emanu-el of Lynbrook (R-UAHC), Saperstein Plaza, Ph: 593-4004. Rabbi S. Geller. Services: Shabbat

MALVERNE
Synagogues

Malverne Jewish Center (C-US), 1 Norwood Ave, Ph: 593-6364. Rabbi T. Steinberg. Services: Daily

MANHASSET
Synagogues

Temple Judea of Manhasset (R-UAHC), 333 Searingtown Rd, Ph: 621-8049. Rabbi A. Bergman. Services: Shabbat

MASSAPEQUA
Synagogues

Congregation Beth El (C-US), 99 Jerusalem Ave, Ph: 541-0740. Rabbi G. Solomon. Services: Daily

Temple Judea (R-UAHC), Jerusalem & Central Aves, Ph: 798-5444. Rabbi S. Jarashow. Services: Friday

Temple Sinai (R), 270 Clocks Blvd, Ph: 795-5015. Rabbi L. Stern. Services: Friday

Young Israel of Massapequa (O-NCYI), 314 Banbury Rd, Ph: 541-2387. Rabbi Y. Bienenfeld. Services: Daily

MERRICK
Synagogues

Temple Beth Am (R-UAHC), Merrick & Kirkwood Aves, Fh: 378-3477. Rabbi R. Brown. Services: Shabbat

Temple Israel of South Merrick (C-US), 2655 Clubhouse Rd, **South Merrick,** Ph: 378-1963. Rabbi M. D. Simckes. Services: Daily

Merrick Jewish Center (C-US), 225 Fox Blvd, Ph: 546-3535. Rabbi C. Klein. Services: Daily

Congregation Ohav Sholom (O-UOJC), 145 S Merrick Ave, Ph: 378-1988. Rabbi C. Klein. Services: Daily

Young Israel of Merrick (O-NCYI), 107 S Hewlett Ave, Ph: 378-2573. Rabbi A. Schechter. Services: Daily

Food

Sheppy's, 2191 Merrick Rd, Ph: 546-2111. Take-out (separate meat and dairy kitchens). Some tables. RS: Rabbi S. Kane (C) of B'nai Israel, Freeport.

Accommodations

Private accommodations; contact the office at Congregation Ohav Sholom, Ph: 378-1988.

MINEOLA
Synagogues

Congregation Beth Sholom (O), 261 Willis Ave, Ph: 746-3211. Rabbi A. Perl. Services: Shabbat and daily p.m.

NEW HYDE PARK
Synagogues

Temple Emanuel (R-UAHC), 3315 Hillside Ave, Ph: 746-1120. Rabbi R. Benjamin. Services: Friday

New Hyde Park Jewish Community Center (C-US), 100 Lakeville Rd, Ph: 354-7583. Rabbi L. Aronson. Services: Daily

Young Israel of New Hyde Park (O-NCYI), 264-15 77th Ave, Ph: (718) 343-0496. Rabbi M. Bilitzky. Services: Daily

Food

New Hyde Park Kosher Meats, 1620 Marcy Ave, Ph: 488-3396.
Glatt meats, poultry, prepared foods for take-out and groceries
(some cholov Yisroel). RS: Vaad Harabonim of Long Island.
Closed Shabbat.

Accommodations

Private accommodations; contact Rabbi M. Bilitzky at Young
Israel of New Hyde Park, Ph: (718) 343-0496.

NORTH BELLMORE (See **BELLMORE**)

OCEANSIDE
Synagogues

Temple Avodah (R-UAHC), 30 Oceanside Rd, Ph: 766-6809.
Rabbi P. Berger. Services: Friday
Darchei Noam (O), Corner of Skillman & Waukema Aves,
Ph: 764-0800. Rabbi D. Friedman. Services: Daily
Jewish Center of Ocean Harbor, Weidner and Royal Aves,
Ph: 536-6481. Rabbi S. Sytner. Services: Shabbat
Oceanside Jewish Center (C-US), 2860 Brower Ave, Ph: 536-6112.
Rabbi E. Rubinger. Services: Daily
Congregation Shaar Hashamayim (O-UOJC), 3309 Skillman Ave,
Ph: 764-6888. Rabbi E. Kasten. Services: Shabbat and Sunday
Young Israel of Oceanside (O-NCYI), 150 Waukena Ave, Ph:
764-1099. Rabbi B. Blech. Services: Daily

Food

Foodtown Supermarket, 3577 Long Beach Rd, Ph: 678-0722.
Bakery (pareve and dairy) is under kosher supervision.
RS: United Kosher Supervision, Rabbi Yaakov Spivak,
Administrator.

Accommodations

Private accommodations:
Rabbi D. Friedman, Darchei Noam, Ph: 764-0800.
Young Israel of Oceanside, Ph: 764-1099.

Mikvah

Mikvah Association of Oceanside, 3397 Park Ave, Ph: 766-3242.

OLD BETHPAGE (See BETHPAGE)

OYSTER BAY
Synagogues

Oyster Bay Jewish Center (C-US), Berry Hill Rd, Ph: 922-6650.
Rabbi M. Zimmerman. Services: Shabbat

PLAINVIEW
Synagogues

Manetto Hill Jewish Center (C-US), 244 Manetto Hill Rd, Ph:
935-5454. Rabbi M. Bernstein. Services: Shabbat and Sunday
Plainview Jewish Center (C-US), 95 Floral Dr, Ph: 938-8610.
Rabbis G. Creditor and J. Goldberg. Services: Daily
Plainview Synagogue (O-Lubav), 255 Manetto Hill Rd,
Ph: 433-6590. Rabbi G. Baras. Services: Daily
Young Israel of Plainview (O-NCYI), 132 Southern Pkwy,
Ph: 433-4811. Rabbi M. Portnoy. Services: Daily

Eating Out

The Promised Land, 397 S Oyster Bay Rd, Ph: 822-0202. Meals:
l,d. Menu: Dairy and vegetarian dishes, fish, Italian, Israeli salads, desserts. RS: Vaad Harabonim of Queens. Closed Shabbat.

Food

Pearl's Bakery, 26 Manetto Hill Mall, Ph: 935-5225. Breads and
pastries. RS: Rabbi M. Portnoy. Closed Shabbat.

Day School

Mid-Island School, 25 Country Dr, Ph: 681-5922.

PORT WASHINGTON
Synagogues

Temple Beth Israel (C-US), Temple Dr, Ph: 767-1708. Rabbi M.
Klayman. Services: Shabbat and Sunday
The Community Synagogue (R-UAHC), 150 Middle Neck Rd,

Ph: 883-3144. Rabbi M. Rozenberg and Rabbi N. Flam.
  Services: Shabbat
The Port Jewish Center (C), 20 Manor Haven Blvd, Ph: 944-7202.
  Rabbi D. Bergman. Services: Shabbat, Fridays only during
  July and August

ROCKVILLE CENTER
Synagogues

Temple B'nai Sholom (C-US), 100 Hempstead Ave, Ph: 764-4628.
  Rabbi B. Schwartz. Services: Daily
Central Synagogue of Nassau County (R-UAHC), 430 DeMott
  Ave, Ph: 766-4300. Rabbi J. Salkin. Services: Shabbat

ROSLYN HEIGHTS
Synagogues

Temple Beth Sholom (C-US), Roslyn Rd & Northern State Pkwy,
  Ph: 621-2288. Rabbi J. Sternstein. Services: Daily
Reconstructionist Synagogue (Recon-FRCH), 1 Willow St,
  Ph: 621-5540. Rabbi L. Friedlander. Services: Friday
Shelter Rock Jewish Center (C-US), Searington & Shelter Rock
  Rds, Ph: 741-4305. Rabbi M. Fenster. Services: Daily
Temple Sinai of Roslyn (R-UAHC), 425 Roslyn Rd, Ph: 621-6800.
  Rabbis A. Petuchowski and S. Schickler. Services: Shabbat

Day School

American Jewish Academy, Remsen Ave, Ph: 621-9500.

SYOSSET
Synagogues

East Nassau Hebrew Congregation (O-UOJC), 310-A S Oyster Bay
  Rd, Ph: 921-9727. Rabbi M. Appleman. Services: Daily
Midway Jewish Center (C-US), 330 S Oyster Bay Rd,
  Ph: 938-8390. Rabbi E. Finkelstein. Services: Daily
North Shore Synagogue (R-UAHC), 83 Muttontown Rd,
  Ph: 921-2282. Rabbi D. Fogel and D. Crystal. Services: Shabbat

Accommodations

Private accommodations; contact the office at East Nassau Hebrew
  Congregation, Ph: 921-9727.

Synagogues cont.

Shabbat hospitality; call Chabad of the North Shore, 116 Jackson Ave, Ph: 364-2233. Rabbi S. Posner.

UNIONDALE
Synagogues

Hebrew Academy of Nassau County (O), 215 Oak St, Ph: 538-8161. Services: Monday-Friday, when school is in session. Call for schedule.

VALLEY STREAM
Synagogues

Congregation Beth Sholom—Sunrise Jewish Center (O-UOJC), 518 Rockaway Blvd, Ph: 561-9245. Rabbi J. Hack. Services: Shabbat and Sunday

Temple Gates of Zion Jewish Center (C-US), 322 N Corona Ave, Ph: 561-2308. Rabbi H. Halpern. Services: Daily

Temple Hillel—Southside Jewish Center (C-US), 1000 Rosedale Rd, Ph: 791-6344. Rabbi M. Friedman. Services: Daily

Congregation Tree of Life (C-US) 502 N Central Ave, Ph: 825-2090. Rabbi J. Dattelkramer. Services: Daily

Accommodations

Private accommodations; contact Rabbi M. Friedman at Temple Hillel—Southside Jewish Center, Ph: 791-6344.

WANTAGH
Synagogues

The Suburban Temple (R-UAHC), 2900 Jerusalem Ave, Ph: 221-2370. Rabbi R. Raab. Services: Shabbat

Wantagh Jewish Center (C-US), 3710 Woodbine Ave, Ph: 785-2445. Rabbi M. Rubin. Services· Daily

WEST HEMPSTEAD
Synagogues

Anshei Shalom (O), 472 Hempstead Ave, Ph: 489-8112. Rabbi Y. Pearl. Services: Daily

Jewish Community Center of West Hempstead (C-US), 711

Dogwood Ave, Ph: 481-7448. Rabbi E. Lankin. Services: Daily
Nassau Community Temple (R-UAHC), 240 Hempstead Ave,
  Ph: 485-1811. Rabbi L. Goodman. Services: Friday
Young Israel of West Hempstead (O-NCYI), 630 Hempstead Ave,
  Ph: 481-7429. Rabbi Y. Kelemer. Services: Daily

Eating Out

Hunki's, 338 Hempstead Ave, Ph: 538-6655. Meals: l,d. Menu:
  Pizza, dairy dishes, salads, cheeses. RS: Vaad Harabonim of
  Queens. Closed Shabbat.

Food

Bagel Craft of Hempstead, 118 Hempstead Tpke, Ph: 485-2314.
  Bagels and bialys (pareve), cakes and sandwiches (dairy).
  RS: Vaad Harabonim of Long Island. Closed Shabbat.

Accommodations

Private accommodations; call Young Israel of West Hempstead,
  Ph: 481-7429.

Mikvah

Mikvah Association of Nassau County, 775 Hempstead Ave,
  Ph: 489-9358.

Day School

Hebrew Academy of Nassau County, 609 Hempstead Ave,
  Ph: 485-7786.

Bookstore

Judaica Unlimited, 433 Hempstead Ave, Ph: 486-3636.

WESTBURY
Synagogues

Temple Beth Torah (C-US), 243 Cantiague Rd, Ph: 334-7979.
  Rabbi M. Katz. Services: Shabbat and Sunday
Community Reform Temple (R-UAHC), 712 Plain Rd,
  Ph: 333-1839. Rabbi M. Gruber. Services: Shabbat
Temple Sholom (C-US), 675 Brookside Ct, Ph: 334-2800.
  Services: Daily

Synagogues cont.

Westbury Hebrew Congregation (C-US), 21 Old Westbury Rd, Ph: 333-7977. Rabbi B. Lerner. Services: Daily

WOODMERE
Synagogues

Congregation Ohr Torah (O-UOJC), 410 Hungry Harbor Rd, **North Woodmere**, Ph: 791-2346. Rabbi T. Jungreis. Services: Daily

Congregation Sons of Israel (C-US), 111 Irving Pl, Ph: 374-0655. Rabbi S. Teplitz. Services: Daily

Young Israel of North Woodmere (O-NCYI), 785 Golf Dr, **North Woodmere**, Ph: 791-5099. Rabbi S. Chill and Rabbi G. Porcelain. Services: Daily

Young Israel of Woodmere (O-NCYI), 859 Peninsula Blvd, Ph: 295-0150. Rabbi H. Billet. Services: Daily

Eating Out

Pizza Pious, 1063 Broadway, Ph: 295-2050. Meals: l,d. Menu: Pizza, Israeli and Italian dishes. RS: Vaad Hakashrus of the Five Towns. Closed Shabbat.

Accommodations

Private accommodations; contact Mr. D. Frankel at Young Israel of Woodmere, Ph: 295-0150.

Mikvah (See **Hewlett**)

NEW YORK CITY

New York City comprises the largest Jewish complex in the Western world, with numerous synagogues. Therefore, information is given here for representative congregations. Further information may be obtained from the following organizations headquartered in the city:

302

Agudath Israel of America
84 William Street
New York, N.Y. 10038
(212) 797-9000

Federation of Reconstructionist Congregations and Havurot
270 W 89th Street
New York, N.Y. 10024
(212) 496-2960

Lubavitch-Chabad World Headquarters
770 Eastern Parkway
Brooklyn, NY 11213
(718) 953-1000

National Council of Young Israel
3 W 16th Street
New York, N.Y. 10011
(212) 929-1525

Union of American Hebrew Congregations
838 Fifth Avenue
New York, N.Y. 10021
(212) 249-0100

The Union of Orthodox Jewish Congregations of America
333 7th Avenue
New York, N.Y. 10001
(212) 563-4000

United Synagogue of America
155 Fifth Avenue
New York, N.Y. 10010
(212) 533-7800

Food
Since New York City includes many Jewish neighborhoods where kosher food shops abound, listings for the **Food** category are omitted. Such information is readily available from local synagogues and rabbis.

Day Schools

There are over one hundred and fifty Jewish day schools in the five boroughs of New York City. Specific information is available from:

The National Society for Hebrew Day Schools
160 Broadway
New York, N.Y. 10038
(212) 227-1000

Solomon Schechter Day School Association
of the United Synagogue of America
155 Fifth Avenue
New York, N.Y. 10010
(212) 260-8450

Union of American Hebrew Congregations
838 Fifth Avenue
New York, N.Y. 10021
(212) 249-0100

BRONX   Area Code (212)   J-pop. 85,000

Synagogues

Beth Shraga Institute (O), 2757 Morris Ave, Ph: 295-3160. Rabbi L. Dulitz. Services: Saturday

Conservative Synagogue Adath Israel (C-US), 250th St & Henry Hudson Pkwy, Ph: 543-8400. Rabbi S. Balter. Services: Daily

Temple Emanu-el of Parkchester (C-US), 2000 Benedict Ave, Ph: 828-3400. Rabbi L. Muroff. Services: Shabbat and daily

Educational Jewish Center (O), 801 Astor Ave, Ph: 881-8074. Rabbi B. Mehler. Services: Daily

Hebrew Institute at Riverdale (O), 3700 Henry Hudson Pkwy, Ph: 796-4730. Rabbi A. Weiss. Services: Daily

Jewish Center of Violet Park (O), 3356 Seymour Ave, Ph: 654-2712. Rabbi I. Sonnenfield. Services: Shabbat

Jewish Center of Williamsbridge (O-UOJC), 2910 Barnes Ave, Ph: 655-4077 or 655-3822. Rabbi A. Predmesky. Services: Daily

Temple Judea (R-UAHC), 615 Reiss Pl, Ph: 881-5118. Rabbi D. Milrod. Services: Call for schedule.

Congregation Khal Adath Yeshurun (O), 2222 Cruger Ave, Ph: 653-4698. Rabbi M. L. Schwartz. Services: Daily

Kingsbridge Center of Israel (O), 3115 Corlear Ave, Ph: 548-1678. Rabbi H. Crupar. Services: Daily

Kingsbridge Heights Jewish Center (O-UOJC), 124 Eames Pl, Ph: 549-4120. Rabbi I. N. Bamberger. Services: Daily

Mosholu Jewish Center (O), 3044 Hull Ave, Ph: 547-1515. Rabbi H. Schachter. Services: Daily

Nathan Straus Jewish Center (Trad), 3512 DeKalb Ave, Ph: 547-1616. Rabbi A. Bardekoff. Services: Daily

Congregation Ohel Moshe (O), 2167 Muliner Ave, Ph: 792-8544. Rabbi M. Stimler. Services: Daily

Ohel Torah Synagogue (O), 629 W 239th St, Ph: 543-5618. Rabbi I. Gottlieb. Services: Daily

Pelham Parkway Jewish Center (C), 900 Pelham Pkwy S, Ph: 792-6450. Rabbi A. Hartstein. Services: Daily

Riverdale Jewish Center (O), 3700 Independence Ave, Ph: 548-1850. Rabbi J. Rosenblatt. Services: Daily

Riverdale Temple (R-UAHC), W 246th St & Independence Ave, Ph: 548-3800. Rabbi S. Franklin. Services: Shabbat

Sephardic Shaare Rahamim, 100 Co-op City Blvd, Ph: 671-8882. Services: Daily

Congregation Sons of Israel of the Bronx (O), 2521 Cruger Ave, Ph: 231-6213. Rabbi M. L. Fuchs. Services: Daily

Van Cortlandt Jewish Center (O), 3880 Sedgwick Ave, Ph: 884-6105. Rabbi J. Sodden. Services: Daily

Young Israel of Astor Gardens (O-NCYI), 1328 Allerton Ave, Ph: 653-1363. Rabbi S. Klammer. Services: Daily

Young Israel of Baychester (O-NCYI), 115 Einstein Loop N, Ph: 379-6920. Rabbi K. Stein. Services: Daily

Young Israel of Co-op City (O-NCYI), 147 Dreiser Loop, Ph: 671-2300. Rabbi S. Berl. Services: Daily

Young Israel of Mosholu Parkway (O-NCYI), 100 E 208th St, Ph: 882-8181. Rabbi Zevulun Charlop. Services: Daily

Young Israel of Parkchester (O), 1375 Virginia Ave, Ph: 822-9576. Rabbi S. Schwartz. Services: Daily

Young Israel of Pelham Parkway (O), 2121 Barnes Ave, Ph: 824-0630. Rabbi S. Rubin. Services: Daily

Synagogues cont.

Young Israel of Riverdale (O-NCYI), 4502 Henry Hudson
Pkwy, Ph: 548-4765. Rabbi M. Willig. Services: Daily

Eating Out

Mr. Bagel of Broadway, 5672 Broadway, Ph: 549-0408. Bagels and
breads (pareve); other baked goods pareve and dairy. Spreads,
sandwiches. Imported Israeli products. RS: Vaad Harabonim of
Riverdale. Closed Shabbat.

The Corner Café, 3552 Johnson Ave, Ph: 601-2861. Meals: b,l,d.
Menu: (Dairy: cholov Yisroel) Dairy and vegetarian fare. Also
fresh baked goods (pareve and dairy). RS: Vaad Harabonim of
Riverdale. Closed Shabbat.

The Main Event, 3702 Riverdale Ave, Ph: 543-1811. Meals: l,d.
Menu: Pizza, falafel, Italian and Israeli dishes, salads (dairy,
vegetarian). RS: Vaad Harabonim of Riverdale. Closed Shabbat.

Moishe's Delicatessen and Restaurant, 157 Dreiser Loop Shopping
Center #1, Co-op City, Ph: 671-3608. Meals: l,d. Menu: (Glatt
meat) Deli. Also take-out. RS: Vaad Harabonim of Co-op City.
Closed Shabbat.

Szechuan Garden, 3717 Riverdale Ave, Ph: 884-4242. Meals: l,d.
Menu: (Glatt meat) Chinese. Also take-out. RS: Vaad Harabonim
of Riverdale. Closed Shabbat.

Accommodations

Home hospitality; call Riverdale Jewish Center, Ph: 548-1850.

Mikvah

Etz Chaim Mikvah, 708 Mace Ave, Ph: 798-6173.
Riverdale Mikvah, 3708 Henry Hudson Pkwy. Call Mrs.
E. Hirschhorn, Ph: 549-8336.

Bookstores

Riverdale Judaica, 3552 Johnson Ave, Ph: 601-7563.

BROOKLYN   Area Code (718)   J-pop. 418,900

Synagogues

Congregation Adath Jacob (O), 1569 47th St, Ph: 438-9230.
Rabbi J. Perlow. Services: Daily

Congregation Agudas Achim Anshei Sfard (O), 1385 E 94th St,
Ph: 272-6933. Rabbi J. Chanes. Services: Daily

Congregation Agudath Sholom of Flatbush (O), 3714 18th Ave,
Ph: 627-1947. Rabbi S. Kornfeld. Services: Daily

Ahi Ezer Congregation (O), 1885 Ocean Pkwy, Ph: 376-4088.
Rabbi S. Maslaton. Services: Daily

Bay Ridge Jewish Center (C-US), 405 81st St, Ph: 836-3103.
Rabbi D. Freidberg. Services: Shabbat, Sunday, Monday and
Thursday mornings

Beth Elohim (R-UAHC), 8th Ave & Garfield Pl, Ph: 768-3814.
Rabbi M. Slome. Services: Shabbat

Beth Sholom People's Temple (R-UAHC), Bay Pkwy & Benson
Ave, Ph: 372-7164. Rabbi A. Lowenberg. Services: Shabbat

Congregation B'nai Isaac (O), 54 Ave O, Ph: 232-3466. Rabbi P.
Singer. Services: Daily

B'nai Jacob of Flatbush (C), 3017 Glenwood Rd, Ph: 434-8855.
Rabbi J. Weitzman. Services: Daily

Brooklyn Heights Synagogue (R-UAHC), 117 Remsen St,
Ph: 522-2070. Rabbi R. Jacobs. Services: Friday

Brooklyn Jewish Center (C-US), 667 Eastern Pkwy, Ph: 493-8800.
Rabbi A Bloch. Services: Saturday and Sunday

Flatbush & Shaare Torah Jewish Center (C-US), 500 Church Ave,
Ph: 871-5200. Rabbi I. Feldman. Services: Daily

Haym Salomon Community Congregation (O), 2300 Cropsey Ave,
Ph: 373-1700. Rabbi I. Gruen. Services: Daily

Kehilath Yaakov Pupa (O), 644 Bedford Ave, Ph: 625-0318.
Services: Daily

Kingsway Jewish Center (O), 2810 Nostrand Ave, Ph: 258-3344.
Rabbi M. Polin. Services: Daily

Congregation of Lanzut (O), 159 Rodney St, Ph: 384-3132.
Rabbi O. Wagshall. Services: Daily

Lubavitch World Headquarters Synagogue (O-Lubav), 770 Eastern
Pkwy, Ph: 953-1000. Rabbi M. Schneerson. Services: Daily

Synagogues cont.

Congregation Mount Sinai (C), 250 Cadman Plaza W, Ph: 875-9126. Rabbi J. Potasnik. Services: Saturday morning, Monday and Thursday

Congregation Shaari Israel (C), 810 E 49th St, Ph: 629-0476. Rabbi A. Feldbin. Services: Shabbat, Monday and Thursday

Congregation Shaare Zion (O-UOJC), 2030 Ocean Pkwy, Ph: 376-0009. Rabbi A. Hecht. Services: Daily

Shore Parkway Jewish Center (C), 8885 26th Ave, Ph: 449-6530. Rabbi H. Horowitz. Services: Daily

Congregation Sons of Israel (O), 2115 Benson Ave, Ph: 372-4830. Rabbi E. Skaist. Services: Daily

Congregation Sons of Judah (O), 5311 16th Ave, Ph: 851-9828. Rabbi I. Kirzner. Services: Daily

Union Temple of Brooklyn (R-UAHC), 17 Eastern Pkwy, Ph: 638-7600. Rabbi S. Salkowitz. Services: Shabbat

Congregation Yetev Lev (O), 152 Rodney St, Ph: 387-2727. Grand Rabbi M. Teitelbaum of Satmar. Services: Daily

Young Israel of Avenue K (O-NCYI), 2818 Ave K, Ph: 258-6666. Rabbi A. Ralbag. Services: Daily

Young Israel of Bedford Bay (O-NCYI), 2114 Brown St, Ph: 332-4120. Rabbi Samuel Fink. Services: Daily

Young Israel of Boro Park (O-NCYI), 4802 15th Ave, Ph: 435-9020. Rabbi I. Schorr. Services: Daily

Young Israel of Brighton Beach (O-NCYI), 293 Neptune Ave, Ph: 648-0843. Rabbi S. Friedler. Services: Daily

Young Israel of Flatbush (O-NCYI), 1012 Ave I, Ph: 377-4400. Rabbi K. Auman. Services: Daily

Young Israel of Kensington (O-NCYI), 305 Church Ave, Ph: 871-4543. Rabbi H. Kurzrock. Services: Daily

Young Israel of Midwood (O-NCYI), 1694 Ocean Ave, Ph: 253-6266. Rabbi M. Greenburg. Services: Daily

Young Israel of Ocean Parkway (O-NCYI), 1781 Ocean Pkwy, Ph: 376-6305. Rabbi H. Bomzer. Services: Daily

Young Israel of Sheepshead Bay (O-NCYI), 2546 E 7th St, Ph: 891-6767. Rabbi Shimon Rabin. Services: Daily

Congregation Zemach Tzedek of Viznitz (O), 118 Lee Ave, Ph: 384-1262. Services: Daily

Eating Out

Ach Tov, 4403 13th Ave, Ph: 438-8494/3266. Meals: l,d. Menu: Dairy and vegetarian. RS: Rabbi C. Pollack. Closed Shabbat.

Brighton Beach Dairy Restaurant, 410 Brighton Beach Ave, Ph: 646-7421. Meals: l,d. Menu: Large variety of dairy dishes. RS: Vaad Harabonim of Flatbush. Closed Shabbat.

Café Ravel, 811 Kings Hwy, Ph: 627-4111. Meals: b,l,d. Menu: (cholov Yisroel) Dairy dishes and pastries. RS: Torah-K. Closed Shabbat.

Carmel Classic Restaurant, 923 Kings Hwy, Ph: 336-2500. Meals: l,d. Menu: Israeli and American. RS: Vaad Harabonim of Flatbush. Closed Shabbat.

Carmel Restaurant, 523 Kings Hwy, Ph: 339-0172. Meals: l,d. Menu: American, Middle Eastern. RS: Vaad Harabonim of Flatbush. Closed Shabbat.

Dagan Pizza, 1560 Ralph Ave, Ph: 209-0636. Meals: l,d. Menu: Pizza, falafel, calzone, salads, dairy dishes. RS: Vaad Harabonim of Flatbush. Closed Shabbat.

D'Zion Restaurant, 4102 18th Ave, Ph: 871-9467. Meals: b,l,d. Menu: (Glatt meat) Mideastern. RS: Torah-K. Closed Shabbat.

Edna's Restaurant & Deli, 125 Church Ave, Ph: 438-8207. Meals: l,d. Menu: (Glatt meat) Traditional, Chinese and deli-style dishes. RS: Vaad Harabonim of Flatbush. Closed Shabbat.

Famous Dairy Restaurant, 4818 13th Ave, Ph: 435-4201. Meals: l,d. Menu: Fish and dairy dishes. RS: Rabbi D. Singer. Closed Shabbat.

Eating Out cont.

Galil Pizza, 3008 Ave J, Ph: 377-8245. Meals: l,d. Menu: Pizza, blintzes, knishes, falafel. RS: Vaad Harabonim of Flatbush. Closed Shabbat.

Glatt Chow, 1204 Ave J, Ph: 692-0001. Meals: l,d. Menu: Chinese and American dishes. RS: Vaad Harabonim of Flatbush

Glatt King, 702 Kings Hwy, Ph: 645-0505. Meals: l,d. Menu: (Meat) Salads, soups, shish kabobs, turkey, chicken, veal, vegetables. RS: Vaad Harabonim of Flatbush. Closed Shabbat.

The Gourmet Cafe, 1622 Coney Island Ave, Ph: 338-5825. Meals: b,l,d. Menu: Vegetarian. RS: Rabbi D. Katz, Torah-K. Closed Shabbat.

Hod Pizza, 1202 Ave J, Ph: 258-1884. Meals: l,d. Menu: (Dairy) Pizza, knishes, egg rolls, salads, soups, falafel. RS: Vaad Harabonim of Flatbush. Closed Shabbat.

Jaffa's Kosher Luncheonette, 1348 Coney Island Ave, Ph: 377-9899. Meals: l. Menu: Soup, sandwiches, dairy dishes. RS: Vaad Harabonim of Flatbush. Closed Shabbat.

Jerusalem II Kosher Pizza, 1312 Ave J, Ph: 338-8156. Meals: l,d. Menu: Pizza, falafel, calzone. RS: Vaad Harabonim of Flatbush. Closed Shabbat.

Jerusalem II Kosher Pizza, 1424 Ave M, Ph: 645-4753. Meals: b,l,d. Menu: Pizza, falafel, Israeli dishes. RS: Vaad Harabonim of Flatbush. Closed Shabbat.

Kosher Castle, 5006 13th Ave, Ph: 436-7474. Meals: b,l,d. Menu: Dairy fast food. RS: O.K. Laboratories. Closed Shabbat.

Kosher Chef, 1906 Ave M, Ph: 376-3440. Meals: l,d. Menu: (Glatt meat) Deli, steaks, chicken; American cuisine. RS: Vaad Harabonim of Flatbush. Closed Shabbat.

Kosher Delight, 4600 13th Ave, Ph: 435-8500. Meals: l,d. Menu: Fast food, soups and salads. RS: Rabbi P. Horovitz. Closed Shabbat.

Kosher Delight, 1223 Ave J, Ph: 377-6873. Meals: l,d. Menu: Fast food, soups and salads. RS: Vaad Harabonim of Flatbush. Closed Shabbat.

Kosher Pizza Plus, 1427 Coney Island Ave, Ph: 258-0392. Meals:

b,l,d. Sun: l,d. Menu: Pizza, falafel, hot dishes. RS: Vaad Harabonim of Flatbush. Closed Shabbat.

Mama's Restaurant, 906 Kings Hwy, Ph: 382-7200. Meals: l,d. Menu: (Meat) Falafel, kabobs, sandwiches. RS: Vaad Harabonim of Flatbush. Closed Shabbat.

Massada Glatt Kosher Restaurant, 2178 Nostrand Ave, Ph: 434-9835. Meals: l,d. Menu: Middle Eastern and American cuisine. RS: Torah-K. Closed Shabbat.

Milk & Honey Delight, 1538 Coney Island Ave, Ph: 377-9883. Meals: b,l,d. Menu: (Dairy: cholov Yisroel) American and Mideastern. RS: Vaad Harabonim of Flatbush. Closed Shabbat.

Natanya Fast Food & Pizza, 1500 Ave J, Ph: 258-5160. Meals: l,d. Menu: Pizza, knishes, egg rolls, salads, falafel. RS: Vaad Harabonim of Flatbush. Closed Shabbat.

Nosheria, 4813 13th Ave, Ph: 436-0400. Meals: l,d. Menu: Chinese and American fast food. RS: Rabbi A. Lehrman. Closed Shabbat.

Ossie's Table, 1314 50th St, Ph: 435-0635. Meals: d; Sunday: l,d. Menu: Seafood. RS: Star-K of Baltimore. Closed Shabbat.

The Pizza Court, 52 Court St, Ph: 237-0226. Meals: b,l. Menu: Pizza, falafel, hot dishes, salads. RS: Vaad Harabonim of Flatbush. Closed Shabbat.

Primavera, 2086 Coney Island Ave, Ph: 627-3904. Meals: l,d. Menu: (Dairy) Italian cuisine. Pasta and fish. RS: Vaad Harabonim of Flatbush. Closed Shabbat.

Primavera Piccola, 2916 Ave M, Ph: 377-6218. Meals: l,d. Menu: Italian Fast Food. Cholov Yisroel. RS: Vaad Harabonim of Flatbush. Closed Shabbat.

Sea Dolphin, 502 Ave M, Ph: 375-9290. Meals: l,d. Menu: (Dairy: cholov Yisroel) Greek-Eastern fish cuisine. RS: Vaad Harabonim of Flatbush. Closed Shabbat.

Shalom Hunan, 1619 Ave M, Ph: 382-6000. Meals: l,d. Menu: (Meat) Chinese cuisine. RS: Vaad Harabonim of Flatbush. Credit cards. Closed Shabbat.

Shang Chai Restaurant, 2189 Flatbush Ave, Ph: 377-6100. Meals: l,d. Menu: (Glatt meat) Chinese and traditional cuisine. RS: Vaad Harabonim of Flatbush. Closed Shabbat.

Eating Out cont.

Shmuel's Kosher Pizza and Falafel, 1621 Kings Hwy, Ph: 339-7884. Meals: l,d. Menu: Pizza, falafel, knishes, special Israeli dishes. RS: Vaad Harabonim of Flatbush. Closed Shabbat.

Taam Eden Dining Room, 5001 13th Ave, Ph: 972-1692. Meals: l,d. Menu: (Dairy) Seafood, vegetarian. RS: Rabbi D. Katz. Closed Shabbat.

Tacos Olé, 1387 Coney Island Ave, Ph: 377-7720. Meals: l,d. Menu: Mexican, meat dishes. RS: Rabbi D. Katz. Closed Shabbat.

The Underground Gourmet (at B'nai B'rith Hillel), Campus Rd & Hillel Pl, Ph: 859-1151. Cafeteria. Meals: l. Menu: Dairy. RS: Vaad Harabonim of Flatbush. Closed Shabbat. Open during school year.

Weiss' Kosher Dairy Restaurant, 1146 Coney Island Ave, Ph: 421-0184. Meals: l,d. Menu: Wide variety of dairy dishes, Jewish-American cuisine, vegetarian, health salads. RS: Vaad Harabonim of Flatbush

Yunkee and Chap-A-Nosh, 1420 Elm Ave, Ph: 627-0072. Meals: d. Menu: (Glatt meat) Chinese food. RS: Association for Reliable Kashruth. Closed Shabbat.

Accommodations

The Crown Palace Hotel, 570 Crown St, Ph: 604-1777. Restaurant open when visiting groups are present. RS: Lubavitch. Shomer Shabbat. Four blocks to Lubavitch headquarters. Visa, MC.

Mikvah

Canarsie Community Mikvah, 1221 Remsen Ave. Ph: 763-5902.

Crown Heights Mikvah, 1506 Union St. Call Mrs. Levertov, Ph: 604-8787 or 493-0852.

Mikvah Israel of Boro Park, 1351 46th St, Ph: 871-6866.

Kehilas Yaakov, 115 Rutledge St. Mikvah attendant, Ph: 384-4899.

Satmar Mikvah, 212 Williamsburg St E, Ph: 387-9388.
Sephardic Mikvah, 810 Ave S, Ph: 339-4600.
Taharath Israel of Flatbush, 1013 E 15th St, Ph: 377-9813.

Bookstores

Crown Heights Judaica, 329 Kingston Ave, Ph: 604-1020.
Eichler's, 1429 Coney Island Ave, Ph: 258-7643.
Eichler's, 5004 13th Ave, Ph: 633-1505.
Flohr's, 4603 13th Ave, Ph: 854-0865.
Frankel's Book Store, 4904 16th Ave, Ph: 851-7766.
Grunfeld's Hebrew Book Store, 4624 16th Ave, Ph: 871-8885.
Hecht Hebrew Book Store, 1265 Coney Island Ave, Ph: 258-9696.
J. Biegeleisen Co., 4409 16th Ave, Ph: 436-1165.
Merkaz Stam, 309 Kingston Ave, Ph: 773-0090.

MANHATTAN   Area Code (212)   J-pop. 274,300

Synagogues

Congregation Ansche Chesed (C), 251 W 100th St, Ph: 864-6637 or
    865-0600. Services: Daily; five minyanim on Shabbat mornings
    and Holidays. Call for details.
Congregation Beth Hillel of Washington Heights (O), 571 W 182nd
    St, Ph: 568-3933. Rabbi S. Kahn. Services: Daily
Congregation Beth Israel—West Side Jewish Center (O), 347 W
    34th St, Ph: 279-0016. Rabbi S. Kahane. Services: Daily
Bialystoker Synagogue (O), 7-11 Bialystoker Pl, Ph: 475-0165.
    Rabbi Y. Singer. Services: Daily
B'nai Jeshurun (C), 270 W 89th St, Ph: 787-7600. Rabbi M. Meyer.
    Services: Shabbat
The Brotherhood Synagogue (C), 28 Gramercy Park S,
    Ph: 674-5750. Rabbi I. Block. Services: Shabbat
Central Synagogue (R-UAHC), 123 E 55th St, Ph: 838-5122.
    Rabbi S. Davis. Services: Daily
Civic Center Synagogue (O), 49 White St, Ph: 966-7141. Rabbi J.
    Glass. Services: Daily
Conservative Synagogue of Fifth Ave (C), 11 E 11th St,
    Ph: 929-6954. Rabbi H. Handler. Services: Shabbat

Synagogues cont.

Congregation Derech Amuno (O), 53 Charles St, Ph: 242-6425. Rabbi M. W. Newman. Services: Daily

East End Temple (R-UAHC), 398 Second Ave, Ph: 254-8518. Rabbi D. Hirsch. Services: Shabbat

East 55th Street Conservative Synagogue (C-US), 308 E 55th St, Ph: 752-1200. Rabbi R. Siegel. Services: Daily

East Side Torah Center (O), 313 Henry St, Ph: 473-3665. Rabbi S. Nulman. Services: Daily

Temple Emanu-El (R-UAHC), 1 E 65th St, Ph: 744-1400. Rabbi R. Sobel. Services: Shabbat

Emunath Israel (O), 236 W 23rd St, Ph: 242-9882. Rabbi M. Leifer. Services: Daily

Ethiopian Hebrew Congregation, 1 W 123rd St, Ph: 534-1058. Services: Saturday

Congregation Ezrath Israel (C), 339 W 47th St, Ph: 245-6975. Rabbi M. Goldberg. Services: Daily

Fifth Avenue Synagogue (O), 5 E 62nd St, Ph: 838-2122. Rabbi S. Roth. Services: Daily

First Roumanian American Congregation (O), 89 Rivington St, Ph: 673-2835. Rabbi J. Speigel. Services: Daily

Fort Tryon Jewish Center (C), 524 Fort Washington Ave, Ph: 795-1391. Rabbi P. Pearl. Services: Daily

Fur Center Synagogue (O), 230 W 29th St, Ph: 594-9480. Rabbi J. Kenny. Services: Daily

Garment Center Congregation (O), 205 W 40th St, Ph: 391-6966. Rabbi N. Listoken. Services: Daily

Congregation Habonim (R-UAHC), 44 W 66th St, Ph: 787-5347. Rabbi J. Rosenbaum. Services: Shabbat

Hebrew Tabernacle Congregation (R-UAHC), 551 Fort Washington Ave, Ph: 568-8304. Rabbi R. Lehman. Services: Shabbat

Inwood Hebrew Congregation (C-US), 111 Vermilyea Ave, Ph: 569-4010. Rabbi A. Yager. Services: Shabbat

Temple Israel (R), 112 E 75th St, Ph: 249-5000. Rabbi M. Zion. Services: Friday

The Jewish Center (O), 131 W 86th St, Ph: 724-2700. Rabbi J. Schacter. Services: Daily

Jewish Theological Seminary (C-US), 3080 Broadway,

Ph: 678-8000. Rabbi J. Meyers. Services: Daily

Congregation Kehilath Jacob (O), 305 W 79th St, Ph: 580-2391.
Rabbi S. Carlebach. Services: Shabbat

Congregation Kehilath Jeshurun (O), 117 E 85th St, Ph: 427-1000.
Rabbi H. Lookstein. Services: Daily

Kehillat Israel Chofetz Chaim (O-Lubav), 310 W 103rd St,
Ph: 864-5010. Rabbi S. Kugel. Services: Shabbat

Congregation K'hal Adath Jeshurun (O), 85 Bennett Ave,
Ph: 923-3582. Rabbi Z. Gelley. Services Daily

Lincoln Square Synagogue (O), 200 Amsterdam Ave,
Ph: 874-6100. Rabbi K. Brander. Services: Daily

Mesivta Tifereth Jerusalem (O), 145 E Broadway, Ph: 964-2830.
Rabbi D. Feinstein. Services: Daily

Metropolitan Synagogue of New York (R), 10 Park Ave,
Ph: 679-8580. Rabbi J. Goor. Services: Shabbat

Millinery Center Synagogue (C), 1025 Avenue of the Americas,
Ph: 921-1580. Rabbi S. D. Davis. Services: Daily

Mount Sinai Jewish Center (O), 135 Bennett Ave, Ph: 928-9870.
Rabbi M. Schnaidman. Services: Daily

Congregation Ohab Zedek (O), 118 W 95th St, Ph: 749-5150.
Rabbi A. Schwartz. Services: Daily

Synagogues cont.

Park Avenue Synagogue (C), 50 E 87th St, Ph: 369-2600. Rabbi P. Graubert. Services: Daily

Park East Synagogue (O), 164 E 68th St, Ph: 737-6900. Rabbi A. Schneier. Services: Daily

Radio City Synagogue (O), 30 W 47th St #305, Ph: 819-0839. Rabbi J. Weinberg. Services: Monday-Thursday

Rodeph Sholom Congregation (R-UAHC), 7 W 83rd St, Ph: 362-8800. Rabbi R. Levine. Services: Shabbat

Congregation Shaaray Tefila (R-UAHC), 250 E 79th St, Ph: 535-8008. Services: Shabbat

Congregation Shaare Zedek (C-US), 212 W 93rd St, Ph: 874-7005. Rabbi J. Wasser. Services: Daily

Congregation Shearith Israel—Spanish Portuguese Synagogue (O), 8 W 70th St, Ph: 873-0300. Rabbi M. Angel, Rabbi H. Tattelbaum. Services: Daily

Society for the Advancement of Judaism (Recon-FRCH), 15 W 86th St, Ph: 724-7000. Rabbi Dr. A. Miller. Services: Saturday

Stephen Wise Free Synagogue (R), 30 W 68th St, Ph: 877-4050. Rabbi H. Friedman. Services: Friday

Sutton Place Synagogue (C-US), 225 E 51st St, Ph: 593-3300. Rabbi D. Kahane. Services: Daily

Talmud Torah Adereth El (O), 135 E 29th St, Ph: 685-4808. Rabbi S. Kleiman. Services: Daily

Town & Village Synagogue (C), 334 E 14th St, Ph: 677-8090. Rabbi H. Glazer. Services: Shabbat, Monday and Thursday

Village Temple (R-UAHC), 33 E 12th St, Ph: 674-2340. Rabbi D. Math. Services: Shabbat

Wall Street Synagogue (O), 47 Beekman St, Ph: 227-7543. Rabbi M. Hager. Services: Daily

Washington Heights Congregation (O), 815 W 179th St, Ph: 923-4407. Rabbi G. Finkelstein. Services: Daily

West End Synagogue (Recon-FRCH), 270 W 89th St, Ph: 769-3100. Rabbi L. Pinsker. Services: First and third Friday; Saturday mornings

West Side Institutional Synagogue (O), 120 W 76th St, Ph: 877-7652. Rabbi M. Morduchowitz. Services: Daily

Yorkville Synagogue—Congregation B'nai Yehuda (O), 352 E 78th

St, Ph: 249-0766. Rabbi J. D. Bleich. Services: Daily

Young Israel of Fifth Avenue (O-NCYI), 3 W 16th St, Ph: 960-5311. Rabbi I. Wohlgelernter. Services: Daily

Young Israel of Manhattan (O-NCYI), 225 E Broadway, Ph: 732-0966. Rabbi S. Siff. Services: Daily

Young Israel of the West Side (O-NCYI), 210 W 91st St, Ph: 787-7513. Rabbi E. Gettinger. Services: Daily

Congregation Zichron Moshe (O), 342 E 20th St, Ph: 567-7392. Rabbi J. Newman. Services: Daily

Eating Out

B.J.'s Bagels, 130 W 72nd St, Ph: 769-3350. Meals: b,l,d. Menu: (Dairy and vegetarian) Bagels, salads, quiches. RS: Tablet-K. Closed Shabbat.

Bernstein's on Essex Street, 135 Essex St, Ph: 473-3900. Meals: l,d. Menu: Chinese and deli-style dishes. RS: Orthodox Union and Rabbi Y. Spiegel. Closed Shabbat. All major credit cards.

Café Masada, 1239 First Ave, Ph: 988-0950. Meals: l,d. Menu: (Glatt meat) Sephardic and Israeli dishes. Also pareve. RS: United Kosher Supervision, Rabbi Yaakov Spivak, Addimistrator. Closed Shabbat.

Chez David, 494 Amsterdam Ave, Ph: 874-4974. Meals: l,d. Menu: Pizza, falafel, Mideastern. RS: Kof-K. Closed Shabbat.

Chez Lanu—Mr. Broadway, 1372 Broadway, Ph: 921-2152. Meals: l,d. Menu: Deli, Mideastern, International. RS: Orthodox Union. Closed Shabbat.

China Shalom II, 686 Columbus Ave, Ph: 662-9676/77. Meals: l,d. Menu: (Glatt Meat). Chinese. RS: Kof-K. Closed Shabbat.

David's Harp Kosher Tower, 150 W 46th St, Ph: 768-3333. Meals: l,d. Menu: (Glatt meat and cholov Yisroel—four kitchens) Chinese, American, Israeli cuisine. RS: Midtown Board of Kashruth. Closed Shabbat.

Deli Glatt Sandwich Shop, 150 Fulton St, Ph: 349-3622. Meals: b,l,d. Menu: Deli, burgers, chicken, salads. RS: Vaad Harabonim of Flatbush. Closed Shabbat.

Deli Kasbah, 251 W 85th St, Ph: 927-1500. Meals: l,d. Menu: Deli, salad, grill. RS: Kof-K. Closed Shabbat.

Eating Out cont.

Eden Terrace, 475 Park Ave S (32nd St), Ph: 545-0455. Meals: l,d. Menu: (Glatt meat) Deli and fast food; also traditional and American cuisine. RS: Kof-K. Closed Shabbat.

Famous Dairy Restaurant, 222 W 72nd St, Ph: 595-8487. Meals: b,l,d. Menu: Dairy dishes. RS: K'hal Adath Jeshurun. Closed Shabbat.

Galil Restaurant, 1252 Lexington Ave, Ph: 439-9886. Meals, l,d. Menu: Mideastern and Israeli. RS: Kof-K. Closed Shabbat.

Gertel's Luncheonette, 53 Hester St, Ph: 982-3250. Meals: b,l. Menu: (Dairy) Sandwiches, RS: Rabbi S. Krausz. Closed Shabbat.

Glatt Yacht, W 23rd St & West Side Hwy, Pier 62, Ph: 869-5400 or (718) 384-4954. Meals: d; Tuesday, Wednesday, Sunday; brunch on Sunday. Menu: (Glatt meat) French continental. RS: O.K. Laboratories.

Great American Health Bar, 15 E 40th St, Ph: 532-3232. Meals: b,l. Menu: Soup, salads, falafel, quiches, hot vegetarian dishes. RS: Rabbi D. Katz. Closed Shabbat.

Great American Health Bar, 35 W 57th St, Ph: 355-5177. Meals: b,l. Menu: Juices, soups, salads, vegetarian dishes, frozen yogurt, tofutti. RS: Tablet-K.

Great American Health Bar, 55 John St, Ph: 227-6100. Meals: b,l. Menu: (Dairy, vegetarian) Pizza, falafel, pasta, fish. RS: Kof-K. Closed Shabbat.

Great American Health Bar, 825 3rd Ave, Ph: 758-0883. Meals: b,l,d. Menu: Juices, soups, salads, yogurt, toffuti. RS: Tablet-K.

Greener Pastures, 119 E 60th St, Ph: 832-3212. Meals: l,d. Menu: Dairy and vegetarian dishes. RS: Orthodox Union. Closed Shabbat.

Hunan New York Restaurant, 1049 2nd Ave, Ph: 888-2256. Meals: l,d. Menu: (Glatt meat) Chinese. RS: Kof-K. Credit Cards. Closed Shabbat.

J 2 Kosher Pizza, 112 Fulton St, Ph: 732-6523. Meals: b,l,d. Menu: Pizza, salads, Israeli and Italian dishes. RS: Vaad Harabonim of Flatbush. Closed Shabbat.

Jerusalem II Kosher Pizza, 1375 Broadway, Ph: 398-1475. Meals:

b,l,d. Menu: Pizza, falafel, Israeli dishes. Also French bakery. RS: Vaad Harabonim of Flatbush. Closed Shabbat.

Kosher Delight, 1365 Broadway, Ph: 563-3366; 1156 6th Ave, Ph: 869-6699. Meals: l,d. Menu: (Glatt meat) Fast food. RS: Vaad Harabonim of Flatbush. Closed Shabbat.

Kosher Roma Pizzeria, 1561 2nd Ave (81st St), Ph: 794-4288. Meals: l,d. Menu: Pizza, falafel, pasta, salads. RS: Midtown Board of Kashruth. Closed Shabbat.

La Kasbah, 70 W 71st St, Ph: 769-1690/93. Meals: d. Menu: Moroccan and Mediterranean. RS: Kof-K. Closed Shabbat.

Levana Restaurant, 141 W 69th St, Ph: 877-8457. Meals: l,d. Menu: (Glatt meat) Continental. RS: Kof-K. Credit cards. Closed Shabbat.

Levy's Kosher Pizza, 330 7th Ave, Ph: 594-4613. Meals: l. Menu: Dairy: cholov Yisroel. RS: Tablet-K. Closed Shabbat.

Ludlow's Dairy Cafe, 85 Ludlow St, Ph: 979-8585. Meals: b,l. Menu: Salads, sandwiches, vegetarian dishes. RS: Orthodox Union. Closed Shabbat.

The Lunch Bunch, 55 W 45th St, Ph: 221-6123. Meals: b,l. Menu: Dairy and vegetarian dishes, salads, sandwiches. RS: Rabbi D. Katz. Closed Shabbat.

Madras Palace, 104 Lexington Ave, Ph: 532-3314. Meals: l,d. Menu: South Indian vegetarian. RS: Rabbi C. Muller. Closed Shabbat.

Mirage, 150 E 39th St, Ph: 867-4690. Meals: l,d. Menu: (Glatt meat) Mideastern, Israeli and American. RS: Star-K of Baltimore. Credit cards. Closed Shabbat.

Mizrachi Kosher Pizza & Falafel, 105 Chambers St, Ph: 964-2280. Meals: b,l,d. Menu: (Dairy: cholov Yisroel) Pizza, falafel, Mideastern foods, fish, soups, salads. RS: Rabbi P. Horowitz. Closed Shabbat.

Mom's Bagels of N.Y., 15 W 45th St, Ph: 764-1566. Meals: b,l. Menu: (Dairy: cholov Yisroel) Spreads, soups, sandwiches, hot dishes. RS: Kof-K. Closed Shabbat.

My most favorite dessert company, 1165 Madison Ave, (85-86th St), Ph: 517-5222/3. Meals: b,l,d. Menu: (Dairy) Vegetarian, sandwiches, Italian, desserts. RS: Midtown Board of Kashruth. Closed Shabbat.

319

Eating Out cont.

My Place, 2553 Amsterdam Ave, Ph: 568-4600. Meals: l,d. Menu: Chili, burgers, chicken, roast beef, Hawaiian, complete dinners. RS: K'hal Adath Jeshurun of Washington Heights. Closed Shabbat.

Naftali's, 77 Fulton St, Ph: 385-9320. Meals: l,d. Menu: Meat dishes, seafood. RS: Star-K of Baltimore. Closed Shabbat.

Pita Factory, 2193 Broadway, Ph: 873-5630. Meals: b,l,d. Menu: Schwarma, falafel, vegeatarian foods, pita, salad. RS: Kof-K. Closed Shabbat.

Pita Pocket, 1207 1st Ave (65-66th St), Ph: 439-6136. Meals: l,d. Menu (Meat): Mideastern, salads, sandwiches, desserts. RS: Kof-K. Closed Shabbat.

Ratner's, 138 Delancey St, Ph: 677-5588. Meals: b,l,d. Menu: (Dairy) Fish, soups, salads. RS: Kof-K. Credit cards. Closed Shabbat.

Rishon II, 2 Lafayette St, Ph: 732-4780. Meals: b,l. Menu: Pizza, falafel, salads. RS: Star-K. Closed Shabbat.

Shalom Kosher Pizza, 1000 6th Ave (37th St), Ph: 730-0008. Meals: b,l,d. Menu: Pizza, falafel, Mideastern, vegetarian, salads. RS: Orthodox Union. Closed Shabbat.

Lou G. Siegel's, 209 W 38th St, Ph: 921-4433. Meals: l,d. Menu: (Glatt meat) American cuisine. Also take-out. RS: Orthodox Union. Closed Shabbat. All major cards.

Stern College for Women (Yeshiva University) Cafeteria, 245 Lexington Ave, Ph: 340-7712. Open Monday-Shabbat during the academic year. Meals: b,l (dairy), d (meat). RS: Rabbi F. Reiss. Advance reservations necessary for Shabbat meals.

Taam Hunan, 212 W 72nd St, Ph: 362-7312. Meals: l,d. Menu: (Glatt meat) Chinese. RS: Orthodox Union. Closed Shabbat.

Teva Natural Foods, 122 E 42nd St, (Chanin Bldg, Lower Arcade), Ph: 599-1265. Meals: l,d. Menu: Dairy and vegetarian dishes. RS: Rabbi N. Josephy. Closed Shabbat.

Tevere, 155 E 84th St, Ph: 744-0210. Meals: l,d. Menu: Italian cuisine. RS: Orthodox Union. Closed Shabbat.

Tevye's Dairy Restaurant, 49 White St, Ph: 966-0234 or (718) 969-9235. Meals:l,d. Menu: (Cholov Yisroel) Vegetarian, fish,

Italian dishes. RS: Vaad Harabonim of Queens. Closed Shabbat.

Va Bene, 1589 2nd Ave, Ph: 517-4448. Meals: d. Menu: Italian cuisine. Fish, pasta, vegetables. RS: Orthodox Union. Closed Shabbat.

Yeshiva University Student Cafeteria, 2501 Amsterdam Ave (Rubin Hall), Ph: 568-2440. This cafeteria is open during the academic year from September to the end of May. Visitors are welcome weekdays. Breakfast and lunch are dairy. Dinner and Sunday lunch are meat. RS: Rabbi F. Reiss.

Mikvah

Mikvah of the East Side, 313 E Broadway. Mrs. Barmenko, Ph: 475-8514.

Mikvah of Mid-Manhattan, 232 W 78th St, Ph: 799-1520.

Mikvah of Washington Heights, Broadway and 186th St. Call mikvah office, Ph: 923-1100.

Bookstores

H & M Skull Cap, 46 Hester St, Ph: 777-2280.
J. Levine Co., 5 W 30th St, Ph: 695-6888.
Jewish Museum Shop. 1109 Fifth Avenue, Ph: 860-1895.
Judaica Emporium, 3070 Broadway, Ph: 864-6501.
Louis Stavsky Co. Inc., 147 Essex St, Ph: 674-1289.
West Side Judaica, 2404 Broadway, Ph: 362-7846.

QUEENS   Area Code (718)   J-pop. 321,200

Synagogues

Astoria Center of Israel (C), 27-35 Crescent St, Long Island City,
    Ph: 278-2680. Rabbi B. Herman. Services: Shabbat
Bayside Jewish Center (C), 203-05 32nd Ave, Bayside,
    Ph: 352-7904. Rabbi W. Orentlicher. Services: Daily
Bell Park Jewish Center (C), 231-10 Hillside Ave, Queens Village,
    Ph: 464-9144. Rabbi M. Kwalbrun. Services: Daily
Temple Beth El (C), 445 Beach 135th St, Belle Harbor,
    Ph: 634-8100. Rabbi A. Blaine. Services: Daily
Temple Beth Sholom (R), 171-39 Northern Blvd, Flushing,
    Ph: 463-4143. Rabbi B. Goldwasser. Services: Friday
Briarwood Jewish Center (C), 139-06 86th Ave, Jamaica,
    Ph: 657-5151. Rabbi E. Elefant. Services: Daily
Clearview Jewish Center (C), 16-50 Utopia Pkwy, Whitestone,
    Ph: 352-6670. Rabbi C. Walkenfeld. Services: Daily
Conservative Synagogue of Jamaica (C-US), 182-69 Wexford
    Terrace, Jamaica, Ph: 658-2587. Rabbi I. Aizenberg. Services:
    Daily
Congregation Darchay Noam—Bayswater Jewish Center (C), 2355
    Healy Ave, Far Rockaway, Ph: 471-7771. Rabbi R. Aronowitz.
    Services: Daily
The Forest Hills Jewish Center (C-US), 106-06 Queens Blvd,
    Forest Hills, Ph: 263-7000. Rabbi S. Katz and Rabbi G.
    Skolnick. Services: Daily
Free Synagogue of Flushing (R-UAHC), 41-60 Kissena Blvd,
    Flushing, Ph: 961-0030. Rabbi C. Agin. Services: Friday
Hillcrest Jewish Center (C-US), 183-02 Union Tpke, Flushing,

Ph: 380-4145. Rabbi M. Efron. Services: Daily

Hollis Hills Jewish Center (C-US), 210-10 Union Tpke, Flushing, Ph: 776-3500. Rabbi H. Simckes. Services: Daily

Holliswood Jewish Center (O-UOJC), 86-25 Francis Lewis Blvd, Jamaica, Ph: 776-8500. Rabbi R. Butler. Services: Daily

International Synagogue, JFK International Airport, Jamaica, Ph: 656-5044. Rabbi A. Poplack, Chaplain. Services: Call for schedule.

Temple Isaiah (R), 75-25 Grand Central Pkwy, Forest Hills, Ph: 544-2800. Rabbi M. Perelmuter. Services: Shabbat

Jewish Center of Forest Hills West (C-US), 63-25 Dry Harbor Rd, Middle Village, Ph: 639-2110. Rabbi S. Geffen. Services: Daily

Jewish Center of Jackson Heights (C), 34-25 82nd St, Jackson Heights, Ph: 429-1150. Rabbi L. Moses. Services: Shabbat, Monday and Thursday

Congregation Kehilas Jakob (O), 612 Beach 9th St, West Lawrence, Ph: 327-0196. Rabbi S. Rubin. Services: Daily

Kew Gardens Anshe Sholom Jewish Center (C), 82-52 Abingdon Rd, Kew Gardens, Ph: 441-2471. Rabbi M. Feldman. Services: Daily

Kissena Jewish Center (O), 43-43 Bowne St, Flushing, Ph: 461-1871. Rabbi H. Frankel. Services: Daily

Congregation Kneseth Israel (O), 728 Empire Ave, Far Rockaway. Ph: 327-7545. Rabbi R. Pelcovitz. Services: Daily

Laurelton Jewish Center (C-US), 228-20 137th St, Laurelton, Ph: 527-0400. Rabbi S. Greenstein. Services: Daily

Little Neck Jewish Center (C-US), 49-10 Little Neck Pkwy, Little Neck, Ph: 224-6017. Rabbi A. Eckstein. Services: Shabbat

Congregation Ohab Zedek (O-UOJC), 134-01 Rockaway Beach Blvd, Belle Harbor, Ph: 474-3300. Rabbi J. Reiner. Services: Daily

Ozone Park Jewish Center (O), 107-01 Cross Bay Blvd, Ozone Park, Ph: 848-4096. Rabbi B. Levin. Services: Daily

Queens Jewish Center (O-UOJC), 66-05 108th St, Ph: 459-8432. Rabbi J. Grunblatt. Services: Daily

Rego Park Jewish Center (C), 97-30 Queens Blvd, Rego Park, Ph: 459-1000. Rabbi S. Blickstein. Services: Daily

Synagogues cont.

Rockwood Park Jewish Center (O), 156-45 84th St, Howard Beach, Ph: 641-5822. Rabbi R. Saffra. Services: Daily

Rosedale Jewish Center (C), 247-11 Francis Lewis Blvd, Rosedale, Ph: 528-3988. Rabbi S. Smerling. Services: Daily

Sephardic Jewish Center of Forest Hills (O), 67-67 108th St, Forest Hills, Ph: 268-2100. Rabbi A. Murciano. Services: Daily

Sephardic Jewish Center of Queens (O), 101-17 67th Dr, Forest Hills, Ph: 544-6932. Rabbi S. Hecht. Services: Daily

Temple Sinai (R), 71-11 112th St, Forest Hills, Ph: 261-2900. Rabbi M. Davis. Services: Shabbat

Sunnyside Jewish Center (C), 45-46 43rd St, Sunnyside, Ph: 784-7055. Rabbi I. Albert. Services: Daily

Congregation Tifereth Israel of Jackson Heights (O), 88th St & 32nd Ave, Jackson Heights, Ph: 429-4100. Rabbi H. Solnica. Services: Daily

Utopia Jewish Center (C-US), 64-41 Utopia Pkwy, Flushing, Ph: 461-8347. Rabbi S. Goldman. Services: Daily

Young Israel of Bayside (O-NCYI), 209-34 26th Ave, Bayside, Ph: 423-3720. Rabbi S. Steinig. Services: Daily

Young Israel of Briarwood (O-NCYI), 84-75 Daniels St, Jamaica, Ph: 657-2880. Rabbi M. Kaufman. Services: Daily

Young Israel of Far Rockaway (O-NCYI), 716 Beach 9th St, Far Rockaway, Ph: 471-6724. Rabbi Y. Goodman. Services: Daily

Young Israel of Forest Hills (O), Yellowstone Blvd & Burns Dr, Forest Hills, Ph: 268-7100. Rabbi F. Wagner. Services: Daily

Young Israel of Hillcrest (O-NCYI), 169-07 Jewel Ave, Flushing, Ph: 969-2990. Rabbi S. Krauss. Services: Daily

Young Israel of Jackson Heights (O-NCYI), 86-23 37th Ave, Ph: 639-8888. Rabbi M. Shapiro. Services: Daily

Young Israel of Jamaica Estates (O-NCYI), 83-10 188th St, Jamaica, Ph: 479-7500. Rabbi S. Hochberg. Services: Shabbat

Young Israel of Kew Gardens Hills (O-NCYI), 150-05 70th Rd, Ph: 261-9723. Rabbi F. Schonfeld. Services: Daily

Young Israel of New Hyde Park (O-NCYI), 264-15 77th Ave, New Hyde Park, Ph: 343-0496. Rabbi M. Bilitzky. Services: Daily

Young Israel of Queens Valley (O-NCYI), 141-55 77th Ave, Flushing, Ph: 263-9073. Rabbi P. Steinberg. Services: Daily

Young Israel of Wavecrest and Bayswater (O-NCYI), 23-60 Brookhaven Ave, Far Rockaway, Ph: 327-8606. Rabbi J. Goldberg. Services: Daily

Young Israel of Windsor Park (O-NCYI), 67-45 215th St, Bayside, Ph: 224-2100. Rabbi L. Bernstein. Services: Daily

Eating Out

Annie's Kitchen, 72-24 Main St, Kew Gardens Hills, Ph: 268-0960. Meals: l,d. Menu: (Glatt meat) Chinese. Also take-out. RS: Vaad Harabonim of Queens. Closed Shabbat.

The Baba Nightclub, 91-33 63rd Dr, Rego Park, Ph: 275-2660. Meals: d. Wed, Sat. night; Sun, l.d. Menu: Israeli, American. RS: Rabbi E. Eisenberg. Closed Shabbat.

Benjy's Kosher Pizza & Falafel, 72-72 Main St, Flushing, Ph: 268-0791. Meals: l,d. Menu: Pizza, falafel, Israeli. RS: Vaad Harabonim of Queens. Closed Shabbat.

Burger Nosh, 69-74 Main St, Flushing, Ph: 793-6927. Meals: l,d. Menu: (Glatt meat) American and deli-style fast food. RS: Vaad Harabonim of Queens. Closed Shabbat.

Cho-Sen Garden 64-43 108th St, Ph: 275-1300. Meals: l,d. Menu: (Glatt meat) Chinese cuisine. RS: Vaad Harabonim of Queens. Closed Shabbat.

Eli's Pizza & Falafel, 63-46 108th St, Forest Hills, Ph: 897-0907. Meals: l,d. Menu: Pizza, falafel, knishes, salads, french fries, soups. RS: Vaad Harabonim of Queens. Closed Shabbat.

Eating Out cont..

Empire Chicken Restaurant, 100-19 Queens Blvd, Ph: 997-7315.
Meals: l,d. Menu: Chicken, turkey, soups, salads. RS: Vaad
Harabonim of Queens. Closed Shabbat.

The Flame Restaurant, 97-04 Queens Blvd, Rego Park,
Ph: 275-1403. Meals: l,d. Menu: (Glatt Meat) Israeli dishes. RS:
Vaad Harabonim of Queens. Closed Shabbat.

Grandma Pizzeria, 189-15 Union Tpke, Flushing, Ph: 217-9090.
Meals: l,d. Menu: Pizza, falafel, calzones, salads. RS: Vaad
Harabonim of Queens. Closed Shabbat.

Hamakom Pizza, 101-11 Queens Blvd, Forest Hills, Ph: 275-3992.
Meals: l,d. Menu: Pizza, falafel, salads, knishes, lasagna.
RS: Vaad Harabonim of Queens. Closed Shabbat.

Hapisgah, 147-25 Union Tpke, Flushing, Ph: 380-4449. Meals: l,d.
Menu: (Glatt meat) Israeli cuisine. RS: Vaad Harabonim of
Queens. Closed Shabbat.

Hazameret Restaurant, 68-36 Main St, Flushing, Ph: 575-0647.
Meals: l,d. Menu: (Glatt meat) Israeli-style fast food. RS: Vaad
Harabonim of Queens. Closed Shabbat.

King Solomon's Pizza, 75-43 Main St, Flushing, Ph: 793-0710.
Meals, b,l,d. Menu: Pizza, falafel, salads, Middle East specialties. RS: Vaad Harabonim of Queens. Closed Shabbat.

Mazur's Market Place & Restaurant, 254-51 Horace Harding Blvd,
Little Neck, Ph: 428-5000. Meals: l,d. Menu: Soup, salad,
entrees. RS: Vaad Harabonim of Long Island. Closed Shabbat.

Menorah, 188-17 Union Tpke, Fresh Meadows, Ph: 465-7032.
Meals: l,d. Menu: (Glatt meat) Mideastern. RS: Vaad
Harabonim of Queens. Closed Shabbat.

Naomi's Kosher Pizza & Falafel, 68-28 Main St, Flushing,
Ph: 520-8754. Meals: l,d. Menu: Pizza, falafel, Israeli dishes.
RS: Vaad Harabonim of Queens. Closed Shabbat.

Pinat Shalom, 69-26 Main St, Ph: 575-1763. Meals: l,d. Menu:
(Glatt meat) Israeli cuisine. RS: Vaad Harabonim of Queens.
Closed Shabbat.

Pizza Roma, 80-55 Kew Gardens Rd, Kew Gardens, Ph: 263-2505.

Meals: l,d. Menu: Pizza, falafel, salad. RS: Vaad Harabonim of Queens. Closed Shabbat.

Shimon's Kosher Pizza, 71-24 Main St, Kew Gardens Hills, Ph: 793-1491. Meals: l,d. Menu: Pizza, falafel, Israel and Italian dishes (dairy). RS: Vaad Harabonim of Queens. Closed Shabbat.

Traditions, 69-78 Main St, Flushing, Ph: 575-1224. Meals: l,d. Menu: (Glatt meat) Deli, Italian cuisine. RS: Vaad Harabonim of Queens.

Zahava's Dairy Restaurant, 69-30 Austin St, Forest Hills, Ph: 544-1400. Meals: l,d. Menu: (Cholov Yisroel) Fish, pasta. RS: Vaad Harabonim of Queens. All major credit cards. Closed Shabbat.

Mikvah

Far Rockaway-Lawrence Mikvah, 1121 Bayport Pl, Far Rockaway. Call mikvah attendant, Ph: 327-9727.

Mikvah Israel, 71-11 Vleigh Pl, Flushing, Ph: 268-6500.

Mikvah of Queens, 75-48 Grand Central Pkwy, Forest Hills. Call mikvah attendant, Ph: 261-6380.

Bookstores

Hebrew Book & Gift World, 72-20 Main St, Flushing, Ph: 261-0233.

Ki-Tov Hebrew Book & Gift Center, 1847 Mott Ave, Far Rockaway, Ph: 471-0963.

STATEN ISLAND   Area Code (718)   J-pop. 31,000

Synagogues

Agudath Achim Anshe Chesed (O-UOJC), 641 Delafield Ave,
Ph: 981-0539. Rabbi M. Zachariash. Services: Daily

Ahavath Israel (C), 7630 Amboy Rd, Ph: 356-8740. Rabbi Y.
Perkin. Services: Friday

Arden Heights Blvd. Jewish Center (C), 1766 Arthur Kill Rd,
Ph: 948-6782. Rabbi S. Davis. Services: Shabbat

Temple B'nai Israel (C), 45 Twombley Ave, Ph: 987-8188.
Rabbi J. Rappoport. Services: Daily

B'nai Jeshurun (C-US), 272 Marling Ave, Ph: 981-5550. Rabbi J.
Neuburger. Services: Shabbat

Temple Israel (R), 315 Forest Ave, Ph: 727-2231. Rabbi D. Katz.
Services: Friday

Springfield Jewish Center—Congregation Shaare Simcha
(O-UOJC), 14 Eli Court, Ph: 983-8063. Rabbi N. Siegel.
Services: Daily

Yeshiva of Staten Island (O), 1870 Drumgoole Rd E, Ph: 356-4323.
Rabbi R. Feinstein. Services: Daily

Young Israel of Eltingville (O-NCYI), 374 Ridgewood Ave,
Ph: 948-1993. Rabbi E. Kaufman. Services: Daily

Young Israel of Staten Island (O-NCYI), 835 Forest Rd,
Ph: 494-6700. Rabbi J. Marcus. Services: Daily

Mikvah

Mikvah Young Israel of Staten Island, 835 Forest Hill Rd,
Ph: 494-6704.

Bookstore

Carmel Gift Center, 10 Carmel Ave, Ph: 761-8480.

NEWBURGH   Area Code (914)

Synagogues

Congregation Agudas Israel (Trad), 290 North St, Ph: 562-5604.
   Rabbi H. Markowitz. Services: Daily
Temple Beth Jacob (R-UAHC), 344 Gidney Ave, Ph: 562-5516.
   Rabbi H. Jaffe. Services: Friday

Food

Broadway Bakery, 356R Windsor Hwy, Ph: 562-2585. Breads
   (pareve) and cakes (dairy). RS: Congregation Agudas Israel.
Gracolicci Bakery, 215 Washington St, Ph: 565-4466. Breads
   (pareve) and cakes (dairy). RS: Congregation Agudas Israel.

Accommodations

Private accommodations; contact Rabbi D. Kramer at
   Congregation Agudas Israel, Ph: 562-5604.

NIAGARA FALLS (See also BUFFALO)
Area Code (716)   J-pop. 395

Synagogues

Temple Beth El (R), 720 Ashland Ave, Ph: 282-2717. Services:
   Friday
Temple Beth Israel (C-US), College & Madison Aves,
   Ph: 285-9894. Rabbi H. Cassorla. Services: Shabbat

OGDENSBURG Area Code (315)

Synagogues

Congregation Anshe Zophen (C), 416 Greene St, Ph: 393-3787.
Rabbi E. Gottesman. Services: Friday

ONEONTA Area Code (607) J-pop. 250

Synagogues

Temple Beth-El (C-US), 83 Chestnut St, Ph: 432-5522. Services:
Call for information.

PORT JERVIS Area Code (914) J-pop. 560

Synagogues

Temple Beth El (C), 88 E Main St, Ph: 856-1722. Rabbi E. Milder.
Services: Shabbat

POUGHKEEPSIE Area Code (914) J-pop. 6,500

Synagogues

Temple Beth-El (C-US), 118 Grand Ave, Ph: 454-0570. Rabbi C.
Feinberg. Services: Daily
Congregation Schomre Israel (O-UOJC), 18 Park Ave,
Ph: 454-2890. Rabbi R. Stein. Services: Daily
Vassar Temple (R-UAHC), 140 Hooker Ave, Ph: 454-2570.
Rabbi S. Arnold. Services: Friday

Accommodations

Private accommodations; contact Congregation Schomre Israel,
Ph: 454-2890.

Mikvah

Congregation Shomre Israel, 18 Park Ave. Call Mrs. Claire May,
Ph: 452-7583 or 454-7300.

Day School

Mid-Hudson Hebrew Day School, 110 Grand Ave, Ph: 454-0474.

QUEENS (See **NEW YORK CITY**)

ROCHESTER   Area Code (716)   J-pop. 23,000

Synagogues

Temple Beth Am (C), 3249 Henrietta Rd, Ph: 334-4855. Services:
  Shabbat

Temple Beth David (C-US, R-UAHC), 3200 St. Paul Blvd,
  Ph: 266-3223. Rabbi L. Skopitz. Services: Daily

Temple Beth El (C-US), 139 S Winton Rd, Ph: 473-1770. Rabbi S.
  Kanter. Services: Daily

Congregation Beth Hakeneses Hachodosh (O), 19 St. Regis Dr,
  Ph: 271-5390 or 244-2740. Rabbi A. Sakoloff. Services: Daily

Temple Beth Hamedrash—Beth Israel (C), 1369 East Ave,
  Ph: 244-2060. Services: Shabbat and Sunday

Beth Joseph Center (O-UOJC), 1150 St. Paul St, Ph: 423-0030.
  Rabbi J. Pearlman. Services: Daily

Congregation Beth Shalom (O-UOJC), 1161 Monroe Ave,
  Ph: 473-1625. Rabbi S. Kilimnick. Services: Daily

Congregation B'nai Israel Ahavas Achim (O), 692 Joseph Ave,
  Ph: 544-9261. Rabbi H. Hyman. Services: Saturdays and
  Holidays

Temple B'rith Kodesh (R-UAHC), 2131 Elmwood Ave,
  Ph: 244-7060. Rabbi J. Cohen-Rosenberg. Services: Shabbat

Chabad Lubavitch (O-Lubav), 4 Chelmsford Rd, Ph: 271-0330.
  Rabbi N. Vogel. Services: Shabbat

Temple Emanu-El of Irondequoit (R-UAHC), 2956 St. Paul Blvd,
  Ph: 544-4642. Rabbi M. Herzbrun. Services: Friday

Etz Chaim (R), P.O. Box 52, **Victor**, Ph: 385-3193. Services:
  Friday

Congregation Light of Israel (O-UOJC-Sephardic), 206 Norton St,
  Ph: 544-1381. Rabbi S. Cohen. Services: Shabbat and Sunday

Temple Sinai (R-UAHC), 363 Penfield Rd, Ph: 381-6890.
  Rabbi A. Katz. Services: Shabbat

Eating Out

B'nai B'rith Hillel at the Rochester Institute of Technology, 1 Lomb

Eating Out cont.

Memorial Dr, Ph: 475-2135. RS: Rabbi P. Saiger (R). Shabbat meals served every other Friday during school year. Call Mr. S. Kolko for information.

B'nai B'rith Hillel Foundation at the University of Rochester, Interfaith Chapel, Ph: 275-4321. RS: Rabbi P. Saiger (R). Shabbat meals every other Friday during the school year.

Jewish Home for the Aged (cafeteria), 2021 S Winton Rd, Ph: 427-7760. Meals: b,l,d. Menu: Soups, salads, fish and meat dishes. RS: Rabbi S. Kilimnik of Beth Shalom. Closed Shabbat.

Food

Lipman's Kosher Market, 1482 Monroe Ave, Ph: 271-7886. Meats, groceries and deli. RS: Rabbi A. Sakoloff of Beth Hakeneses Hachodosh. Closed Shabbat.

Lea Malek's Bakery, 1795 Monroe Ave, Ph: 461-1720. Breads and pastries. RS: Rabbi A. Sakoloff. Closed Shabbat.

Quality Bakery, 687 Joseph Ave, Ph: 544-2100. Breads and pastries. RS: Rabbi H. Hyman of B'nai Israel Ahavas Achim.

Accommodations

Private accommodations; contact Rabbi N. Vogel of Chabad Lubavitch, Ph: 271-0330.

Mikvah

Beth Hatvilah, 27 St. Regis Dr N, Ph: 442-0245.

Day School

Hillel School, 191 Fairfield Dr, Ph: 271-6877.

Bookstore

Tradition, 1697 Monroe Ave, Ph: 244-3540.

ROCKLAND COUNTY   Area Code (914)   J-pop. 60,000

HAVERSTRAW
Synagogues

Congregation Sons of Jacob (Trad), 37 Clove Ave, Ph: 429-4644. Rabbi S. Wohlberg. Services: Shabbat and Holidays

MONSEY (See also SPRING VALLEY and SUFFERN)
Synagogues

Congregation Ayshel Avraham (O), 225 Maple Ave, Ph: 352-0630. Rabbi Y. Spivak. Services: Daily

Congregation Bais Torah (O), 36 Carlton Rd, **Suffern,** Ph: 578-9515. Rabbi B. Wein. Services: Daily

Congregation Beth Israel, 92 Main St, Ph: 356-2135. Rabbi N. Horowitz. Services: Daily

Congregation Beth Tefilla (O), Maplewood Lane, Ph: 356-5089. Rabbi S. Breslauer. Services: Daily

B'nai Jeshurun (O), Park Lane, Ph: 356-9472. Rabbi I. Flam. Services: Daily

Community Synagogue (O-UOJC), 11 Cloverdale Lane, Ph: 356-2720. Rabbi M. Tendler. Services: Daily

Etz Chaim (O), 63 Carlton Rd, Ph: 426-3583. Rabbi I. Dahan. Services: Shabbat and daily a.m.

Congregation Hadar (O), 70 Highview Rd, Ph: 357-1515. Rabbi N. Muschel. Services: Daily

Congregation K'hal Torath Chaim Viznitz, 25 Phyllis Terr, Ph: 356-6666. Rabbi M. Hager. Services: Daily

Monsey Jewish Center (C), 101 Rte 306, Ph: 352-6444. Rabbi D. Chanofsky. Services: Daily

NCFJE (O-Lubav), 4 Phyllis Terrace, Ph: 352-7642. Rabbi S. Werner. Services: Shabbat and daily p.m.

Congregation Ohaiv Israel (O), 30 Blueberry Hill Rd, Ph: 425-3315. Rabbi C. Chait. Services: Daily

Young Israel of Monsey (O-NCYI), 58 Parker Blvd, Ph: 362-1838. Rabbi N. Fromowitz. Services: Shabbat and Sunday

Eating Out

Bagels N' More Dairy Restaurant, 106B Rte 59, Ph: 352-0710. Meals: b,l,d. Menu: Bagels, danish, soups, salads, fish, dairy dishes. Cholov Yisroel. RS: Star-K of Baltimore. Closed Shabbat.

Chai Pizza and Falafel, 94 Rte 59, Ph: 356-2424. Meals: l,d. Menu: Pizza, falafel, salads. Cholov Yisroel. Also take-out. RS: Rabbi N. Horowitz. Closed Shabbat.

Cyrk Café, 162 Rte 59 (near Remsen), Ph: 356-3006. Meals: l,d.
Menu: (Dairy) Soups, salads, sandwiches, fresh fish, omelettes,
home-made ice cream, desserts (cholov Yisroel). RS: Rabbi
M. Bernstein. Closed Shabbat.

Deli-N-More, 3D Rte 59, Atrium Plaza, Ph: 352-0000 or
356-0000. Meals: l,d. Menu: (Glatt meat) Deli. RS: Star-K.
Closed Shabbat.

59 West Family Restaurant, 118 Rte 59, (corner Saddle River Rd),
Ph: 578-9560. Meals: l,d. Menu: Deli, meat grill, fried chicken,
side dishes; also take-out. RS: Rabbi S. Breslauer of Beth
Tefilla. Closed Shabbat.

Oasis, 3D Rte 59, Atrium Plaza, Ph: 352-0000 or 356-0000.
Meals: l,d. Menu: (Glatt meat) Chinese. Also take-out. RS:
Star-K. Closed Shabbat.

Tov Tam Kosher Dairy Restaurant, 32 Main St, Ph: 352-0207.
Meals: l,d. Menu: Pizza, falafel, salad and side dishes. RS:
Satmar. Closed Shabbat.

Food

A & B Fish Market, 84 E Rte 59, Ph: 425-0900. Fresh fish and
ready-to-cook gefilte fish. RS: Rabbi N. Horowitz. Closed
Shabbat and Sunday.

European Home Made Foods, 82 Rte 59, Ph: 356-9555.
Traditional prepared foods for take-out; also bakery and some
grocery items. RS: Rabbi N. Horowitz. Closed Shabbat.

Kosher Town, 46 Main St, Ph: 425-0350. Kosher groceries, produce, bakery goods, cholov Yisroel, health foods, vitamins.
Closed Shabbat.

Meal Mart, 41 Main St, Ph: 352-9008. Prepared foods; some frozen and packaged items. RS: Rabbi Y. Roth of Boro Park.
Closed Shabbat.

Meat Showcase, 106 Rte 59 & 306, Ph: 426-2333. Fresh meat and
poultry; complete kosher grocery. RS: Rabbi S. Breslauer.
Closed Shabbat.

Food cont.

Mendlowitz Glatt Kosher Meat, 84A Rte 59, Ph: 356-2376. Fresh meat and poultry and deli meats; kosher groceries and frozen foods. RS: Rabbi N. Horowitz. Closed Shabbat.

Monsey Fish, 46 Main Street, Ph: 356-8877. Fresh fish & ready-to-cook gefilte fish. RS: K'hal Adath Yeshurun of Washington Heights. Open Mon-Thur. Closed Shabbat.

Monsey Fruit and Vegetable Market, 19 Main St, Ph: 356-5310, 5311. Produce, groceries. Closed Shabbat.

Monsey Kosher Bake Shop, 51 Main St, Ph: 352-6435. Breads, cakes, cookies, some groceries. RS: Rabbi M. Neuschloss of New Square. Closed Shabbat.

Nagel's Superette, 40 Main St, Ph: 356-5123. Complete kosher grocery, bakery items and produce. Closed Shabbat.

One Stop Kosher, 34 Main St, Ph: 425-2266. Complete supermarket including produce and bakery items. Closed Shabbat.

Pathmark Supermarket, 45 Rte 59, Ph: 352-0178. Very large kosher section. Also cholov Yisroel milk and dairy products.

Sweet Occasions, 199 Rte 59, Ph: 352-3400. Packaged and bulk items. RS: Star-K of Baltimore. Closed Shabbat.

Mikvah

Mikvah Beth Israel, Maple Leaf Rd. Contact Mikvah office, Ph: 356-1000.

Mikvah of Concord, 19 Bartlett Rd, Ph: 425-8598.

Day Schools

Adolph H. Schreiber Hebrew Academy of Rockland County, Yeshivas Hadar Avrohom Tzvi, 70 Highview Rd, Ph: 357-1515 or 357-1516 or 357-1517.

Bais Mikroh, 23 W Maple Ave, Ph: 425-4880.

Bais Rochel School for Girls, 145 Saddle River Rd, Ph: 352-5000.

Bas Mikroh, 28 W Maple Ave, Ph: 356-0807; 352-5296.

B'nos Yisroel Girls School of Viznitz, 1 School Terr, Ph: 356-2322.

Rockland Hebrew Day School, 101 Rte 306, Ph: 352-6629.

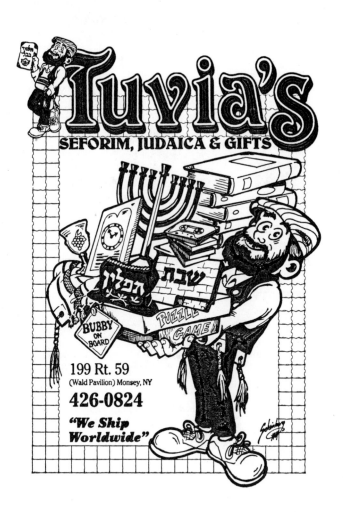
337

Day Schools cont.

United Talmudical Academy—Monsey Torah V'Yirah, Beth Esther D'Satmar, 89 S Main St, Ph: 425-6758.

Yeshiva Beth David, 20 W Maple Ave, Ph: 352-3100.

Yeshiva of Spring Valley, 230 Maple Ave, Ph: 356-1400.

Yeshiva Viznitz, 15 Elyon Rd, Ph: 356-1010; 425-4242.

Bookstores

Judaica Home & Gift Center, 33 Main St, Ph: 425-9399.

Monsey Books, 44 Main St, Ph: 425-8530.

Tuvia's Judaica, 203 Rte 59, Ph: 426-0824.

NANUET
Synagogues

Nanuet Hebrew Center (C-US), 34 S Middletown Rd, Ph: 623-3735. Rabbi S. Potok. Services: Daily

NEW CITY
Synagogues

Temple Beth Sholom (R-UAHC), 228 New Hempstead Rd, Ph: 638-0770. Rabbi D. Fass. Services: Shabbat

Chabad Lubavitch of Rockland (O-Lubav), 315 N Main St, Ph: 634-0951. Rabbi A. Kotlarsky. Services: Shabbat and Sunday a.m.

New City Jewish Center (C-US), Old Schoolhouse Rd, Ph: 634-3619. Rabbi H. Sosland. Services: Daily

Mikvah

Mikvah Chana, 315 N Main St, Ph: 634-0951. (Due for completion summer 1991).

NEW SQUARE (See also MONSEY and SPRING VALLEY)
Synagogues

Congregation Zemach David of New Square (O), 13 Truman Ave, Ph: 354-9736. Rabbi D. Twersky. Services: Daily

Mikvah

Mikva of New Square, 33 Truman Ave, Ph: 354-6578

Day Schools

Gruss Girls School of New Square, 15 Roosevelt Ave, Ph: 354-0874.

Yeshiva of New Square, 766 N Maine St, Ph: 354-1201.

ORANGEBURG
Synagogues

Orangetown Jewish Center (C-US), Independence Ave, Ph: 359-5920. Services: Daily

Young Israel of Orangeburg (O-NCYI), 15 Edgewood St, Ph: 365-2877. Rabbi A. Morduchowitz. Services: Shabbat, except July and August; Holidays

PEARL RIVER
Synagogues

Beth Am Temple (R-UAHC), 60 E Madison Ave, Ph: 735-5858. Rabbi D. Pernick. Services: Shabbat

POMONA (See also SPRING VALLEY)
Synagogues

Pomona Jewish Center (C-US), 106 Pomona Rd, Ph: 354-2226. Rabbi J. Case. Services: Daily

Day School

Bais Yaakov Chofetz Chaim of Pomona, Camp Hill Rd, Ph: 362-3166; 354-6682.

SPRING VALLEY (See also MONSEY and SUFFERN)
Synagogues

Bais Knesset of New Hempstead (O), 653 Union Rd, Ph: 354-4948. Rabbi M. Tendler.

Temple Beth El (R-UAHC), 415 Viola Rd, Ph: 356-2000. Rabbi L. Frishman. Services: Friday

Synagogues cont.

Jewish Community Center (C-US), 250 N Main St, Ph: 356-3710.
Services: Daily

Kehilath Israel (O), Old Nyack Turnpike, Ph: 352-2429. Rabbi
A. M. Gluck.

Ramat Shalom (Recon), 21 Lomand Ave, Ph: 623-7604. Rabbi
D. Small.

Congregation Shaarey Tfiloh (C), 972 S Main St, Ph: 356-2225.
Rabbi A. Michaelson. Services: Shabbat

Congregation Sons of Israel (C), 80 Williams Ave, Ph: 352-6767.
Rabbi S. Zeides. Services: Shabbat

West Clarkstown Jewish Center, 277 W Clarkstown Rd,
Ph: 352-0017. Rabbi L. Gordon. Services: Shabbat

Young Israel of Spring Valley (O-NCYI), 23 N Union Rd,
Ph: 356-3363. Rabbi M. Schwartz. Services: Daily

Eating Out

Little David's, 303 N Main St, Ph: 356-8777. Menu: (Glatt meat)
Shwarma, falafel. RS: Rabbi B. Wosner. Closed Shabbat.

Oneg Pizza, 33 Maple Ave, Ph: 356-3560. Meals: l,d. Menu:
Mediterranean, vegetarian and dairy dishes. Cholov Yisroel.
RS: O.K. Laboratories. Closed Shabbat.

Food

Ahdor Fish Market, 37 Maple Ave, Ph: 425-7776. Fresh fish. RS:
Rabbi S. Stern, Boro Park. Closed Shabbat.

Glauber's Kosher Bakery, 33 Maple Ave (in rear), Ph: 352-4683.
Everything pareve, except cheesecake. RS: Rabbi B. Gruber of
Williamsburg. Closed Shabbat.

Glauber's Appetizing Store, 33 Maple Ave (in rear), Ph: 425-4949.
Separate meat and dairy sections (separate kitchens). RS: Rabbi
L. Horowitz (meat side); Rabbi B. Gruber of Williamsburg
(dairy side). Closed Shabbat.

Hazlochah Grocery, 33 Maple Ave, Ph: 425-9220. Complete
kosher grocery, cholov Yisroel. Closed Shabbat.

Lenny's Village Kosher Market, 303A N Main St, Ph: 356-0241.
   Meat, poultry, groceries, take-out. RS: Rabbi M. Zuber. Closed
   Shabbat.
Neiman's Fish, 55 Myrtle Ave, Ph: 425-7704. Fresh fish and frozen
   gefilte fish. RS: K'hal Toras Chaim Viznitz. Closed Shabbat.
Our Favorite Kosher Bakery, 33 Maple Ave, Ph: 425-9161. Breads
   (pareve), cakes (pareve and dairy). RS: Orthodox Union. Closed
   Shabbat.

Day School

Reuben Gittelman Hebrew Day School, 4 Widman Ct,
   Ph: 356-1800.
Talmud Torah D'Khal Adas Yereim, 33 Union Rd, Ph: 425-5678.
Yeshiva Degel Hatorah, 137 Union Rd, Ph: 356-4610.

SUFFERN (See also MONSEY and SPRING VALLEY)
Synagogues

Reform Temple of Suffern (R), 70 Haverstraw Rd, Ph: 357-5872.
   Rabbi E. Frishman. Services: Shabbat
Congregation Sons of Israel (C-US), Suffern Pl, Ph: 357-9827.
   Rabbi P. Schuchalter. Services: Shabbat and mornings

UPPER NYACK
Synagogues

Temple Beth Torah (R-UAHC), Rte 9W, Ph: 358-2248. Rabbi
   G. Stern. Services: Shabbat
Congregation Sons of Israel (C-US), 300 N Broadway,
   Ph: 358-3767. Rabbi J. Hoffman. Services: Shabbat and Sunday

ROME   Area Code (315)

Synagogues

Congregation Adas Israel (C-US), 705 Hickory St, Ph: 337-3170.
   Rabbi J. Cohen. Services: Shabbat.

SARATOGA SPRINGS   Area Code (518)   J-pop. 500

Synagogues

Congregation Shaare Tfille (C), 260 Broadway, Ph: 584-2370.
  Rabbi L. Alpern. Services: Saturday, Monday and Thursday
Temple Sinai (R-UAHC), 509 Broadway, Ph: 584-8730. Rabbis L.
  Motzkin, J. Rubenstein. Services: Friday

SCHENECTADY   (See also **ALBANY**)
  Area Code (518)   J-pop. 5,200

Synagogues

Congregation Agudat Achim (C-US), 2117 Union St, Ph: 393-9211.
  Rabbi S. Kieffer. Services: Daily
Congregation Beth Israel (O-UOJC), 2195 Eastern Pkwy,
  Ph: 377-3700. Rabbi J. Horowitz. Services: Daily
Congregation Gates of Heaven (R-UAHC), 852 Ashmore Ave,
  Ph: 374-8173. Rabbi B. Bloom. Services: Shabbat

Food

New Mt. Pleasant Bakery, 941 Crane St, Ph: 374-7577. Breads and
  pastries (pareve and dairy; Pas Yisroel, except donuts). RS:
  Vaad Hakashrut of the Capital District.
New York City Bagel, 1859 State St, Ph: 370-1800. Challahs,
  bagels (pareve, other baked goods dairy). RS: Vaad Hakashrut
  of the Capital District (endorsed products available Tuesday-
  Friday only.
Schenectady J.C.C. Snack Bar, 265 Balltown Rd, Ph: 377-8803. At
  swimming pool. Menu: (Glatt meat) Hamburgers, hot dogs,
  sandwiches, salads. RS: Vaad Harabonim of the Capital District.
  Summers only. Closed Shabbat.

Accommodations

Private accommodations; contact Rabbi J. Horowitz at Congregation
  Beth Israel, Ph: 377-3700.

SHARON SPRINGS   Area Code (518)

Accommodations

Adler's Spa, Ph: 284-2285. Shomer Shabbat hotel. Synagogue on premises. Glatt meat. RS: Orthodox Union. Open June-August.

SOUTH FALLSBURG (See CATSKILL REGION)

STATEN ISLAND (See NEW YORK CITY)

SUFFOLK COUNTY   Area Code (516)   J-pop. 106,200

AMITYVILLE
Synagogues

Beth Sholom Center (C-US), 79 County Line Rd, Ph: 264-2891. Rabbi L. Spielman. Services: Daily

BABYLON
Synagogues

Congregation Beth Sholom (C-US), 441 Deer Park Ave, Ph: 669-9797. Rabbi R. Smith. Services: Daily

BAYSHORE
Synagogues

Temple Beth Am (C), 28 6th Ave. Rabbi S. Berger. Services: Shabbat

Jewish Centre of Bay Shore (C-US), 34 N Clinton Ave, Ph: 665-1140. Rabbi G. Schwartz. Services: Daily

Sinai Reform Temple (R-UAHC), 39 Brentwood Rd, Ph: 665-5755. Rabbi R. Slavkin. Services: Friday

CENTER MORICHES
Synagogues

Jewish Center of the Moriches (C-US), 227 Main St, Ph: 878-0388. Services: Friday

CENTEREACH
Synagogues

Temple Beth Torah (Trad), 26 Ronkonkoma Blvd, Ph: 736-0505.
Rabbi B. Gottlieb. Services: Saturday

COLD SPRING HARBOR
Synagogues

Congregation Kehillath Shalom (Recon), 58 Goose Hill Rd,
Ph: 367-4589. Rabbi A. Schwartz. Services: Shabbat

COMMACK
Synagogues

Temple Beth David (R-UAHC), 100 Hauppauge Rd, Ph: 499-0915.
Rabbi L. Troupp. Services: Shabbat

Commack Jewish Center (C-US), 83 Shirley Ct, Ph: 543-3311.
Rabbi W. Berman. Services: Daily

Congregation Lubavitch (O-Lubav), 65 Valleywood Rd,
Ph: 462-6640. Rabbi T. Teldon. Services: Shabbat

Young Israel of Commack—Etz Chaim (O-NCYI), 40 Kings Park
Rd, Ph: 543-1441. Rabbi R. Wizman. Services: Shabbat and
Sunday

Eating Out

Y.M.H.A. of Commack, 74 Hauppage Rd, Ph: 462-9800. Dairy
lunchroom which serving the Solomon Schechter School (C) is
open to visitors for breakfast and lunch Monday-Friday. Call for
information.

Food

Commack Kosher Meats, 132 Jericho Tpke, Ph: 543-2300. Fresh
meat and poultry; traditional dishes prepared for take-out; small
kosher grocery. RS: Rabbi W. Berman of Commack Jewish
Center. Closed Shabbat.

Entrees N' Much More, 223 Commack Rd, Ph: 499-9763. Take-
out. A few tables. Traditional, Chinese, continental cuisine. RS:
Rabbi R. Wizman of Young Israel. Closed Shabbat.

Accommodations

Courtesy Inn, 1126 Jericho Tpke, Ph: 864-3500. Three-quarters of a mile to Young Israel.

Private hospitality; contact Rabbi T. Teldon at Congregation Lubavitch, Ph: 462-6640.

Mikvah

Suffolk Community Mikvah, 74 Hauppauge Rd, Ph: 462-6075.

Day School

Solomon Schechter Day School of Suffolk County (C), 74 Hauppauge Rd, Ph: 462-5999.

CORAM
Synagogues

Coram Jewish Center (O-UOJC), 981 Old Town Rd, Ph: 732-9768. Rabbi M. Golshevsky. Services: Shabbat and Sunday

DEER PARK
Synagogues

Suffolk Jewish Center (C-US), 330 Central Ave, Ph: 667-7695. Rabbi G. Maza. Services: Shabbat

DIX HILLS
Synagogues

Temple Beth Torah (R-UAHC), 35 Bagatelle Rd, Ph: 643-1200. Rabbi M. Gellman. Services: Shabbat

Dix Hills Jewish Center (C-US), 555 Vanderbilt Pkwy, Ph: 499-6644. Rabbi N. Steinberg. Services: Daily

EAST HAMPTON
Synagogues

Jewish Center of the Hamptons (R), 44 Woods Lane, Ph: 324-9858. Rabbi D. Greenberg. Services: Friday

EAST NORTHPORT
Synagogues

East Northport Jewish Center (C-US), 328 Elwood Rd,
Ph: 368-6474. Rabbi R. Adler. Services: Daily
Young Israel of East Northport (O-NCYI), 547 Larkfield Rd,
Ph: 368-5880. Rabbi C. Bausk. Services: Daily

Accommodations

Private hospitality; contact Rabbi C. Bausk at Young Israel of East
Northport, Ph: 368-5880.

EAST ROCKAWAY
Synagogues

Hewlett East Rockaway Jewish Center (C-US), 295 Main St,
Ph: 599-2634. Rabbi S. Platek. Services: Daily

FARMINGDALE
Synagogues

Farmingdale Jewish Center (C-US), 425 Fulton St, Ph: 694-2343.
Rabbi R. Marcus. Services: Daily

GLEN COVE
Synagogues

North Country Reform Temple (R-UAHC), Crescent Beach Blvd,
Ph: 671-4760. Rabbi L. Kotok. Services: Shabbat
Congregation Tifereth Israel (C-US), Hill St & Landing Rd,
Ph: 676-5080. Rabbi M. Weisenberg. Services: Daily

HAUPPAUGE
Synagogues

Temple Beth Chai (C-US), 870 Townline Rd, Ph: 724-5807. Rabbi
H. Buechler. Services: Daily

HUNTINGTON
Synagogues

Temple Beth El (R-UAHC), 660 Park Ave, Ph: 421-5835.
Rabbi B. Shallat. Services: Friday

Huntington Hebrew Congregation (C-US), 510 Park Ave,
Ph: 427-1089. Rabbi N. Kurshan. Services: Daily
South Huntington Jewish Center (C-US), 2600 New York Ave,
Melville, Ph: 421-3224. Rabbi E. Kideckel. Services: Daily

Eating Out

Fuchsberg Law Center of Touro College Cafeteria, 300 Nassau Rd,
Ph: 421-2244 Ext. 373. Meals: b,l,d. Menu: (Glatt meat)
Sandwiches. Hot food. RS: Rabbi M. Portnoy of Young Israel of
Plainview. Open when school is in session; Monday-Thursday 8
a.m.-8:30 p.m.; Friday 8 a.m. to 2:30 p.m.

Bookstore

Zion Lion, 444 W Jericho Tpke, **Huntington Station**,
Ph: 549-5155.

LAKE GROVE (See also **RONKONKOMA**)

Eating Out

Ben's Lake Grove, 135 Alexander Ave, Ph: 979-8770. Meals: l,d.
Menu: Deli-style dishes. RS: Rabbi H. Buechler, Temple Beth
Chai, Hauppauge.

LINDENHURST
Synagogues

Lindenhurst Hebrew Congregation (C), 225 N 4th St & W John St,
Ph: 226-2022. Rabbi R. Rhodes. Services: Shabbat

OAKDALE
Synagogues

B'nai Israel Reform Temple (R-UAHC), 67 Idle Hour Blvd and
Biltmore Ave, Ph: 563-1660. Rabbi S. Moss. Services: Friday

PATCHOGUE
Synagogues

Temple Beth El of Patchogue (C-US), 45 Oak St, Ph: 475-1882.
Rabbi R. Thaler. Services: Daily
Young Israel of Patchogue (O-NCYI), 28 Mowbray St,
Ph: 654-0882. Rabbi S. Richmond. Services: Daily

PORT JEFFERSON
Synagogues

North Shore Jewish Center (C-US), 384 Old Town Rd,
Ph: 928-3737. Rabbi M. Edelman. Services: Daily

Food

Mel Weitz Food Town, 1108 Rt 112, Ph: 474-0212. Good selection
of kosher products.

RIVERHEAD
Synagogues

Temple Israel of Riverhead (C-US), 490 Northville Tpke,
Ph: 727-3191. Rabbi C. Gerlitz. Services: Shabbat and Sunday

RONKONKOMA
Synagogues

Torah Community Center (O-Lubav), 821 Hawkins Ave,
Ph: 585-0521. Rabbi M. Ossey. Services: Shabbat and Holidays

SAG HARBOR
Synagogues

Temple Adas Israel (R), Elizabeth St & Atlantic Ave, Ph:
725-0904. Dr. P. Steinberg. Services: Friday (summers only)

SAYVILLE
Synagogues

Temple Shalom (Trad), 225 Greeley Ave, Ph: 589-9722. Rabbi J.
Wartenberg. Services: Daily

SMITHTOWN
Synagogues

Temple Beth Sholom (C-US, Recon), Edgewood Ave & River Rd,
Ph: 724-0425. Rabbi E. Spar and Rabbi A. Axelrud. Services:
Shabbat

Day School

Hebrew Academy of Suffolk County, 525 Veterans Hwy,
Ph: 543-3377.

STONY BROOK
Synagogues

B'nai B'rith Hillel Foundation at SUNY, Stony Brook. Two
services each Shabbat during academic year (O, C). Summers:
Saturdays only (O), Ph: 632-6565. Mr. J. Topek, Director.

Temple Isaiah (R-UAHC), 1404 Stony Brook Rd, Ph: 751-8518.
Rabbi A. Fisher. Services: Shabbat

Eating Out

B'nai B'rith Hillel at SUNY, Stony Brook (cafeteria), Stony Brook
Campus, Ph: 632-6565. Daily kosher meals can be ordered
through Hillel during the academic year. Summers, frozen dinners are available. Advance reservations are required.
RS: National Council of Young Israel.

WESTHAMPTON BEACH
Synagogues

The Westhampton Synagogue (O), 75 Mill Rd, Ph: 288-0534.
Rabbi M. Schneier. Services: Shabbat (summers only)

SYRACUSE   Area Code (315)   J-pop. 9,000
Synagogues

Temple Adath Yeshurun (C-US), 450 Kimber Rd, Ph: 445-0002.
Rabbi C. Sherman. Services: Daily

Temple Beth El (Trad), 3528 E Genesee St, Ph: 446-5858. Rabbi
D. Sheinkopf. Services: Daily

Congregation Beth Sholom Chevra Shas (C-US), 5205 Jamesville
Rd, **Dewitt**, Ph: 446-9570. Rabbi D. Jezer. Services: Shabbat
and Sunday

B'nai B'rith Hillel Foundation (Hendricks Chapel), Syracuse
University, Ph: 443-2904. Rabbi A. Iser. Services: Friday (C)
and Saturday (O) during the school year.

Chabad Lubavitch (O-Lubav), 113 Berkeley Dr, Ph: 424-0363.
Rabbi Y. Rapoport. Services: Friday. (Saturday morning services at Hillel, Syracuse University; meal following.)

Synagogues cont.

Congregation Ner Tamid (C), 5061 W Taft Rd, **North Syracuse**,
Ph: 458-2022. Services: Friday

Sephardic Congregation of Syracuse (O), 119 Doll Pkwy,
Ph: 446-0760. Services: High Holidays

Temple Society of Concord (R-UAHC), 910 Madison St,
Ph: 475-9952. Rabbi S. Ezring. Services: Friday

Young Israel-Shaarei Torah (O-NCYI), 4313 E Genesee St,
Ph: 446-6194. Rabbi E. Shore. Services: Daily

Eating Out

B'nai B'rith Hillel Foundation, Syracuse University. Meals: d,
Monday-Friday. For further information, contact Rabbi A. Iser
(C), Ph: 443-2904.

Jewish Community Center, 5655 Thompson Rd S, **Dewitt**,
Ph: 445-2360. Senior's kosher lunch program (Monday-Friday),
open to the public. RS: The Syracuse Va'ad Ha'ir.

Food

For additional information on kosher products and supervision,
call the Syracuse Va'ad Ha'ir, Ph: 446-6194.

The Dewitt Bagelry, 4451 E Genesee St, **Dewitt**, Ph: 445-0959.
Bagels and challahs (pareve), pastries (dairy). Some groceries.
RS: Syracuse Va'ad Ha'ir.

Elsaha Bakery, 100 Fairgrounds Dr, **Manlius**, Ph: 682-2780. Fresh
baked pita bread (pareve). RS: Syracuse Va'ad Ha'ir.

Fins and Tails Seafood Store, 3012 Erie Blvd E, Ph: 446-5417.
Within the store, there is a kosher fresh fish section. RS:
Syracuse Va'ad Ha'ir. Purchases must be requested as kosher.

Harrison Bakery, 1306 W Genesee St, Ph: 422-1468. Breads and
pastries (breads and rolls are pareve; all other items are made
pareve by request only). RS: Syracuse Va'ad Ha'ir.

Martin's & Tenenbaum's Kosher Meat Market, 2914 E Genesee St,
Ph: 446-3254. Fresh meats, poultry and full line of kosher
groceries. RS: Syracuse Va'ad Ha'ir. Closed Shabbat.

P & C, 4410 E Genesee St, **Dewitt**, Ph: 446-6421. Kosher appetizing section. RS: Syracuse Va'ad Ha'ir. Also fresh and frozen kosher items.

Patrician Bakery, 1951 E Fayette St, Ph: 472-4476. Breads and rolls (pareve). Croissants and other items (dairy). RS: Syracuse Va'ad Ha'ir. Closed Shabbat.

Pickles Kosher Deli, 4410 E Genesee St, **Dewitt**, Ph: 445-1294. Sandwiches, deli, appetizers and packaged kosher foods. RS: Syracuse Va'ad Ha'ir.

Snowflake Pastry Shoppe, 2012 E Fayette St, Ph: 472-3041. Breads and rolls (pareve). Croissants and other items (dairy). RS: Syracuse Va'ad Ha'ir.

Accommodations

Dewitt Inn, 3300 Erie Blvd E, Ph: 446-3300. Walk to Young Israel.

Genesee Inn, 1060 E Genesee St, Ph: 476-4212. Fifteen-minute walk to Chabad House.

Sheraton University Inn, 801 University Ave, Ph: 475-3000. Close to Chabad House.

Private accommodations; call the Sephardic Congregation of Syracuse, Ph: 446-0760.

Shabbat hospitality; call Young Israel, Ph: 446-6194.

Chabad House hospitality; call Rabbi Y. Rapoport at Chabad, Ph: 424-0363.

Mikvah

Syracuse Mikvah, 2200 E Genesee St. Call Mrs. Rose Rosenzweig, Ph: 475-7606.

Day School

Syracuse Hebrew Day School, 5655 Thompson Rd, **Dewitt**, Ph: 446-1900.

TONOWANDA (See BUFFALO)

TROY (See also ALBANY)   Area Code (518)   J-pop. 800

Synagogues

Temple B'rith Sholom (R-UAHC), 167 3rd St, Ph: 272-8872. Rabbi J. Wolkoff. Services: Friday

Synagogues cont.

Temple Beth-El (C-US), 411 Hoosick St, Ph: 272-6113. Rabbi A.
  Weinman. Services: Daily

Beth Tephila Synagogue (O-UOJC), 82 River St, Ph: 272-3182.
  Rabbi A. Fruchter. Services: Daily

Accommodations

Holiday Inn, 1800 6th Ave, Ph: 274-3210. Within walking distance
  of Beth Tephila Synagogue.

Hospitality, call Rabbi L. Morrison of Chabad, Ph: 274-5572.

Mikvah

Mikvah Israel, 2306 15th St. Contact Ms. E. Morrison,
  Ph: 274-5572.

TUPPER LAKE   Area Code (518)

Synagogues

Beth Joseph Synagogue, Hill & Lake Sts; call Janet Chapman,
  Ph: 359-9594. Services: Friday, in summer. Historic site.

UTICA   Area Code (315)   J-pop. 1,900

Synagogues

Temple Beth El (C-US), 1607 Genesee St, Ph: 724-4751. Rabbi S.
  Gerstein. Services: Daily

Temple Emanuel (R), 2710 Genesee St, Ph: 724-4177. Rabbi H.
  Bamberger. Services: Friday

Congregation Zvi Jacob (O-UOJC), 110 Memorial Pkwy,
  Ph: 724-8357. Rabbi E. Engel. Services: Daily

Food

De Iorio's Bakery, 624 Elizabeth St, Ph: 732-7617. RS: Rabbi E.
  Engel (breads only).

Star Bakery, 1212 Catherine St, Ph: 733-6603. Breads and pastries
  (pareve and dairy). RS: Rabbi E. Engel.

Mikvah

Congregation Zvi Jacob, 110 Memorial Pkwy, Ph: 733-0125.

Accomodations

Travelodge, 1700 Genesee St, Ph: 724-2101. Walk to Temple Beth El and Congregation Zvi Jacob.

WALDEN   Area Code (914)

Synagogues

Congregation Beth Hillel/Walden JCC (C), 20 Pine St, Ph: 778-7374. Services: Friday

WEST POINT   Area Code (914)

Synagogues

West Point Jewish Chapel, West Point Military Academy, Ph: 446-7706. Chaplain (Cpt.) D. Beck-Berman. Services: Friday, during the academic year.

WESTCHESTER COUNTY   Area Code (914)
J-pop. 122,600

ARMONK
Synagogues

B'nai Israel (R-UAHC), 485 Bedford Rd, Ph: 273-2220. Rabbi D. Krantz. Services: Friday

BEDFORD HILLS
Synagogues

Shaaray Tefila of Westchester (R-UAHC), Baldwin Rd, Ph: 666-3133. Services: Friday

Yeshivah Ohel Shmuel (O), 165 Haines Rd, Ph: 241-2700. Rabbi R. Blum. Services: Daily

Mikvah

Mikvah, 165 Haines Rd. Call Mrs. R. Blum, Ph: 666-4391.

BREWSTER
Synagogues

Temple Beth Elohim (R), Rte 22, Ph: 279-4585. Rabbi S. Acrish. Services: Friday

New York WESTCHESTER COUNTY

BRIARCLIFF MANOR
Synagogues

Congregation Sons of Israel (C-US), 1666 Pleasantville Rd, Ph: 762-2700. Rabbi D. Isaak. Services: Shabbat

CHAPPAQUA
Synagogues

Temple Beth El of Northern Westchester (R-UAHC), 220 S Bedford Rd, Ph: 238-3928. Rabbis C. Stern and R. Rheins. Services: Shabbat

CROTON-ON-HUDSON
Synagogues

Croton Jewish Center (C-US), 52 Scenic Dr, Ph: 271-2218. Services: Saturday
Temple Israel of Northern Westchester (R-UAHC), Glengary Rd, Ph: 271-4705. Rabbi M. Levy. Services: Shabbat

DOBBS FERRY
Synagogues

Greenburg Jewish Center (C-US), 515 Broadway, Ph: 693-4260. Rabbi B. Kenter. Services: Daily

HARRISON
Synagogues

Jewish Community Center of Harrison (C-US), Union Ave, Ph: 835-2850. Rabbi N. Shargel. Services: Daily
Young Israel of Harrison (O-NCYI), 207 Union Ave, Ph: 835-4656. Rabbi Y. Bienenfeld. Services: Shabbat & Sunday

Food

Kosher Konsultants, 64 Halstead Ave, Ph: 835-4700. Fresh meat and poultry. Also baked goods, roast chickens, salads, side dishes. RS: Vaad Hakashrus of Westchester. Closed Shabbat.

HASTINGS-ON-HUDSON
Synagogues

354

Temple Beth Shalom (R-UAHC), 740 N Broadway, Ph: 478-3833. Rabbi E. Schechter. Services: Friday

LARCHMONT
Synagogues

Congregation Beth Emeth (C-US), 2111 Boston Post Rd, Ph: 834-1093. Rabbi H. Portnow. Services: Shabbat

Larchmont Temple (R-UAHC), 75 Larchmont Ave, Ph: 834-6120. Rabbis H. Poller and V. Hollander. Services: Shabbat

MAHOPAC
Synagogues

Temple Beth Shalom (C-US), Rte 6, Croton Falls Rd, Ph: 628-6133. Rabbi P. Fleischer. Services: Shabbat

MAMARONECK
Synagogues

Westchester Jewish Center (C-US), Rockland & Palmer Aves, Ph: 698-2960. Rabbi J. Segelman. Services: Daily

Day School

Westchester Day School, 856 Orienta Ave, Ph: 698-8900.

MOUNT KISCO
Synagogues

Beth Torah (C-US), 60 Smith Lane, Ph: 666-7595. Rabbi F. Fine. Services: Daily

Congregation Beth Medrash Chemed (O), Pines Bridge Rd. Rabbi S. Unger. Services: Daily

Mikvah

Congregation Beth Medrash Chemed, Pines Bridge Rd. Call Mrs. R. Schwartz, Ph: 241-0175 or Mrs. L. Kalisch, Ph: 666-3652.

Day School

Talmud Torah Bais Yechiel-Yeshiva of Nitra, Beth Miriam-Leah-Nitra, Pines Bridge Rd, Ph: 666-2087/2929; (718) 387-0422.

MOUNT VERNON
Synagogues

Congregation Brothers of Israel (O-UOJC), 116 Crary Ave, Ph: 664-8945. Rabbi S. Freilich. Services: Daily

Emanu-El Jewish Center (C-US), 261 E Lincoln Ave, Ph: 667-0161. Rabbi D. Haymovitz. Services: Daily

Fleetwood Synagogue (O-UOJC), 11 E Broad St, Ph: 664-9053. Rabbi J. Chait. Services: Daily

Free Synagogue of Westchester (R-UAHC), 500 N Columbus Ave, Ph: 664-1727. Rabbi J. Perman. Services: Shabbat

Sinai Temple (R), 132 Crary Ave, Ph: 668-9471. Rabbi D. Cahn-Lipman. Services: Shabbat

Food

Sabers Cake Nook, 33 W Grand St, Ph: 664-5796. Pastries and dairy products. RS: Rabbi S. Freilich.

Westchester Glatt Kosher Meat & Poultry Market, 25 W Grand St, Ph: 664-4313; 664-6818. Prepared chicken, meat and kosher groceries. RS: Vaad Hakashrus of Westchester. Closed Shabbat.

Accommodations

For private accommodations, call:

Rabbi J. Chait at the Fleetwood Synagogue, Ph: 664-7643.

Rabbi S. Freilich of Brothers of Israel, Ph: 664-8945.

NEW ROCHELLE
Synagogues

Congregation Anshe Shalom (O-UOJC), 50 North Ave, Ph: 632-9220. Rabbi P. Weinberger. Services: Daily

Beth El Synagogue (C-US), Northfield Rd & North Ave, Ph: 235-2700. Rabbi M. Sirner. Services: Daily

Temple Israel (R-UAHC), 1000 Pinebrook Blvd, Ph: 235-1800. Rabbis A. Wohl and J. Singer. Services: Shabbat

Young Israel of New Rochelle (O-NCYI), 1228 North Ave, Ph: 636-2215. Rabbi R. Fink. Services: Daily

Eating Out

Pizza-Pasta-Pita, 1295 North Ave (Wykagyl Shopping Center), Ph: 235-7100. Meals: l,d. Menu: (Cholov Yisroel) Pizza, falafel, soups, salads. Also take-out. RS: Vaad Hakashrus of Westchester. Closed Shabbat.

Food

G & M Kosher Take-Out, 1284 North Ave, Ph: 576-8505. Glatt meat. Traditional and Chinese dishes; chicken, salads. RS: Vaad Hakahrus of Westchester. Closed Shabbat.

Top's Bakery, 1321 North Ave, Ph: 235-8201. Dairy and pareve baked goods. RS: Vaad Hakashrus of Westchester. Closed Shabbat.

Accommodations

Ramada New Rochelle, 1 Ramada Plaza, Ph: 576-3700. Within walking distance of Congregation Anshe Shalom.

PEEKSKILL
Synagogues

First Hebrew Congregation (C), 1821 E Main St, Ph: 739-0500. Rabbi E. C. Radler. Services: Shabbat

First Hebrew Congregation (C), 813 Lower Main St, Ph: 737-8155. Rabbi E. C. Radler. Services: Daily

Synagogue of Pine Lake Park (C), Furnace Dock Rd, Ph: 737-2408. Services: Saturday (summers only)

PELHAM MANOR
Synagogues

Pelham Jewish Center (C), 451 Esplanade, Ph: 738-6008. Rabbi R. Harris. Services: Shabbat

PORT CHESTER
Synagogues

Congregation Kneses Tifereth Israel (C-US), 575 King St, Ph: 939-1004. Rabbi A. Winter. Services: Daily

PUTNAM VALLEY
Synagogues

Reform Temple of Putnam Valley (R-UAHC), Church Rd, Ph: 528-4774. Rabbi Z. Davidowitz. Services: Friday

RYE
Synagogues

Community Synagogue (R-UAHC), 200 Forest Ave, Ph: 967-6262. Rabbi R. Rothman. Services: Friday

Congregation Emanu-El of Westchester (R-UAHC), Kenilworth Rd, Ph: 967-4382. Rabbi D. Wolk. Services: Friday

SCARSDALE
Synagogues

Scarsdale Synagogue—Tremont Temple (R-UAHC), 2 Ogden Rd, Ph: 725-5175. Rabbi S. Klein. Services: Friday

The Sephardic Community of New Rochelle-Scarsdale (O), 1313 Weaver St (Young Israel of Scarsdale), Ph: 636-8686. Services: Shabbat

Westchester Reform Temple (R-UAHC), 255 Mamaroneck Rd, Ph: 723-7727. Rabbi J. Stern Jr. Services: Shabbat

Young Israel of Scarsdale (O-UOJC), 1313 Weaver St, Ph: 636-8686. Rabbi J. Rubenstein. Services: Daily

Food

M'hadrin Kosher Food Shop, 1066 Wilmot Rd, Ph: 472-2240/1. Meats, kosher groceries and take-out. RS: Rabbi M. Grauer of White Plains. Closed Shabbat.

Accommodations

Private accommodations; call the Sisterhood office at Young Israel of Scarsdale, Ph: 636-8686.

Mikvah

Young Israel of Scarsdale, 1313 Weaver St, Ph: 961-6971.

TARRYTOWN
Synagogues

Temple Beth Abraham (R-UAHC), 25 Leroy Ave, Ph: 631-9661. Rabbi P. Siegel. Services: Friday

TUCKAHOE
Synagogues

Genesis Agudas Achim Congregation (C-US), 25 Oakland Ave, Ph: 961-3766. Rabbi S. Grossman. Services: Shabbat

WHITE PLAINS
Synagogues

Bet Am Shalom Synagogue (Recon-FRCH), 295 Soundview Ave, Ph: 946-8851. Rabbi L. Bronstein. Call for schedule.

Hebrew Institute of White Plains (O-UOJC), 20 Greenridge Ave, Ph: 948-3095. Rabbis M. Grauer and S. Schlam. Services: Daily

Temple Israel Center (C-US), 280 Old Mamaroneck Rd, Ph: 948-2800. Rabbis A. Turetsky, J. Finkelstein. Services: Daily

Jewish Community Center of White Plains (R-UAHC), 252 Soundview Ave, Ph: 949-4717. Rabbi S. Milgrom, Rabbi M. Davis (Emeritus). Services: Shabbat

Woodlands Community Temple (R-UAHC), 50 Worthington Rd, Ph: 592-7070. Rabbi A. Magid. Services: Shabbat

Young Israel of White Plains (O-NCYI), 84 Gedney Way, Ph: 949-4742. Rabbi S. Greenberg. Services: Daily

Food

Ken-Mar Kosher, 333 Mamaroneck Ave, Ph: 761-8046. Fresh meat and poultry, barbecued chickens, deli, frozen foods and kosher groceries. RS: Rabbi M. Grauer. Closed Shabbat.

Accommodations

Shabbat hospitality; call the Hebrew Institute of White Plains, Ph: 948-3095.

Private hospitality; call the office of the Temple Israel Center, Ph: 948-2800.

The following are located within walking distance of the Hebrew Institute of White Plains (frozen kosher dinners are available if requested in advance):

Holiday Inn Crown Plaza, 66 Hale Ave, Ph: 682-0050.

Accommodations cont.

LaReserve, 5 Barker Ave, Ph: 761-7700. Suites with kitchens.
White Plains Hotel, S Broadway and Lyon Pl, Ph: 761-8100.

Day School

Solomon Schechter School of Westchester (C), 30 Dellwood Rd,
Ph: 948-3111.

Bookstore

The Jewish Quarter, 150 Mamaroneck Ave, Ph: 946-2121.

YONKERS
Synagogues

Temple Emanu-El (R-UAHC), 306 Rumsey Rd, Ph: 963-0575.
Rabbi A. Klausner. Services: Friday
Greystone Jewish Center (O-UOJC), 600 N Broadway,
Ph: 963-8888. Rabbi W. Herskowitz. Services: Shabbat and
Sunday
Lincoln Park Jewish Center (C-US), 311 Central Park Ave,
Ph: 965-7119. Rabbi S. Sternstein. Services: Daily
Midchester Jewish Center (C-US), 236 Grandview Blvd,
Ph: 779-3660. Rabbi B. Rosenberg. Services: Daily
Northeast Jewish Center (C-US), 11 Salisbury Rd, Ph: 337-0268.
Rabbi J. Lefkowitz. Services: Daily
Congregation Ohab Zedek (O-UOJC), 63 Hamilton Ave,
Ph: 356-5728. Services: Saturday
Congregation Sons of Israel (O-UOJC), 105 Radford Ave,
Ph: 969-4453. Rabbi I. Rosner. Services: Daily
Young Israel of North Riverdale (O-NCYI), 25 Clifton Ave,
Ph: 963-9448. Rabbi N. Cohen. Services: Daily

Eating Out

Mazel Wok, 2700 Central Park Ave, Ph: 472-7579/7597. Meals: l,d.
Menu: (Glatt meat) Chinese. RS: Vaad Hakashrus of Westchester.
Closed Shabbat.

Food

Centuck Butcher Shop, 662 Tuckahoe Rd, Ph: 779-3683. Fresh meat and poultry. Frozen products and packaged items. RS: Vaad Hakashrus of Westchester. Closed Shabbat.

Yonkers Glatt Kosher Meat, 636 McLean Ave, Ph: 965-5802. RS: Vaad Hakashrus of Westchester. Closed Shabbat.

Accommodations

Private accommodations; call Congregation Sons of Israel, Ph: 969-4453.

Day School

Yeshiva Day School of Lincoln Park, 311 Central Park Ave, Ph: 965-7082.

YORKTOWN HEIGHTS
Synagogues

Temple Beth Am (R-UAHC), 203 Church Pl, Ph: 962-7500. Rabbi L. Schofer. Services: Friday

Yorktown Jewish Center (C-US), 2966 Crompond Rd, Ph: 245-2324. Rabbi S. Urbas. Services: Shabbat

Accommodations

Private accommodations; call the office at Yorktown Jewish Center, Ph: 245-2324.

North Carolina

ASHEVILLE   Area Code (704)   J-pop. 1,350

Synagogues

Congregation Beth Ha'Tephila (R-UAHC), 43 N Liberty St,
   Ph: 253-4911. Rabbi R. Bluming. Services: Friday
Beth Israel Synagogue (C-US), 229 Murdock Ave, Ph: 252-8431.
   Rabbi S. Birnham. Services: Shabbat and Sunday

CARY   (See also RALEIGH)   Area Code (919)

Synagogues

Beth Shalom (R-UAHC), P.O. Box 5161, 27511, Ph: 481-1880.
   Rabbi E. Gottman. Services: Every other Friday; call for
   location.

CHARLOTTE   Area Code (704)   J-pop. 4,000

Synagogues

Temple Beth El-V'Shalom (R-UAHC), Meets at JCC, 5007
   Providence Rd, Ph: 366-1948. Rabbi R. Seigel. Services: Friday
Temple Israel (C-US), 1014 Dilworth Rd, Ph: 376-2796. Rabbi H.
   Millgram. Services: Daily
Lubavitch of North Carolina (O), 921 Jefferson Dr, Ph: 366-3984.
   Rabbi Y. Groner. Services: Shabbat and Sunday

Food

Phil's Deli, 198 S Sharon Amity Rd, Ph: 366-5405. Kosher grocery
   and frozen packaged items.

Mikvah

Lubavitch of North Carolina, 6500 Newhall Rd. Contact Ms.
   Mariasha Groner, Ph: 366-3984.

Day School

Lubavitch Day School, 921 Jefferson Dr, Ph: 366-3984.

DURHAM   (See also RALEIGH)   Area Code (919)   J-pop. 2,800

362

Synagogues

Beth-El Synagogue (C-US), 1004 Watt St, Ph: 682-1238. Rabbi S. Sager. Services: Shabbat

Judea Reform Congregation (R-UAHC), 2115 Cornwallis Rd, Ph: 489-7062. Rabbi J. Friedman. Services: Shabbat

Orthodox Kehilla (O-UOJC), meets at Beth-El Synagogue. Services: Saturday. Call Mr. Leon Dworsky for further information, Ph: 220-6001.

Eating Out

B'nai B'rith Hillel at the University of North Carolina-Chapel Hill, 210 W Cameron Ave, **Chapel Hill**. Friday evening Shabbat dinner is served twice a month during the school year. Call Rabbi F. Fischer for information and reservations, Ph: 942-4057.

Accommodations

For information on accommodations near the Orthodox Kehilla, contact Mr. Leon Dworsky, 1100 Leon St, Durham, NC 27705, Ph: 220-6001.

FAYETTEVILLE   Area Code (919)   J-pop. 300

Synagogues

Congregation Beth Israel (C-US), 2204 Morganton Rd, Ph: 484-6462. Rabbi B. Shoter. Services: Call for schedule.

GASTONIA   Area Code (704)   J-pop. 240

Synagogues

Temple Emanuel (R-UAHC), 320 South St, Ph: 865-1541. Rabbi D. Zielonka. Services: Friday

GREENSBORO   Area Code (919)   J-pop. 2,700

Synagogues

Beth David Synagogue (C-US), 804 Winview Dr, Ph: 294-0007. Rabbi A. Chorny. Services: Shabbat

Synagogues cont.

Temple Emanuel (R-UAHC), 713 N Greene St, Ph: 275-6316.
Rabbi R. Harkevy. Services: Friday

GREENSVILLE   Area Code (919)   J-pop. 300

Synagogues

Congregation Bayt Shalom (C), 1420 E 14th St, Ph: 830-1138.
Rabbi M. Cain. Services: Fridays and second Saturday

HENDERSONVILLE   Area Code (704)   J-pop. 135

Synagogues

Congregation Agudas Israel (C-US), 328 N King St, Ph: 693-9838.
Call for schedule.

HIGHPOINT   Area Code (919)

Synagogues

B'nai Israel Synagogue (C-US), 1207 Kensington Dr,
Ph: 884-5522. Rabbi R. Sandman. Call for schedule.

Mikvah

B'nai Israel Synagogue, 1207 Kensington Dr, Ph: 884-5522.

KINSTON   Area Code (919)

Synagogues

Temple Israel (R-UAHC), Vernon & Laroque Sts, Ph: 523-2057.
Rabbi D. Rose. Services: Friday

RALEIGH   Area Code (919)   J-pop. 2,500

Synagogues

Beth Meyer Synagogue (C-US), 504 Newton Rd, Ph: 848-1420.
Rabbi D. Ornstein. Services: Shabbat and Wednesday
Temple Beth Or (R-UAHC), 5315 Creedmoor, Ph: 781-4895. Rabbi
J. Bleiberg. Services: Shabbat

Congregation Sha'arei Israel—Lubavitch (O-Lubav), 7400 Falls of
the Neuse Rd, Ph: 847-8986. Rabbi P. Herman. Services: Shabbat

Food

Sha'arei Israel, 7400 Falls of the Neuse Rd, Ph: 847-8986. The
synagogue keeps a full selection of kosher meats and frozen
products on the premises. Call for further information.

Accommodations

Shabbat hospitality; call Rabbi P. Herman at Lubavitch,
Ph: 847-8986.

Mikvah

Sha'arei Israel—Lubavitch, 7400 Falls of the Neuse Rd. Call
Helena Herman, Ph: 846-0426 or 847-8986.

STATESVILLE   Area Code (704)

Synagogues

Congregation Emanuel (C-US), Kelly St & W End Ave,
Ph: 873-7611. Services: Friday

WILMINGTON   Area Code (919)   J-pop. 500

Synagogues

B'nai Israel Synagogue (C), 2601 Chestnut St, Ph: 762-1117. Rabbi
R. Waxman. Services: Shabbat
Temple of Israel (R-UAHC), 4th & Market Sts, Ph: 762-0000.
Rabbi A. Gordon. Services: Friday

WINSTON-SALEM   Area Code (919)   J-pop. 440

Synagogues

Beth Jacob Congregation (C-US), 1833 Academy St, Ph: 725-3880.
President: Dr. R. David. Services: Friday
Temple Emanuel (R-UAHC), 201 Oakwood Dr, Ph: 722-6640.
Rabbi T. Liebschutz. Services: Shabbat

North Dakota

BISMARK   Area Code (701)

Synagogues

Bismark Hebrew Congregation (R), 703 N 5th St, Ph: 223-1768.
  Services: High Holidays

FARGO   Area Code (701)   J-pop. 500

Synagogues

Temple Beth El (R-UAHC), 809 11th Ave S, Ph: 232-0441.
  Services: Friday
Fargo Hebrew Congregation (O), 901 S 9th St, Ph: 232-5192 or
  Joe Paper, President, Ph: 237-5629. Call for schedule.

GRAND FORKS   Area Code (701)   J-pop. 150

Synagogues

B'nai Israel (C), 601 Cottonwood St, Ph: 775-5124. Services:
  Shabbat

Ohio

AKRON (See also CLEVELAND)   Area Code (216)
  J-pop. 6,000

Synagogues

Congregation Anshe Sfard (Trad-UOJC), 646 N Revere Rd,
  Ph: 867-7292. Rabbi A. Leibtag. Services: Daily
Beth El Congregation (C-US), 464 S Hawkins Ave, Ph: 864-2105.
  Rabbi S. Kamens. Services: Daily
B'nai B'rith Hillel (R, C), 202 N Lincoln, Ph: 678-0397. Rabbi
  S. Adams. Services: Friday, during the academic year.
Temple Israel (R-UAHC), 133 Merriman Rd, Ph: 762-8617.
  Rabbi D. Horowitz. Services: Friday

Eating Out

B'nai B'rith Hillel at Kent State University, 202 N Lincoln,
Ph: 678-0397. Shabbat dinner and Sunday brunch are served
regularly. RS: Rabbi S. Adams (R). For information contact
Rabbi Adams or Ms. S. Gibbons.

Accommodations

Days Inn, 3150 W Market St, Ph: 836-8431. One-half mile to
Chabad House.

Shabbat hospitality; call Rabbi M. Sasonkin at Chabad House, Ph:
867-6798.

Day School

Jerome Lippman Jewish Community Day School, 750 White Pond
Dr, Ph: 836-0419.

ATHENS   Area Code (614)   J-pop. 100

Synagogues

B'nai B'rith Hillel Center at Ohio University, 21 Mill St,
Ph: 592-1173. Rabbi M. Newton. Services: Every other Friday
during the academic year. Call for information.

Eating Out

B'nai B'rith Hillel Center at Ohio University, 21 Mill St,
Ph: 592-1173. Shabbat meal every other Friday evening after
services. RS: Rabbi M. Newton. Call for reservations.

Accommodations

Home hospitality; call B'nai B'rith Hillel, Ph: 592-1173.

BEACHWOOD (See CLEVELAND)

CANTON   Area Code (216)   J-pop. 2,400

Synagogues

Temple Israel (R-UAHC), 333 25th St NW, Ph: 455-5197.
Rabbi J. Spitzer. Services: Friday

Synagogues cont.

Shaaray Torah Synagogue (C-US), 432 30th St NW, Ph: 492-0310. Rabbi M. Miller. Services: Daily

Young Israel of Canton (O-NCYI), 2508 Market St N, Ph: 456-8781. Rabbi M. Sasonkin. Services: Shabbat, Sunday, Monday and Thursday.

CINCINNATI   Area Code (513)   J-pop. 23,000

Synagogues

Congregation Adath Israel (C-US), 3201 E Galbraith Rd, Ph: 793-1800. Services: Daily

Congregation Agudas Israel—Golf Manor Synagogue (O-UOJC), 6442 Stover Ave, Ph: 531-6654. Rabbis H. Balk and S. Lavenda. Services: Daily

Agudath Achim Roselawn Synagogue (O-UOJC), 7600 Reading Rd, Ph: 761-7755. Services: Daily

Bene Israel Rockdale Synagogue (R-UAHC), 8501 Ridge Rd, Ph: 891-9900. Rabbi M. Goldman. Services: Shabbat

Congregation Beth Adam (Humanistic), 1720 Section Rd #107, Ph: 396-7730. Rabbi R. Barr. Services: Shabbat and Holidays

Congregation B'nai Tzedek (O), 1580 Summit Rd, Ph: 821-0941. Services: Shabbat and Holidays

Chabad House (O-Lubav), 1636 Summit Rd, Ph: 821-5100. Rabbi S. Kalmanson. Services: Shabbat and Sunday

The Isaac M. Wise Temple (R-UAHC), 8329 Ridge Rd, Ph: 793-2556. Rabbi L. Kamrass. Services: Shabbat

Kehilas B'nai Israel (O), 1546 Kenova Ave, Ph: 761-5200. Rabbi Z. Sharfstein. Services: Shabbat and Holidays

Keneseth Israel Synagogue (O), 1515 Section Rd, Ph: 948-2208. Rabbi J. Lustig. Services: Daily

New Hope Congregation (O-UOJC), 1625 Crest Hill Ave, Ph: 821-6274. Rabbi M. Rabenstein and Rabbi B. Hollander. Services: Daily

North Avondale Synagogue (O), 3870 Reading Rd, Ph: 281-3243. Rabbi R. Stein. Services: Shabbat

Northern Hills Synagogue—Congregation B'nai Avraham (C-US),

715 Fleming Rd, Ph: 931-6038. Rabbi G. Barnard. Services: Shabbat and Sunday

Congregation Ohav Shalom (Trad), 1834 Section Rd, Ph: 531-4676. Rabbi S. Marcu. Services: Daily

Temple Sholom (R-UAHC), 3100 Longmeadow Lane, Ph: 791-1330. Rabbi G. Walter. Services: Shabbat

The Valley Temple (R-UAHC), 145 Springfield Pike, Ph: 761-3555. Rabbi S. Greenberg. Services: Friday

Eating Out

B'nai B'rith Hillel Foundation at the University of Cincinnati, 2615 Clifton Ave, Ph: 221-6728. Friday evening Shabbat dinner and Monday dinner are served weekly. RS: Vaad Ho'ier. For further information contact Rabbi A. Ingber at the Hillel office.

Food

Bilker's Fine Foods, 7648 Reading Rd, Ph: 821-6800. Complete line of kosher groceries.

Golf Manor Bakery, 2000 Losantiville Ave, Ph: 631-4550. Breads and pastries. RS: Vaad Ho'ier. Closed Shabbat.

Marx Hot Bagels, 477 E Kemper Rd, Ph: 671-0278; 7617 Reading Rd, Ph: 821-0103; 9701 Kenwood Rd, Blue Ash, Ph: 891-5561. Menu: Soups, salads, bagel sandwiches, desserts and soft drinks. RS: Vaad Ho'ier.

Pilder's Kosher Foods, 7601 Reading Rd, Ph: 821-7050. Fresh meats (Glatt) and poultry; frozen, refrigerated and grocery products. Also take-out (sandwiches and salads). RS: Vaad Ho'ier. Closed Shabbat.

Accommodations

Private hospitality; contact Rabbi S. Kalmanson at Chabad House, Ph: 821-5100.

Carrousel Motel, 8001 Reading Rd, Ph: 821-5110. Some kitchenettes. Within walking distance of Agudath Achim Synagogue, Chabad House, Congregation Keneseth Israel, New Hope Congregation and Congregation Ohav Shalom.

Vernon Manor Hotel, 400 Oak St, Ph: 281-3300. Twenty-minute walk to Hillel at the University of Cincinnati.

369

Mikvah

Beth Tvillah Mikvah Society, 1546 Kenova Ave. Call mikvah office, Ph: 821-6679. For further information, call Vaad Ho'ier, Ph: 761-5200.

Day Schools

Cincinnati Hebrew Day School, 7855 Dawn Rd, Ph: 761-1614.
Yavneh Day School, 8401 Montgomery Rd, Ph: 984-3770.

CLEVELAND   Area Code (216)   J-pop. 65,000

Jewish Information Service of The Jewish Community Federation, Ph: 371-3999.

Synagogues

Ahavath Israel (O-UOJC), 3448 Euclid Heights Blvd, Ph: 371-3665. Rabbi A. Berger. Services: Daily

Congregation Beth Am (C-US), 3557 Washington Blvd, **Cleveland Heights**, Ph: 321-1000. Rabbi M. Hecht. Services: Daily

Temple Beth El (Trad), 15808 Chagrin Blvd, Ph: 991-6044. Services: Daily

Beth Israel The West Temple (R-UAHC), 14308 Triskett Rd, Ph: 941-8882. Rabbi S. Stone. Services: Call for schedule.

Bethaynu (C), 27900 Gates Mills Blvd, Ph: 292-2931. Rabbi M. Rube. Services: Shabbat, Sunday

Chabad House (O-Lubav), 4481 University Pkwy, Ph: 382-5050. Rabbi L. Alevsky. Services: Shabbat

Cleveland Hillel Foundation at Case Western Reserve, 11291 Euclid Ave, Ph: 231-0040. Rabbi A. Lettofsky, Executive Director. Services: (Trad) Fridays, during the academic year. Call for further information.

Temple Emanu El (R-UAHC), 2200 S Green Rd, Ph: 381-6600. Rabbi D. Roberts. Services: Friday

Fairmount Temple-Anshe Chesed (R-UAHC), 23737 Fairmount Blvd, Ph: 464-1330. Rabbi D. Gelfand. Services: Shabbat

Green Road Synagogue (O-UOJC), 2437 S Green Rd, **Beachwood**, Ph: 381-4757. Rabbi M. Granatstein. Services: Daily

Heights Jewish Center (O-UOJC), 14270 Cedar Rd, Ph: 382-1958.
Rabbi D. Schur. Services: Daily
Temple Israel (R), 1732 Lander Rd, Ph: 473-5120. Rabbi
F. Eisenberg. Services: Friday
K'hal Yereim (O), 1771 S Taylor Rd, **Cleveland Heights,**
Ph: 321-5855. Rabbi Y. Blum. Services: Daily
Menorah Park Center for the Aging (O), 27100 Cedar Rd,
Ph: 831-6500. Rabbi D. Bader. Services: Daily
Temple Ner Tamid—Euclid Jewish Center (R-UAHC), 24950
Lake Shore Blvd, **Euclid,** Ph: 261-2280. Rabbi B. Abrams.
Services: Friday
Congregation Oer Chodosh Anshe Sfard (O-UOJC), 3466
Washington Blvd, **University Heights,** Ph: 932-7739. Rabbi
E. Nisenbaum. Services: Daily
The Park Synagogue (C), 3300 Mayfield Rd, Ph: 371-2244. Rabbi
A. Cohen, Rabbi J. Skoff. Services: Daily
Park Synagogue East (C), 27575 Shaker Blvd, **Pepper Pike,**
Ph: 831-5363. Rabbi P. Horowitz. Services: Shabbat
Rinath Israel (C), 2308 Warrensville Center Rd, Ph: 932-7664.
Rabbi A. Bensoussan. Services: Daily
Congregation Shaarey Tikvah (C-US), 26811 Fairmount Blvd,
Beachwood, Ph: 765-8300. Rabbi J. Shtull. Services: Shabbat
and Sunday
Shomre Shaboth (O), 1801 S Taylor Rd, **Cleveland Heights,**
Ph: 932-2619. Rabbi Y. Grumer. Services: Daily
Sinai Synagogue (O-UOJC), 3246 De Sota Ave, **Cleveland
Heights,** Ph: 932-0206. Rabbi I. Pickholtz. Services: Daily
The Suburban Temple (R-UAHC), 22401 Chagrin Blvd,
Ph: 991-0700. Rabbi M. Oppenheimer. Services: Friday
Taylor Road Synagogue—Oheb Zedek (O-UOJC), 1970 S Taylor
Rd, **Cleveland Heights,** Ph: 321-4875. Rabbi D. Zlatin.
Services: Daily. Special Saturday adult beginners service.
Telshe Yeshiva (O), 28400 Euclid Ave, **Wickliffe,** Ph: 943-5300.
Services: Daily
The Temple (R-UAHC), University Circle at Silver Park,
Ph: 791-7755. Rabbi B. Kamin. Services: Friday. Sunday morn-
ing service held at 26000 Shaker Blvd, except in summer.

Synagogues cont.

The Temple on the Heights—B'nai Jeshurun (C-US), 27501 Fairmount Blvd, Ph: 831-6555. Rabbi S. Schachter. Services: Daily

Torah U'tefilah (O), 1861 S Taylor Rd, Ph: 371-5872. Rabbi M. Einstadter. Services: Saturday

Congregation Tzemach Tzedek (O), 1922 Lee Rd, **Cleveland Heights**, Ph: 321-5169. Rabbi Z. Kazan. Services: Daily

Warrensville Center Synagogue (O-UOJC), 1508 Warrensville Center Rd, **Cleveland Heights**, Ph: 382-6566. Rabbi L. Zierler. Services: Daily

Young Israel (O-NCYI), 14141 Cedar Rd, Ph: 382-5740. Services: Daily; Branch: Hebrew Academy of Cleveland, 1860 S Taylor Rd, **Cleveland Heights**, Ph: 321-5838. Services: Daily

Young Israel of Beachwood (O), Call for location, Ph: 691-9007. Rabbi Y. Feitman. Services: Daily

Zichron Chaim (O), 2203 S Green Rd, Ph: 291-5000; 381-9175. Rabbi M. Garfunkel. Services: Daily

Eating Out

For kosher food information, call Rabbi I. Pickholtz, Chairman, Orthodox Rabbinical Council of Cleveland (ORC), Ph: 321-0078.

Center Café at Mandel JCC, 26001 S Woodland Rd, Ph: 831-0700. Meals: b,l. Menu: Dairy for breakfast: bagels, cream cheese, eggs. Meat (Glatt) or pareve for lunch: sandwiches, hamburgers, hot dogs, vegetables, salads. Closed Shabbat.

Cleveland Hillel Foundation at Case Western Reserve University, 11291 Euclid Ave, Ph: 231-0040. RS: Rabbi M. Granatstein of the Green Road Synagogue. Meat lunches Monday through Friday at The Hillel Deli Cellar, during the academic year. For information, contact Rabbi A. Lettofsky, Executive Director.

Chez "J", Mayfield JCC, 3505 Mayfield Rd, Ph: 382-4000. Meals: l. Menu: Dairy. RS: ORC. Closed Shabbat.

Kinneret Kosher Restaurant, 1869 S Taylor Rd, **Cleveland Heights**, Ph: 321-1404. Meals: l,d. Menu: (Dairy: cholov Yisroel) Israeli dishes. RS: ORC. Closed Shabbat.

Peking Kosher Chinese Restaurant, 1841 S Taylor Rd, **Cleveland Heights,** Ph: 371-2223. Meals: l,d. Menu: (Meat) Chinese. RS: ORC. Credit cards. Closed Shabbat.

Yakov's Vegetarian Restaurant, 13969 Cedar Rd, **University Heights,** Ph: 932-8848. Meals: l,d. Menu: (Dairy: cholov Yisroel) Israeli, Italian and fish. RS: ORC. Closed Shabbat.

Food

Academy Party Center, 4182 Mayfield Rd, **South Euclid,** Ph: 381-2066. Call in advance for individual meals to take out. RS: ORC. Closed Shabbat.

Acme Supermarket, 4401 Mayfield Rd, **South Euclid,** Ph: 382-6500. Good selection of kosher items.

Altman's Quality Kosher Meat Market, 2185 S Green, Ph: 381-7615. Kosher grocery, fresh meat (Glatt), poultry and deli. RS: ORC. Closed Shabbat.

Basch's Kosher Meats, 1944 S Taylor Rd, **Cleveland Heights,** Ph: 321-1911. Fresh meat (Glatt) and poultry. RS: ORC. Closed Shabbat.

Boris' Kosher Meat Market, 14406 Cedar Rd, **University Heights,** Ph: 382-5330. Frozen prepared dishes, fresh meats (Glatt) and poultry. RS: ORC. Closed Shabbat.

Coventry Poultry, 1825 Coventry Rd, **Cleveland Heights,** Ph: 371-0555. Fresh poultry. RS: ORC. Closed Shabbat.

David's Gourmet Catering & Take-out, 1918 S Taylor Rd, **Cleveland Heights,** Ph: 932-6670. Gourmet meat, chicken and fish dishes, desserts. Call ahead for take-out orders. RS: ORC. Closed Shabbat.

Davis Kosher Caterers, 1805 S Taylor Rd, **Cleveland Heights,** Ph: 321-7945. Will prepare meals for travelers. RS: ORC. Closed Shabbat.

Lax & Mandel Bakery, 2070 S Taylor, **Cleveland Heights,** Ph: 932-6445. Breads and pastries (pareve and dairy). Also dairy products. RS: ORC. Closed Shabbat.

Leo's Kosher Meats, 1839 S Taylor, **Cleveland Heights,** Ph: 932-9212. Fresh meat (Glatt), poultry and cold cuts. RS: ORC. Closed Shabbat.

Food cont.

Unger's Kosher Bakery, 1831 S Taylor Rd, **Cleveland Heights**, Ph: 321-7176. Breads, pastries, deli, full take-out menu and kosher grocery. RS: ORC. Closed Shabbat.

University Food Centre, 13908 Cedar Rd, Ph: 321-9494. Kosher bakery within the supermarket. Wednesday-Friday, kosher fish is available. RS: ORC.

Accommodations

For Shabbat and Holiday hospitality and general Jewish information, call Rabbi M. Mendelson of Chabad House of Cleveland Heights, Ph: 371-3679 or Rabbi and Mrs. L. Alevsky, Ph: 382-1878 or 382-5050.

For Shomer Shabbat accommodation and kosher information call Dr. A. Spero, Ph: 321-3845.

The following motels are within walking distance of the Telshe Yeshiva:

Holiday Inn, 28500 Euclid Ave, **Wickliffe**, Ph: 585-2750

Ramada Inn, 27981 Euclid Ave, **Euclid**, Ph: 731-5800

Kosher meals for travelers can be arranged at the Telshe Yeshiva, Ph: 943-5300.

Mikvah

Chabad Mikvah, 2479 S Green Rd, call Mrs. Sheindl Chaikin, Ph: 381-8567.

Cleveland Community Mikvah, 1744 Lee Rd, Ph: 321-0270 or Mrs. Debby Berger, Ph: 321-6728.

Day Schools

Agnon School, 26500 Shaker Blvd, Ph: 464-4055.

Bet Sefer Mizrachi of Cleveland, 2301 Fenwick Rd, **University Heights**, Ph: 932-0220.

Hebrew Academy of Cleveland, 1860 S Taylor Rd, **Cleveland Heights**, Ph: 321-5838.

Mosdos Ohr Hatorah, Boys Division: 1508 Warrensville Center Rd, **Cleveland Heights**, Ph: 382-6248; Girls Division: 1970 S Taylor Rd, **Cleveland Heights**, Ph: 321-1547.

Ratner Day School, 4900 Anderson Rd, Ph: 291-0034.

Solomon Schechter Day School of Cleveland (C), 3300 Mayfield Rd, Ph: 397-2900.

Bookstores

Frank's Hebrew Book Store, 1647 Lee Rd, Ph: 321-6850.
Jacob's Judaica, 13962 Cedar Rd, **University Heights**, Ph: 321-7200.

COLUMBUS   Area Code (614)   J-pop. 15,000

Synagogues

Agudas Achim Synagogue (O-Trad-UOJC), 2767 E Broad St, Ph: 237-2747. Rabbi A. Ciner. Services: Shabbat and Holidays
Congregation Ahavas Shalom (O-UOJC), 2568 E Broad St, Ph: 252-4815. Services: Daily
Congregation Beth Jacob (O-UOJC), 1223 College Ave, Ph: 237-8641. Rabbi D. Stavsky. Services: Daily
Beth Shalom (R-UAHC), 3100 E Broad St, Ph: 231-4598. Rabbi H. Apothaker. Services: Friday
Congregation Beth Tikvah (R-UAHC), 6121 Olentangy River Rd, **Worthington**, Ph: 885-6286. Rabbi G. Huber. Services: Friday
Chabad House (O-Chabad), 207 E 15th Ave, Ph: 294-3296. Rabbi C. Capland. Services: Shabbat and Holidays
Temple Israel (R-UAHC), 5419 E Broad St, Ph: 866-0010. Rabbi B. Bleefeld. Services: Shabbat
Congregation Tifereth Israel (C-US), 1354 E Broad St, Ph: 253-8523. Rabbi H. Berman. Services: Shabbat

Eating Out

Block's Hot Bagels, 6115 McNaughton Center, Ph: 863-0470; also 3415 E Broad, Ph: 235-2551. RS: Vaad Ho'ier, for bagels and bread only (pareve).
B'nai B'rith Hillel Foundation at Ohio State University, 46 E 16th Ave, Ph: 294-4797. Dinner is served Monday through Friday, during the school year. RS: Rabbi S. Abrams (O), Director. For fees and reservations contact Rabbi Abrams.

Eating Out cont.

Chabad House, 207 E 15th Ave, Ph: 294-3296. Shabbat dinner and lunch are served regularly. Also, "The Kosher Buckeye Restaurant" is open Sunday nights during the school year. Menu: "Fast food and gourmet." RS: Rabbi C. Capland, Director. Contact Rabbi C. Capland for reservations.

Food

Leah's Bakery, 2996 E Broad St, Ph: 231-8700. Breads and pastries (pareve and dairy). RS: Vaad Ho'ier.

Martin's Food, 3685 E Broad St, Ph: 231-3653. Complete super-market including kosher meat (Glatt), poultry and delicatessen. Meat, dairy and fish dishes for take-out. RS: Vaad Ho'ier. Closed Shabbat.

Accommodations

Holiday Inn, 238 W Lane Ave (across from Ohio State U), Ph: 294-4848. Twenty-minute walk to Chabad House.

Shabbat hospitality:

Congregation Ahavas Shalom, Ph: 252-4815.

Congregation Beth Jacob, Ph: 237-8641.

Rabbi C. Capland at Chabad House, Ph: 294-3296.

For private accommodations and hospitality, contact Rabbi A. Ciner at Agudas Achim Congregation, Ph: 237-2747.

Mikvah

Community Mikvah (Taharas Society), Beth Jacob Synagogue, 1223 College Ave, Ph: 239-0070, Mrs. T. Press, Ph: 237-1068 or Mrs. R. Seidman, Ph: 252-9348.

Day School

Columbus Torah Academy (O), 181 Noe Bixby Rd, Ph: 864-0299.

DAYTON   Area Code (513)   J-pop. 6,000

Synagogues

Beth Abraham Synagogue (C-US), 1306 Salem Ave, Ph: 275-7403. Rabbi S. Press. Services: Daily

376

Beth Jacob Congregation (Trad), 7020 N Main St, Ph: 274-2149.
   Rabbi S. Fox. Services: Daily
Temple Beth Or (R), 5275 Marshall Rd, **Kettering**, Ph: 435-3400.
   Rabbi J. Chessin. Services: Friday
Temple Israel (R-UAHC), 1821 Emerson Ave, Ph: 278-9621.
   Rabbi P. I. Bloom. Services: Shabbat
Shomrei Emunah—Young Israel of Dayton (O-UOJC, NCYI),
   1706 Salem Ave, Ph: 274-6941. Services: Daily

Food

Rinaldo's Bake Shoppe, 910 W Fairview Ave, Ph: 274-1311. Pareve
   breads and pastries. RS: Congregation Shomrei Emunah.

Accommodations

For private hospitality; contact Shomrei Emunah, Ph: 274-6941.

Mikvah

Mikvah, 556 Kenwood Ave. Call Mrs. J. Segal, Ph: 274-1662 or
   Mrs. M. Lewitin, Ph: 277-3579

Day School

Hillel Academy of Dayton (O), 100 E Woodbury Dr, Ph: 277-8966.

ELYRIA   Area Code (216)   J-pop. 250

Synagogues

Temple B'nai Abraham (R-UAHC), 530 Gulf Rd, Ph: 366-5537.
   Rabbi D. Weber. Services: Shabbat

EUCLID (See **CLEVELAND**)

HAMILTON   Area Code (513)

Synagogues

Beth Israel Congregation (C), Sixth & Butler Sts, Ph: 868-2049.
   Rabbi B. Adler. Services: Shabbat and Holidays

LORAIN   Area Code (216)   J-pop. 600

Synagogues

Agudath B'nai Israel (C-US), 1715 Meister Rd, Ph: 282-3307.
  Rabbi D. Mayer. Services: Shabbat

MANSFIELD   Area Code (419)   J-pop. 250

Synagogues

Emanuel Jacob Congregation (R-UAHC), 973 Larchwood Rd,
  Ph: 756-7355. Rabbi S. Marks. Services: Shabbat

MARION   Area Code (614)   J-pop. 110

Synagogues

Temple Israel (R), Seffner Ave at Mount Vernon, Ph: 387-2663.
  Services: Shabbat

MAYFIELD HEIGHTS (See CLEVELAND)

MENTOR   Area Code (216)

Synagogues

Am Shalom-Lake County Jewish Center (R), 7599 Center St,
  Ph: 255-1544. Rabbi P. Horowitz. Services: Friday

MIDDLETOWN   Area Code (513)

Synagogues

Temple Beth Sholom (R-UAHC), 610 Gladys Dr, Ph: 422-8313.
  Rabbi D. Adler. Services: Friday

PEPPER PIKE (See CLEVELAND)

SANDUSKY   Area Code (419)   J-pop. 130

Synagogues

Oheb Shalom (R), 1521 E Perkins Ave, Ph: 625-0160. Services:
  Friday

SPRINGFIELD   Area Code (513)   J-pop. 250

Synagogues

Temple Sholom (R-UAHC), 2424 N Limestone St, Ph: 399-1231.
  Rabbi L. Goldman. Services: Friday

STEUBENVILLE   Area Code (614)   J-pop. 180

Synagogues

Temple Beth Israel (R), 300 Lovers Lane, Ph: 264-5514. Services:
  Shabbat

SOUTH EUCLID (See CLEVELAND)

SYLVANIA (See TOLEDO)

TOLEDO   Area Code (419)   J-pop. 6,300

Synagogues

Temple B'nai Israel (C-US), 2727 Kenwood Blvd, Ph: 531-1677.
  Rabbi A. Bienstock. Services: Daily
Congregation Etz Chayim (O-UOJC), 3853 Woodley Rd,
  Ph: 473-2401. Rabbi E. Garsek. Services: Daily
The Temple—Congregation Shomer Emunim (R-UAHC), 6453
  Sylvania Ave, **Sylvania**, Ph: 885-3341. Rabbi A. Sokobin.
  Services: Shabbat

Eating Out

Zayde's Place, 6725 W Central Ave, Ph: 843-3354. Meals: b,l,d.
  Menu: (Meat-some Glatt) Sandwiches, soups, salads. Also take-
  out. RS: Rabbi E. Garsek. Closed Shabbat.

Food

Zayde's Place, 6725 W Central Ave, Ph: 843-3354. Fresh meat
  (Glatt) and poultry, frozen meats, kosher groceries and wines. RS:
  Rabbi Z. Garsek. Closed Shabbat.

Accommodations

Red Roof Inn, 3530 Executive Pkwy, Ph: 536-0118. Less than a
mile from Etz Chaim; about a mile to Chabad House.

Sheraton Westgate, 3536 Secor Rd, Ph: 535-7070. Less than a mile
from Etz Chaim; aabout a mile to Chabad House.

Private accommodations; contact Chabad House, Rabbi Y.
Shemtov, Ph: 535-1930.

Mikvah

Congregation Etz Chayim, 3853 Woodley Rd, Ph: 473-2401

Day School

Hebrew Academy of Toledo, 6465 Sylvania Ave, **Sylvania**,
Ph: 885-4584.

UNIVERSITY HEIGHTS (See CLEVELAND)

WARREN   Area Code (216)   J-pop. 400

Synagogues

Beth Israel Temple Center (C-US), 2138 E Market St,
Ph: 395-3877. Rabbi A. Graubart. Services: Shabbat

WICKLIFFE (See CLEVELAND)

WOOSTER   Area Code (216)   J-pop. 125

Synagogues

Knesseth Israel Temple (C), 1670 Cleveland Rd, Ph: 262-3516.
Rabbi P. Roff. Services: Friday

WORTHINGTON (See COLUMBUS)

YOUNGSTOWN   Area Code (216)   J-pop. 4,000

Synagogues

Congregation Children of Israel (O-UOJC), 3970 Logan Way,
Ph: 759-2167. Rabbi D. Merkin. Services: Daily

Temple El Emeth (C-US), 3970 Logan Way, Ph: 759-1429. Rabbi
D. Steinhardt. Services: Shabbat

Congregation Ohev Tzedek Shaare Torah (C-US), 5245 Glenwood Ave, Ph: 758-2321. Rabbi M. Kornspan. Services: Daily

Congregation Rodef Sholom (R-UAHC), Elm St & Woodbine Ave, Ph: 744-5001. Rabbi J. Brown. Services: Shabbat

Accommodations

For private accommodations, contact Congregation Children of Israel, Ph: 759-2167.

To inquire about kosher meals, call Jewish Family and Children's Service, Mr. A. Goldberg, Director, Ph: 746-3251.

Mikvah

Congregation Children of Israel—Temple El Emeth, 3970 Logan Way. Contact Rabbi D. Merkin, Ph: 759-8692 or 759-2167.

Day School

Altshuler Akiva Academy, 505 Gypsy Lane, Ph: 747-0452.

ZANESVILLE   Area Code (614)   J-pop. 120

Synagogues

Beth Abraham Synagogue (C), 1740 Blue Ave, Ph: 453-5391. Rabbi N. Langer. Services: Shabbat

Oklahoma

OKLAHOMA CITY   Area Code (405)   J-pop. 2,300

Synagogues

Temple B'nai Israel (R-UAHC), 4901 N Pennsylvania Ave, Ph: 848-0965. Rabbi A. Packman. Services: Friday

Congregation Emanuel (C-US), 900 NW 47th St, Ph: 528-2113. Rabbi C. Shalman. Services: Shabbat

Food

For kosher food information call Jerry or Helen Friedman, Ph: 524-2881 (home) or 521-8449 (office).

Food cont.

Crescent Market, 6409 Avondale, Ph: 842-5755. Empire chicken
and turkey products, some deli, cheeses and packaged
kosher items.

Plett's I.G.A. Supermarket, 715 NW 50th St, Ph: 842-6695. Full line
of packaged kosher foods in separate kosher section, including glatt kosher meats and cholov Yisroel dairy products.

Accommodations

For Shabbat hospitality or a kosher meal, call Jerry or Helen
Friedman, a Shomer Shabbat family, Ph: 524-2881 (home) or
521-8449 (office).

Mikvah

Congregation Emanuel (C-US), 900 NW 47th St, Ph: 528-2113.

Day School

Solomon Schechter Academy of Oklahoma City (C), 900 NW 47th
St, Ph: 521-9945.

TULSA   Area Code (918)   J-pop. 2,750

Synagogues

Congregation B'nai Emunah (C-US), 1719 S Owasso Ave,
Ph: 583-7121. Rabbi M. Fitzerman. Services: Shabbat

Temple Israel (R-UAHC), 2004 E 22nd Pl, Ph: 747-1309.
Rabbi C. Sherman. Services: Friday

Food

For kosher food information, call Rabbi Y. Weg at Chabad House,
Ph: 493-7006.

Homeland Supermarket, 31st & Harvard, Ph: 744-4414. Sinai
frozen meats, Empire frozen chickens, kosher cheeses.

Accommodations

Private hospitality; for a kosher meal, call Rabbi Y. Weg at Chabad
House, 6701 S Utica, Ph: 493-7006; 492-4499.

Sheraton-Kensington Hotel, 1902 E 71st St, Ph: 493-7000. Walk to
Chabad House.

Day School

Heritage Academy Day School, 2021 E 71st St, Ph: 494-0953.

Oregon

ASHLAND   Area Code (503)

Synagogues

Temple Emek Shalom (R-UAHC), 1082 E Main, Ph: 488-2909.
Rabbi D. Isaac. Services: Shabbat

EUGENE   Area Code (503)   J-pop. 2,300

Synagogues

Temple Beth Israel (R,C-US), 2550 Portland St, Ph: 485-7218.
Rabbi M. Kinberg. Services: Shabbat

PORTLAND   Area Code (503)   J-pop. 9,000

Synagogues

Beth Israel (R-UAHC), 1931 NW Flanders St, Ph: 222-1069.
Rabbi E. Rose. Services: Shabbat
Kesser Israel (O-UOJC), 136 SW Meade St, Ph: 222-1239.
Services: Daily
Neveh Shalom (C-US), 2900 SW Peaceful Lane, Ph: 246-8831.
Rabbi J. Stampfer. Services: Daily
Shaarie Torah (Trad), 920 NW 25th Ave, Ph: 226-6131. Rabbi Y.
Geller. Services: Daily

Food

Albertson's, 5415 SW Beaverton-Hillsdale Hwy, Ph: 246-1713.
Packaged kosher meats, cheeses and frozen entrees.
Ikeda Pastry Shop, 6330 SW Capitol Hwy, Ph: 244-7573. Breads
and pastries. RS: Rabbi Y. Geller.
Rose's Bakery, 35 NW 20th Pl, Ph: 227-4875. Breads and pastries.
RS: Rabbi Y. Geller.

Accommodations

Private accommodations; call Rabbi Y. Geller at Congregation
Shaarie Torah, Ph: 226-6131.

Caravan Motor Motel, 2401 SW Fourth, Ph: 226-1121. Five-minute
walk to Kesser Israel.

Carriage Inn, 2025 NW Northrup, Ph: 224-0543. Rooms with
kitchens are available. Three-block walk to Shaarie Torah.

Red Lion Inn, 310 SW Lincoln, Ph: 221-0450. Ten-minute walk to
Kesser Israel.

Mikvah

Portland Jewish Ritualarium, 1425 SW Harrison St, Ph: 224-3409
or Lillian Corcas, Ph: 241-0916.

Day School

The Portland Jewish Academy, 6651 SW Capitol Hwy,
Ph: 244-0126.

SALEM   Area Code (503)

Synagogues

Temple Beth Shalom (C), 1795 Broadway NE, Ph: 362-5004.
Services: Friday

Pennsylvania

ABINGTON (See also PHILADELPHIA)   Area Code (215)

Synagogues

Old York Road Temple Beth Am (R-UAHC), 971 Old York Rd,
Ph: 886-8000. Rabbi R. S. Leib. Services: Shabbat

ALLENTOWN   Area Code (215)   J-pop. 6,000

Synagogues

Congregation Am Haskalah (Recon-FRCH), St. Timothy's
Lutheran Church, Ott & Walnut Sts, Ph: 435-3775. Services:
Shabbat

Temple Beth El (C-US), 1702 Hamilton St, Ph: 435-3521. Rabbi
E. Wernick. Services: Daily

Congregation Keneseth Israel (R-UAHC), 2227 Chew St,
Ph: 435-9074. Rabbi M. Beifield. Services: Friday

Congregation Sons of Israel (O-UOJC), 2715 Tilghman St,
Ph: 433-6089. Rabbi S. Horowitz. Services: Daily

Eating Out

For kosher information, call Rabbi M. Raven, Ph: 434-3109.

Leader Nursing & Rehabilitation Center II (cafeteria), 2020
Westgate Dr, Ph: 861-0100. RS: Lehigh Valley Kashruth
Commission. The home's kosher kitchen arranges meals for
travelers. Call one day in advance.

Snack Bar in the Jewish Community Center (planned), 702 N 22nd
St, Ph: 435-3571. Meals: l,d. Menu: (Glatt meat) Fast food and
dinners. RS: Lehigh Valley Kashruth Commission. Closed
Shabbat.

Food

Bob's Bake Shop, 1500 Cedarcrest Blvd, Crest Plaza Shopping
Center, Ph: 395-3662. Challahs (pareve), breads, cakes and
pastries (dairy). RS: Lehigh Valley Kashruth Commission.

Accommodations

Home hospitality; call Rabbi S. Horowitz, Ph: 433-6089.

Mikvah

Hebrew Family League Mikvah Association, 1834 Whitehall St,
Call Congregations Sons of Israel, Ph: 433-6089.

Day School

Jewish Day School of Allentown, 2313 Pennsylvania St,
Ph: 437-0721.

ALTOONA   Area Code (814)   J-pop. 480

Synagogues

Congregation Agudath Achim (C-US), 1306 17th St, Ph: 944-5317.
Rabbi M. Berger. Services: Daily

Synagogues cont.

Temple Beth Israel (R-UAHC), 3004 Union Ave, Ph: 942-0057. Rabbi R. A. Zionts. Services: Shabbat

ARDMORE (See PHILADELPHIA)

BALA-CYNWYD (See PHILADELPHIA)

BENSALEM (See also PHILADELPHIA)   Area Code (215)

Synagogues

Congregation Tifereth Israel of Lower Bucks County (C-US), 2909 Bristol Rd, Ph: 752-3468. Rabbi M. Saks. Services: Shabbat

BERWYN (See PHILADELPHIA)

BETHLEHEM (See also ALLENTOWN)
Area Code (215)   J-pop. 810

Synagogues

Congregation Agudath Achim (O-UOJC), 1550 Linwood St. Call for schedule. Dr. M. Bader, President, Ph: 868-1311. Services: Saturdays

Congregation Brith Sholom (C-US), 1190 W Macada Rd, Ph: 866-8009. Rabbi A. Juda. Services: Daily

BLOOMSBURG   Area Code (717)

Synagogues

Beth Israel Congregation (C), 144 E 4th St, Ph: 784-5778. Services: High Holidays

BLUE BELL (See PHILADELPHIA)

BRADFORD   Area Code (814)   J-pop. 110

Synagogues

Temple Beth El (R-UAHC), 111 Jackson Ave, Ph: 368-8204. Services: Call for schedule.

BRISTOL (See also **PHILADELPHIA**)   Area Code (215)

Synagogues

Bristol Jewish Center (C), 216 Pond St, Ph: 788-7548. Rabbi
M. Jacobi. Services: Shabbat

BROOMALL (See **PHILADELPHIA)**

BUTLER   Area Code (412)   J-pop. 285

Synagogues

Congregation B'nai Abraham (C-US), 519 N Main St,
Ph: 287-5806. Rabbi W. Boninger. Services: Fridays and second
Saturdays

CHAMBERSBURG   Area Code (717)   J-pop. 470

Synagogues

Congregation Sons of Israel (C), 2nd & E King Sts, Ph: 264-2915.
Rabbi H. Gilner. Services: Shabbat

CHELTENHAM (See **PHILADELPHIA)**

COATESVILLE (See also **PHILADELPHIA**   Area Code (215)

Synagogues

Congregation Beth Israel (C-US), 25 S 5th Ave, **Coatesville,**
Ph: 384-1978. Rabbi M. Charnay. Services: Shabbat

DOYLESTOWN (See also **PHILADELPHIA)**   Area Code (215)

Synagogues

Temple Judea of Bucks County (R-UAHC), 300 Swamp Rd,
Doylestown, Ph: 348-5022. Rabbi B. Goldman-Wartell.
Services: Call for schedule.

DRESHER (See **PHILADELPHIA)**

EASTON   Area Code (215)   J-pop. 1,200

Synagogues

B'nai Abraham Synagogue (C-US), 16th & Bushkill Sts,
   Ph: 258-5343. Rabbi J. Sales. Services: Shabbat
Temple Covenant of Peace (R-UAHC), 1451 Northampton St,
   Ph: 253-2031. Rabbi M. Yudkin. Services: Friday

ELKINS PARK (See PHILADELPHIA)

ERDENHEIM (See PHILADELPHIA)

ERIE   Area Code (814)   J-pop. 800

Synagogues

Temple Anshe Hesed (R-UAHC), 930 Liberty St, Ph: 454-2426.
   Rabbi S. Weinstein. Services: Shabbat

Brith Sholom Jewish Centre (C-US), 3207 State St, Ph: 454-2431.
   Rabbi L. Lifshen. Services: Saturday, Monday & Thursday

FALLSINGTON (See PHILADELPHIA)

FEASTERVILLE (See PHILADELPHIA)

GREENSBURG   Area Code (412)   J-pop. 425

Synagogues

Temple Emanu-El Israel (R-UAHC), 222 N Main St,
   Ph: 834-0560. Rabbi S. Perman. Services: Shabbat

HARRISBURG   Area Code (717)   J-pop. 6,500

Synagogues

Beth El Temple (C-US), 2637 N Front St, Ph: 232-0556. Rabbi M.
   Greenspan. Services: Shabbat
Congregation Chisuk Emuna (C-US), Fifth & Division Sts,
   Ph: 232-4851. Rabbi E. Snitkoff. Services: Daily
Congregation Kesher Israel (O-UOJC), 2500 N 3rd St,
   Ph: 238-0763. Rabbi C. Schertz. Services: Daily

Machzeikei Hadas (O), 3029 N Front St, Ph: 236-2934.
Services: Shabbat
Temple Ohev Shalom (R-UAHC), 2345 N Front St, Ph: 233-6459.
Services: Friday

Food

Quality Kosher, 2911 N 7th St, Ph: 234-6777. Fresh meats (Glatt)
and small kosher grocery, deli sandwiches to take out.
RS: Rabbi C. Schertz. Closed Shabbat.
Giant Food Store Bakery, 4450 Oakhurst Blvd, Ph: 652-7795.
Breads and pastries (pareve and dairy). RS: Rabbi C. Schertz
(baked goods only). This supermarket carries a large selection of
kosher products.
Pathmark, 50-70 Jonestown Rd, Ph: 652-0550. Large selection of
kosher products.

Accommodations

Days Inn, 3919 N Front St, Ph: 233-3100. A mile to Kesher Israel.

Excellent Inn, 4125 N Front St, Ph: 233-5891. One and one-half
miles to Kesher Israel.

Mikvah

Taharas Mishpacha, 3601 N 4th St. Contact Mrs. E. Levine after
3 p.m., Ph: 234-0097.

Day School

Yeshiva Academy of Harrisburg, 100 Vaughn St,
Ph: 238-2074/1458.

HAVERTOWN (See PHILADELPHIA)

HAZELTON   Area Code (717)   J-pop. 410

Synagogues

Agudas Israel Synagogue (C-US), Pine & Oak Sts, Ph: 455-2851.
Rabbi R. Miller. Services: Daily
Beth Israel Temple (R-UAHC), 98 N Church St, Ph: 455-3971.
Rabbi B. Perelmuter. Services: Friday

HERSHEY   Area Code (717)

Food

G. Memmi & Sons Bakery, 204 Hillcrest Rd, Ph: 533-9859.
Breads. RS: Star-K.

HUNTINGDON   Area Code (814)

Synagogues

Congregation Agudath Achim (C), 1009 Washington St,
Ph: 643-3591. Services: Call for schedule.

HUNTINGDON VALLEY (See also PHILADELPHIA)
Area Code (215)

Synagogues

Temple Zion of Huntingdon Valley (R), 1620 Pine Rd,
Ph: 947-9302. Rabbi Dr. D. Parker. Services: Shabbat

INDIANA   Area Code (412)

Synagogues

Beth Israel Synagogue (C), 5th & Washington Sts, Ph: 465-6721.
Rabbi E. Epstein. Services: Friday

JOHNSTOWN   Area Code (814)   J-pop. 485

Synagogues

Beth Shalom Congregation (C-US, R-UAHC), 700 Indiana St,
Ph: 536-0647. Rabbi A. Soloff. Services: Shabbat

KING OF PRUSSIA (See PHILADELPHIA)

KINGSTON (See also WILKES-BARRE)   Area Code (717)

Synagogues

Temple B'nai B'rith (R-UAHC), 408 Wyoming Ave, Ph: 287-9606.
Rabbi A. Shevlin. Services: Shabbat

Congregation Ohav Zedek (branch), United Hebrew Institute, 3rd Ave, and Institute Lane, Ph: 825-6619. Rabbi Dr. M. J. Yeres. Services: Shabbat and Holidays

Food

Basically Bagels, 3rd Ave (Kingston Plaza), Ph: 288-6000. RS: Rabbi Dr. M. J. Yeres (bagels and challahs only).
Giant Food Store, 750 Wyoming Ave, Ph: 287-0655. Large selection of kosher products.
Pierce Bakery, 334 Pierce St, Ph: 288-5456. Breads and pastries. RS: Rabbi Dr. M. J. Yeres.
Shop Rite, 3rd Ave, Ph: 287-4591. Many kosher products.

Mikvah

The Ritualarium, 139 3rd Ave. Contact Mrs. S. Perlman, Ph: 283-1961; 287-6336.

Day School

Israel Ben Zion Academy/United Hebrew Institute, 3rd Ave & Institute Lane, Ph: 287-9608.

LAFAYETTE (See also PHILADELPHIA)   Area Code (215)

Synagogues

Congregation Or Ami (R-UAHC), Ivy Ridge J.C.C., 708 Ridge Pike, **Lafayette Hill**, Ph: 828-9066. Rabbi S. Prystowsky. Services: Friday

LANCASTER   Area Code (717)   J-pop. 2,100

Synagogues

Temple Beth El (C-US), 25 N Lime St, Ph: 392-1379. Rabbi Y. Atkins. Services: Shabbat and Monday
Degel Israel Synagogue (O-UOJC), 1120 Columbia Ave, Ph: 397-0183. Rabbi G. Weinberg. Services: Daily
Congregation Shaarai Shomayim (R-UAHC), 508 N Duke St, Ph: 397-5575. Rabbi D. Sofian. Services: Friday

Food

Giant Food Store Bakery, 1360 Columbia Ave, Ph: 291-9678.
Breads and pastries (pareve and dairy). RS: Rabbi G. Weinberg
(baked goods only). The supermarket also carries a large
selection of kosher products.

Accommodations

Nissly Tourist Home, 624 W Chestnut, Ph: 392-2311. This small inn
is located within walking distance of the Degel Israel
Synagogue. Rooms with kitchenettes and suites with kitchens.
Call for reservations.

Day School

The Jewish Day School, 2120 Oregon Pike, Ph: 560-1904.

LANSDALE   Area Code (215)

Synagogues

Congregation Beth Israel (C-US), 1080 Sumneytown Pike,
Ph: 752-3468. Rabbi R. Dobrusin. Services: Shabbat

LEBANON   Area Code (717)   J-pop. 400

Synagogues

Congregation Beth Israel (C-US), 411 S 8th St, Ph: 273-2669.
Rabbi L. Zivic. Services: Daily

LEVITTOWN (See PHILADELPHIA)

LUZERNE   Area Code (717)

Synagogues

Achavas Achim (O), Academy & Walnut Sts, Ph: 287-2032. Rabbi
M. Pernikoff. Services: Shabbat

Food (See **Kingston**)

Mikvah (See **Kingston**)

McKEESPORT (See also PITTSBURGH)   Area Code (412)

Synagogues

Temple B'nai Israel (R-UAHC), 536 Shaw Ave, Ph: 678-6181.
  Rabbi L. Helman. Services: Friday
Gemilas Chesed (Trad-UOJC), 1400 Summit St, **White Oak**,
  Ph: 678-8859. Rabbi I. Chinn. Services: Daily
Tree of Life-Sfard (C), 2025 Cypress Dr, **White Oak**,
  Ph: 673-0938. Services: Shabbat and Sunday

Mikvah

Congregation Gemilas Chesed, 1545 Ohio Ave. Contact Mikvah
  attendant, Ph: 678-2725 or 678-2264.

MECHANICSBURG   Area Code (717)

Synagogues

Temple Beth Shalom (Recon-FRCH), 913 Allendale Rd,
  Ph: 697-2662. Rabbi C. Choper. Services: Friday; one Saturday a
  month

MEDIA (See PHILADELPHIA)

MELROSE PARK (See also PHILADELPHIA)
  Area Code (215)

Day School

Forman Center (C), 7601 Old York Rd, Ph: 635-3130.

MERION (See PHILADELPHIA)

NEW KENSINGTON (See also PITTSBURGH)
  Area Code (412)

Synagogues

Beth Jacob Congregation (C-US), 1040 Kenneth Ave,
  Ph: 335-8524. Rabbi Y. Dick. Services: Shabbat

NEWTOWN (See also **TRENTON, NJ**)   Area Code (215)

Synagogues

Shir Ami—Bucks County Jewish Congregation (R-UAHC), 101 Richboro Rd, Ph: 968-3400. Rabbi E. Strom. Services: Friday

OIL CITY   Area Code (814)   J-pop. 145

Synagogues

Congregation Tree of Life (Trad), 316 W 1st St, Ph: 677-4082. Rabbi S. Schwartzman. Services: Saturday

PENN VALLEY (See **PHILADELPHIA**)

PHILADELPHIA   Area Code (215)   J-pop. 250,000

Synagogues

Temple Adath Israel of the Main Line (C-US), Old Lancaster Rd & Highland Ave, **Merion**, Ph: 664-5150. Rabbi F. Kazan. Services: Daily

Congregation Adath Jeshurun (C-US), York & Ashbourne, **Elkins Park**, Ph: 635-6611. Rabbi S. Rosenbloom. Services: Daily

Adath Shalom (C-US), Marshall & Ritner Sts, Ph: 463-2224. Rabbi B. Goldman. Services: Shabbat

Adath Tikvah-Montefiore (C), Summerdale Ave & Hoffnagle St, Ph: 742-9191, Rabbi I. Abraham. Services: Daily

Adath Zion Congregation (Trad), Pennway & Friendship Sts, Ph: 742-8500. Rabbi M. Goldman. Services: Daily

Congregation Ahavas Torah—Rhawnhurst Torah Center (O-UOJC), 7525 Loretto Ave, Ph: 725-3610. Rabbi Y. Kaganoff. Services: Daily

Aitz Chaim Synagogue Center (O-UOJC), 7600 Summerdale Ave, Ph: 742-4870. Rabbi A. Novitsky. Services: Shabbat and Sunday

Congregation Beth Ahavah (R), YM & YWHA, Broad & Pine Sts, Ph: 790-0603. Services: Call for schedule.

Congregation Beth Am Israel (C-US), 1301 Hagys Ford Rd, **Penn Valley**, Ph: 667-1651. Rabbi M. Margolius. Services: Shabbat and Sunday

Temple Beth Ami (C-US), 9201 Old Bustleton Ave, Ph: 673-2511. Rabbi Dr. M. Goldman. Services: Daily

Congregation Beth Chaim (Trad, C), 350 E Street Rd, **Feasterville**, Ph: 355-3626 or 357-7130. Rabbi M. Novoseller. Services: Shabbat and daily p.m.

Beth David Reform Congregation (R-UAHC), 1130 Vaughans Lane, **Gladwyne**, Ph: 896-7485. Rabbi H. Cohen. Services: Friday

Congregation Beth El of Lower Bucks County (C-US), 21 Penn Valley Rd, **Fallsington**, Ph: 945-9500. Rabbi W. Fierverker. Services: Daily

Congregation Beth El Suburban (C-US), 715 Paxon Hollow Rd, **Broomall**, Ph: 356-8700. Rabbi B. Blum. Services: Daily

Congregation Beth Emeth—B'nai Yitzhok (C-US), Bustleton & Unruh Aves, Ph: 338-1533. Rabbi C. Krause. Services: Daily

Beth Hamedrosh Hagodol—Beth Yaacov (O-UOJC), 6018 Larchwood Ave, Ph: 747-3116. Rabbi C. Budnick. Services: Saturday

Beth Hamedrosh of Overbrook Park (O), 7505 Brookhaven Rd, Ph: 473-1019. Rabbi S. Caplan. Services: Daily

Temple Beth Hillel/Beth El (C-US), Remington Rd & Lancaster Ave, **Wynnewood**, Ph: 649-5300. Rabbi M. Maltzman. Services: Daily

Congregation Beth Israel of Media (Recon-FRCH), Gayley Terr, **Media**, Ph: 566-4645. Rabbi L. Berner. Services: Friday

Beth Sholom Congregation (C-US), Foxcroft & Old York Rd, **Elkins Park**, Ph: 887-1342. Rabbi A. Landes. Services: Daily

Congregation Beth Solomon Suburban of Somerton (O), 11006 Audubon Ave, Ph: 698-1180. Rabbi S. Isaacson. Services: Daily

Beth Tefilath Israel—Rodeph Zedek (C), 2605 Welsh Rd, Ph: 464-1242. Rabbi J. Lauterbach. Services: Daily

Beth T'Fillah of Overbrook Park (C-US), 7630 Woodbine Ave, Ph: 477-2415. Rabbi B. Rosen. Services: Daily

Beth Tikvah—B'nai Jeshurun (C-US), 1001 Paper Mill Rd, **Erdenheim**, Ph: 233-5356 or 836-5677. Rabbi D. Klatzker. Services: Daily

Synagogues cont.

Temple Beth Torah (R-UAHC), 608 Welsh Rd, Ph: 677-1555.
Rabbi B. Frank. Services: Friday

Congregation Beth Tovim (Trad), 5871 Drexel Rd, Ph: 879-1100.
Rabbi A. Novoseller. Services: Daily

Beth Uziel Congregation (C), Rorer St & Wyoming Ave,
Ph: 329-0250. Rabbi Dr. O. Kramer. Services: Daily

Beth Zion—Beth Israel (C-US), 18th & Spruce Sts, Ph: 735-5148.
Rabbi I. Stone. Services: Daily

Temple Brith Achim (R-UAHC), 481 S Gulph Rd, **King of
Prussia**, Ph: 337-2222. Rabbi R. Ourach. Services: Friday

Congregation B'nai Abraham (O), 521-27 Lombard St,
Ph: 627-3123. Services: Daily

Congregation B'nai Israel—Ohev Zedek (O-UOJC), 8201 Castor
Ave, Ph: 742-0400. Rabbi A. Felder. Services: Daily

Congregation B'nai Jacob—Dershu Tov (O-UOJC), 1145-47
Gilham St, Ph: 725-5182. Rabbi B. Leizerowski. Services: Daily

Center City Havurah Minyan (Recon-FRCH), A.J.C. Daroff
House, 255 S 16th St. Services: Saturday. For information call
Carmi Levine, Ph: 568-7073.

Far Northeast Congregation, 11001 Bustleton Ave, Ph: 464-6206.
Services: Shabbat and Sunday a.m.

Germantown Jewish Centre (C-US), Lincoln Dr & Ellet St,
Ph: 844-1507. Rabbi S. Hahn. Services: Daily

Har Zion Temple (C-US), Hagys Ford at Hollows Rd, **Penn Valley**,
Ph: 839-1250. Rabbi G. Wolpe. Services: Daily

Temple Israel of Upper Darby (C-US), Bywood Ave & Walnut St,
Upper Darby, Ph: FL2-2125. Rabbi M. Rubenstein. Services:
Shabbat

Kensington Synagogue (C), 2033 E Allegheny Ave, Ph: 634-4428.
Rabbi H. Cole. Services: High Holidays

Kesher Israel (Trad), 412 Lombard St, Ph: 922-7736. Services:
Daily

Congregation Kneses Israel—Anshei S'fard (O), 6716 Bustleton
Ave, Ph: 332-7655. Rabbi S. Lewis. Services: Shabbat

Congregation Knesseth Israel (R-UAHC), Old York & Township

Line Rds, **Elkins Park**, Ph: 887-8700. Rabbi S. Maslin. Services: Shabbat

Lower Merion Synagogue (O), 123 Old Lancaster Rd, **Bala-Cynwyd**, Ph: 664-5626. Rabbi A. Levene. Services: Daily

Congregation Lubavitch (O-Lubav), 7622 Castor Ave, Ph: 725-2030. Rabbi A. Shemtov. Services: Daily

Main Line Reform Temple—Beth Elohim (R-UAHC), 410 Montgomery Ave, **Wynnewood**, Ph: 649-7800. Rabbi M. Hausen. Services: Shabbat

Congregation Melrose B'nai Israel Emanu-El (C-US), Cheltenham Ave & 2nd St, **Cheltenham**, Ph: 635-1505. Rabbi I. Moseson. Services: Shabbat

Temple Menorah—Keneseth Chai (C-US), 4301 Tyson Ave, Ph: 624-9600; 332-2335. Rabbi N. Goldstein. Services: Friday

Congregation Mikveh Israel (C-US), Independence Mall E, 44 N 4th St, Ph: 922-5446. Rabbi A. Lazaroff. Services: Saturday

Congregation Mishkan Shalom (Recon-FRCH), Stratford Friends School, Darby & Llandillo Rds, **Havertown**, Ph: 446-4068. Rabbi B. Walt. Services: Shabbat

Congregation Ner Zedek—Ezrath Israel (C-US), Bustleton Ave & Oakmont St, Ph: 728-1155. Rabbi M. Z. Dembowitz. Services: Daily

Congregation Ohev Shalom (C-US), 2 Chester Rd, **Wallingford**, Ph: 874-1465. Rabbi Dr. L. Kaplan. Services: Daily

Ohev Shalom (C-US), 944 Second St Pike, **Richboro**, Ph: 322-9595. Rabbi E. Perlstein. Services: Shabbat

Congregation Or Shalom (C-US), 835 Darby-Paoli Rd, **Berwyn**, Ph: 644-9086. Rabbi W. Kaplan. Services: Shabbat

Oxford Circle Jewish Community Center (C-US), 1009 Unruh Ave, Ph: 342-2400. Rabbi J. Romirowsky. Services: Daily

Congregation Raim Ahuvim (O-UOJC), 5854 Drexel Rd, Ph: 878-8477. Rabbi I. Axelrod. Services: Daily

Congregation Rodeph Shalom (R-UAHC), 615 N Broad St, Ph: 627-6747. Rabbi A. Fuchs. Services: Shabbat

Rodef Shalom Suburban Center (R-UAHC), 8201 High School Rd, Ph: 635-2500. Rabbi A. Fuchs. Services: Friday

Synagogues cont.

Congregation Shaare Shamayim-Beth Judah (C-US), 9768 Verree Rd, Ph: 677-1600. Rabbi I. Grussgott. Services: Daily

Temple Shalom (R-UAHC), 2901 Edgely Rd, **Levittown**, Ph: 945-4154. Rabbi A. Tuffs. Services: Friday

Shearit Israel—Northeast Sephardic Congregation, 1603 Colima Rd, Ph: 698-2691 or 342-1452. Rabbi A. Gabay. Services: Holidays

Temple Sholom (C-US), Large St & Roosevelt Blvd, Ph: 288-7600. Rabbi P. Chazin. Services: Friday

Temple Sholom in Broomall (R-UAHC), 55 N Church Lane, **Broomall**, Ph: 356-5165. Rabbi M. Selekman. Services: Shabbat

Temple Sinai (C-US), Limekiln Pike & Dillon Rd, **Dresher**, Ph: 643-6510. Rabbi S. Greenberg. Services: Daily

Society Hill Synagogue (C-US), 418 Spruce St, Ph: 922-6590. Rabbi I. Caine. Services: Shabbat

Suburban Jewish Community Center—B'nai Aaron (C-US), 560 Mill Rd, **Havertown**, Ph: 446-1967. Rabbi M. Sandberg. Services: Daily

Talmudical Yeshiva of Philadelphia (O), 6063 Drexel Rd, Ph: 477-1000. Rabbi S. Kamenetsky. Services: Daily

Congregation Tiferes B'nai Israel (C), 2478 Street Rd, **Warrington**, Ph: 343-0155. Services: Call for schedule.

Tiferet Bet Israel (C-US), 1920 Skippack Pike, **Blue Bell**, Ph: 275-8797. Rabbi D. Maharam. Services: Friday

Tikvoh Chadoshoh (C-US), 5364 W Chew Ave, Ph: 438-1508. Rabbi Dr. W. Eisenberg. Services: Saturday

Vilna Congregation (Trad), 509 Pine St, Ph: 592-9433. Rabbi M. Schmidt. Services: Saturday

Young Israel of Elkins Park (O-NCYI), High School Rd & Montgomery Ave, **Elkins Park**, Ph: 635-5295. Rabbi D. Brisman. Services: Shabbat and daily a.m.

Young Israel Synagogue of Oxford Circle (O-NCYI), 6427 Large St, Ph: 743-2848. Rabbi J. Meles. Services: Daily

Young Israel of Wynnefield (O-NCYI), 5300 Wynnefield Ave, Ph: 473-3511. Rabbi M. Young. Services: Daily

Young Peoples Congregation, Shari Eli (C-US), 728 W
Moyamensing Ave, Ph: 339-9897. Rabbi I. Wolmark. Services:
Shabbat

Congregation of the YM/YWHA Branch (C), 401 S Broad St,
Ph: 545-4400. Rabbi N. Waldman. Services: Shabbat

Eating Out

Dragon Inn, 7628 Castor Ave, Ph: 742-2575. Meals: l,d. Menu:
(Glatt meat) Chinese cuisine. RS: Rabbi D. Brisman. Closed
Shabbat.

European Dairy, 20th & Sansom St, Ph: 568-1298. Meals: l,d.
Menu: Dairy and fish dishes. RS: Orthodox Vaad of
Philadelphia. Amex, Discover, Diners. Closed Shabbat.

Kosher Fare Restaurant, 7534 Haverford Ave, Ph: 877-8310.
Meals: l,d. Menu: (Glatt meat) Deli, Jewish, American, Israeli.
Also take-out. RS: Orthodox Vaad of Philadelphia. Closed
Shabbat.

Jonathan's, 130 S 11th St, Ph: 829-8101. Meals: l,d. Menu: (Glatt
meat) Mediterranean cuisine; deli, soups, sandwiches, entrees,
salads, desserts. RS: Rabbi D. Brisman. Closed Shabbat.

Marcelle's, 7518 Castor Ave, Ph: 742-5320. Meals: l,d. Menu:
(Glatt meat) Israeli and Moroccan specialties. RS: Rabbi D.
Brisman. Closed Shabbat.

Tiberias Cafeteria, 8010 Castor Ave, Ph: 725-7444. Meals: l,d.
Menu: (Dairy: cholov Yisroel) Pizza, dairy dishes.
RS: Orthodox Vaad of Philadelphia. Closed Shabbat.

Tiberias Chinese Restaurant, 7638 Castor Ave, Ph: 725-5666.
Meals: l,d. Menu: (Glatt meat) Chinese and American.
RS: Orthodox Vaad of Philadelphia. Closed Shabbat.

University of Pennsylvania Hillel Cafeteria, 202 S 36th St,
Ph: 898-7391. Lunch and dinner are served daily during the
academic year. RS: Orthodox Vaad of Philadelphia. For information and reservations, contact Rabbi J. Brochin, Director.

Food

Best Value, 8566 Bustleton Ave, Ph: 342-1902. Fresh meat (Glatt)
and poultry. Complete kosher grocery. RS: Rabbi D. Brisman.
Closed Shabbat.

Food cont.

Coventry Market, 737 Valley Rd, **Elkins Park**, Ph: 635-2328. Take-out meat, poultry, side dishes and some kosher groceries. RS: Rabbi S. Issacson.

Kosher Fare, 7534 Haverford Ave, Ph: 877-8311. Complete kosher grocery. RS: Orthodox Vaad of Philadelphia. Closed Shabbat.

Michael's Bakery, 6635 Castor Ave, Ph: 745-1423. Breads and pastries (pareve and dairy). RS: Rabbi D. Brisman.

Milk N' Honey, 7618 Castor Ave, Ph: 342-3224. Complete kosher grocery, frozen meat and poultry. Closed Shabbat.

Rhawnhurst Kosher Meat Market, 8259 Bustleton Ave, Ph: 742-5287. Fresh meat and poultry (Glatt on request), hot and cold deli-style food to go. RS: Vaad Hakashrus of Philadelphia, Rabbi B. Leizerowski. Closed Shabbat.

Simon's Kosher Meat, 6926 Bustleton Ave, Ph: 624-5695. Fresh meat and poultry; also deli meats. RS: Vaad Hakashrus of Philadelphia. Closed Shabbat.

Accommodations

Abraham & Sarah Kadis Hachnosas Orchim Home (affiliated with Congregation Beth Tovim), 5871 Drexel Rd, Ph: 879-1100. The Kadis Hostel provides Jewish travelers (men only) with beds and a shower free of charge.

Private accommodations; contact Congregation B'nai Jacob, Ph: 725-5182; Lubavitch Center, Ph: 725-2030; or Young Israel of Oxford Circle, Ph: 535-9328.

Mikvah

Congregation Ahavas Torah, 7525 Loretto Ave, Ph: 722-7574.
Torah Academy, Argyle & Wynnewood Rds, Ph: 642-8679.

Day School

Hebrew Academy of N.E. Philadelphia, 9225 Old Bustleton Ave, Ph: 969-5960.

Solomon Schechter Day School of Philadelphia (C), Stern Center, Old Lancaster Rd & Highland Ave, **Bala-Cynwd**, Ph: 664-5480.

Torah Academy of Greater Philadelphia, Wynnewood and Argyle Rds, **Ardmore**, Ph: 642-7870.

Bookstores

Bala Judaica Center, 222 Bala Ave, **Bala-Cynwyd**, Ph: 664-1303.

Jerusalem Gift Shop, 7818 Castor Ave, Ph: 342-1452.

National Museum of Jewish History Museum Shop, Independence Mall E, Ph: 923-0262.

Rosenberg Hebrew Book Store, 409 Old York Rd, **Jenkintown**, Ph: 884-1728.

Rosenberg Hebrew Book Store, 6408 Castor Ave, Ph: 744-5205.

PHOENIXVILLE   Area Code (215)

Synagogues

Congregation B'nai Jacob Synagogue (C-US), Starr & Manovon Sts, Ph: 933-5550. Rabbi H. M. Kamsler. Services: Shabbat

PITTSBURGH   Area Code (412)   J-pop. 45,000

Synagogues

Adath Israel Congregation (O), 3257 Ward St, Ph: 682-6020. Services: Call for schedule.

Congregation Adath Jeshurun—Cneseth Israel (O-UOJC), 5643 E Liberty Blvd, Ph: 361-0176. Rabbi Dr. M. Landes. Services: Daily

Agudath Achim (C), United Jewish Community Center, Rte 51, **Beaver Falls**, Ph: 846-5696. Rabbi M. Asper. Services: Call for schedule.

Temple Beth Am (R), 1000 Watkins Ave, Ph: 684-8290. Services: Friday

Beth El Congregation of South Hills (C-US), 1900 Cochran Rd, Ph: 561-1168. Rabbi K. Stern. Services: Daily

Beth Hamedrash Hagadol—Beth Jacob (O), 1230 Colwell St, Ph: 471-4443. Rabbi S. Savage. Services: Shabbat

Beth Israel Center (C), 118 Gill Hall Rd, **Pleasant Hills**, Ph: 655-9806. Services: Friday

Beth Samuel Jewish Center (C), 810 Kennedy Dr, **Ambridge**, Ph: 266-5238. Rabbi S. Bell. Services: Call for schedule.

Congregation Beth Shalom (C-US), 5915 Beacon St, Ph: 421-2288. Rabbi S. Steindel. Services: Daily

Synagogues cont.

Congregation B'nai Emunoh (O-UOJC), 4315 Murray Ave, Ph: 521-1477. Rabbi J. Weiss. Services: Daily

Congregation B'nai Israel of East End (C-US), 327 N Negley Ave, Ph: 661-0252. Rabbi R. Marcovitz. Services: Daily

B'nai Zion Congregation (O), 6404 Forbes Ave, Ph: 521-1440. Services: Call for schedule.

Bohnei Yisrael/Young People's Synagogue (O), P.O. Box 8141, 15217, Ph: 521-6407. Services: Saturday

Temple David (R), 4415 Northern Pike, **Monroeville**, Ph: 372-1200. Rabbi J. Edelstein. Services: Friday

Temple Emanuel of South Hills (R-UAHC), 1250 Bower Hill Rd, Ph: 279-7600. Rabbi M. Mahler. Services: Friday

Congregation Kether Torah (O), 5706 Bartlett St, Ph: 521-9992. Rabbi E. Rosenblum. Services: Daily

Lubavitch Center Synagogue (O-Lubav), 2100 Wightman St, Ph: 422-7315 or Rabbi Y. Rosenfield, Ph: 421-8441. Services: Daily

New Light Congregation (C), 1700 Beechwood Blvd, Ph: 421-1017. Rabbi D. Lazar. Services: Shabbat and Sunday

Temple Ohav Shalom (R), 2201 Duncan Ave, **Allison Park**, Ph: 486-7374. Rabbi N. Klein. Services: Call for schedule.

Parkway Jewish Center—Shaar Ha-Shamayim (C-US), 300 Princeton Dr, Ph: 823-4338. Rabbi D. Rubin. Services: Shabbat

Congregation Poale Zedeck (O-UOJC), Phillips & Shady Aves, Ph: 421-9786. Rabbi Y. Miller. Services: Daily

Rodef Shalom Congregation (R-UAHC), 4905 5th Ave, Ph: 621-6566. Rabbi Dr. W. Jacob. Services: Shabbat, Wednesday and Thursday

Congregation Shaare Tefillah (O-UOJC), 5741 Bartlett St, Ph: 521-9911. Rabbi S. Kagan. Services: Daily

Congregation Shaare Torah (O-UOJC), 2319 Murray Ave, Ph: 421-8855. Rabbi Dr. B. Poupko and Rabbi M. Kletenik. Services: Daily

Temple Sinai (R-UAHC), 5505 Forbes Ave, Ph: 421-9715. Rabbi J. A. Gibson. Services: Friday

Torath Chaim Congregation (O), 728 N Negley Ave, Ph: 362-7736. Services: Daily

Congregation Tree of Life (C-US), Wilkins & Shady Aves, Ph: 521-6788. Rabbi A. Berkun. Services: Daily

Young Israel—Shaare Zedek (O-NCYI), 5751 Bartlett St, Ph: 421-7224. Rabbi C. Weiss. Services: Shabbat & Sunday

Eating Out

King David Restaurant, 2020 Murray Ave, Ph: 422-3370. Meals: l,d. Menu: (Glatt meat) Chinese and American. RS: Rabbinical Council of Pittsburgh. Closed Shabbat.

Yacov's Vegetarian Restaurant, 2109 Murray Ave, Ph: 421-7208. Meals: l,d. Menu: Dairy, vegetarian. RS: Rabbinical Council of Pittsburgh. Closed Shabbat.

Food

Brauner's Emporium, 2023 Murray Ave, Ph: 422-6100. Kosher gourmet specialties: candies, dried fruits, cheeses (some are cholov Yisroel), nuts, etc. Closed Shabbat.

Greenberg's Kosher Poultry, 2223 Murray Ave, Ph: 421-9455. Fresh meat (Glatt) and poultry. RS: Rabbi Dr. B. Poupko. Closed Shabbat.

Koshermart Inc., 2121 Murray Ave, Ph: 421-4450. Traditional kosher dishes, sandwiches and side dishes for take-out. Complete kosher grocery. RS: Rabbi I. Chinn. Closed Shabbat.

Pastries Unlimited, 2119 Murray Ave, Ph: 521-6323. Breads and pastries (pareve and dairy). RS: Rabbinical Council of Pittsburgh. Closed Shabbat.

Prime Kosher, 1916 Murray Ave, Ph: 421-1015. Meat, poultry and side dishes for take-out and complete kosher grocery. RS: Rabbi M. Kletenik. Closed Shabbat.

Accommodations

For private accommodations, contact:

Rabbi Y. Rosenfeld, Lubavitch Center, Ph: 422-7315 or 521-5119.

Rabbi M. Kletenik, Congregation Shaare Torah, Ph: 421-8855.

The following motels are thirty to forty minutes' walk from Congregation Shaare Torah:

Hampton Inn-Oakland, 3315 Hamlet, Ph: 681-1000.

Accommodations cont.

Holiday Inn University Center, 100 Lytton Ave, Ph: 682-6200.

Howard Johnson University Motel, 3401 Blvd of the Allies, Ph: 683-6100.

Mikvah

Jewish Women's League for Taharas Hamishpacha, 2336 Shady Ave. Call Mikvah office, Ph: 422-7110.

Day Schools

Community Day School (C), 6401 Forbes Ave, Ph: 521-5127.

Hillel Academy of Pittsburgh, 5685 Beacon St, Ph: 521-8131.

Yeshiva Achei Tmimim for Boys, Nechama Minsky School for Girls, 2100 Wightman St, Ph: 422-7779/7300.

Bookstore

Pinsker's, 2028 Murray Ave, Ph: 421-3033.

POTTSTOWN   Area Code (215)   J-pop. 700

Synagogues

Congregation Mercy & Truth (C-US), 575 N Keim St, Ph: 326-1717. Rabbi S. Shanken. Services: Daily

POTTSVILLE   Area Code (717)   J-pop. 250

Synagogues

Oheb Zedeck Community Center (C), 2300 Mahantongo St, Ph: 622-5890. Rabbi S. Hashash. Services: Shabbat

READING   Area Code (215)   J-pop. 2,800

Synagogues

Kesher Zion Synagogue (C-US), 1245 Perkiomen Ave, Ph: 374-1763. Rabbi J. Weintraub. Services: Daily

Temple Oheb Sholom (R-UAHC), Perkiomen & 13th St, Ph: 373-4623. Rabbi A. Weitzman. Services: Friday

Shomrei Habrith Congregation (O-UOJC), 2320 Hampton Blvd, Ph: 921-0881. Rabbi M. Eskowitz. Services: Shabbat, daily p.m.

404

Food

Giant Food Store Bakery, 1100 Rockland St, Ph: 921-2773. Breads
and challahs (pareve) and cakes (dairy). RS: Rabbi M. Eskowitz.

Giant Food Store Bakery, 2641 Shillington Rd, **West Reading**,
Ph: 678-3286. RS: Rabbi J. Weintraub (C) of Kesher Zion.

Pathmark, 4201 Perkiomen Ave, Ph: 779-7234. Some kosher baked
goods. RS: Rabbi J. Weintraub (C) of Kesher Zion.

RICHBORO (See PHILADELPHIA)

SCRANTON   Area Code (717)   J-pop. 3,150

Synagogues

Congregation Beth Shalom (O), Clay Ave & Vine St,
Ph: 346-0502. Rabbi A. Herman. Services: Daily

Temple Hesed (R-UAHC), Knox St & Lake Scranton Rd,
Ph: 344-7201. Rabbi S. Wylen, Rabbi M. Richman (Emeritus).
Services: Friday

Temple Israel (C-US), Monroe Ave & Gibbon St, Ph: 342-0350.
Rabbi Y. Rone. Services: Daily

Congregation Machzikeh Hadas (O-UOJC,NCYI), 901 Olive St,
Ph: 342-6271. Rabbi M. Fine. Services: Daily

Congregation Ohev Zedek (O), Prescott Ave & Mulberry St,
Ph: 343-2717. Rabbi M. Fine. Services: Saturday, Sunday a.m.

Yeshivath Beth Moshe (O), 930 Hickory St, Ph: 346-1747.
Services: Daily

Food

For kosher food information, call Scranton Orthodox Rabbinate:
Rabbi M. Fine, Ph: 342-6271 or Rabbi A. Herman,
Ph: 346-0502.

Ari's Pizza, Madison & Linden, Ph: 344-3638. Variety of pizzas to
take out. RS: Star-K. Closed Shabbat.

Community Bake Shop, 321 Lackawanna Ave, Ph: 346-7404.
Breads and pastries (pareve and dairy). RS: Rabbi M. Fine.

Giant Market, 320 Meadow Ave, Ph: 961-9030. Frozen Empire
products and other kosher items.

Food cont.

Linden Bake Shop, 422 S Main Ave, Ph: 343-8826. Challahs, breads and pastries (pareve and dairy) and pizza. Cholov Yisroel. RS: Rabbi A. Herman.

NGM Meat Market, 1502 Vine St, Ph: 342-3886. Meat (Glatt) and poultry; kosher frozen foods and groceries. RS: Scranton Orthodox Rabbinate. Closed Shabbat.

Yeshiva Bais Moshe, 930 Hickory St, Ph: 963-5699; if no answer call the pay phone, 961-8161. The yeshiva runs a kosher co-op selling cholov Yisroel and pas Yisroel products.

National Bakery, 1100 Capouse Ave, Ph: 343-1609 or 961-3945. Italian bakery. Breads, pastries (pareve and dairy). Pizza (cholov Yisroel). RS: Scranton Orthodox Rabbinate.

Accommodations

Royce Hotel, 700 Lackawanna Ave, Ph: 342-8300. Four blocks to Machzikeh Hadas; five blocks to Beth Shalom.

Sheraton Inn, 300 Meadow Ave, Ph: 344-9811. Four blocks to Yeshivath Beth Moshe.

For Shabbat hospitality, contact:

Rabbi A. Herman at Congregation Beth Shalom, Ph: 346-0502.

Rabbi M. Fine at Congregation Machzikeh Hadas, Ph: 342-6271.

Mikvah

Mikvah Yisroel of Scranton, 917 Gibson St. Contact Mrs. Rivka Gass, Ph: 344-5138. Also separate men's mikvah for daily use.

Day School

Scranton Hebrew Day School, 540 Monroe Ave, Ph: 346-1576.

SHAMOKIN   Area Code (717)

Synagogues

Congregation B'nai Israel (O), 3 E Sunbury St, Ph: 648-2281. Services: Shabbat

SHARON   Area Code (412)   J-pop. 260

Synagogues

Temple Beth Israel (R-UAHC), 840 Highland Rd, Ph: 346-4754.
Rabbi S. Sniderman. Services: Friday

SPRING HOUSE (See also PHILADELPHIA)   Area Code (215)

Synagogues

Congregation Beth Or (R-UAHC), Penllyn Pike & Dager Rd,
Ph: 646-5806. Rabbi G. S. Marx. Services: Shabbat

SPRINGFIELD (See also PHILADELPHIA)   Area Code (215)

Synagogues

Congregation Ner Tamid of Delaware County (C-US), 300 W
Woodland Ave, Ph: 543-4241. Rabbi R. Libowitz. Services:
Shabbat

STROUDSBURG   Area Code (717)   J-pop. 400

Synagogues

Temple Israel (C-US), 660 Wallace St, Ph: 421-8781. Rabbi
A. Berg. Services: Shabbat

SUNBURY   Area Code (717)   J-pop. 160

Synagogues

Congregation Beth El (C-US), 249 Arch St, Ph: 286-1127. Rabbi
D. Silverman. Services: Friday

UNIONTOWN   Area Code (412)   J-pop. 290

Synagogues

Temple Israel (R-UAHC), 119 E Fayette St, Ph: 437-6431. Rabbi
S. David. Services: Call for schedule.
Congregation Tree of Life (C-US), Pennsylvania Ave,
Ph: 438-0801. Services: Shabbat

UPPER DARBY (See PHILADELPHIA)

WALLINGFORD (See PHILADELPHIA)

WARRINGTON (See PHILADELPHIA)

WASHINGTON   Area Code (412)   J-pop. 250

Synagogues

Congregation Beth Israel (C-US), 265 North Ave, Ph: 225-7080.
Rabbi A. Goldman. Services: Shabbat

WEST CHESTER   Area Code (215)   J-pop. 300

Synagogues

Kesher Israel Congregation (Trad), 100 Pottstown Pike, Ph:
696-7210/1153. Rabbi M. Portal. Services: Shabbat and Sunday

WILKES-BARRE (See also KINGSTON)
Area Code (717)   J-pop. 3,500

Synagogues

Temple Israel (C-US), 239 S River, Ph: 824-8927. Rabbi
J. Michaels. Services: Daily
Congregation Ohav Zedek (O-UOJC), 242 S Franklin,
Ph: 825-6619. Rabbi Dr. M. J. Yeres. Services: Daily. (Branch
in **Kingston**)
United Orthodox Synagogue (O), 13 S Welles St, Ph: 824-1781.
Rabbi E. Freed. Services: Daily

Eating Out

Jewish Community Center Snack Bar, 60 S River St,
Ph: 824-4646. Meals: l. Menu: (Meat and dairy) Pizza, ham-
burgers, snack foods. RS: Vaad Hakashrus of Lucerne County.
Closed Shabbat.
Pennsak's Kosher Deli, 41 E North Hampton, Ph: 823-0764.
Meals: b,l,d. Menu: Meat and fish dishes and take-out. Also
kosher grocery. The owner, Mr. M. Pennsak, is a member of
Congregation Ohev Zedek.

Food (See **Kingston**)

408

Accomodations

Ramada Inn, Public Square, Ph: 824-7100. Walk to all three synagogues.

Genetti Best Western Motor Inn, Market & Pennsylvania Ave, Ph: 823-6152. Walk to all three synagogues.

Mikvah (See Kingston)

WILLIAMSPORT   Area Code (717)   J-pop. 415

Synagogues

Beth Hashalom (R), 425 Center St, Ph: 323-7751.

Congregation Ohev Shalom (C-US), 1501 Cherry St, Ph: 322-4209. Rabbi N. Singer. Services: Daily

Food

Giant Food Store, The Golden Strip, Ph: 326-6578. Best selection of kosher products.

Mikvah

Congregation Ohev Shalom, 1501 Cherry St. Contact Rabbi N. Singer, Ph: 322-7050.

WYNCOTE (See also PHILADELPHIA)   Area Code (215)

Synagogues

Temple Micah (R), 116 Greenwood Ave, Suite 300, Ph: 887-4300. Rabbi R. Alper.

Reconstructionist Congregation Or Hadash (Recon-FRCH), Church Rd and Greenwood Ave, Ph: 576-0800. Rabbi V. Schirn. Services: Friday and every other Saturday

WYNNEWOOD (See PHILADELPHIA)

YARDLEY (See also TRENTON, NJ)   Area Code (215)

Synagogues

Knesset Hasefer, Educational Synagogue of Yardley (O), 31 W College Ave, Ph: 493-0286. Rabbi T. Kilstein. Services: Shabbat

Synagogues cont.

Congregation Kol Emet (Recon-FRCH), 65 N Main St, Ph: 493-8522. Rabbi E. Weiner-Kaplow. Services at Friends Meeting Hall, 85 Main St: every other Friday

Day School

Abrams Hebrew Academy, 31 W College Ave, Ph: 493-1800.

YORK   Area Code (717)   J-pop. 1,500

Synagogues

Temple Beth Israel (R-UAHC), 2090 Hollywood Dr, Ph: 843-2676. Rabbi K. Cohen. Services: Friday
Congregation Ohev Sholom (C-US), 2251 Eastern Blvd, Ph: 755-2714. Rabbi A. Kogen. Services: Daily

Eating Out

Kaplan's Delicatessen & Meat Market, 2300 E Market St, Ph: 757-4025. Meals: b,l,d. Menu: Deli-style dishes; also fresh meat and poultry. RS: Rabbi K. Cohen.

Rhode Island

BARRINGTON   Area Code (401)

Synagogues

Temple Habonim (R-UAHC), 165 New Meadow, Ph: 245-6536. Rabbi J. Rosenberg. Services: Friday

BRISTOL   Area Code (401)

Synagogues

United Brothers Synagogue (C), 215 High St, Ph: 253-3460. Services: High Holidays

CRANSTON (See also PROVIDENCE) Area Code (401)

Synagogues

Temple Sinai (R-UAHC), 30 Hagan Ave, Ph: 942-8350. Rabbi
    G. Astrachan. Services: Shabbat
Temple Torat Yisrael (C-US), 330 Park Ave, Ph: 785-1800. Rabbi
    D. Rosen. Services: Daily

Food

Marty Weissman's Kosher Meat Market, 88 Rolfe St,
    Ph: 467-8903. Fresh meat, poultry and some frozen food. RS:
    Vaad Hakashrut of Rhode Island. Closed Shabbat.

KINGSTON Area Code (401)
Washington County J-pop. 1,200

Synagogues

B'nai B'rith Hillel Foundation at the University of Rhode Island, 34
    Lower College Rd, Ph: 792-2740. Rabbi R. Wolfgang, Director.
    Services: (Recon) Friday during the academic year. Dinner served
    afterwards. Call for information.

MIDDLETOWN (See also NEWPORT) Area Code (401)

Synagogues

Temple Shalom (C-US), Valley Rd, Ph: 846-9002. Rabbi
    M. Jagolinzer. Services: Shabbat

NARRAGANSETT Area Code (401)

Synagogues

Congregation Beth David (C), Kingstown Rd, Ph: 789-3437. Mr.
    A. Gabrilowitz, Pres. Services: Shabbat

NEWPORT Area Code (401) J-pop. 700

Synagogues

Touro Synagogue (O), 85 Touro St, Ph: 847-4794. Rabbi Dr.
    C. Shapiro. Services: Shabbat. Historic site.

Accommodations (See also **Providence**)

Newport Marriott, 25 America's Cup Ave, Ph: 849-1000. Two blocks from Touro Synagogue.

PAWTUCKET (See also **PROVIDENCE**) Area Code (401)

Synagogues

Congregation Ohawe Sholam (O-UOJC), 671 East Ave, Ph: 722-3146. Services: Daily

Accommodations

Private accommodations; call Congregation Ohawe Shalom, Ph: 722-3146.

Howard Johnson Motel, 2 George St, Ph: 723-6700. Walk to Congregation Ohawe Shalom.

PROVIDENCE Area Code (401)
Providence Area J-pop. 14,200

Synagogues

Temple Beth-El (R-UAHC), 70 Orchard Ave, Ph: 331-6070 or 521-0343. Rabbi L. Gutterman. Services: Daily

Congregation Beth Sholom—Sons of Zion (O-UOJC), 275 Camp St, Ph: 331-9393. Rabbi C. Marder. Services: Daily

Chabad House (O-Lubav), 48 Savoy St, Ph: 273-7238. Rabbi Y. Laufer. Services: Shabbat and Holidays

Temple Emanu-El (C-US), 99 Taft Ave, Ph: 331-1616. Rabbi W. Franklin. Services: Daily

Congregation Mishkon Tfiloh (O), 203 Summit Ave, Ph: 521-1616. Services: Shabbat

New England Academy of Torah (O), (High School), Blackstone Blvd, Ph: 331-5327. Services: Daily

Providence Hebrew Day School (O), 450 Elmgrove Ave, Ph: 331-5327. Rabbi S. Strajcher. Services: Daily

Congregation Shaare Zedek—Sons of Abraham (O-UOJC), 688 Broad St, Ph: 751-4936. Services: Daily

Congregation Sons of Jacob (O-UOJC), 24 Douglas Ave, Ph: 274-5260. Rabbi Y. Dubovick. Services: Daily

Eating Out

B'nai B'rith Hillel Foundation at Brown University, 80 Brown St,
Ph: 863-2805. Dinners are served Sunday through Thursday
from 5:30 until 6:30 during the academic year. RS: Rabbi Y.
Dubovick, Kosher Supervision of Rhode Island. Please call in
advance. Contact Elaine Strajcher, Ph: 751-1443 or 274-8017.

Café De-Lite, 758 Hope St, Ph: 454-5652. Meals: l,d. Menu:
(Dairy) Pizza (cholov Yisroel), lasagna, falafel, vegetarian
dishes, fish, soup, sandwiches, salads. Also take-out. Pas
Yisroel. RS: Kosher Supervision of Rhode Island. Closed
Shabbat.

Food

Catering by Elaine, 21 Lincoln Ave, Ph: 751-1443 or 274-8017.
Will prepare kosher dinners for travelers. Glatt meat. Baked
goods are Pas Yisroel. RS: Kosher Supervision of Rhode Island.
Closed Shabbat.

Davis Dairy, 721 Hope St, Ph: 331-4239. Complete kosher
grocery; pre-packaged meat and dairy products.

Kaplan's Bakery, 756 Hope St, Ph: 621-8107. Breads and pastries
(all pareve). RS: Rabbi C. Marder, Vaad Hakashrut of Rhode
Island.

Spiegel's Kosher Meats & Deli, 243 Reservoir Ave, Ph: 461-0425.
Fresh meat, poultry and deli. (Some Glatt available). Full kosher
grocery, hot sandwiches. RS: Vaad Hakashrut of Rhode Island.
Closed Shabbat.

Accommodations

Chabad House Jewish Hospitality Center, 360 Hope St,
Ph: 273-7238. Rooms for rent daily, weekly and weekends.
Kosher kitchen on premises.

Providence Marriott Hotel, Charles and Orms St, Ph: 272-2400.
Two blocks to Congregation Sons of Jacob.

For private hospitality; call the Providence Hebrew Day School,
Ph: 331-5327.

Mikvah

Mikvah, 401 Elmgrove Ave. Call Mrs. Ruth Weiner, Ph: 751-0025.

Day Schools

Alperin Schechter Day School (C), 99 Taft Ave, Ph: 421-5364.
Providence Hebrew Day School, 450 Elmgrove Ave, Ph: 331-5327.

Bookstore

Melzer's Hebrew Book Store, 97 Overhill Rd, Ph: 831-1710.
  Please call first.

WARWICK   Area Code (401)

Synagogues

Temple Am David (C-US), 40 Gardiner St, Ph: 463-7944. Rabbi
  H. White. Services: Daily

WESTERLY (See also NEW LONDON and NORWICH, CT)
Area Code (401)

Synagogues

Congregation Shaare Zedek (C), Union St. Contact J. Lewiss,
  President, Ph: 596-4621. Services: High Holidays

WOONSOCKET   Area Code (401)

Synagogues

Congregation B'nai Israel (C-US), 224 Prospect St, Ph: 762-3651.
  Rabbi M. Wasserman. Services: Daily

South Carolina

AIKEN   Area Code (803)

Synagogues

Congregation Adath Jeshurun (C), 154 Greenville St NW.
  President: Irene Rudnick, Ph: 648-5080 or 648-2565 (office).
  Services: first Friday, except summer

ANDERSON   Area Code (803)

Synagogues

Temple B'nai Israel (R-UAHC), Oakland Ave, Ph: 226-0310.
  Services: Friday

BEAUFORT   Area Code (803)

Synagogues

Congregation Beth Israel (C-US), Scott St, Ph: 524-9103.
  Services: Friday

CHARLESTON   Area Code (803)   J-pop. 4,000

Synagogues

Brith Sholom Beth Israel (O-UOJC), 182 Rutledge Ave,
  Ph: 577-6599. Rabbi D. Radinsky. Services: Daily
Synagogue Emanu-El (C-US), 5 Windsor Dr, Ph: 571-3264. Rabbi
  L. Rosenblum. Services: Daily
Kahal Kadosh Beth Elohim (R-UAHC), 86 Hasell St, Ph:
  723-1090. Rabbi W. Rosenthall. Services: Shabbat. Historic site.

Eating Out

Nosh with Josh, 217 Meeting St, Ph: 577-6674. Meals: b,l,d. Menu:
  (Dairy) Israeli, Mediterranean. Falafel, humous, salads, yogurt.
  RS: Rabbi D. Radinsky.

Food

Circus Donuts, 1091 Savannah Hwy, Ph: 571-2378. Donuts and
  coffee. RS: Rabbi D. Radinsky.
Lash Meat Market, 1107 King St, Ph: 577-6501. Fresh meat,
  poultry and deli. (Glatt on request). Full line of frozen kosher
  foods. RS: Rabbi D. Radinsky. Closed Shabbat.
South Windermere Piggly Wiggly, 74 Folly Rd, Ph: 571-1522. Full
  line of kosher groceries, packaged deli and Empire products.

Accommodations

Comfort Inn Riverview, 144 Bee St, Ph: 577-2224. Six blocks to
  Brith Sholom Beth Israel.

Accommodations cont.

Howard Johnson's, Spring St, Ph: 722-4000. Seven blocks to Brith
Sholom Beth Israel.

Sheraton Charleston Hotel, 170 Lockwood Pl, Ph: 723-3000. Eight
blocks to Brith Sholom Beth Israel.

(Downtown inns and hotels are one to two miles from Brith
Sholom Beth Israel)

Shabbat hospitality; call Brith Sholom Beth Israel, Ph: 577-6599.

Mikvah

Brith Sholom Beth Israel, 182 Rutledge Ave. Contact Rabbi
D. Radinsky, Ph: 577-6599.

Day School

Addlestone Hebrew Academy, 1639 Wallenberg Blvd,
Ph: 571-1105.

COLUMBIA   Area Code (803)   J-pop. 2,000

Synagogues

Congregation Beth Shalom (C-US), 5827 N Trenholm Rd,
Ph: 782-2500. Rabbi P. Silverstein. Services: Daily

Chabad House, 6338 Goldbranch Rd, Ph: 782-1831. Rabbi
N. Epstein. Services: Shabbat and Sunday a.m.

Tree of Life Congregation (R-UAHC), 2701 Heyward St,
Ph: 787-2182. Rabbi S. Marcus. Services: Friday

Accommodations

Shabbat hospitality; call Rabbi H. Epstein at Chabad House,
Ph: 782-1831.

FLORENCE   Area Code (803)   J-pop. 210

Synagogues

Temple Beth Israel (R-UAHC), 316 Park Ave, Ph: 669-9724. Rabbi
L. Mahrer. Services: Friday

416

GEORGETOWN   Area Code (803)

Synagogues

Temple Beth Elohim (R), Screven St. Services: Friday

GREENVILLE   Area Code (803)   J-pop. 800

Synagogues

Beth Israel Synagogue (C-US), 425 Summit Dr, Ph: 232-9031.
   Rabbi J. Futornick. Services: Shabbat
Temple of Israel (R-UAHC), 400 Spring Forest Rd, Ph: 292-1782.
   Rabbi J. Cohn. Services: Friday

KINGSTREE   Area Code (803)

Synagogues

Temple Beth Or (C), 107 Hirsch St, Ph: 354-6425. Services: Friday

MYRTLE BEACH   Area Code (803)   J-pop. 425

Synagogues

Chabad of Myrtle Beach, 2803 N Oak St, Ph: 448-0035. Rabbi
   J. Naparstek. Services: Saturday and daily a.m. Kiddush follows
   Shabbat services.

Accommodations

The following hotels and motels, among others, are within four
   blocks of Chabad of Myrtle Beach:
American Hotel, 2803 N Ocean Blvd, Ph: 448-7780.
Breakers Resort, 21st Ave N & Ocean Blvd, Ph: 626-5000.
Patricia Grand Hotel, 2710 N Ocean Blvd, Ph: 448-8453.
Sahara Motel, 2903 N Ocean Blvd, Ph: 448-6114.
Shangri-La Motel, 2700 N Kings Hwy, Ph: 448-6436.
Voyager Motel, 2904 N Kings Hwy, Ph: 448-3009.

Day School

The Chabad Academy, 2803 N Oak St, Ph: 448-0035.

417

SPARTANBURG   Area Code (803)   J-pop. 320

Synagogues

Temple B'nai Israel (C-US), 146 Heywood Ave, Ph: 582-2001.
  Rabbi R. Unger. Services: Friday

SUMTER   Area Code (803)   J-pop. 175

Synagogues

Congregation Sinai (R-UAHC), 11 Church St, Ph: 773-2122.
  Rabbi R. Leviton. Services: Friday

South Dakota

ABERDEEN   Area Code (605)

Synagogues

Congregation B'nai Isaac (C-US), 202 N Kline St, Ph: 225-3404
  or 225-7360. Services: Call for schedule.

RAPID CITY   Area Code (605)

Synagogues

Synagogue of the Hills, Main Chapel, Ellsworth Air Force Base,
  Ph: 385-1597 or Mr. S. Adelstein, Ph: 342-9524. Services: first
  and third Fridays

SIOUX FALLS   Area Code (605)   J-pop. 135

Synagogues

Mount Zion Temple (R-UAHC), 523 W 14th St, Ph: 338-5454.
  Services: Friday

Tennessee

CHATTANOOGA   Area Code (615)   J-pop. 2,000

Synagogues

Beth Sholom Synagogue (O-UOJC), 20 Pisgah Ave, Ph: 894-0801.
Rabbi E. Kay. Services: Shabbat and daily a.m.

B'nai Zion Synagogue (C-US), 114 McBrien Rd, Ph: 894-8900.
Rabbi R. Sherwin. Services: Daily

Congregation Mizpah (R-UAHC), 923 McCallie Ave,
Ph: 267-9771. Rabbi K. Kanter. Services: Shabbat

Food

Red Food Store, 5080 S Terrace (off Moore Rd exit of freeway),
Ph: 894-9451. Some kosher products, including packaged deli,
cheeses and Empire poultry.

Accommodations

Shoney's Inn, 5505 Brainerd Rd, Ph: 894-2040. Close to Beth
Sholom Synagogue.

Mikvah

Beth Sholom Congregation, 20 Pisgah Ave, Ph: 894-0801.

Day School

Chattanooga Jewish Day School, 5326 Lynnland Terrace,
Ph: 892-2337.

JACKSON   Area Code (901)   J-pop. 100

Synagogues

Congregation B'nai Israel (R-UAHC), Campbell & Grand,
Ph: 427-6141. Services: Friday

KNOXVILLE   Area Code (615)   J-pop. 1,350

Synagogues

Temple Beth El (R-UAHC), 3037 Kingston Pike, Ph: 524-3521.
Rabbi H. Simon. Services: Shabbat

Heska Amuna Congregation (C-US), 3811 Kingston Pike,
Ph: 522-0701. Rabbi A. Weiner. Services: Daily

Food

Harold's, 131 S Gay St, Ph: 523-5315. Kosher freezer section and
some kosher cheeses.

Kosher Karry Outs, 520 Cherokee Blvd, Ph: 522-1133. Challahs,
prepared dinners by Marion Goldstein. RS: Rabbi A. Weiner of
Heska Amuna. Please call first.

MEMPHIS   Area Code (901)   J-pop. 10,000

Synagogues

Congregation Anshei Sphard Beth El Emeth (O-UOJC), 120 E
Yates Road N, Ph: 682-1611. Rabbi A. M. Levin. Services: Daily

Baron Hirsch Synagogue (O-UOJC), 400 S Yates Rd,
Ph: 683-7486. Rabbi R. Grossman. Services: Daily

Congregation Beth Sholom (C-US), 482 S Mendenhall Rd,
Ph: 683-3591. Rabbi P. Light. Services: Daily

Temple Israel (R-UAHC), 1376 E Massey Rd, Ph: 761-3130. Rabbi
H. Danziger. Services: Shabbat

Eating Out

M. I. Gottlieb's Deli Restaurant, 5062 Park Ave, Ph: 763-3663.
Meals: l,d. Menu: (Meat) Hot dishes, salads, sandwiches,
desserts. RS: Rabbi N. Greenblatt. Closed Shabbat.

Rubenstein's Kosher Food, 4965 Summer Ave, Ph: 682-3801.
Meals: l. Menu: Sandwiches. RS: Vaad Hakahillos, Rabbi N.
Greenblatt. Closed Shabbat.

Food

Carl's Bakery, 1688 Jackson Ave, Ph: 276-2304. Breads & pastries (pareve). RS: Rabbi N. Greenblatt. Closed Monday and Shabbat.

Kroger's Supermarket, 540 Mendenhall Rd S, Ph: 683-8841. Large selection of kosher products, including Empire.

Piggly Wiggly, 888 White Station Rd, Ph: 767-0256. Some Empire products.

Rubenstein's Kosher Food, 4965 Summer Ave, Ph: 682-3801. Kosher grocery. Closed Shabbat.

Seesel's Supermarket, 576 S Perkins, Ph: 765-4880. Large selection of kosher products.

Mikvah

Congregation Anshei Sphard, 120 E Yates Road N. Call synagogue office, Ph: 682-1611.

Baron Hirsch Mikvah, 400 S Yates Rd. Call synagogue office, Ph: 683-7485.

Day Schools

Solomon Schechter Day School (C), 482 S Mendenhall Rd, Ph: 683-2313.

Memphis Hebrew Academy, Yeshiva of the South, 390 S White Station Rd, Ph: 682-2409.

NASHVILLE   Area Code (615)   J-pop. 5,520

Synagogues

Congregation Sherith Israel (O-UOJC), 3600 West End Ave, Ph: 292-6614. Rabbi Z. Posner. Services: Daily

The Temple—Congregation Ohabai Sholom (R-UAHC), 5015 Harding Rd, Ph: 352-7620. Rabbi B. Davidson and Rabbi S. Fuchs. Services: Shabbat

West End Synagogue—Khal Kadesh Adath Israel (C-US), 3814 W End Ave, Ph: 269-4592. Rabbi R. Roth. Services: Daily

Food

HG Hill, 4340 Harding Rd, Ph: 383-1482. Some Empire products.

Mikvah

Congregation Sherith Israel, 3600 W End Ave. Call Mrs. Posner,
   Ph: 385-3730.

Day School

Akiva School, 3600 West End Ave, Ph: 292-6614.

OAK RIDGE   Area Code (615)   J-pop. 200

Synagogues

Jewish Congregation of Oak Ridge (C-US), 101 W Madison Lane,
   Ph: 483-3581. Rabbi V. Rashkofsky. Services: Shabbat

Texas

ABILENE   Area Code (915)

Synagogues

Temple Mizpah (R-UAHC), 849 Chestnut St. Services: Call Dr.
   Herman Schaffer for schedule, Ph: 692-7141.

AMARILLO   Area Code (806)   J-pop. 190

Synagogues

Temple B'nai Israel (R-UAHC), 4316 Albert St, Ph: 352-7191.
   Rabbi J. Dobin. Services: Friday

ARLINGTON (See also DALLAS and FORT WORTH)

   Area Code (817)

Synagogues

Beth Shalom (R), 1211 Thannisch Dr, Ph: 860-5448. Rabbi K.
   Stern. Services: Friday

AUSTIN   Area Code (512)   J-pop. 5,000

Synagogues

Congregation Agudas Achim (C-US), 4300 Bull Creek Rd, Ph: 459-3287. Rabbi M. Sack. Services: Shabbat

Temple Beth Israel (R-UAHC), 3901 Shoal Creek Blvd, Ph: 454-6806. Rabbi L. Firestein. Services: Shabbat

B'nai B'rith Hillel Foundation at the Universiy of Texas-Austin (C, R), 2105 San Antonio, Ph: 476-0125. Services: Friday, when school is in session. Call for further information.

Chabad House—Jewish Student Center (O-Lubav), 2101 Nueces St, Ph: 472-3900. Rabbi Y. Levertov. Services: Shabbat

Food

Tom Thumb, 5311 Balcones Dr, Ph: 452-9497. Some kosher products, including frozen Empire poultry.

Accommodations

Private accommodations for Shabbat; call Rabbi Y. Levertov at Chabad House, Ph: 472-3900.

Mikvah

Mikvah at Chabad House, 2101 Nueces St, Ph: 478-8222.

BEAUMONT   Area Code (409)   J-pop. 800

Synagogues

Temple Emanuel (R-UAHC), 1120 Broadway, Ph: 832-6131. Rabbi P. Hyman. Services: Shabbat

CORPUS CHRISTI   Area Code (512)   J-pop. 1,400

Synagogues

Temple Beth El (R-UAHC), 4402 Saratoga, Ph: 857-8181. Rabbi S. Wolf. Services: Friday

Congregation B'nai Israel (C-US), 3434 Fort Worth Ave, Ph: 855-7308. Rabbi L. Heim. Services: Shabbat, Monday and Thursday

DALLAS Area Code (214) J-pop. 34,000

For kosher food information, call the Vaad Hakashrus of Dallas,
Rabbi D. Shawel, Administrator, Ph: 750-8223.

Synagogues

Congregation Anshai Emet (C), 1301 Custer Rd #1810, **Plano,**
Ph: 578-9903. Services: Shabbat

Congregation Beth Emunah (C), 3401 Conflans Rd, **Irving,**
Ph: 790-3868. Rabbi S. Groesberg. Services: Saturday

Beth Torah (C-US), 720 Lookout Dr, **Richardson**, Ph: 234-1542.
Rabbi J. Leynor. Services: Shabbat

Chabad House (O-Lubav), 7008 Forest Lane, Ph: 361-8600. Rabbi
M. Dubrawsky. Services: Daily

Temple Emanu-El (R-UAHC), 8500 Hillcrest Rd, Ph: 368-3613.
Rabbi S. Zimmerman. Services: Shabbat

Forest Lane Shul (O-Lubav), 7008 Forest Lane, Ph: 361-8600.
Rabbi M. Dubrawsky. Services: Daily

Congregation Ner Tamid (R), 4443 N Josey, **Carrollton,**
Ph: 416-9738. Rabbi N. Kasten. Services: Friday

Congregation Ohev Shalom (O), 6959 Arapaho #575,
Ph: 991-6115 or 701-8433. Rabbi A. Rodin. Shabbat, Monday
and Thursday

Congregation Shaare Tefilla (O-UOJC), 6131 Churchill Way,
Ph: 661-0127. Rabbi H. Wolk. Services: Daily.

Temple Shalom (R-UAHC), 6930 Alpha Rd, Ph: 661-1810. Rabbi
K. Roseman. Services: Friday

Shearith Israel (C-US), 9401 Douglas Ave, Ph: 361-6606. Rabbi J.
Ofseyer. Services: Daily

Congregation Tiferet Israel (Trad), 10909 Hillcrest Rd,
Ph: 691-3611. Rabbi S. Weiss. Services: Daily

Young Israel of Dallas (O-Sephardic), 1450 Preston Forest Square,
Ph: 386-7162. Rabbi D. Shawel. Services: Shabbat and Sunday.

Eating Out

J.C.C. Kosher Kids' Café, 7900 Northaven Rd, Ph: 739-2737.
Meals: l. Menu: Hamburgers, hot dogs (Glatt on request).
Sundays (closed summers).

Reichman's Kosher Meat & Delicatessen, 7517 Campell Rd, Ph: 248-3773. Meals: b,l,d. Menu: Deli-style food, sandwiches. RS: Dallas Vaad Hakashrut. Closed Shabbat.

Food

Most supermarkets are well-stocked with kosher products.

Highland Park Bakery breads (with Vaad Hakashrus of Dallas label only) are available at Tom Thumb Supermarkets.

Preizler's Bakery, 116 Preston Valley Shopping Center, Ph: 458-8896. Take-out deli, fish, appetizers, breads and pastries. RS: Vaad Hakashrut. Closed Shabbat.

Reichman's Kosher Meat & Delicatessen, 7517 Campell Rd, Ph: 248-3773. Fresh meat and poultry, kosher grocery and deli-style food to go. RS: Vaad Hakashrut. Closed Shabbat.

Tom Thumb Bakery & Kosher Deli, in Tom Thumb Supermarket, 11920 Preston Rd, Ph: 392-2501. Bakery: breads and rolls (pareve), cakes and pastries (as marked). All packages must be sealed with Vaad label. Separate kosher deli (Glatt meat): all sandwiches and trays must be sealed with Vaad label. RS: Vaad Hakashrus of Dallas. This supermarket has a large selection of other kosher products.

Accommodations

Preston Suites Hotel, 6104 LBJ Freeway (corner Preston), Ph: 458-2626. Suites with kitchens. One mile from Shaare Tefilla.

Private accommodations:

Rabbi D. Jacobson at Akiba Academy, Ph: 239-7248;

Rabbi H. Wolk at Shaare Tefilla, Ph: 661-0217;

Shabbat hospitality; Rabbi M. Dubrawsky, Chabad Lubavitch, Ph: 361-8600.

Mikvah

The Mikvah Society, Congregation Tiferet Israel, 10909 Hillcrest, Ph: 368-1787 or 691-3611.

Day Schools

Akiba Academy, 6210 Churchill Way, Ph: 239-7248.

Day Schools cont.

Solomon Schechter Academy (C), 18011 Hillcrest Rd,
Ph: 248-3032.

EL PASO   Area Code (915)   J-pop. 4,800

Synagogues

Congregation B'nai Zion (C-US), 805 Cherry Hill Lane,
Ph: 833-2222. Rabbi S. Leon. Services: Daily

Chabad House (O-Lubav), 6505 Westwind Dr, Ph: 584-8218.
Rabbi I. Grinberg. Services: Shabbat.

Temple Mount Sinai (R-UAHC), 4408 N Stanton, Ph: 532-5959.
Rabbi K. Weiss. Services: Shabbat

Eating Out

Alex's Meat Market and Delicatessen, 1000 Wyoming St, Ph:
533-8524. Meals: b,l,d. Menu: Meat, dairy and fish. RS: Rabbi
S. Leon. Separate service for meat and dairy. Closed Shabbat.

Food

Lomart, 6600 N Mesa, Ph: 854-3731. Sinai 48 meat, Empire
products, kosher cheeses.

Accommodations

For private accommodations, contact Congregation B'nai Zion,
Ph: 833-2222.

For a Shabbat meal, call Rabbi I. Grinberg, Chabad House,
Ph: 833-5711.

Mikvah

Chabad Mikvah, 6505 Westwind Dr. Call Chana Grinberg,
Ph: 584-8218.

Day School

El Paso Hebrew Day School, 805 Cherry Hill Lane, Ph: 833-0808.

FORT WORTH   Area Code (817)   J-pop. 5,000

Synagogues

Congregation Ahavath Shalom (C), 4050 S Hulen, Ph: 731-4721. Rabbi A. Stiebel. Services: Daily

Congregation Beth-El (R-UAHC), 207 W Broadway, Ph: 332-7141. Rabbi R. Mecklenburger. Services: Friday

Day School

Fort Worth Hebrew Day School (Unaffiliated), 6795 Dan Danciger Rd, Ph: 370-0777.

GALVESTON   Area Code (409)   J-pop. 800

Synagogues

Congregation Beth Jacob (C-US), 2401 Ave K, Ph: 762-7267. Rabbi H. Trusch. Services: Daily

Temple B'nai Israel (R-UAHC), 3008 Ave O, Ph: 765-5796. Rabbi J. Kessler. Services: Shabbat

HOUSTON   Area Code (713)   J-pop. 42,000

Synagogues

Congregation Beth Am (C-US), 1431 Brittmoore Rd, Ph: 461-7725. Services: Shabbat

Congregation Beth El (R), 2200 Farm Market #1092, **Missouri City**, Ph: 980-1310. Services: Friday

Congregation Beth Israel (R-UAHC), 5600 N Braeswood Blvd, Ph: 771-6221. Rabbi S. Karff. Services: Shabbat

Congregation Beth Rambam (O), 11333 Braesridge, Ph: 723-3030. Services: Shabbat

Congregation Beth Shalom (R-UAHC), P.O. Box 7711, **The Woodlands**, 77387, Ph: 363-4090. Rabbi T. Sanders. Services: First and third Fridays

Congregation Beth Yeshurun (C-US), 4525 Beechnut Blvd, Ph: 666-1881. Rabbi J. Segal. Services: Daily

Congregation Brith Shalom (C-US), 4610 Bellaire Blvd, Ph: 667-9201. Rabbi S. Osadchey. Services: Shabbat and Sunday

Synagogues cont.

Chabad House at Texas Medical Center, 1955 University Blvd, Ph: 522-2004. Rabbi M. Traxler. Services: Shabbat and Holidays

Chabad Lubavitch Center (O-Lubav), 10900 Fondren Rd, Ph: 777-2000. Rabbi S. Lazaroff. Services: Daily

Congregation Emanu El (R-UAHC), 1500 Sunset Blvd, Ph: 529-5771. Rabbi R. Walter. Services: Shabbat

Congregation Jewish Community North (R-UAHC), 18519 Klein Church Rd, **Spring**, Ph: 376-0016. Rabbi R. Sharff. Services: Friday

Congregation for Reform Judaism (R-UAHC), 801 Bering Dr, Ph: 782-4162. Rabbi M. Brownstein. Services: Friday

Congregation Shaar Hashalom (C-US), 16020 El Camino Real, Ph: 488-5861. Rabbi S. Levy. Services: Shabbat

Congregation Shaarei Tsedek (Unaffiliated), 15825 Memorial Dr, Ph: 556-6952. Rabbi E. Treister. Services: first and third Fridays; second and fourth Saturdays

Temple Sinai (Trad), 783 Country Place Dr, Ph: 496-5950. Rabbi H. Rabinowitz. Services: Friday

United Orthodox Synagogues (O-UOJC), 4221 S Braeswood, Ph: 723-3850. Rabbi J. Radinsky. Services: Daily

Young Israel of Houston (O-NCYI), 11523 Bob White St, Ph: 729-0719. Rabbi Y. Wender. Services: Daily

Eating Out

Mama's & Papa's Snack Bar, Jewish Community Center, 5601 S Braeswood Blvd, Ph: 729-3200. Meals: b,l.d. Menu: Israeli dishes, hamburgers, hot dogs. RS: Vaad Hakashrut of Houston. Closed Shabbat.

Simon's Gourmet Kosher Foods, 5411 S Braeswood Blvd, Ph: 729-5333. Meals: l,d. Menu: (Glatt meat) Deli and entrees. Also take-out. RS: Vaad Hakashrut of Houston. Closed Shabbat.

Wonderful Vegetarian Restaurant, 7549 Westheimer, Ph: 977-3137. Meals: l,d. Menu: Large variety of vegetarian dishes made with tofu. RS: Vaad Hakashrut of Houston. Closed Monday.

Food

Ashcraft Bakery, 1301 N 1st, **Bellaire**. Breads and pastries. RS: Vaad Hakashrut of Houston.

Belden Supermarket, Chimney Rock & N Braeswood, Ph: 723-5670. Large selection of kosher items, including packaged meats and Cholov Yisroel products.

Bubbie & Zaida's Brick Oven, 3601 Westheimer, Ph: 622-4357. Montreal style bagel shop. RS: Vaad Hakashrut of Houston.

Le Moulin European Bakery, 5645 Beechnut, Ph: 779-1678. Breads, pastries and cakes. RS: Vaad Hakashrut of Houston.

New York Bagel, 9724 Hillcroft, Ph: 723-5879. Bagels and breads. RS: Vaad Hakashrut of Houston.

Randall's Supermarket Bakeries, S Post Oak & Bellfort, Ph: 771-8991; Fondren & Bissonet, Ph: 271-0250; Gessner & W Bellfort, Ph: 771-8991. Breads and cakes (pareve and dairy) RS: Vaad Hakashrut of Houston.

Simon's Gourmet Kosher Foods, 5411 S Braeswood Blvd, Ph: 729-5333. Fresh meat (Glatt) and poultry, prepared meat and poultry dishes, appetizers, salads and groceries. RS: Vaad Hakashrut of Houston. Closed Shabbat.

Three Brothers Bakery, 4036 S Braeswood Blvd, Ph: 666-2551. Breads and pastries. RS: Vaad Hakashrut of Houston.

Accommodations

Private accommodations:
Chabad House, Ph: 522-2004.
Rabbi J. Radinsky, United Orthodox Synagogue, Ph: 723-3850.
Young Israel of Houston, Ph: 729-0719.

Mikvah

Mikvah Taharas Yisrael, 10900 Fondren Rd. Contact Rebbitzin Lazaroff, Ph: 777-2000 (day), 981-1000 (evening).
United Orthodox Synagogue, 9001 Greenwillow, Ph: 723-3850.

Day Schools

Hebrew Academy of Houston, 5435 S Braeswood, Ph: 723-7170.

Day Schools cont.

The Irvin M. Schlenker School of Congregation Beth Israel (R), 5600 N. Braeswood Blvd, Ph: 270-6127.

Torah Day School of Houston (Lubavitch), 10900 Fondren Rd, Ph: 777-2000.

LAREDO   Area Code (512)   J-pop. 200

Synagogues

Congregation Agudas Achim (C-US), 1301 Malinche Ave, Ph: 723-4435. Rabbi H. Leiberman. Services: Shabbat

LONGVIEW   Area Code (903)   J-pop. 200

Synagogues

Temple Emanu-el (R-UAHC), 1205 Eden Dr, Ph: 753-6512. Rabbi B. Honan. Services: Friday

LUBBOCK   Area Code (806)   J-pop. 225

Synagogues

Temple Shaareth Israel (R-UAHC), 7111 82nd St, Ph: 794-7517. Rabbi S. Stein. Services: Friday

McALLEN   Area Code (512)   J-pop. 475

Synagogues

Temple Emanuel (R-UAHC), 1803 N Main, Ph: 686-9432. Rabbi J. Elson. Services: Friday

SAN ANGELO   Area Code (915)   J-pop. 100

Synagogues

Congregation Beth Israel (C), 1825 W Beauregard, Ph: 655-6781. Services: Friday

SAN ANTONIO   Area Code (512)   J-pop. 9,000

Synagogues

Congregation Agudas Achim (C-US), 1201 Donaldson Ave, Ph: 736-4216. Rabbi R. Spiegel. Services: Daily

Temple Beth-El (R-UAHC), 211 Belknap Pl, Ph: 733-9135. Rabbi:
Dr. S. Stahl. Services: Shabbat

Congregation Rodfei Sholom (O-UOJC), 3003 Sholom Blvd,
Ph: 493-3557. Rabbi A. Scheinberg. Services: Daily

Food

DELIcious Foods, 7460 Callaghan Rd, Suite 300, Ph: 366-1844.
Bakery: challah, breads, bagels, cakes (mostly pareve).
Delicatessen, sandwiches, frozen meats, kosher groceries.
RS: Rabbi A. Scheinberg. Closed Shabbat.

Pen Food Bakery, 8101 Callaghan Rd, Ph: 349-3671. All bakery
products kosher (pareve and dairy). RS: Rabbi A. Scheinberg
(bakery only). Also frozen kosher packaged foods.

Accommodations

For a Shabbat meal, contact Rabbi C. Block, Chabad House,
Ph: 735-4656 or Rabbi A. Scheinber, Rodfei Sholom,
Ph: 493-3557.

Mikvah

Congregation Rodfei Sholom, 3003 Sholom Blvd, Ph: 493-3557
(days) or call Mrs. Scheinberg, Ph: 492-3979 (evenings).

Day School

Jonathan Netanyahu Academy, 103 E Rampart Dr, Ph: 341-0735.

Bookstore

L'Chayim Gift Shop, Magic Court Center, 7460 Callaghan Rd #310,
Ph: 341-5045.

SHERMAN   Area Code (903)   J-pop. 125

Synagogues

Temple Beth Emeth (R-UAHC), 304 N Rusk St, Ph: 892-9326.
  Services: Friday

TEXARKANA   Area Code (903)

Synagogues

Temple Sinai (R-UAHC), 1310 Walnut St, Ph: 792-2394.
  Services: Friday

TYLER   Area Code (903)   J-pop. 450

Synagogues

Congregation Ahavas Achim (C-US), 3501 S Donnybrook St,
  Ph: 561-4284. Rabbi A. W. Flicker. Services: Shabbat
Temple Beth El (R-UAHC), 1102 S Augusta Ave, Ph: 597-2917.
  Rabbi S. Gold. Services: Friday

VICTORIA   Area Code (512)

Synagogues

Temple B'nai Israel (R-UAHC), 606 N Main, Ph: 578-5140.
  Services: Friday

WACO   Area Code (817)   J-pop. 500

Synagogues

Congregation Agudath Jacob (C), 4925 Hillcrest Dr, Ph: 772-1451.
  Rabbi R. Aronowitz. Services: Call for schedule.
Temple Rodef Sholom (R-UAHC), 1717 N New Rd, Ph: 754-3703.
  Rabbi J. Taub. Services: Call for schedule.

Utah

OGDEN   Area Code (801)

Synagogues

Congregation B'rith Sholem (C), 2750 Grant Ave, Ph: 621-3729.
  Services: Friday

SALT LAKE CITY   Area Code (801)

Synagogues

Chavurah B'yachad (Recon-FRCH), 509 E Northmont Way,
  Ph: 364-7060. Services: Call for schedule.
Congregation Kol Ami (C-US, R-UAHC), 2425 E Heritage Way,
  Ph: 484-1501. Rabbi F. Wenger. Services: Friday (R),
  Saturday (C)

Vermont

BENNINGTON   Area Code (802)   J-pop. 100

Synagogues

Congregation Beth El (Unaffiliated), North St and Adams,
  President: Patricia Barr, Ph: 447-0543. Services: Friday, once a
  month. (Schedule is posted in Spice N' Nice, 223 North St.)

BRATTLEBORO   Area Code (802)   J-pop. 150

Synagogues

Brattleboro Area Jewish Community (Unaffiliated), Meets at West
  Village Meeting House, South St W, West Brattleboro,
  Ph: 257-1959. Rabbi S. Freeman. Services: Call for information.

BURLINGTON   Area Code (802)   J-pop. 3,000

Synagogues

Congregation Lubavitch (O-Lubav), 317 Maple St, Ph: 865-2770 or
  658-7612. Rabbi Y. Raskin. Services: Saturdays and Holidays

Synagogues cont.

Congregation Ohavi Zedek (C-US), 188 N Prospect St, Ph: 864-0218. Rabbi M. Wall. Services: Saturday

Temple Sinai (R-UAHC), 899 Dorset St, **South Burlington**, Ph: 862-5125. Rabbi J. Glazier. Services: Friday

Food

Grand Union, 516 Shelburne Rd, Ph: 863-8260. Carries Empire frozen chickens.

Martin's Foods, 217 Dorset St, University Mall, Ph: 863-6311. Carries Empire frozen chickens.

Accommodations

Private hospitality; call Rabbi Y. Raskin, Ph: 658-7612.

Mikvah

Mikvah Chaya Muschka, 221 Summit St. Contact Mrs. Z. Raskin, Ph: 865-2770.

MANCHESTER   Area Code (802)

Synagogues

Israel Congregation (Unaffiliated), Rte 7A N, Ph: 362-4578. Rabbi M. Cohen. Services: Shabbat

MONTPELIER   Area Code (802)   Montpelier-Barre J-pop. 500

Synagogues

Beth Jacob Synagogue (Unaffiliated), 10 Harrison Ave, Ph: 229-9429. Services: Friday; two Saturdays a month and Holidays

RUTLAND   Area Code (802)   J-pop. 550

Synagogues

Rutland Jewish Center (C-US), 96 Grove St, Ph: 773-3455. Rabbi S. Goldberg. Services: Shabbat

Food

Grand Union, N Main St, Ph: 775-6984. Empire frozen poultry.
Price Chopper, Merchant's Row, Ph: 775-5933. Carries Empire
frozen poultry and other Empire products.

Virginia

Jewish Information & Referral Service: (301) 770-4848

ALEXANDRIA   Area Code (703)   J-pop. (Alexandria, Falls Church, Arlington and Fairfax Counties) 35,100

Synagogues

Agudas Achim Congregation (C-US), 2908 Valley Dr,
Ph: 243-3382. Rabbi J. Moline. Services: Shabbat
Beth El Hebrew Congregation (R-UAHC), 3830 Seminary Rd,
Ph: 370-9400. Rabbi J. Kraus. Services: Shabbat

ARLINGTON   Area Code (703)

Synagogues

Arlington-Fairfax Jewish Congregation (C-US), 2920 Arlington
Blvd, Ph: 979-4466. Rabbi Dr. M. Bash. Services: Daily

CHARLOTTESVILLE   Area Code (804)   J-pop. 950

Synagogues

Temple Beth Israel (R-UAHC), 301 E Jefferson St, Ph: 295-6382.
Rabbi D. S. Alexander. Services: Shabbat
B'nai B'rith Hillel Foundation at the University of Virginia (C, R),
1824 University Circle, Ph: 295-4963. Services: Friday, during
the academic year

Eating Out

B'nai B'rith Hillel Foundation at the University of Virginia, 1824
University Circle, Ph: 295-4963. Friday night dinner is served
every week during the academic year. Call for information.

Food

Giant Supermarket, Seminole Square, Ph: 973-7860. Good selection of kosher products, including Empire.

DANVILLE   Area Code (804)   J-pop. 100

Synagogues

Beth Sholom Temple (R-UAHC), 127 Sutherlin Ave, Ph: 792-3489. Rabbi A. Ponn. Services: Friday

FAIRFAX   Area Code (703)

Synagogues

Chabad Lubavitch of Northern Virginia, 3976 Bradwater St, Ph: 764-0239. Rabbi S. Deutsch. Services: Saturday
Congregation Olam Tikvah (C-US), 3800 Glenbrook Rd, Ph: 425-1880. Rabbi Y. Klirs. Services: Daily

FALLS CHURCH   Area Code (703)

Synagogues

Temple Rodef Shalom (R-UAHC), 2100 Westmoreland St, Ph: 532-2217. Rabbi L. Berkowits. Services: Shabbat

FREDERICKSBURG   Area Code (703)   J-pop. 140

Synagogues

Beth Sholom Temple (R-UAHC), 515 Charlotte St, Ph: 373-4834. Services: Friday

HAMPTON   Area Code (804)

Synagogues

B'nai Israel Congregation (Trad), 3116 Kecoughtan Rd, Ph: 722-0100. Rabbi N. Golner. Services: Shabbat and Sunday a.m.
Temple Rodef Sholom (C-US), 318 Whealton Rd, Ph: 826-5894. Rabbi S. Lindemann. Services: Daily

436

Food

Food Carnival, 608 E Mercury Blvd, Ph: 723-0771. Empire
products.

HARRISONBURG   Area Code (703)

Synagogues

Temple Beth-El (R-UAHC), Old Furnace Rd, Ph: 434-2744. Rabbi
L. Rappaport. Services: Friday

LYNCHBURG   Area Code (804)

Synagogues

Agudath Sholom Congregation (R-UAHC), 2055 Langhorne Rd,
Ph: 846-0739. Rabbi M. Shapiro. Services: Friday

MARTINSVILLE   Area Code (703)

Synagogues

Congregation Ohev Zion (R-UAHC), 801 Parkview Ave,
Ph: 632-2828. Services: Friday

NEWPORT NEWS   Area Code (804)
J-pop. (including Hampton and Williamsburg) 2,500

Synagogues

Congregation Adath Jeshurun (O-UOJC), 12646 Nettles Dr,
Ph: 930-0820. Rabbi E. Weinbach. Services: Daily
Temple Sinai (R-UAHC), 11620 Warwick Blvd, Ph: 596-8352.
Rabbi M. Golub. Services: Friday

Eating Out

Adath Jeshurun, 12646 Nettles Dr, Ph: 930-0820. Tuesday 5 to 9
p.m. (Bingo night). Meat and pareve snacks are available.
RS: Rabbi E. Weinbach.

Food

Not Just Bagels, 1159 J. Clyde Morris, Newport Square,
Ph: 599-3556. RS: Rabbi E. Weinbach (bagels, bread and
muffins only).

Food cont.

Superfresh Supermarket, 11008 Warwick Blvd, Ph: 596-5305. Good selection of kosher products.

Warwick Bakery, 240 31st St, Ph: 244-1362. Breads and pastries. RS: Rabbi E. Weinbach. Closed Shabbat.

Accommodations

Private accommodations; call Rabbi E. Weinbach at Congregation Adath Jeshurun, Ph: 930-0820 or 930-3385 (home).

Mikvah

Congregation Adath Jeshurun, 12646 Nettles Dr, Ph: 599-0820. Call in advance.

NORFOLK   Area Code (804)
J-pop. (including Virginia Beach and Portsmouth) 18,000

For kosher food information, call Rabbi S. Goder, Rabbinic Administrator, Vaad Hakashrus of Tidewater, Ph: 627-7358.

Synagogues

Congregation Beth El (C-US), 422 Shirley Ave, Ph: 625-7821. Rabbi A. Ruberg. Services: Daily

Congregation B'nai Israel (O-UOJC), 420 Spotswood Ave, Ph: 627-7358. Rabbi S. Goder. Services: Daily

Temple Israel (C-US), 7255 Granby St, Ph: 489-4550. Rabbi S. Altshuler. Services: Daily

Temple Ohef Sholom (R-UAHC), 530 Raleigh Ave, Ph: 625-4295. Rabbi L. Forman. Services: Shabbat

Food

Farm Fresh Supermarkets, 201 W 21st St, Ph: 623-5933; 1300 Colonial Ave, Ph: 623-9889. Good selection of kosher items, including Empire frozen poultry.

Something Special Bakery, 118 W Little Creek Rd, Ph: 489-2365. Challahs, cakes, pastries (pareve and dairy). RS: Vaad Hakashras of Tidewater.

Superfresh at Ward's Corner, 7635 Granby St, Ph: 423-1766. Good selection of kosher items, including Empire frozen poultry.

Accommodations

Hospitality: call Congregation B'nai Israel, Ph: 627-7358.

Madison Hotel, 345 Granby St, Ph: 622-6682. About a mile from
    Congregation B'nai Israel.

Mikvah

Congregation B'nai Israel, 420 Spotswood Ave, Ph: 627-7358
    (days); or Mrs. Mitzi Berman, Ph: 627-1997 (evenings).

PETERSBURG   Area Code (804)   J-pop. 550

Synagogues

Congregation Brith Achim (C-US), 314 South Blvd, Ph: 732-3968.
    Rabbi O. Fleishaker. Services: Shabbat

PORTSMOUTH   Area Code (804)   J-pop. 1,900

Synagogues

Congregation Gomley Chesed (C-US), 3110 Sterling Point Dr,
    Ph: 484-1019. Rabbi P. Krohn. Services: Daily
Temple Sinai (R-UAHC), 4401 Hatton Point Dr, Ph: 484-1730.
    Rabbi A. Steinberg. Services: Friday

RESTON   Area Code (703)

Synagogues

Beth Emeth (C-US), 12523 Lawyers Rd, Ph: 860-4515. Services:
    Shabbat
Northern Virginia Hebrew Congregation (R-UAHC), 1441 Wiehle
    Ave, Ph: 437-7733. Rabbi R. Gold. Services: Friday

RICHMOND   Area Code (804)   J-pop. 8,000

Synagogues

Congregation Beth Ahaba (R-UAHC), 1111 W Franklin St,
    Ph: 358-6757. Rabbi J. Spiro. Services: Shabbat
Temple Beth-El (C-US), 3330 Grove Ave, Ph: 355-3564. Rabbi Dr.
    M. Berman. Services: Shabbat

Synagogues cont.

Keneseth Beth Israel Congregation (O-UOJC), 6300 Patterson Ave, Ph: 288-7953. Rabbi D. Gorelick. Services: Daily

Lubavitch Center (O-Lubav), 212 Gaskins Rd, Ph: 740-2000. Rabbi Y. Kranz. Services: Daily

Congregation Or Ami (R-UAHC), 3406 Huguenot Rd, Ph: 272-0017. Rabbi J. Spiro. Services: Friday

Congregation Or Atid (C-US), 501 Parham Rd, Ph: 740-4747. Rabbi J. Chazin. Services: Shabbat

Young Israel of Richmond-Kol Emes (O-UOJC), 4811 Paterson Ave, Ph: 353-5831. Services: Daily

Food

Nick's, 1911 W Main St, Ph: 359-0842. Full line of kosher products including frozen chicken and wines.

Ukrop's Supermarket, Gayton Crossing Shopping Center, Ph: 740-9167. Good selection of kosher products.

Accommodations

Lubavitch Retreat and Hotel Center, 212 Gaskins Rd, Ph: 740-2000. Meals: b, box lunch, d. Shabbat hotel and meal package available.

Private accommodations; call Keneseth Beth Israel, Ph: 288-7953.

Mikvah

Young Israel—Kol Emes, 4811 Patterson Ave. Contact Mrs. C. Buehler, Ph: 288-8816.

Day School

The Joseph and Fannie Rudlin Torah Academy, 6801 Patterson Ave, Ph: 288-7610.

ROANOKE   Area Code (703)   J-pop. 1,050

Synagogues

Beth Israel Synagogue (C-US), 920 Franklin Rd SW, Ph: 343-0289. Rabbi J. Fox. Services: Shabbat, Monday, and Thursday

Temple Emanuel (R-UAHC), 1163 Persinger Rd SW, Ph: 342-3378. Rabbi F. Muller. Services: Friday

Food

Harris Teeter, Towers Mall, 2121 Colonial Ave SW, Ph: 342-1017. Empire frozen poultry.

Kroger Cave Spring, Brambleton Ave, Cave Spring corners, Ph: 774-0861. Empire frozen poultry.

SPRINGFIELD   Area Code (703)

Synagogues

Congregation Adat Reyim (C), 6500 Westbury Oaks Ct, Ph: 455-1444. Rabbi Z. Porath. Services: Shabbat and Holidays

Eating Out

Hunan Gourmet, 7081 Brookfield Plaza, Ph: 451-1213/1960. Meals: l,d. Menu: (Meat) Chinese. Amex, MC, V. RS: Star-K of Baltimore. Closed Shabbat.

STAUNTON   Area Code (703)   J-pop. 375

Synagogues

Temple House of Israel (R), 19 N Market St, Ph: 886-4091. Rabbi D. Fink. Services: Call for schedule.

VIRGINIA BEACH   Area Code (804)

Synagogues

Beth Chaverim (R-UAHC), P.O. Box 5130, Ph: 468-4115. Rabbi I. Zoberman. Services: Friday

Chabad Lubavitch of Tidewater (O-Lubav), 533 Gleneagle Dr, Ph: 499-0507. Rabbi A. Margolin. Services: Saturday and Holidays

Temple Emanuel (C-US), 25th St & Baltic Ave, Ph: 428-2591. Rabbi D. Abrams. Services: Shabbat

Kehillat Bet Hamidrash (C-US), 925 Indian Lakes Blvd, Ph: 495-8510. Services: Friday

Day School

Hebrew Academy of Tidewater, 1244 Thompkins Lane, Ph: 424-4327.

WILLIAMSBURG   Area Code (804)

Synagogues

Temple Beth El (Unaffiliated), 600 Jamestown Rd, Ph: 220-1205. Services: Call for information.

WOODBRIDGE   Area Code (703)

Synagogues

Congregation Ner Shalom (R), meets at Community Baptist Church, 15012 Dumfries Rd, **Manassas**, Ph: 494-3251. Rabbi J. Abrams. Services: Friday

Washington

ABERDEEN   Area Code (206)

Synagogues

Temple Beth Israel (R), 1254 N "L" St, Ph: 532-7485. Services: High Holidays

BELLINGHAM   Area Code (206)   J-pop. 300

Synagogues

Congregation Beth Israel (R), 2200 Broadway, Ph: 733-8890. Rabbi M. Oblath. Services: Friday

BOTHELL   Area Code (206)

Synagogues

Northshore Jewish Community (Recon), P.O. Box 1773, 98011, Ph: 481-3024. Services: Friday, once a month; High Holidays

BREMERTON (See also SEATTLE)   Area Code (206)

Synagogues

Community Center (C), 11th & Veneta Sts, Ph: 373-9884.
   Services: third Friday

FORT LEWIS   Area Code (206)

Synagogues

Fort Lewis Jewish Chapel (Trad), Liggett Ave & 12th,
   Ph: 967-6590. Chaplain (Major) M. Applebaum. Services:
   (Open to military and civilians) Friday; 1st Saturday

RICHLAND   Area Code (509)

Synagogues

Congregation Beth Sholom (C-US), 312 Thayer Dr, Ph: 943-9457.
   Services: Shabbat

Accommodations

Nendels Motor Inn, 615 Jadwin Ave, Ph: 943-4611. Some kitchens.
   A mile to Congregation Beth Sholom.

SEATTLE   Area Code (206)   J-pop. 19,500

Synagogues

Temple Beth Am (R-UAHC), 8015 27th Ave NE, Ph: 525-0915.
   Rabbi N. Hirsh. Services: Friday
Congregation Beth Shalom (C-US), 6800 35th NE, Ph: 524-0075.
   Rabbi D. Gartenberg. Services: Shabbat
Congregation Bikur Cholim—Machzikay Hadath (O-UOJC), 5145
   S Morgan St, Ph: 723-0970. Rabbi M. Londinski. Services:
   Daily
B'nai Torah (R-UAHC), 6195 92nd Ave SE, Ph: 232-7243. Rabbi
   J. Mirel. Services: Friday
Chabad House (O-Lubav), 4541 19th Ave NE, Ph: 527-1411. Rabbi
   Y. Kornfeld. Services: Saturday and daily a.m.
Temple De Hirsch Sinai (R-UAHC), 1511 E Pike St, Ph: 323-8486.
   Rabbi E. Starr. Services: Shabbat

Synagogues cont.

Emanuel Congregation (O), 3412 NE 65th St, Ph: 525-1055. Services: Shabbat

Congregation Ezra Bessaroth (O-UOJC), 5217 S Brandon, Ph: 722-5500. Rabbi Dr. W. Greenberg. Services: Daily

Congregation Herzl—Ner Tamid (C-US), 3700 E Mercer Way, **Mercer Island**, Ph: 232-8555. Rabbi H. D. Rose. Services: Shabbat and daily a.m.

Congregation Shaarei Tefilah Lubavitch (Lubav), 6803 40th NE (plans to move to nearby location), Ph: 523-1323. Rabbi S. Levitin. Services: Shabbat and Holidays

Sephardic Bikur Holim Congregation (O-UOJC), 6500 52nd Ave S, Ph: 723-3028. Rabbi S. Benzaquen. Services: Daily

South Island Jewish Center (O), **Mercer Island**, Ph: 232-6434. President, Dr. Z. Young, Ph: 236-2386. Services: Daily. Call for information.

Congregation Tikvah Chadashah (R), (Gay and Lesbian), Meets at Prospect Congregational Church, 1919 E Prospect St, Ph: 329-2590. Services: second and fourth Friday

Yeshiva Gedola of Greater Seattle (O), 5220 20th Ave NE, Ph: 527-1100. Rabbi A. Kaplan. Services: Daily

Food

Bagel Deli, 340 15th Ave E, Ph: 322-2471. Bagels and "fragels." (For a bagel, cream cheese and lox sandwich, request the kosher knife.) RS: Seattle Kashruth Board (the above items only).

Brenner's Bakery, 12000 Bellevue-Redmond Rd, **Bellevue**, Ph: 454-0600. Breads and pastries (pareve and dairy). RS: Seattle Kashruth Board (bakery only).

Great Harvest Bread Co., 5408 Sand Point Way NE, Ph: 524-4873. Breads, challahs (pareve); cookies, brownies, muffins, (pareve and dairy). RS: Rabbi M. Londinski.

Noah's Grocery, 4700 50th Ave S, Ph: 725-4267. Kosher products: Deli, breads, frozen chicken, wine and groceries.

Q.F.C., Corner SE 68th and 84th SE, Ph: 232-0102. Packaged kosher items; also fresh bakery goods from Brenner's and Great Harvest.

Varon's Kosher Meats, 3931 S Empire Way, Ph: 723-0240. Fresh
  meat. Full line of kosher groceries, packaged deli and frozen
  foods. RS: Seattle Kashruth Board. Closed Shabbat.

Accommodations

Shabbat hospitality; call Congregation Bikur Cholim,
  Ph: 723-0970.
Private accommodations; call Chabad House, Ph: 527-1411.
Travelodge, 4725 25th NE, Ph: 525-4612. Walk to Congregation
  Shaarei Tefilah.
University Motel, 4731 12th NE, Ph: 522-4724. Kitchens. About
  nine blocks from Chabad House.
University Motor Inn, 4140 Roosevelt NE, Ph: 632-5055.
  Kitchenettes. About a mile from Chabad House.

Mikvah

Congregation Bikur Cholim, 5145 S Morgan St. Call Mrs. Solny,
Ph: 725-7620.

Day Schools

Chabad House Cheder, 4541 19th Ave NE, Ph: 527-1411.
Jewish Day School of Metropolitan Seattle, 15749 NE 4th St,
Ph: 641-3335.
Seattle Hebrew Academy, 1617 Interlaken Dr E, Ph: 323-5750.

SPOKANE   Area Code (509)   J-pop. 800

Synagogues

Temple Beth Shalom (C-US), 1322 E 30th Ave, Ph: 747-3304.
Rabbi J. Izakson. Services: Shabbat

TACOMA (See also SEATTLE)   Area Code (206)   J-pop. 1,100

Synagogues

Temple Beth El (R-UAHC), 5975 S 12th St, Ph: 564-7101. Rabbi
R. Rosenthal. Services: Shabbat

West Virginia

BLUEFIELD   Area Code (304)

Synagogues

Congregation Ahavath Sholom (R-UAHC), 632 Albemarie St,
Ph: 325-9372. Rabbi E. Sapinsley. Services: Friday

CHARLESTON   Area Code (304)   J-pop. 1,025

Synagogues

Congregation B'nai Jacob (Trad), 1599 Virginia St, Ph: 344-4167.
Rabbi V. Urecki. Services: Daily
Temple B'nai Israel (R-UAHC), 2312 Kanawha Blvd,
Ph: 342-5852. Rabbi I. Koller. Services: Friday

Food

Dutchess Bakery, 715 Bigley Ave, Ph: 356-3210. Cakes and breads
(pareve and dairy). RS: Rabbi V. Urecki

Kroger's Ashton Place, 1100 Emerald Rd, **South Hills,**
Ph: 342-8807. Large selection of kosher products, including deli
and frozen poultry.

Mikvah

Congregation B'nai Jacob, 1599 Virginia St. Contact Mrs. Marilyn
Urecki, Ph: 343-3217 or 344-4167.

CLARKSBURG   Area Code (304)   J-pop. 115

Synagogues

Tree of Life Synagogue (C-US), W Pike at Fifth St, Ph: 622-3453.
Rabbi A. Raich. Services: Shabbat

HUNTINGTON   Area Code (304)   J-pop. 275

Synagogues

B'nai Sholom (C-US,R-UAHC), 949 10th Ave, Ph: 522-2980.
Rabbi D. E. Wucher. Services: Shabbat

Food

Victor's Delicatessen, 625 8th St, Ph: 522-4123. Good selection of
kosher groceries, kosher deli and Empire frozen poultry.

MARTINSBURG   Area Code (304)

Synagogues

Congregation Beth Jacob (R), 126 W Martin St, President: M.
Apfeldorf, Ph: 267-6824. Services: one Friday a month and
High Holidays

MORGANTOWN   Area Code (304)   J-pop. 150

Synagogues

Tree of Life Temple (R), 242 S High St, Ph: 292-7029.
Services: Friday

WHEELING   Area Code (304)   J-pop. 300

Synagogues

Temple Shalom—Congregation Leshem Shomayim (R-UAHC),
23 Bethany Pike, Ph: 233-4870. Rabbi D. Lowy. Services:
Shabbat

WILLIAMSON   Area Code (304)

Synagogues

Temple B'nai Israel (R-UAHC), College Hill, Ph: 235-2947. Rabbi
I. B. Koller. Services: Friday

Wisconsin

APPLETON   Area Code (414)   J-pop. 250

Synagogues

Congregation Moses Montefiore (C-US), 3131 N Meade St,
Ph: 733-1848. Rabbi M. Eskowitz. Services: Shabbat

BELOIT   Area Code (608)   J-pop. 120

Synagogues

B'nai Abraham (R-UAHC), 2400 Oxford Lane, Ph: 364-4916 or
365-3081. Rabbi A. Bregman. Services: Call for information.

EAU CLAIRE   Area Code (715)

Synagogues

Temple Sholom (C-US), 1223 Emery St, Ph: 832-1231 or
834-4667. Services: Call for schedule.

FOND DU LAC   Area Code (414)

Synagogues

Temple Beth Israel (C), 149 E Division St, Ph: 922-1590. Rabbi M.
Shalowitz. Services: High Holidays

GREEN BAY   Area Code (414)

Synagogues

Congregation Cnesses Israel (C-US), 222 S Baird St,
Ph: 437-4841. Rabbi S. Vineburg. Services: Shabbat

KENOSHA   Area Code (414)   J-pop. 200

Synagogues

Beth Hillel Temple (R-UAHC), 6050 8th Ave, Ph: 654-2716. Rabbi
D. Feingold. Services: Friday

LA CROSSE   Area Code (608)   J-pop. 150

Synagogues

Congregation Sons of Abraham (Trad), 1820 Main St,
Ph: 784-2708. Services: Shabbat

MADISON   Area Code (608)   J-pop. 4,500

Synagogues

Temple Beth El (R-UAHC), 2702 Arbor Dr, Ph: 238-3123. Rabbi
J. Brahms. Services: Friday

Beth Israel Center (C-US), 1406 Mound St, Ph: 256-7763. Rabbi
M. Re'em. Services: Daily

B'nai B'rith Hillel Foundation, 611 Langdon St, Ph: 256-8361.
Services: Friday

Chabad House (O-Lubav), 1722 Regent St, Ph: 231-3450. Rabbi Y.
Matusof. Services: Shabbat

Shaarei Shamayim Madison Jewish Reconstructionist Community,
P.O. Box 55061, 53705-8861.

Eating Out

B'nai Brith Hillel Foundation at the University of Wisconsin,
611 Langdon St, Ph: 256-8361. Shabbat dinners are served during
the school year. Contact Irving Saposnik, Director.

Food

Cornucopia, 716 S Whitney Way, Ph: 271-6500. Some kosher
products, including Sinai kosher meats.

Food cont.

Kohl's, 3770 University Ave, Ph: 231-1391. Some kosher products, including deli.

Mikvah

Mikvah Chaya Mousya; Call Mrs. Faygie Matusof, Ph: 251-8764 or 231-3450.

MANITOWOC   Area Code (414)   J-pop. 100

Synagogues

Anshe Poale Zedek Synagogue (Trad), 435 N 8th St, Ph: 682-4511. Rabbi M. Relles. Services: Saturday

MEQUON (See also MILWAUKEE)   Area Code (414)

Synagogues

Beth El Ner Tamid Synagogue (C-US), 2909 W Mequon Rd, Ph: 242-6900. Rabbi G. Goldenholz. Services: Daily
Congregation Chabad of North Shore (O-Lubav), 2233 W Mequon Rd, Ph: 242-2235. Rabbi D. Rappaport. Services: Saturday and Holidays

MILWAUKEE   Area Code (414)   J-pop. 29,000

Synagogues

Congregation Agudas Achim (O-UOJC), 5820 W Burleigh St, Ph: 442-2296. Rabbi I. Feldman. Services: Daily
Congregation Anshai Lebowitz (O), 3100 N 52nd St, Ph: 444-9640. Rabbi B. Reichman. Services: Daily
Anshe Sfard—Kehillat Torah (O), 6717 N Green Bay, Ph: 228-9296. Rabbi N. Levine. Services: Shabbat and daily a.m.
Congregation Beth Israel (C-US), 6880 N Green Bay Ave, Ph: 352-7310. Rabbi H. Panitch. Services: Daily
Congregation Beth Jehuda (O), 2700 N 54th St, Ph: 442-5730. Rabbi M. Twerski. Services: Daily
Congregation Emanu-el B'ne Jeshurun (R-UAHC), 2419 E

Kenwood Blvd, Ph: 964-4100. Rabbi F. Silberg. Services: Shabbat

Lake Park Synagogue (O), 3207 N Hackett Ave, Ph: 962-5508. Services: Shabbat

Lubavitch House (O-Lubav), 3109 N Lake Dr, Ph: 961-6100. Rabbi I. Shmotkin. Services: Daily

Temple Menorah (Trad), 9363 N 76th St, Ph: 355-1120. Rabbi I. Lerer. Services: Daily

Milwaukee Jewish Home Chapel (O-UOJC), 1414 N Prospect Ave, Ph: 276-2627. Rabbi S. Pontos. Services: Daily

Congregation Shalom (R-UAHC), 7630 N Santa Monica Blvd, Ph: 352-9288. Rabbi R. Shapiro. Services: Shabbat

Congregation Shir Hadash (Recon), President Marti Fine, Ph: 228-9050. Rabbi K. Karnofsky. Services: three Fridays and one Saturday a month

Congregation Sinai (R-UAHC), 8223 N Port Washington Rd, Ph: 352-2970. Rabbi T. Bookman. Services: Shabbat

Wisconsin Institute for Torah Study (O), 3288 N Lake Dr, Ph: 963-9317. Rabbi Y. Cheplowitz, Rabbi R. Wachsman and Rabbi A. B. Rauch. Services: Daily

Eating Out

Milwaukee Jewish Home, 1414 N Prospect Ave, Ph: 276-2627. Serves kosher lunches. RS: Rabbi S. Pontos. Please call ahead.

Food

Bagel Nosh Bakery, 3875 N Teutonia, Ph: 873-4200. Breads, challahs, cakes (pareve). RS: Chicago Rabbinical Council. Closed Shabbat.

Kosher Meat Klub, 4731 W Burleigh, Ph: 871-3273. Prepared food platters, cold cuts and complete kosher grocery. RS: Orthodox Rabbinical Council, Rabbi I. Feldman, Chairman. Closed Shabbat.

Kramer's Kosher Corner, 5101 W Keefe Ave, Ph: 442-2625. Complete kosher grocery, including a kosher deli counter, sandwiches and take-out. RS: Orthodox Rabbinical Council. Closed Shabbat.

Accommodations

Private hospitality; call Rabbi M. Twerski at Congregation Beth Jehuda, Ph: 442-5730.

Park East Hotel, 916 E State, Ph: 276-8800. About one-half hour's walk to Chabad.

Mikvah

Congregation Agudas Achim, 5820 W Burleigh. Contact Mrs. J. Dressler, Ph: 445-5705.

Congregation Beth Jehuda, 2700 N 54th St. Contact Ms. S. Glazer, Ph: 447-7727.

Mikvah Israel, 3109 N Lake Dr. Contact Mrs. R. Pontos, Ph: 961-2266.

Day Schools

Hillel Academy, 6401 N Santa Monica Blvd, Ph: 962-9545.

Milwaukee Jewish Day School (Unaffiliated), 6401 N Santa Monica, Ph: 964-1499.

Yeshiva Elementary School, 3447 N 51st Blvd, Ph: 871-9376.

Bookstore

Judaica Express, 5401 E Keefe Ave, Ph: 449-3403. Please call first.

OSHKOSH   Area Code (414)   J-pop. 150

Synagogues

Temple B'nai Israel (R), 1121 Algoma Blvd, Ph: 235-4270. Services: Friday

RACINE   Area Code (414)   J-pop. 375

Synagogues

Congregation Beth Israel Sinai (C), 944 Main St, Ph: 633-7093. Rabbi S. Lipson. Services: Shabbat

SHEBOYGAN   Area Code (414)   J-pop. 160

Synagogues

Congregation Beth El (C-US), 1007 North Ave, Ph: 452-5828.
Rabbi P. Mehler. Services: Daily

WAUKESHA   Area Code (414)

Synagogues

Congregation Emanu-el (R), 830 W Moreland Blvd, Ph: 547-7180.
Services: Every other Friday

WAUSAU   Area Code (715)

Synagogues

Mount Sinai Congregation (R-UAHC), 622 4th St, Ph: 845-7461.
Rabbi E. Danson. Services: Friday

Wyoming

CASPER   Area Code (307)

Synagogues

Temple Beth El (R), 4105 S Poplar, Ph: 237-2330. Services: 2nd and
4th Friday

CHEYENNE   Area Code (307)   J-pop. 230

Synagogue

Congregation Mount Sinai (C), 2610 Pioneer Ave, Ph: 634-3052.
Services: Shabbat

Food

Safeway, 2512 Pioneer Ave, Ph: 638-6337. Glatt hamburger meat,
Empire chickens; Cole Shopping Center, Ph: 778-8590. Empire
turkeys, etc.

LARAMIE   Area Code (307)

Synagogues

Jewish Community Center of Laramie (R-UAHC), P.O. Box 202,
82070. Services: High Holidays

Puerto Rico

SAN JUAN   Area Code (809)   J-pop. 1,500

Synagogues

Shaare Zedeck Synagogue (C-US), Jewish Community Center, 903 Ponce de Leon Ave, Ph: 724-4110/4157. Rabbi A. B. Felch. Services: Shabbat and Sunday

Temple Beth Shalom (R-UAHC), 101 San Jorge St, corner Loiza, Ph: 721-6333. Services: Friday

Food

Bertha's Bakery, Caparra Terrace, Rio Piedras, Ph: 781-5945. Challahs. RS: Rabbi A. B. Felch (challahs only).

Multi Bakery, 954 Ponce de Leon Ave, Ph: 725-7490. Cakes. RS: Rabbi A. B. Felch.

Pueblo Supermarket, De Diego St, Ph: 725-1095. Kosher packaged deli, Empire products and some kosher groceries.

U.S. Virgin Islands

ST. THOMAS   Area Code (809)   J-pop. 300

Synagogues

Hebrew Congregation of St. Thomas (R-UAHC), Crystal Gade, Ph: 774-4312. (Mailing address: P.O. Box 266, St. Thomas, U.S.V.I., 00804). Rabbi B. H. Boxman, Services: Friday, Saturday (September-June). Closed Saturday afternoon through Sunday. Historic site, est. 1796.

CANADA
Alberta

CALGARY   Area Code (403)

For kosher food information, call the Kashrut Coordinator at the
Calgary Jewish Community Council, Ph: 253-7915.

Synagogues

Beth Tzedec (C), 1325 Glenmore Trail SW, Ph: 255-8688. Rabbi
R. Tanenbaum. Services: Daily

Temple B'nai Tikvah (R), 1607 90th Ave SW, (in Calgary Jewish
Centre), Ph: 252-1654. Rabbi J. Goldson. Services: Friday

House of Jacob—Mikve Israel (O), 1613 92nd Ave SW,
Ph: 259-3230. Rabbi D. Lichtman. Services: Daily

Eating Out

Cafe Merkaz, Calgary Jewish Centre, 1607 90th Ave SW,
Ph: 255-5311. Separate dairy and meat kitchens. Meals: b,l,d.
Meat menu: burgers, sandwiches. Dairy menu: soups, salads,
sandwiches, pastries. Also take-out. Picnic baskets, Shabbat
meals on prior notice. RS: CK*. Closed Shabbat.

Wolf's Kosher World & Deli, Macleod Plaza (94th Ave & Macleod
Trail), Ph: 253-3354. Four tables. Meals: l,d. Menu: Deli,
chicken, sandwiches, salads. RS: CK*. Closed Shabbat.

Food

Bakery in Carriage House Inn, 9030 Macleod Trail S,
Ph: 253-1101. **Unsliced breads only**. Challah available on
Fridays. RS: CK*.

Baskin Robbins, Chinook Shopping Centre, Macleod Trail, N of
Glenmore Trail, Ph: 258-2266. Many products and some cones
under RS: COR (Rabbinical Vaad Hakashruth of Toronto).

Daniels' Bagel & Baguette, 414 36th Ave SE, Ph: 243-3207.
Wholesale bakery open to the public only on Friday mornings.
Challah available.

*Calgary Rabbinical Council

Food cont.

Oakridge Calgary Co-op, Oakridge Shopping Centre, 2580 Southland Dr SW, Ph: 281-0333. Kosher grocery section. Aravah cheeses, Palm dairy products.

Safeway-Glenmore Landing, Glenmore Landing Shopping Centre, 90th Ave and 14th St SW. Kosher section. Carries Empire products, Sinai deli products, locally made Aravah kosher cheeses; also kosher breads and dairy products.

Schayer's Kosher Meats & Delicatessen, 2515 90th Ave SW, Ph: 251-2552. Also kosher groceries. RS: CK*. Closed Shabbat.

Wolf's Kosher World & Delicatesen, Macleod Plaza, 94th Ave & Macleod Trail S, Ph: 253-3354. Butcher, bakery, groceries. Meat and pareve foods. RS: CK*. Closed Shabbat.

Accommodations

Shabbat accommodations:

Hospitality Committee of House of Jacob—Mikve Israel; call Ellie, Ph: 281-9066;

Rabbi M. Matusof of Chabad House, Ph: 238-4880.

Mikvah

Community Mikvah, Calgary Jewish Academy, 6700 Kootenay St SW. Call Mrs. Linda Wolf, Ph: 252-2485 or Mrs. Lisa Lichtman, Ph: 238-2196.

Day Schools

Akiva Academy, 140 Haddon Rd SW, Ph: 258-1312.

Calgary Jewish Academy, 6700 Kootenay St SW, Ph: 253-3992.

EDMONTON   Area Code (403)

For kosher food information, call the Jewish Community Center, Ph: 487-0585.

Synagogues

Beth Israel Synagogue (O), 10205 119th St, Ph: 488-2840 (office); 482-5095 (rabbi). Rabbi S. Mann. Services: Daily

*Calgary Rabbinical Council

Temple Beth Ora (R), 7200 156th St, Ph: 487-4817. Student rabbi.
Services: Friday

Beth Shalom (C), 11916 Jasper Ave, Ph: 488-6333 (office);
482-3033 (rabbi). Rabbi J. Rosner. Services: Shabbat, Monday
and Thursday a.m.

Eating Out

Marc's Gourmet Choices, 7200 156th St, (JCC) Ph: 444-4460.
Meals: b,l,d. Menu: (b) Pancakes, waffles, eggs; (l) Israeli
dishes, falafel, hamburgers, hot dogs; (d) Israeli and traditional.
Also take-out: fresh and frozen meals for travelers. RS:
Edmonton Vaad Hakashruth. Closed Shabbat.

Food

Andy's Valleyview IGA, 9106 142nd St, Ph: 483-1525. Kosher frozen meats, deli, baked goods, dairy & cheeses.

The Bagel Bin Bakery, 7552 178th St, Ph: 481-5721. Dairy and
pareve. RS: Edmonton Vaad Hakashruth.

Bon Ton Bakery Ltd., 8720 149th St, Ph: 489-7717. Dairy and
pareve. RS: Edmonton Vaad Hakashruth.

Edmonton Kosher Meat & Deli, 10983 127th St, Ph: 451-0774. RS:
Edmonton Vaad Hakashruth. Closed Shabbat.

Hulls Foods, 11720 Jasper Ave, Ph: 488-2100. Good selection of
kosher items; also cheeses.

Accommodations

Hilton Hotel, 10235 101st St, Ph: 428-7111. 25-minute walk to
synagogues.

Mayfair Hotel, 10815 Jasper Ave, Ph: 423-1650. 10-15-minute walk
to synagogues.

Tower-on-the-Park, 9715 110th St, Ph: 420-1212. Suites with kitchens. 20-minute walk to synagogues.

Westin Hotel, 10135 100th St, Ph: 426-3636. 25-minute walk to
synagogues.

Mikvah

Beth Israel Synagogue, 10205 119th St, Ph: 488-2840/482-5095 or
Rabbi Mann, Ph: 482-3990.

Day School

Edmonton Talmud Torah, 13213 106th Ave, Ph: 455-9114.

LETHBRIDGE   Area Code (403)

Synagogues

Beth Israel (C), 914 15th St, Ph: 327-8621.

MEDICINE HAT   Area Code (403)

Synagogues

Sons of Abraham (R), 540 5th St SE, Ph: 526-3880. Services: High
   Holidays

British Columbia

VANCOUVER   Area Code (604)

For kosher food information, call Rabbi S. Crandall at
   Congregation Schara Tzedeck, Ph: 736-7607.

Synagogues

Congregation Beth Hamidrash (O-Sephardic), 3231 Heather St,
   Ph: 872-4222. Rabbi D. Bassous. Services: Daily
Beth Israel (C), 4350 Oak St, Ph: 731-4161. Rabbi W. Solomon.
   Services: Daily
Beth Tikvah (C), 9711 Geal Rd, **Richmond**, Ph: 271-6262. Rabbi
   M. Cohen. Services: Shabbat
Chabad Lubavitch Centre (O-Lubav), 5750 Oak St, Ph: 266-1313.
   Rabbi Y. Wineberg. Services: Daily
Eitz Chaim Synagogue (O), 8080 Francis Rd, **Richmond**,
   Ph: 275-0007. Rabbi A. Feigelstock. Services: Shabbat
Har-El Congregation & North Shore Jewish Centre (C), 1735
   Inglewood, **West Vancouver**, Ph: 922-8245. Rabbi I. Balla.
   Services: Shabbat
Or Shalom (Egalitarian), 4764 Quebec St, Ph: 872-1614. Rabbi Y.
   Marmorstein. Services: Shabbat
Congregation Schara Tzedeck (O), 3476 Oak St, Ph: 736-7607.
   Rabbi M. Feuerstein. Services: Daily

Temple Sholom (R), 7190 Oak St, Ph: 266-7190. Rabbi P. Bregman. Services: Shabbat, Sunday, Monday and Wednesday a.m.

Eating Out

Cafe Mercaz, at Jewish Community Centre, 950 W 41st Ave, Ph: 266-9111. Meals: b,l,d. Menu: (Dairy). RS: ORCBC*.

Food

Leon's Kosher Korner, "Kosher Specialists," 3710 Oak St, Ph: 736-5888. Butcher, bakery, grocery and take-out deli. RS: ORCBC*. Closed Shabbat.

Accommodations

Ramada Inn, 898 W Broadway, Ph: 872-8661. 10-15-minute walk to Schara Tzedeck and Beth Hamidrash.

Holiday Inn, 711 W Broadway, Ph: 879-0511. 10-15-minute walk to Schara Tzedeck and Beth Hamidrash.

Mikvah

Lubavitch Centre, 5750 Oak St, Ph: 266-1313.

Schara Tzedeck, 3476 Oak St, Ph: 736-7607.

Day Schools

Maimonides High School, 5465 Bailee St, Ph: 263-9700.
Vancouver Hebrew Academy, 5750 Oak St, Ph: 266-1245.
Vancouver Talmud Torah, 998 W 26th Ave, Ph: 736-7307.

Bookstore

Shalom Books, 3712 Oak St, Ph: 734-1106.

VICTORIA   Area Code (604)

Synagogues

Congregation Emanu-El (C-US), 1461 Blanshard St, Ph: 382-0615. Rabbi V. Reinstein. Services: Saturday

*Orthodox Rabbinical Council of British Columbia

Manitoba

WINNIPEG   Area Code (204)

For Winnipeg information, call the Winnipeg Jewish Community
Council, Ph: 943-0406

Synagogues

Ashkenazi Congregation (O), 297 Burrows Ave, Ph: 589-1517.
Services: Daily

Beth Israel, H.S.B.A. (C), 1007 Sinclair St, Ph: 582-2353.
Services: Call for information.

B'nai Abraham (Trad), 235 Enniskillen Ave, Ph: 339-9297. Rabbi
P. Weizman. Services: Daily

Chabad Lubavitch Centre (O-Lubav), 2095 Sinclair St, Ph:
339-8737/4756. Rabbi A. Altein. Services: Daily

Chavurat Tefilla—Fellowship of Prayer (O), 459 Hartford Ave,
Ph: 338-9451. Services: Daily

Chevra Mishnayes (O), 700 Jefferson Ave, Ph: 338-8503. Services:
Daily

Herzlia-Adas Yeshurun (O), 620 Brock St, Ph: 489-6262/6668.
Rabbi J. Krupnick. Services: Daily

Rosh Pina (C), 123 Matheson Ave E, Ph: 589-6306. Rabbi J.
Kogen. Services: Daily

Shaarey Zedek (C), 561 Wellington Crescent, Ph: 452-3711. Rabbi
H. Balser. Services: Daily

Temple Shalom (R), 1077 Grant Ave, Ph: 453-1625. Rabbi J. Gale.
Services: Shabbat

Talmud Torah—Beth Jacob (O), 427 Matheson Ave, Ph: 589-5345.
Services: Daily

Eating Out

Cafe Shalom, Y.M.H.A. Jewish Community Centre, 370 Hargrave
St, Ph: 942-6625. Meals: l,b,d. Menu: (Dairy and pareve) Israeli
style dishes. RS: WK*.

Desserts Plus, 1595 Main St, Ph: 339-1957. Meals: l,d. Menu:
(Dairy - vegetarian) soups, salads, sandwiches, lasagna, fish,
blintzes and pastries. RS: WK*. Closed Shabbat.

The Gwen Secter Creative Living Center, 1588 Main St, Ph: 339-1701. Meals: l and Erev Shabbat. Menu: (Glatt meat and pareve). Very reasonable. RS: WK*. Please call ahead.

Miracle Bakery, 1385 Main St, Ph: 586-6140. Meals: b,l. Menu: Pastries, salads and coffee. RS: WK*.

Food

Acme Produce (fresh chicken), 525 Jarvis Ave, Ph: 589-6454. RS: WK*.

City Bread, 238 Dufferin Ave, Ph: 586-8409. Wholesale outlet, Arlington Street. RS: WK*.

Eliyohu's Food Mart, 686 MacGregor St, Ph: 586-4514. Kosher grocery, frozen meats and poultry. Closed Shabbat.

Goodie's Bake Shop, 2 Donald Ave, (this location only), Ph: 949-2480. RS: WK*.

Gunn's Bakery, 247 Selkirk Ave, (this location only), Ph: 582-2364/586-4361. RS: WK*.

Hearthstone Bakery, 634 Leila Avenue, Ph: 339-8929. RS: WK*.

Miracle Bakery, 1385 Main St, Ph: 586-6140. RS: WK*.

Omnitsky's Kosher Meats, 1428 Main St, Ph: 586-8271. Glatt meat and poultry. Take-out deli and sandwiches. RS: WK*.

Tuxedo I.G.A., 1853 Grant Ave, Ph: 488-9667. Has a full-service kosher meat (Glatt) section. RS: WK*. Also carries a wide variety of kosher products.

Accommodations

Garden City Inn, 2100 McPhillips, Ph: 635-0024. Walk to Beth Israel, Lubavitch Centre and Chavurat Tefila.

Shabbat Hospitality: Call Mrs. M. Gerber of Chabad Lubavitch, Ph: 334-2624.

Mikvah

Mikvah Chabad Lubavitch, 455 Hartford Ave, Ph: 338-4761. In an emergency, call Mrs. Altein, Ph: 589-2547. Please call 24 hours in advance.

*Vaad Ha'ir of Winnipeg, Inc., Ph: 943-0406 ext. 242

Day Schools

Joseph Wolinsky Collegiate, 437 Matheson Ave, Ph: 589-5345.
Oholei Torah Day School, 2095 Sinclair St, Ph: 334-8222.
Ramah Hebrew School, 705 Lanark St, Ph: 453-4136.
Talmud Torah/I.L. Peretz Folk School, 427 Matheson Ave, Ph: 586-8366.

New Brunswick

FREDERICTON   Area Code (506)

Synagogues

Congregation Sgoolai Israel (O), 168 Westmorland St, Ph: 454-9698 or 455-8425. Rabbi D. Spiro. Services: Shabbat.

Food

Most supermarkets will carry some kosher products with the COR, MK, OU and other kashruth symbols. However, travelers to New Brunswich and Nova Scotia are advised to bring the bulk of their kosher supplies from Bangor, Maine or Montreal.
Victory Meat Market, King Street, Ph: 458-8480. This non-kosher store and mini supermarket carries kosher frozen Marved chickens with the "MK" symbol, from Montreal

Mikvah

Congregation Sgoolai Israel, 168 Westmorland St. Call Rabbi D. Spiro, Ph: 455-8425. The mikvah is available for use when the rabbi is in town. Please call several days in advance.

MONCTON   Area Code (506)

Synagogues

Tiferes Israel Congregation (O), 56 Steadman St, Ph: 858-0258. Rabbi F. Nebel. Services: Shabbat

Food

For kosher food information, call Tiferes Israel Congregation, Ph: 858-0258.

Mikvah

Tiferes Israel Congregation, 56 Steadman St, Ph: 858-0258.

ST. JOHN   Area Code (506)

Synagogues

Congregation Shaarei Zedek (C), 76 Coburgh St, Ph: 657-4790.
  Services: Shabbat.

Newfoundland

ST. JOHN'S   Area Code (709)

Synagogues

Hebrew Congregation of Newfoundland (C), Elizabeth Ave,
  P.O.B. 724, A1C 5L4, Ph: 726-0480.

Nova Scotia

GLACE BAY   Area Code (902)

Synagogues

Sons of Israel (O), 1 Prince St, B1A 3C8, Ph: 849-8605. Services:
  Shabbat

HALIFAX   Area Code (902)

Synagogues

Beth Israel Synagogue (O), 1480 Oxford St, Ph: 422-1301.
  Rabbi M. Pritzker. Services: Daily
Shaar Shalom Synagogue (C), 1981 Oxford St, Ph: 423-5848.
  Rabbi J. Chinitz. Services: Shabbat

Mikvah

Beth Israel Synagogue, 1480 Oxford St, Ph: 422-1301.

SYDNEY   Area Code (902)

Synagogues

Temple Sons of Israel (C), Whitney Ave, P.O.B. 311, B1P 6H2,
Ph: 564-4650. Services: Shabbat

Ontario

BELLEVILLE   Area Code (613)

Synagogues

Sons of Jacob Congregation (C), 211 Victoria St, K8N 2C2,
Ph: 962-1433.

BRAMPTON   Area Code (416)

Synagogues

Har Tikvah Congregation (R), P.O.B. 2094, L6T 3B1, Ph:
792-7589 or 453-7949. Rabbi L. Lander. Services: Shabbat and
Holidays

BRANTFORD   Area Code (519)

Synagogues

Beth David Congregation (O), 50 Waterloo St, N3T 3R8,
Ph: 752-8950.

CHATHAM   Area Code (519)

Synagogues

Children of Jacob (C), c/o 66 Bedford St, N7L 2V3, Ph: 352-3544.

CORNWALL   Area Code (613)

Synagogues

Beth El Congregation (C), 321 Amelia St, Ph: 933-6322. Services:
Saturday and once a month on Friday.

DOWNSVIEW (See GREATER TORONTO)

GUELPH   Area Code (519)

Synagogues

Beth Isaiah Congregation (O), 47 Surrey St, **West Guelph**,
Ph: 822-8487. Rabbi T. Berman. Services: Shabbat

HAMILTON   Area Code (416)

Synagogues

Adas Israel Congregation (O), 125 Cline Ave S, Ph: 528-0039.
Rabbi M. Green. Services: Daily
Temple Anshe Sholom (R), 215 Cline Ave N, Ph: 528-0121.
Rabbi I. Zeplowitz. Services: Friday
Beth Jacob Congregation (C), 375 Aberdeen Ave, Ph: 522-1351.
Rabbi I. N. Silverman. Services: Daily

Day School

Hamilton Hebrew Academy, 60 Dow St, Ph: 528-0330.

KINGSTON   Area Code (613)

Synagogues

Beth Israel Congregation (O), 116 Centre St, Ph: 542-5012.
Services: Shabbat, Monday and Thursday
Temple Iyr Ha-Melech (R), c/o Dr. Michael Levinson, 203
Glengary Rd, Ph: 544-3088. Services: Friday at Queens
University, Ph: 542-1159.

Mikvah

Beth Israel Congregation, 116 Centre St, Ph: 542-5012.

KITCHENER   Area Code (519)

Synagogues

Beth Jacob Congregation (O), 161 Stirling Ave S, Ph: 743-8422.
Rabbi D. J. Levy. Services: Saturday
Temple Shalom (R), 116 Queen St N, Ph: 743-0401. Services:
Call for information.

LONDON   Area Code (519)

Synagogues

Congregation Beth Tefilah (O), 1210 Adelaide St N, Ph: 433-7081.
Rabbi S. Kurtz. Services: Daily
Or Shalom Synagogue (C), 534 Huron St, Ph: 438-3081. Services:
Shabbat
Temple Israel (R), 313 Grangeover Ave, Ph: 679-9977. Rabbi
J. Wittstein. Services: Friday

Food

For kosher food information, contact Marilyn Sober, Ph: 438-7486.
A&P, 1030 Adelaide St N, Ph: 672-8994. Many kosher items; also
Hermes Kosher breads, rolls and challahs from Toronto.
London Kosher, in J.C.C., 536 Huron St, Ph: 438-7486. Meat and
meat products from Perl's Glatt Meat, Toronto. (RS: COR).

Mikvah

Congregation Beth Tefilah, 1210 Adelaide St N. Call Mrs.
S. Kurz, Ph: 672-4168 or Mrs. L. Block, Ph: 439-4828.

Day School

London Community Hebrew Day School, 247 Epworth Ave,
Ph: 439-8419.

MISSISSAUGA   Area Code (416)

Synagogues

Solel Congregation (R), 2399 Folkway Dr, Ph: 820-5915. Rabbi
L. Englander. Services: Shabbat

NIAGARA FALLS   Area Code (416)

Synagogues

B'nai Jacob Congregation (C), 5358 Ferry St, L2G 1R7,
Ph: 354-3934.

NORTH BAY   Area Code (705)

Synagogues

Sons of Jacob Synagogue (O), 302 McIntyre W, P1B 2Z1, Ph: 474-2170.

OAKVILLE   Area Code (416)

Synagogues

Shaarei Beth El Congregation (R,C), 186 Morrison Rd, Ph: 849-6000. Rabbi E. Goldfarb. Services: Saturday and High Holidays

OSHAWA   Area Code (416)

Synagogues

Beth Zion Congregation (O), 144 King St E, L1H 1B6, Ph: 723-2353.

OTTAWA   Area Code (613)

Synagogues

Adath Shalom Congregation (C), Box 106 Station "B", K1P 6C3, Ph: 228-0570. Services: Saturday

Agudath Israel Congregation (C), 1400 Coldrey Ave, Ph: 728-3501. Rabbi A. Fine. Services: Daily

Beth Shalom Congregation (O), 151 Chapel St, Ph: 232-3501. Rabbi S. Aranov. Services: Daily

Beth Shalom West (O), 15 Chartwell Ave, **Nepean**, Ph: 723-1800. Rabbi H. Finkelstein. Services: Daily

Chabad House (O), 64 Templeton St, Ph: 565-1818. Rabbi P. Sperlin. Services: Shabbat, during the school year

Hillel Lodge (O), 125 Wurtemberg, Ph: 236-7132/7133. Services: Daily

Machzikei Hadas Congregation (O), 2310 Virginia Dr, Ph: 521-9700. Rabbi Dr. R. Bulka. Services: Daily

Temple Israel (R), 1301 Prince of Wales Dr, Ph: 224-1802. Rabbi I. Tanenbaum. Services: Shabbat

Young Israel of Ottawa (O-NCYI), 627 Kirkwood Ave, Ph: 722-8394. Rabbi M. Berger. Services: Daily

Eating Out

Ottawa Kosher Deli and Nosh, 2730 Iris St, **Nepean**, Ph: 726-9391. Meals: l,d. Menu: (Glatt meat) soups, deli, sandwiches, meat and fish entrees, salads, side dishes. RS: Ottawa Vaad Hakashruth. Closed Shabbat.

Yudi's Deli-Diner-Salad Bar, 250 Greenbank Rd, **Nepean**, Ph: 721-DELI. Meals: b,l,d. Menu: (Glatt meat) hamburgers, falafel, sandwiches, barbecued chicken, salads, desserts. Also complete take-out. RS: Ottawa Vaad Hakashruth. Closed Shabbat.

Food

Greenbank IGA, 250 Greenbank Rd, **Nepean**, Ph: 828-9321. Good selection of kosher items.

Ottawa Kosher Deli, 2730 Iris St, **Nepean**, Ph: 726-9391. Fresh meat and poultry, deli, bread, salads, kosher groceries. RS: Ottawa Vaad Hakashruth. Closed Shabbat.

Rideau Bakery, 384 Rideau St, Ph: 234-1019; 1066 Bank St, Ph: 737-3355. RS: Ottawa Vaad Hakashruth (breads, challahs, rolls only)

United Kosher Meat & Deli, 378 Richmond Rd, Ph: 722-6556. Butcher, deli, prepared foods; full line of kosher groceries. RS: Chabad, Ottawa Vaad Hakashruth. Closed Shabbat.

Yudi's Deli, 250 Greenbank Rd, **Napean**, Ph: 721-DELI. Prepared foods for take-out. RS: Ottawa Vaad Hakashruth. Closed Shabbat.

Accommodations

All downtown hotels are within walking distance of Hillel Lodge.

Embassy West Hotel, 1400 Carling Ave at Queensway, Ph: 729-4331. Short walk to Young Israel.

Mikvah

Mikvah Israel, 127 Kirkwood Ave; call Chabad, Ph: 565-1818.

Day Schools

Hillel Academy Day School, 881 Broadview Ave, Ph: 722-0020.
Maimonides School, 25 Esquimault St, **Nepean**, Ph: 820-9484.

468

Bookstore

All Occasions Judaica, Mrs. G. Sheffield, 767 Canterbury Ave, Ph: 521-1875. Please call first.

OWEN SOUND   Area Code (519)

Synagogues

Congregation Beth Ezekiel (C), 313 11th St, N4K 1V1, Ph: 376-8774.

PEMBROKE   Area Code (613)

Synagogues

Beth Israel Congregation (O), 322 William St, K8A 1P3. Call Jeff Eisen, Ph: 785-5987.

PETERBOROUGH   Area Code (705)

Synagogues

Beth Israel Congregation, P.O. Box 144, Weller St, K9J 6Y5, Ph: 745-8398.

RICHMOND HILL   Area Code (416)

Synagogues

Shaarei Haim Synagogue of York Region (C), 9711 Bayview Ave, Ph: 884-8400;884-3353. Rabbi L. Troster. Services: Shabbat, Sunday and Holidays

Day School

United Synagogue Day School (C), 31 Spruce Ave, Ph: 781-5658.

ST. CATHERINE   Area Code (416)

Synagogues

Congregation B'nai Israel (C), 190 Church St, Ph: 685-6767. Rabbi J. Ben-David. Services: Shabbat, Monday and Thursday

Temple Tikvah (R), 83 Church St, Ph: 682-4191. Services: Call for information.

SARNIA   Area Code (519)

Synagogues

Ahavas Isaac Synagogue (C), 202 Cobden St, Ph: 337-9281.

SAULT STE. MARIE   Area Code (705)

Synagogues

Beth Jacob Congregation (C), 147 Bruce St, Ph: 256-8061.
   Services: Call for information.

STRATFORD   Area Code (519)

Synagogues

Beth Israel Congregation, 122 Downie St, N5A 1X1, Ph: 271-0235.
   Services: Minyan as needed; High Holidays

SUDBURY   Area Code (705)

Synagogues

Shaar Hashamayim Congregation (O), 159 John St, P3E 1P4,
   Ph: 673-0831.

THUNDER BAY   Area Code (807)

Synagogues

Shaarey Shomayim Congregation (C), 627 Grey St, Ph: 622-4867.
   Services: first and third Fridays; Holidays

GREATER TORONTO   Area Code (416)

Toronto Jewish Information Service, Ph: 635-5600
Kosher Information Service of Rabbinical Vaad Hakashruth
   (COR), Ph: 635-9550.

DOWNTOWN TORONTO

Synagogues

Anshe Minsk (O), 10 St. Andrew's St, Ph: 595-5723. Services:
   Daily

Bloor J.C.C. Chapel (O), 750 Spadina Rd, Ph: 924-6211. Services: Sunday, Monday, Thursday and Rosh Chodesh a.m.

Shaare Tzedec (O), 397 Markham St, Ph: 923-5828/534-2904. Services: Shabbat and Holidays

Eating Out

Bagels Galore Dairy Restaurant, First Canadian Pl, Ph: 363-4233. Meals: b,l,d. Menu: Bagels, spreads, soups. RS: COR.

Jewish Community Centre, South Branch Bloor "Y", 750 Spadina Ave, Ph: 924-6211. Meals: b,l,d. Menu: (Dairy) Soups, pierogies, vegetables, fish. RS: COR.

Lower East Side Cafe B'nai B'rith Hillel Foundation, University of Toronto, 604 Spadina Ave, Ph: 923-9861. Meals: l,d. Menu: Hamburgers, hot dogs, pizza, falafel. Open during the academic year. RS: COR.

Food

Bagels Galore (dairy, take-out), First Canadian Pl, Ph: 363-4233. RS: COR.

SOUTH BATHURST

Synagogues

Agudath Israel of Toronto (O), 129 McGillivray Ave, Ph: 789-5514. Rabbi M. Lowy. Services: Daily

Associated Hebrew School Chapel (O), 3630 Bathurst St, Ph: 789-7471. Services: Daily

Beth Lida Forest Hill Synagogue (O), 22 Gilgorm Rd, Ph: 489-2550. Services: Shabbat and Holidays

Beth Sholom (C), 1445 Eglinton Ave W, Ph: 783-6103. Rabbi L. Schechter. Services: Daily

Beth Torah (C), 47 Glenbrook Ave, Ph: 782-4495. Rabbi C. Freundlich. Services: Saturday and Holidays

Beth Tzedec (C), 1700 Bathurst St, Ph: 781-3511. Rabbi B. Friedberg. Services: Daily

Chevra Shas (O), 3545 Bathurst St, Ph: 782-0849. Services: Daily

Chasidei Bobov (O), 3703 Bathurst St, Ph: 789-0971 or 661-3173. Rabbi J. Fuhrer. Services: Daily

Synagogues cont.

Congregation Habonim (Liberal), 5 Glen Park Ave, Ph: 782-7125. Services: One Friday a month and Holidays

Holy Blossom Temple (R), 1950 Bathurst St, Ph: 789-3291. Rabbi D. Marmur. Services: Daily

Congregation Imrei Noam (O), 84 Stormont Ave, Ph: 782-7995 or 499-9977. Rabbi M. Adler. Services: Daily

Kielcer Congregation (O), 2941 Bathurst St, Ph: 783-0522. Services: Daily

Kiever Congregation (Rodfei Shalom-Anshei Kiev) (O), 25 Bellevue Ave, Ph: 593-9702 or 593-9956. Services: Shabbat and Holidays

Mesivta Yessodei Hatorah (O), 2949 Bathurst St, Ph: 789-7153. Services: Daily

Minyan Avreichim (Boat Shul) (O), 2919 Bathurst St, Ph: 789-4731. Rabbi Y. Y. Sofer. Services: Daily

Temple Sinai (R), 210 Wilson Ave, Ph: 487-4161. Rabbi J. Pearlson. Services: Shabbat and Holidays

Shaarei Shomayim (O), 470 Glencairn Ave, Ph: 789-3213. Rabbi H. Hoschander. Services: Daily

Congregation Shaare Tefilah (O), 3600 Bathurst St, Ph: 787-1631. Rabbi M. Stern. Services: Daily

Shomrai Shaboth Chevra Mishnayoth (O), 585 Glengrove Ave W, Ph: 782-8849. Rabbi Y. Felder. Services: Daily

Torah Emeth Jewish Centre (O), 1 Viewmont Ave, Ph: 782-9621. Rabbi M. Ochs. Services: Daily

Yavneh Zion (O), 788 Marlee Ave, Ph: 781-1611. Services: Shabbat, Sunday and Holidays

Yeshiva Yessodei Hatorah (O), 77 Glen Rush Blvd, Ph: 787-1101. Services: Daily

Zichron Schneur (Toronto Lakewood Minyan) (O), 2801 Bathurst St, Ph: 781-0136. Rabbi D. Pam. Services: Daily

The following restaurants and food stores are under the supervision of the Rabbinical Vaad Hakushruth of the Kashruth Council, Orthodox Division, Toronto Jewish Congress. "COR" is their logo. They are all closed Shabbat.

472

Eating Out

Chopstix, 3426 Bathurst St, Ph: 787-0345. Meals: d. Menu: (Meat) Chinese. RS: COR. Major cards.

Dairy Treats European Cafe and Bakery, 3522 Bathurst St, Ph: 787-0309. RS: COR.

Jewish Community Centre, North Branch North "Y", 4588 Bathurst St, Ph: 633-4660. Meals: b,l,d. Menu: (Meat and dairy) Chicken, tuna, salads, soups. RS: COR.

Kosher King, 3500 Bathurst St, Ph: 787-8610. Meals: l,d. Menu: (Glatt meat) Fast food and Israeli dishes. RS: COR.

Mati's Fallafel & Pizza, 3430 Bathurst St, Ph: 783-9505. Meals: l,d. Menu: Pizza, falafel. RS: COR.

Milk'n Honey Restaurant, 3457 Bathurst St, Ph: 789-7651. Meals: l,d. Menu: Dairy and fish dishes. RS: COR. Major cards.

My Zaidy's Bagel, 3456 Bathurst St, Ph: 789-0785. Meals: l,d. Menu: Pizza, bagels, baked items. Also take-out. RS: COR.

Food

Boro Park Kosher Mart, 3023 Bathurst St, Ph: 782-6865. RS: COR.

Carmel Bakery, 3856 Bathurst St, Ph: 633-5315. RS: COR.

Cohen's Bakery, 2839 Bathurst St, Ph: 787-6791. RS: COR.

Dairy Treats European Cafe and Bakery, 3522 Bathurst St, Ph: 787-0309. RS: COR.

Food City (Oshawa Foods), Clark and Hilda, Ph: 764-3770. Fresh fish department under COR supervision; Bathurst and Steeles, Ph: 223-8585. Kosher meat department RS: COR.

Gershon's Fish Market, 3019 Bathurst St, Ph: 782-6056. Fresh Fish. RS: COR.

Grocer's Delight, 4117 Bathurst St, Ph: 633-7876. Complete kosher grocery, including packaged meats and poultry. Also prepared foods. RS: COR.

H. Perl, 3013 Bathurst, Ph: 787-4234. Butcher, small selection of groceries and frozen foods. RS: COR.

Hermes Bakery, 2885 Bathurst St, Ph: 787-1234; 3543 Bathurst St, Ph: 787-2611; 652 Sheppard Ave W, Ph: 635-1932. RS: COR.

Isaac's Bakery Ltd., 3390 Bathurst St, Ph: 789-7587. RS: COR.

Food cont.

Joe Kirshen's Kosher Butcher Shop, 3544 Bathurst St, 781-7767. RS: COR.

Kosher City, 3515 Bathurst St, Ph: 782-6788; 782-4982. Kosher grocery. RS: COR.

Kosher 'N' Natural Foods, 3413 Bathurst St, Ph: 789-7173. Nuts, dried fruits, candies and gift baskets. RS: COR.

Kosher Meats & Treats, 2825 Bathurst St, Ph: 783-4231. Butcher and take-out. RS: COR.

Manor Kosher Meat Market, 662 Sheppard Ave W, Ph: 636-2000. RS: COR.

Prime Kosher Meats—Loblaws, 270 Wilson Ave, Ph: 638-8287. RS: COR.

Richman's Bakery, 4119 Bathurst St, Ph: 636-9710. Breads and cakes (pareve). RS: COR.

Springers Butcher, 3393 Bathurst St, Ph: 787-3971. RS: COR.

Stroli's Butcher, 3459 Bathurst St, Ph: 789-5333. RS: COR.

Sweet York Desserts, 1700 Bathurst St, Ph: 782-1798. RS: COR.

Mikvah

Agudath Israel, 129 McGillivray Ave, Ph: 789-5514.

Beth Jacob Elementary School, 85 Stormont Ave, Ph: 781-2073 or 787-5958.

Shomrei Shabboth, 583-585 Glengrove Ave W, Ph: 782-8849.

Torath Emeth Jewish Centre, 1 Viewmont Ave, Ph: 782-9621.

Day Schools

Associated Hebrew Schools of Toronto, 3630 Bathurst St, Ph: 789-7471

Bialik Hebrew Day School (Secular Zionist), 12 Viewmont Ave, Ph: 783-3346.

Bais Yaakov Elementary School, 85 Stormont Ave, Ph: 783-6181.

Eitz Chaim Yeshiva, 1 Viewmont Ave, Ph: 789-4366.

Netivot HaTorah Day School, 55 Yeomans Rd, Ph: 636-4050; 210 Wilson Ave, Ph: 322-5589.

United Synagogue Day School (C), 1700 Bathurst St, (Beth Tzedec) Ph: 781-5658.

Yeshiva Bnei Zion of Bobov, 250 Carmichael Ave, Ph: 785-1594.
Yeshiva Nachlas Zvi, 475 Lawrence Ave W, Ph: 787-4176.
Yeshiva Yesodei Hatorah, 77 Glen Rush Blvd, Ph: 787-1101.

Bookstores

Aleph Beth Judaic, 3453 Bathurst St, Ph: 781-2133.
Israel's the Judaica Centre, 897 Eglinton Ave, Ph: 256-1010.
Ma-Tov Books & Gifts, 3173 Bathurst St, Ph: 782-7075.
Miriam Book & Religious Supplies, 3007 Bathurst St, Ph: 781-8261.
Negev Book & Gift Store, 3509 Bathurst St, Ph: 781-9356.
Sinai Religious Articles, 11 Fairholme Ave, Ph: 787-9292.

NORTH BATHURST

Synagogues

Adath Israel Synagogue (C), 37 Southbourne Ave, Ph: 635-5340. Rabbi S. Saltzman. Services: Daily

Adath Sholom Synagogue, 864 Sheppard Ave W, Ph: 635-0131. Services: Shabbat and Holidays

Beth David B'nai Israel Beth Am (C), 55 Yeomans Rd, Ph: 633-5500. Rabbi P. Scheim. Services: Daily

Beth Emeth Bais Yehuda (C), 100 Elder St, Ph: 633-3838. Rabbi D. Kelman. Services: Daily

Beth Jacob (O), 147 Overbrook Pl, Ph: 638-5955. Rabbi M. Burak. Services: Daily

Beth Joseph Lubavitch Anshei New York (O), 44 Edinburgh Dr, Ph: 731-7000. Services: Daily

Beth Meyer, 816 Sheppard Ave W, Ph: 633-5711. Services: Saturday

Clanton Park (O), 11 Lowesmoor Ave, Ph: 633-4193. Rabbi Y. Kerzner. Services: Daily

Congregation Darchei Noam (Recon), 15 Hove St, Ph: 638-4783. Services: Shabbat and Holidays

Lodzer Centre Holocaust Congregation, 12 Heaton St, Ph: 636-6665. Services: Shabbat and Holidays

Magen David Sephardic Congregation (O), 10 McAllister, Ph: 636-0865. Rabbi Y. Benayon. Services: Daily

Mishkan Abraham (Ulpanot Orot Chapel) (O), 45 Canyon Ave, Ph: 630-6772/638-5434. Services: Daily

Moria Institute Congregation (O), 11 Kaimona Ave, Ph: 636-6820. Services: Shabbat and Holidays

Petach Tikva Anshei Castilla Congregation (O-Sephardic), 20 Danby Ave, Ph: 636-4719. Services: Daily

Tiferet Israel (O-Sephardic), 756 Sheppard Ave W, Ph: 633-1874. Services: Daily

Torah V'Avodah (Bnei Akiva) (O), 296 Wilson Ave, Ph: 630-6772. Services: Daily

Ulpanat Orot-Mishkan Avraham (O), 45 Canyon Ave, Ph: 630-6772. Services: Shabbat

Yeshiva Or Chaim (O), 159 Almore Ave, Ph: 630-6772. Services: Daily

The following restaurants and food stores are under the supervision of the Rabbinical Vaad Hakushruth of the Kashruth Council, Orthodox Division, Toronto Jewish Congress. "COR" is their logo. They are all closed Shabbat.

Eating Out

Isaac's Cafe/Restaurant, 221 Wilmington Ave, Ph: 630-1678. Meals: b,l. Menu: Dairy. RS: COR.

Marky's Delicatessen, 280 Wilson Ave, Ph: 638-1081. Meals: b,l,d. Menu: Deli, fish, salads, American and Continental cuisine. RS: COR.

Marky's Fine Dining, 355 Wilson Ave, Ph: 636-0163. Meals: l,d. Menu: (Glatt meat) "Nouvelle" cuisine, meat, fish, and vegetarian dishes. Reservations recommended. Sunday-Thursday. All major credit cards. RS: COR.

Food

Akiva's Kosher Food Market, 3858 Bathurst St, Ph: 635-0470. RS: COR.

Anito Bengio Patisserie, 870 Steeprock Dr, Ph: 638-3051. Cakes and pastries (pareve). RS: COR.

B. Goldstein Products, 308 Wilson Ave, Ph: 633-9642. Butcher shop, prepared food for take-out. RS: COR.

Isaac's Bakery Ltd., 221 Wilmington Ave, Ph: 630-1678. RS: COR.

Kosher Delicious Ltd., 99 Dolomite Dr, Ph: 650-5774. Baked goods (pareve). RS: COR.

Kosher Food Warehouse, 75 Doncaster Ave, Ph: 764-7575. Bulk foods, natural and organic products; also regular kosher groceries. RS: COR.

Rachel's Catering, 243 Wilmington Ave, Ph: 633-6661. Kosher grocery and take-out. RS: COR.

Mikvah

Chabad Lubavitch, 44 Edinburgh Dr, Ph: 633-4608.
Clanton Park Mikvah, 11 Lowesmoor Ave, Ph: 633-4193.

Mikvah cont.

Mikvah Society for Family Sanctity, 694 Sheppard Ave W, Ph: 633-4729. For women only

Day Schools

Netivot HaTorah Day School, 55 Yeomans Rd, Ph: 636-4050.
Or Haemet Sefardic School, 37 Southborne Ave, Ph: 635-9881.
Shearim Hebrew Day School, 100 Elder St, Ph: 633-8247. Grades 1-8, for children with learning problems.

Bookstore

Pardes Hebrew Book Shop, 4119 Bathurst St, Ph: 633-7113.

THORNHILL

Synagogues

Beth Avraham Yoseph of Toronto (O), 613 Clark Ave W, Ph: 886-3810. Rabbi B. Taub. Services: Daily
Bet Hamedrash (O), 269 Arnold Ave, Ph: 731-7855 or 784-4602. Services: Daily
B'nai Shalom Congregation, 275 Arnold Ave, Ph: 731-2797. Rabbi S. Z. Domb. Services: Saturday and Holidays
Chabad Lubavitch Community Centre (O), 770 Chabad Gate, Ph: 731-7000. Rabbi Z. Grossbaum. Services: Daily
Chabad Lubavitch of Markham, 55 Guardsman Rd, Ph: 886-0420. Rabbi A. Plotkin. Services: Shabbat and Holidays
Temple Har Zion (R), 7360 Bayview Ave, Ph: 889-2252. Rabbi M. S. Stroh. Services: Shabbat and Holidays
Ner Israel Yeshiva (O), 8950 Bathurst St, Ph: 731-1224. Services: Daily
Shaar Shalom (C), 2 Simonston Blvd, Ph: 889-4975. Rabbi H. Markose. Services: Shabbat and Sunday

The following restaurants and food stores are under the supervision of the Rabbinical Vaad Hakushruth of the Kashruth Council, Orthodox Division, Toronto Jewish Congress. "COR" is their logo. They are all closed Shabbat.

Eating Out

Café Olé, 7241 Bathurst St (at Chabad Gate Plaza), Ph: 764-8957.
    Meals: b,l,d. Menu: (Dairy: cholov Yisroel) Omelettes, pasta,
    fish, pizza, sandwiches, salads. RS: COR.
My Zaidy's Pizza, 441 Clark Ave W, Ph: 731-3029. Meals: l,d.
    Menu: Pizza, falafel and french fries. RS: COR.

Food

Abram's Kosher Meat, 7241 Bathurst St, Ph: 731-4112. RS: COR.
Daniel's Kitchen, 57 Glen Cameron Rd, Unit 8, Ph: 886-6967.
    Take-out foods and catering service. RS: COR.
Happy Days, 441 Clark Ave W, Ph: 789-4438. Candies, nuts, gift
    baskets. RS: COR.
Kosher City, 7380 Bathurst St, Ph: 882-2214. RS: COR.
Tastefully Yours, 2300 John St, Ph: 731-1735. Prepared foods for
    take-out (meat). RS: COR.
San Diego's, 800 Steeles Ave W, Unit B15A, Ph: 738-1322. Meals:
    l. Menu: Falafel, sandwiches, frozen yogurt. RS: COR.

Mikvah

Chabad Lubavitch, 770 Chabad Gate, Ph: 731-7000.

Day School

Etz Chaim Yeshiva, Spring Farm Campus, 80 York Hill Blvd,
    Ph: 764-6633.

Bookstore

Israel's the Judaica Centre, Spring Farm Market Place, 441 Clark
    Ave W, Ph: 881-1010.

WILLOWDALE (includes East of Yonge St)

Synagogues

Associated Hebrew School Chapel (O), 252 Finch Ave W,
    Ph: 223-4845. Services: Shabbat, Sunday and Holidays
Beth Tikvah (C), 3080 Bayview Ave, Ph: 221-3433/3434.
    Rabbi W. Allen. Services: Daily

Synagogues cont.

B'nai Torah Congregation (O), 465 Patricia Ave, Ph: 226-3700. Rabbi R. Marus. Services: Daily

Temple Emanu-El (R), 120 Old Colony Rd, Ph: 449-3880. Services: Sabbath and Holidays

Jewish Russian Community Centre (O), 18 Rockford Rd, Ph: 665-9600. Rabbi Y. Zaltzman. Services: Daily

Kehillat Shaarei Torah (O), 2640 Bayview Ave, Ph: 229-2600. Rabbi S. Cohen. Services: Daily

Pride of Israel Temple, 59 Lissom Cres, Ph: 226-0111. Services: Daily

Shomer Israel Congregation (O), 60 Rockford Rd, Ph: 665-4815. Services: Shabbat, Sunday and Holidays

Willowdale Orthodox Jewish Congregation (O), 623 Finch Ave W, Ph: 665-4683. Services: Daily

The following restaurants and food stores are under the supervision of the Rabbinical Vaad Hakushruth of the Kashruth Council, Orthodox Division, Toronto Jewish Congress. "COR" is their logo. They are all closed Shabbat.

Eating Out

Hakerem Restaurant, 1045 Steeles Ave W, Ph: 736-7227. Meals: l,d. Menu: (Glatt meat) Israel Yemenite; falafel, humous, shwarma, soups, salads. Also take-out. RS: COR.

Pikanti Gourmet Foods, 5887 Bathurst St, Ph: 229-9090. Meals: l,d. Menu: Mediterranean, Moroccan, Israeli. Also take-out. RS: COR.

Tov-Li Pizza & Falafel, 5972 Bathurst St, Ph: 650-9800. Meals: l,d. Menu: Pizza, falafel, salads. RS: COR.

Food

Baskets N' Stuff, 6211 Bathurst St, Ph: 250-9116. Confectionery, gift baskets. RS: COR.

Hartman's Kosher Meats, 5974 Bathurst St, Ph: 663-7779. Butcher, some prepared meals, groceries. RS: COR.

My Zaidy's Bakery, 7241 Bathurst St, Ph: 731-3831. RS: COR.

Mikvah

B'nai Torah, 465 Patricia Ave, Ph: 255-6620 or 221-9899.

Day Schools

Associated Hebrew Schools of Toronto, 252 Finch Ave W, Ph: 223-4845; 6100 Leslie St, Ph: 494-7666.

Eitz Chaim Yeshiva—Willowdale, 475 Patricia Ave, Ph: 225-1187.

The Leo Baeck Day School (R), 34 Kenton Dr, Ph: 222-9220.

United Synagogue Day School (C), 3080 Bayview Ave, (Beth Tikvah), Ph: 225-1143.

WILLOWDALE (See GREATER TORONTO)

WINDSOR   Area Code (519)

Synagogues

Congregation Beth El (R), 2525 Mark Ave, Ph: 969-2422. Rabbi H. Folb. Services: Friday

Congregation Shaar Hashomayim (O), 115 Giles Blvd E, Ph: 256-3123. Services: Daily

Shaaray Zedek Synagogue (O), 610 Giles Blvd E, Ph: 252-1594. Services: Saturday

Quebec

MONTREAL   Area Code (514)

Jewish Information & Referral Service, Ph: 735-3541.

Synagogues

Adath Israel (O), 223 Harrow Crescent, **Hampstead,** Ph: 482-4252. Rabbi M. Kramer. Services: Daily

Adat Re'im (C), 60 Anselme Lavigne Blvd, **Dollard des Ormeaux,** Ph: 683-5253. Rabbi E. Malomet. Services: Daily

Anshei Ozeroff (O), 5380 Bourret St, Ph: 738-2012. Rabbi I. Siropa. Services: Shabbat and Holidays

Beth El (C), 100 Lucerne Rd, **Mount Royal,** Ph: 738-4766. Rabbi K. Katz. Services: Daily

Synagogues cont.

Beth Hamedrash Hagadol Tifereth Israel (O), 4605 Mackenzie St,
Ph: 733-5356. Rabbi Y. Rosner. Services: Daily

Congregation Beth Hillel (O), 6230 Coolbrook Ave, Ph: 731-8708.
Rabbi M. Kizelnick. Services: Daily

Beth Israel Beth Aaron (O), 6800 Mackle Rd, **Cote St. Luc,**
Ph: 487-1323. Rabbi R. J. Poupko. Services: Daily

Beth Ora (O), 2600 Badeau St, **St. Laurent,** Ph: 748-6559. Rabbi
M. H. Jablon. Services: Daily p.m.

Beth Tikvah (O), 136 Westpark Blvd, **Dollard des Ormeaux,**
Ph: 683-5610. Rabbi M. Zeitz. Services: Daily

Beth Zion (O), 5740 Hudson Ave, Ph: 489-8411. Rabbi S. Shoham.
Services: Daily

Centre Chabad (O-Lubav), 4691 Van Horne, Ph: 738-4654. Rabbi
S. Chriqui. Services: Daily (men only)

Synagogue du Centre Communautaire Juif (O), 5480 Westbury,
Ph: 735-5565. Services: Daily

Centre Merkaz Sepharade (O), 3917 Van Horne, Ph: 738-3155.
Rabbi E. Ezagui. Services: Daily

Centre Sepharade Rabbinique (O), 5850 Victoria Ave,
Ph: 738-1004. Rabbi D. Sabbah. Services: Daily

Chabad Lubavitch (O-Lubav), 3429 Peel St, Ph: 842-6616. Rabbi
R. Fine. Services: Afternoons

Chevra Kadisha B'nai Jacob Synagogue (O), 5237 Clanranald Ave,
Ph: 482-3366. Rabbi B. Hauer. Services: Daily

Chevra Shas Adath Jeshurun Hadrath Kodesh (O), 5855 Lavoie,
Ph: 739-2448. Rabbi N. Kops. Services: Daily

Chevra Thillim Pinsker Kinyan Torah (O), 1904 Van Horne Ave,
Ph: 737-6206. Rabbi M. Werner. Services: Daily

Communaute Sepharade Hekhal Shalom (O), 825 Gratton, **Ville
St. Laurent,** Ph: 747-4530. Rabbi M. Arzouane. Services: Daily

Dorshei Emet Reconstructionist Synagogue (Recon), 18 Cleve Rd,
Hampstead, Ph: 486-9400. Rabbi R. Aigen. Services: Saturday

Temple Emanu-El Beth Sholom (R), 4100 Sherbrooke St W,
Westmount, Ph: 937-3575. Rabbi L. Lerner. Services: Friday

Hungarian Jewish Memorial Synagogue (O), 3910 de Courtrai

Ave, Ph: 733-8007. Rabbi M. Schnurmacher. Services: Shabbat and Holidays

Synagogue Or Sefarad (O), 4860 Notre Dame Blvd, **Chomedey,** Ph: 682-6606. Rabbi D. Banon. Services: Daily

Synagogue Petah Tikvah de Ville St. Laurent (O), 2650 St. Louis, **Ville St. Laurent,** Ph: 744-3434. Rabbi N. Lancry. Services: Daily

Rabbinical College—Lubavitch (O-Lubav), 6405 Westbury Ave, Ph: 735-2201. Services: Friday (men only), Saturday (men and women), Daily (men only)

Rodeph Shalom (R), 96 Fredmir Blvd, **Dollard des Ormeaux,** Ph: 626-2173. Rabbi L. Kaplan. Services: Friday

Congregation Sepharade Beth Rambam (O), 5780 Westminster, **Cote St. Luc,** Ph; 481-7217. Rabbi M. Chriqui. Services: Daily

Congregation Sepharade Beth Yossef Young Israel (O), 6235 Hillsdale, Ph: 844-3865 or 738-6444. Services: Shabbat and daily a.m.

Congregation Sepharade de Langue Francaise (Beth Hamedrash Hagadol), 4605 McKenzie, Ph: 733-5356. Services: Shabbat

Congregation Sepharade Maghen David (O), 4691 Van Horne, Ph: 731-1960; 739-4902. Rabbi Cabessa.

Congregation Sepharade Or Hahayim (O), 5700 Einstein, **Cote St. Luc,** Ph; 489-1301. Rabbi M. Ohana. Services: Shabbat, Monday and Thursday a.m.

Shaar Hashomayim (C), 450 Kensington, **Westmount,** Ph: 937-9471. Rabbi W. Shuchat and Rabbi A. Nadler. Services: Daily

Shaar Shalom (C), 4880 Notre Dame Blvd, **Chomedey,** Ph: 688-8100.

Shaare Zedek (C), 5305 Rosedale Ave, Ph: 484-1122. Rabbi B. Leffell. Services: Daily

Shaare Zion (C), 5575 Cote St. Luc Rd, Ph: 481-7727. Rabbi L. Perlman. Services: Daily

Shomrim Laboker (O), 5151 Plamondon Ave, Ph: 731-6831. Rabbi C. Denburg. Services: Daily

Spanish and Portuguese Synagogue (Shearith Israel) (O), 4894 St. Kevin Ave, Ph: 737-3695. Rabbi H. Joseph. Services: Daily

Synagogues cont.

Tifereth Beth David Jerusalem (O), 6519 Baily Rd, **Cote St. Luc,**
   Ph: 489-3841; 3842. Rabbi J. H. Schmidman. Services: Daily
Young Israel of Chomedey (O-NCYI), 1025 Elizabeth Blvd,
   Chomedey, Ph: 681-2571. Rabbi S. J. Spiro. Services: Daily
Young Israel of Montreal (O-NCYI), 6235 Hillsdale Rd,
   Ph: 737-6589. Rabbi H. Kaufman. Services: Daily
Young Israel of Val Royal (O-NCYI), 2855 Victor Dore,
   Ph: 334-4610. Services: Shabbat
Zichron Kedoshim (O), 5215 Westbury Ave, Ph: 735-2113. Rabbi
   Zlotnick. Services: Daily

Eating Out

For kosher information, call the Jewish Community Council
(Vaad Ha'Ir), Ph: 739-6363. "MK" is the logo of the Vaad Ha'Ir.
All establishments under the "MK" are closed Shabbat.

BBQ McDavid, 5611 Cote des Neiges Rd, Ph: 341-1633. Meals: l,d.
   Menu: (Meat) Hamburgers, falafel, complete meals. RS: MK.
   Open after Shabbat.
Deli Cachere, 419 des Recollets, Ph: 849-0283. Meals: b,l,d.
   Menu: Deli sandwiches, hamburgers, falafel, salads. Take-out
   and delivery. RS: MK.
Deli Peking, 6900 Decarie Blvd, Decor Decarie Shopping Centre,
   Ph: 738-2844. Meals: l,d. Menu: (Glatt meat) Cantonese and
   Szechuan. Also take-out and delivery. RS: MK. Open after
   Shabbat.
El Morocco II, 3450 Drummond Ave, Ph: 844-6888. Meals: l,d.
   Menu: (Meat) Middle Eastern. Credit cards. RS: MK. Open
   after Shabbat.
Foxy's Pizza, 5987 Victoria Ave, Ph: 739-8777. Meals: l,d. Menu:
   (Dairy: cholov Yisroel) Pizza, falafel, dairy dishes. RS: MK.
   Open after Shabbat.
The Golden Spoon, 5217 Decarie Blvd, Ph: 481-3431. Meals: l,d.
   Menu: (Dairy: cholov Yisroel) Pizza, vegetarian dishes. Also
   take-out. Visa. RS: MK. Open after Shabbat.
Hillel House—McGill University, 3460 Stanley St, Ph: 845-9171.

Meals: l,d. Menu: (Meat and pareve) Soup, sandwiches, complete meals. RS: MK. Open during the academic year.

Jerusalem Snack Bar, 4961 Queen Mary Rd, Ph: 344-4095. Meals: l,d. Menu: (Meat) Israeli. Shwarma, falafel, latkes, salad etc. RS: MK.

Kosher Place, 206 Bernard Ave, Ph: 495-7862. Meals: l,d. Menu: (Glatt meat) hamburgers, hot dogs, chicken. Also take-out. RS: MK.

Kotel Restaurant (Chabad House), 3429 Peel St, Ph: 987-9875. Meals: l,d. Menu: (Glatt meat) Shwarma, chicken, falafel, soup, salad. RS: MK. Also Shabbat. Call for reservations.

Mitchell's Y.M.H.A. Cafeteria, 5500 Westbury Ave, Ph: 737-8704. Meals: b,l,d. Sunday: b,l. Menu: (Meat and dairy) Soups, sandwiches, hamburgers, hot dogs; dairy snacks. RS: MK.

Odelia Snack Bar, 5897-A Victoria Ave, Ph: 733-0984. Meals: l,d. Menu: (Glatt meat) Middle Eastern. RS: MK.

Pita Pizza, 5710 Victoria Ave, Ph: 731-7482. Meals: l,d. Menu: (Dairy: cholov Yisroel) Pizza, falafel, salads. RS: MK.

Food

Club Kosher, in Esposito Farms, 340 Laurentian Blvd, **Ville St. Laurent**, Ph: 744-2979. Kosher meat department only. RS: MK.

European Bakeries, 206 St. Viateur St W, Ph: 274-4633; 1587 Van Horne Ave W, Ph: 272-3003; RS: MK.

France Cachere Patisserie, 4655 Van Horne Ave, Ph: 735-9822. Prepared foods. Meat (Glatt), fish, salads, pastires. RS: MK.

Home Made Kosher Bakery, 1085 Bernard St W, Ph: 276-2105; 6795 Darlington St, Ph: 342-1991; 6685 Victoria Ave, Ph: 733-4141; 5638 Westminster Ave, **Cote St. Luc**, Ph: 486-2024. RS: MK.

Hypermarche, 6855 Clanranald Ave, Decor Decarie Shopping Centre, Ph: 735-2755. Kosher meat department only. RS: MK.

J'ae Delicatessen, 4879 Notre Dame St, **Chomedey**, Ph: 687-6184. Take-out deli, grocery, bakery. RS: MK.

Knick Nosh, 5204 Decarie Blvd, Ph: 481-0331. Kosher groceries. Also deli sandwiches, chicken, salads for take-out. RS: MK.

Kosher Quality Bakery, 5855 Victoria Ave, Ph: 731-7883. Also prepared foods for take-out (Glatt meat). RS: MK.

Food cont.

Mendy's, 6735 Darlington, Ph: 738-3207. Take-out (Glatt meat): Entrees, soups, salads, sandwiches. Complete kosher grocery. RS: MK.

Montreal Kosher Bakery, 2865 Van Horne Ave, Ph: 737-0393; 7005 Victoria Ave, Ph: 739-3651. RS: MK.

New Home Made Kosher Bakery, 6915 Kuerbes, Ph: 270-5567. Breads and pastries (pareve and dairy). Also some prepared foods. RS: MK.

Sabra, 7018 Cote St. Luc Rd, Ph: 486-9547. Shabbat dinners delivered to your hotel room or home. Order in advance. Also bakery. RS: MK.

Steinberg Kosher Department, 5800 Cavendish, **Cote St. Luc**, Ph: 482-4710. Kosher meat department only. RS: MK.

Steinberg Plus, 3291 Sources Blvd, **Dollard des Ormeaux**, Ph: 685-0071. Kosher meat department only. RS: MK.

Mikvah

Mikveh Israel, 7015 Kildare, **Cote St. Luc**, Ph; 487-5581.

Mikveh du Rabbinat, 5850 Victoria Ave, Ph: 738-6320.

Ritualarium of Montreal, 6235 Hillsdale Rd (in rear of Young Israel building), Ph: 737-2625 (evenings) or call Mrs. Cohen, Ph: 733-1485 (days).

Young Israel of Chomedey Mikveh, 1025 Elizabeth Blvd, Ph: 681-2103.

Day Schools

The Akiva School, 450 Kensington Ave, **Westmount**, Ph: 939-2430.

Bais Tzipora-Skver, 6019 Durocher Ave, **Outrement**, Ph: 279-4425.

Belz Boys School, 5565 Jeanne Mance St, **Outremont**, Ph: 270-5086.

Beth Esther School, 1239 Van Horne Ave, Ph: 272-4988.

Beth Jacob School, 1750 Glendale Ave, Ph: 739-3614.

Beth Rikvah Academy for Girls, 5001 Vezina Ave, Ph: 731-3681.

Beth Zion Hebrew Day School, 5740 Hudson Ave, **Cote St. Luc**, Ph: 486-5423.

Bnos Jerusalem Girls' School, 1495 Ducharme Ave, **Outrement,**
    Ph: 271-9464; 271-0611.
Ecole Maimonide, 7450 Cote St. Luc Rd, **Cote St. Luc,**
    Ph: 486-7003; 6520 Gouin Blvd W, **St. Laurent,** Ph: 331-6310.
Hassidic Community School, 1495 Ducharme Ave, **Outremont,**
    Ph: 271-0611.
Hebrew Academy, 8205 Mackle Rd, **Cote St. Luc,**
    Ph: 489-5321.
Hebrew Foundation School, 2 Hope Dr, **Dollard Des Ormeaux,**
    Ph: 684-6270.
Jewish People's & Peretz Schools, 7946 Wavell Rd, **Cote St. Luc,**
    Ph: 488-2541; 5710 Van Horne Ave, Ph: 731-6456.
Rabbinical College of Canada Tomche Tmimim Lubavitch, 6405
    Westbury Ave, Ph: 735-2201.
Rabbinical College of Toras Moshe, 5214 St. Urbain,
    Ph: 277-6931.
Sephardic Academy of Montreal (Ecole Sepharade), 2915 Marcel
    St, **Ville St. Laurent,** Ph: 333-4060.
Solomon Schechter Academy (C), 5555 Cote St. Luc, **Cote St.
    Luc,** Ph: 485-0866.
Summit School for Exceptional Children, 1750 Deguire St, **St.
    Laurent,** Ph: 744-2867.
Talmud Torah Jacob Joseph, 1235 Ducharme Ave, **Outremont,**
    Ph: 274-8241.
United Talmud Torahs of Montreal, 4894 St. Kevin Ave,
    Ph: 739-2291; 5554 Robinson Ave, **Cote St. Luc,** Ph: 484-1151;
    4850 St. Kevin Ave, Ph: 739-2291; 2205 Rue de L'Eglise, **St.
    Laurent,** Ph: 337-4566.
Yeshiva Gedola Merkaz HaTorah, 6155 Deacon Rd, **Outremont,**
    Ph: 735-6611.

Bookstores

Gan Eden Inc., 4705 Van Horne, Ph: 733-1947.
Kotel Hebrew Book and Gift Store, 6414 Victoria Ave,
    Ph: 739-4142; 739-8839.
Merkaz S'tam of Montreal, 4661 Van Horne, Ph: 737-0756.
Rodal's Hebrew Book Store, 4689 Van Horne, Ph: 733-1876.

QUEBEC CITY   Area Code (418)

Synagogues

Congregation Beth Israel Ohev Sholom (O), 20 Cremazie St E,
Ph: 692-5733. Rabbi S. Prager. Services: Saturday and Holidays

ST. AGATHE-DES-MONTS   Area Code (819)

Synagogues

House of Israel (O), 31 Albert St, Ph: 326-4320. Rabbi E.
Carlebach. Services: Daily during the summer; Saturday and
Sunday during the winter

Saskatchewan

REGINA   Area Code (306)

Synagogues

Beth Jacob (O), 1640 Victoria Ave, Ph: 757-8643. Rabbi S.
Truzman. Services: Shabbat

SASKATOON   Area Code (306)

Synagogues

Agudas Israel (R), 715 McKinnon Ave, Ph: 343-7023.
Rabbi R. V. Pavey.